An Artist in Treason

BY THE SAME AUTHOR

Measuring America

The Fabric of America

AN ARTIST IN TREASON

*The Extraordinary Double Life
of General James Wilkinson*

ANDRO LINKLATER

WALKER

Published by Walker Publishing Company, Inc., New York

All papers used by Walker & Company are natural, recyclable products
made from wood grown in well-managed forests. The manufacturing processes
conform to the environmental regulations of the country of origin.

LIBRARY OF CONGRESS CATALOGING-IN-PUBLICATION DATA HAS BEEN APPLIED FOR.

ISBN-13: 978-0-8027-1720-7

Visit Walker & Company's Web site at www.walkerbooks.com

First U.S. edition 2009

1 3 5 7 9 10 8 6 4 2

Typeset by Westchester Book Group
Printed in the United States of America by Quebecor World Fairfield

CONTENTS

EAST OF THE MISSISSIPPI RIVER
• CIRCA 1790 •

Lake Superior

BRITISH TERRITORY

(MASS.)

Mississippi R.

Lake Michigan

Lake Huron

Lake Ontario

NEW YORK   N.H.

FORT GEORGE

MASS.

Lake Erie

Detroit

CONN.   R.I.

FORT MIAMI

Presq'Isle

New York City

Maumee R.

FORT FAYETTE

PENNSYLVANIA

FORT WASHINGTON

Eel R.

OHIO (1803)

Pittsburgh

Philadelphia

FORT WAYNE

FORT RECOVERY

NEW JERSEY

NORTHWEST TERRITORY

FORT GREENVILLE

DELAWARE

MARYLAND

INDIANA TERRITORY

Ohio R.

Louisville   Lexington

VIRGINIA

Frankfort

Allegheny Mountains

FORT MASSAC

KENTUCKY (1792)

FORT NEW MADRID

SPANISH TERRITORY

TENNESSEE (1796)

NORTH CAROLINA

Memphis

Mississippi R.

SOUTH CAROLINA

MISSISSIPPI TERR.

GEORGIA

Vicksburg

Natchez

Atlantic Ocean

FORT ADAMS

WEST FLORIDA

EAST FLORIDA

New Orleans

Gulf of Mexico

0 Miles   200   400

0 Kilometers   400

© 2009 Jeffrey L. Ward

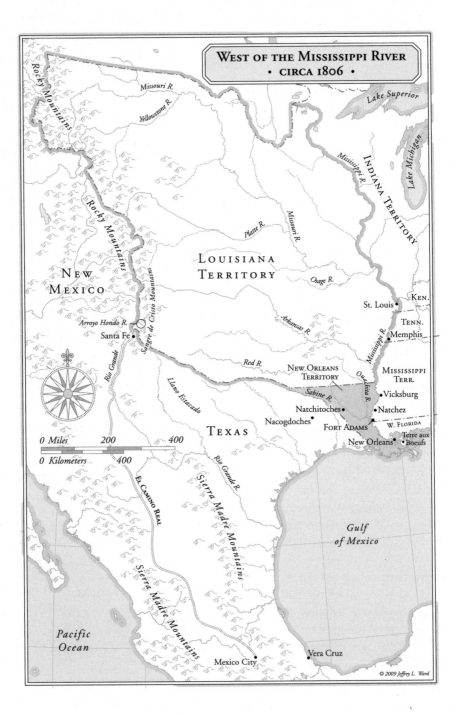

WEST OF THE MISSISSIPPI RIVER
· CIRCA 1806 ·

Rocky Mountains

Missouri R.

Yellowstone R.

Lake Superior

Mississippi R.

INDIANA TERRITORY

Lake Michigan

Rocky Mountains

Platte R.

Missouri R.

LOUISIANA
TERRITORY

Osage R.

NEW
MEXICO

Sangre de Cristo Mountains

St. Louis

KEN.

Arroyo Hondo R.

Arkansas R.

TENN.
Memphis

Santa Fe

Rio Grande

Red R.

NEW ORLEANS
TERRITORY

Mississippi R.

MISSISSIPPI
TERR.

Llano Estacado

Sabine R.

Ouachita R.

Vicksburg

Natchitoches

Natchez

Nacogdoches

FORT ADAMS

TEXAS

W. FLORIDA

0 Miles   200   400

New Orleans

Terre aux
Boeufs

0 Kilometers   400

El Camino Real

Sierra Madre Mountains

Rio Grande R.

Gulf
of Mexico

Sierra Madre Mountains

Pacific
Ocean

Mexico City

Vera Cruz

© 2009 Jeffrey L. Ward

INTRODUCTION

A TEST OF LOYALTY

LIEUTENANT COLONEL THOMAS CUSHING, commanding officer of the Second Regiment, could remember precisely the moment when his general held the fate of the country in his hands. "On the 8th of October 1806, I was sitting at the dining-table in my quarters at Natchitoches with general Wilkinson when a gentleman entered the room." The newcomer was a young New Yorker named Samuel Swartwout. His ostensible purpose in coming to the tiny settlement, situated on what was then the southwestern border of the United States, was to volunteer to serve in the forthcoming war with Spain. Since the two officers had been deployed to Natchitoches together with a force of twelve hundred troops in anticipation of such a war, Cushing found, as he said, nothing in Swartwout's explanation "which could excite a suspicion against him."

The cause of the approaching hostilities was a dispute between the United States of America and His Catholic Majesty Carlos IV about the border between the Spanish province of Texas and the western extent of the Louisiana Purchase. Trouble had been brewing ever since France sold the vast territory to the United States in 1803. The quarrel now threatened to boil over. The Spanish had stationed more than one thousand troops in Nacogdoches in Texas and occupied positions on what the United States regarded as its territory. In response, President Thomas Jefferson's administration had ordered General James Wilkinson, commander of the U.S. army, to "counteract the hostile views or obvious intentions of the invaders." Already on its way to Washington was Wilkinson's assurance that with the forces available "I shall be able to drive our opponents before me and take Nacodoches."

It would be a popular war. People within the United States, and especially in the west, had a pent-up desire to attack their giant neighbor. In Tennessee and Kentucky, militia generals such as Andrew Jackson and John Adair had promised to lead thousands of citizen-soldiers into Spanish territory once the conflict began. All it required was the first shot to be fired and the first blood spilt.

Routine business called the colonel from his office, leaving Swartwout alone with the general. "The next morning," Cushing recalled, "I was walking on the gallery, in front of my quarters, when general Wilkinson came up, and taking me aside, informed me that he had something of a serious nature to communicate to me."

While the colonel was out of the room, Swartwout had handed the general a package that included a letter from former vice president Aaron Burr. It told Wilkinson, his old friend, of Burr's plan to seize New Orleans and use it as a base to attack Mexico. "A great number of individuals possessing wealth, popularity and talents," Wilkinson informed Cushing, "are, at this moment, associated for purposes inimical to the government of the United States: colonel Burr is at their head, and the young gentleman . . . is one of his emissaries." The letter explicitly stated that Wilkinson was to be regarded as Burr's lieutenant. It also made clear that the success of the conspiracy depended upon war with Spain. Until then, Cushing later explained, he had never heard of the Burr Conspiracy. He recalled that Wilkinson dismissed any suggestion of having collaborated with the former vice president. What the general wanted to discuss was the danger of giving Burr inadvertent help by attacking Nacogdoches.

War with Spain would force the army to fight on the frontier, leaving New Orleans defenseless. There would be nothing to stop Burr from seizing the city and putting into effect a project that might dismember the fragile United States. On the hand, if Wilkinson retreated to deal with Burr, the border would be left undefended. The general's choice would determine the future of the United States. Although the straightforward Cushing did not realize it, another, more secret outcome weighed equally heavily with the general. Whether he turned against Aaron Burr or helped him, James Wilkinson risked being exposed as a traitor himself.

EVER SINCE 1797, James Wilkinson had been the senior general in the U.S. army. Throughout that period, he was also Agent 13 in the Spanish secret service. At a time when Spain's empire dominated North America, occupying until 1803 an area three times that of the United States, General Wilkinson not only passed on his country's strategic secrets, he sought to detach

Kentucky from the Union and wrote detailed plans advising the Spanish authorities on the best way to prevent American expansion beyond the Mississippi. In the words of Frederick Jackson Turner, Wilkinson was "the most consummate artist in treason the nation has ever possessed."

That evocative description aptly conveys the reputation that Wilkinson enjoys today. Yet one aspect of his career as a secret agent should make one pause. It was hardly secret at all. For most his life, he was repeatedly referred to as a "Spanish pensioner." Letters were sent to the first four presidents warning of his activities. Numerous pamphlets were printed accusing him of being a traitor. In Kentucky an entire newspaper, the *Western World*, was devoted to exposing him. Accusations of collusion were made by congressmen of every political persuasion. Nor were these charges overlooked. Presidents George Washington, John Adams, Thomas Jefferson, and James Madison, together with half a dozen different secretaries of war, not to mention a score of their cabinet colleagues, were all aware of his close contacts with the Spanish authorities in New Orleans and Madrid. No fewer than four official inquiries were mounted into the allegations against the general.

It is impossible to disguise the unease that treachery arouses. To excuse it is to risk losing sight of one of the yardsticks—love of country—by which moral living is measured. Yet one administration after another chose to confirm Wilkinson in command of the U.S. army. Unless a collective blindness was at work, his political contemporaries found in him some other quality that outweighed suspicions about his loyalty.

What makes the story of James Wilkinson's double life truly compelling is the light that it casts upon the early years of the United States. The federal union was newly knit, and its government untested. Its very identity was more tenuous than seems imaginable today. There was no certainty that "the experiment in democracy" would take hold, no inevitability about the survival of liberty, no guarantee about the growth of power and territory. Failure threatened every political choice.

In the republic's barely formed state, the loyalty of the army posed a particular danger. The military structure—its rigid hierarchy and unquestioning obedience to orders from above—resembled an absolutist monarchy and was thought to make professional soldiers sympathetic to the values of autocratic rulers. In Whig mythology, "a standing army" was, therefore, always viewed as a threat to democratic, civilian government. The nightmare was acted out in France on November 9, 1799, when Napoléon used his troops to sweep aside a government and constitution approved by half a million French voters. To many of the founding generation of Americans, and especially to Thomas Jefferson's followers, it was clear that the republic had to counter this inescapable threat. Successive administrations gambled that the general's influence in taming the army would outweigh the risk of his tendency to treachery.

The bet paid off. Every postrevolutionary government in the American hemisphere has had to undergo the ordeal of a military coup, with the exception of the United States. The key to its good fortune was the prolonged, intricate collusion that took place between the founding fathers and the artist in treason.

Thus the paradox running through James Wilkinson's career is the service he performed for the United States while he was unmistakably betraying it. That tortured relationship reached its peak with Thomas Jefferson, who not only confirmed Wilkinson as commander of the U.S. army, but appointed him to the posts of governor of Louisiana Territory and commissioner of Indian affairs. No president trusted Wilkinson more, or asked so much in return, or, at the apogee of Aaron Burr's conspiracy, came closer to a catastrophic misjudgment of Wilkinson's uncertain loyalties. As Congressman John Randolph pointed out, "The agency of the Army was the whole pivot on which that plot turned." Why then did James Wilkinson choose to defend his country at the cost, as it turned out, of his career?

THE FEAR OF BEING FOUND out haunted the general throughout his life as a spy. His tradecraft was exemplary. He rarely met his handlers. He communicated through a wide range of ciphers and codes, some of whch remain unbreakable because the source books have been lost. He took pains to ensure that his payment in silver dollars came hidden in casks of coffee and sugar and was laundered through banks and real estate deals. To explain away any transfers of money that came to light, he had a watertight cover story backed by forged documents and false testimonials showing them to be the outcome of commercial deals.

The effectiveness of his methods was such that although he faced four official investigations, and many more private and newspaper inquiries, none turned up any hard evidence that he had actually passed information on to Spain in return for money. Nevertheless, Wilkinson was well aware that in one area he remained vulnerable. He could do nothing about the bureaucratic efficiency of the Spanish imperial government.

Once deciphered, his reports were copied in duplicate, sometimes in triplicate, so that local officials in New Orleans, their regional superiors in Havana, and their central masters in Madrid would all be aware of what

Agent 13, the key Spanish operative in North America, had to disclose. Repeatedly, he begged his handlers to destroy his letters, "to hide them in deepest oblivion." When the empire began to crumble, his anxieties became acute. To reasure him, one of his last Spanish contacts, Governor Don Vizente Folch of West Florida, grandly promised him that every incriminating document had been sent to Havana, and "before the United States shall be in a position to conquer that capital, you and I, Jefferson, Madison, with all the secretaries of the different departments . . . will have made many days' journey on the voyage to the other world."

So it proved, and Wilkinson died before his secret was uncovered. But in the last years of the nineteenth century a cache of papers relating to his activities was found in Baton Rouge, Louisiana. Not until the first quarter of the twentieth century, however, when a succession of dogged historians began to dig through the estimated two hundred thousand documents sent back from Havana to Madrid in 1888, was the smoking gun found. Hundreds of letters, reports, comments, and assessments exchanged between Wilkinson, his handlers, and their superiors, the secretary of the Indies and the royal council in Madrid, testify to the scale and importance of his activities. Seventy years ago, they gave rise to two biographies that traced his life but shrank from exploring either the full extent of his treachery or the reasons why successive administrations were ready to tolerate and in some circumstances collude with his activities. To make real sense of the behavior detailed in those documents, it is necessary to see the world through his eyes, and to understand why he found it so rewarding to lead a double life.

HIS BITTEREST ENEMIES testified to his charm. According to an early Kentucky historian, Humphrey Marshall, who came to hate Wilkinson after being cheated on a land deal, the general was not only "easy, polite and gracious" but possessed that seductive trait of focusing "assured attention, cordiality and ease" on each person he talked to. His language was lively and inventive. In a letter to George Washington, Wilkinson dismissed an allegation of taking Spanish money as the sort of attack that was inevitable "in these times of general calumny, when slander on stilts stalks over the fences of reputation." He was musical, widely read, and imaginative enough to choose the perfect present for those he wished to impress—maps and Indian artifacts for Jefferson, thoroughbred horses for a Spanish commandant, and an exotic Alpine strawberry plant for a frontier governor.

To explain his taste for espionage, a CIA profiler might apply the four classic motives for treachery—money, ideology, coercion, or excitement—and conclude that the general was driven by his fear of poverty and boredom. Probing more deeply, a psychologist might guess that the general's infectious enthusiasm, intoxicating confidence, instinctive lying, and sudden contempt for rivals suggested a narcissistic personality.

Yet neither of these explanations quite captures the cold detachment that underlay the vanity, energy, and extravagance. Both as soldier and spy, Wilkinson always hungered for intelligence. It gave him a sense of power. He did not care about the source—gossip, maps, and explorers were equally acceptable—so long as it told him something about the love life of a rival, a path through the mountains, or the ground that a battle might be fought on. As a result, he possessed an exceptionally well-informed, clear-eyed view of the rapidly changing era in which he lived, and of the advantages to be wrung from it. When Aaron Burr expected his collaboration in a conspiracy to tear the United States apart, it was this calculating appraisal that shaped Wilkinson's response.

It is impossible to deny the psychological fascination of James Wilkinson's ability to live a double existence in public view for so many years. Indeed, to judge him by the dark canons of treachery, his long record as commander and spy must rank as one of the most extraordinary careers as a secret agent in the history of espionage. But the lasting value of his divided loyalty is the unique perspective it offers of the young, vulnerable republic taking shape and gathering strength. Viewed through General James Wilkinson's chilly, binocular vision, the struggle to establish the identity of the United States appears as it really was, an uncertain adventure in dangerous times.

1

The Penniless Aristocrat

E XCESS WAS BRED INTO HIM. It showed in his large aspirations, his wild
expenditure, his undisciplined behavior, and his gigantic autobiography. In *Memoirs of My Own Times*, James Wilkinson spread himself across
more than two thousand highly colored pages, but, as he confessed to
friends, he had still only been able "to glance at one fifth of my public life."

A tendency to grandiose living was habitual in the society into which he
was born on March 24, 1757, the colonial aristocracy of Maryland
planters. His grandfather Joseph Wilkinson, a tobacco merchant from England, had arrived in the province in the early years of the eighteenth century. This was the era when Europeans suddenly realized that the great
landmass of British America contained uncountable acres that could be
surveyed and converted into property. Anyone with enough money to pay
his passage might hope to own an estate that would have made him a squire
or a petty lord in Europe. The result was a growing flood of immigrants,
especially to the middle colonies of Maryland, Pennsylvania, and northern
Virginia, that threatened to engulf the proprietorial rights of the great families, the Calverts, the Penns, and the Fairfaxes, who had overall possession
of the land.

A sharp divide soon opened up between the established settlements near
the coasts and rivers, where the ground was already measured out by the
proprietors for sale or rent, and the interior where the poorer immigrants
settled, often squatting rent-free on territory beyond the proprietors' control. *Banditti* was the word commonly used to describe these savage incom-
ers, mostly Presbyterian Scots-Irish from Ulster and Germans from the
Palatine state in the Rhine valley, who occupied the land as though it were

their own. William Byrd of Virginia compared them to "the Goths and Vandals of old," while in Pennsylvania James Logan, in charge of the Penn family's affairs, complained of the disrespect "these bold and indigent strangers"
showed for eighteenth-century conventions, "saying as their excuse when
challenged for titles [to property], that we had solicited for colonists and they
had come accordingly."

Joseph Wilkinson had money enough to buy a plantation of almost nine
hundred acres in Calvert County, a thumb of coastal land bordered on the
east by Chesapeake Bay and on the west and south by the slow waters of
the Patuxent River as it broadened into the bay. The location ensured that
his family would grow up with values quite distinct from the egalitarian
and rebellious impulses of those farther west.

The Calverts, who owned Maryland, maintained better control than
their neighbors the Penns. As early as 1718, the assembly, under presure
from Charles Calvert, the earl of Baltimore and "Absolute Lord and Pro-
prietary of this Province of Maryland," passed legislation requiring each
county to employ a team of nine public surveyors to parcel out the land.
The best of it was sold in large units, as much as ten thousand acres to the
nobly born or well moneyed, but a hundred acres of indifferent soil were
available free to a single individual who paid his or her own passage or
worked for a number of years as an indentured servant. Although frequently breached, this plan proved surprisingly effective as social engineer-
ing and helped bring about the growth of a society with class distinctions
as well-defined as in aristocratic England.

"The Manners of Maryland are somewhat peculiar," a bemused John
Adams observed in 1777 when he visited for the first time. "They have but
few Merchants . . . The Lands are cultivated, and all Sorts of Trades are exercised by Negroes, or by transported Convicts, which has occasioned the
Planters and Farmers to assume the Title of Gentlemen, and they hold their
Negroes and Convicts, that is all labouring People and Tradesmen, in such
Contempt, that they think themselves a distinct order of Beings. Hence
they never will suffer their Sons to labour or learn any Trade, but they
bring them up in Idleness or, what is worse, in Horse Racing, Cock fighting, and Card Playing."

This was an exaggeration—the rapidly growing port of Baltimore had
many merchants, and industrial enterprises such as the giant water mills
erected by the Ellicott brothers on the Patapsco River in the 1760s were
creating a middle class. Nevertheless, the structure of colonial Maryland did
remain remarkably feudal right up to the Revolution. To a New England

lawyer such as Adams, it could only appear alien, but to James Wilkinson, who grew up in it, hierarchy appeared not only natural, but the proper way for society to be organized.

Stoakley Manor, the Wilkinsons' plantation, lay beside a meandering river called Hunting Creek, about four miles north of Prince Frederick, the present county capital. Other properties in Calvert County were more than three times its size, but Stoakley was large enough to justify the family's belief that they belonged to the distinct order of gentlemen. They were related to the Mackalls, the richest family in the county, and Joseph Wilkinson's son, another Joseph, married Althea Heighe, whose siblings and cousins owned seven or eight other plantations. It must have seemed a good match at the time. The young Joseph had inherited Stoakley in 1734 on the death of his father, and Althea, generally known as Betty, had 150 acres of her own, as well as "one feather bed and furniture" left to her by her wealthy father.

Although some of the land was devoted to wheat and other crops, tobacco underpinned Maryland's economy, and to such an extent that until 1733 when paper money was introduced, tobacco leaf was an official currency alongside silver dollars and gold sovereigns, even for such payments as rents, taxes, and fines. Throughout the 1730s, the international demand for it rose, so that within a decade prices doubled. For a time, all tobacco planters prospered, the Wilkinsons among them. But shortly before young Joseph married Betty Heighe and took over the running of Stoakley, the boom began to tail away. By the time that their son James was born in 1757, the youngest of four children, the family was in debt, and the plantation heavily mortgaged.

Any one of several difficulties could have overwhelmed an inexperienced young planter. From the 1740s, Maryland's producers had to accept increasingly complex bureaucratic controls introduced by the assembly to improve the quality of the province's tobaccco. Their French customers caused a sharp fall in prices by manipulating the market, while Dutch merchants abruptly changed fashion from the bright-flavored tobacco known as Sweetscented to the heavier Oronoco leaf. But in the long term, the most crucial decision facing every tobacco planter during this period was whether to rely on European convicts and indentured servants for labor or to switch to the new fashion for African slaves. Perhaps Joseph Wilkinson had scruples about using slaves or perhaps he overstretched himself financially in buying them at thirty-five pounds sterling (approximately $175) a head; perhaps he had been brought up as an idle gentleman with no head for business, or perhaps he had gambled and lost heavily on cockfighting or cardplaying. No record of bankruptcy exists, but the estate was broken up and sold soon after Joseph's premature death in 1764 at the age of thirty-three.

James Wilkinson was just six years old when Joseph died. Into his absence, the son projected the picture of the ideal gentleman, and of the way he should behave under duress. "The last words my father spoke to me," Wilkinson declared, "were 'My son, if you ever put up with an insult, I will disinherit you.' " Whether the dying Joseph actually uttered such baleful words is questionable—as the younger son, James was not the heir—but the idea they expressed was branded deep into his son's personality. In adult life, the merest hint that Wilkinson had not behaved properly would be met with an explosion of anger and, frequently, a challenge to settle the matter with sword or pistol. His violent reaction, almost hysterical at times, must have had its roots in the psychological pressure of seeing his father ground down by debt.

In the absence of banks, Maryland planters borrowed from each other—Stoakley's broad acres ended up in the hands of three of Calvert County's most prominent families. Thus the creditors Joseph Wilkinson was staving off would have been his friends. Among the excuses he must have offered them, the deceits he must have practiced, and the slow, corrosive experience of letting down those who had trusted him most, the one thing he evidently clung to, the single asset that no one could take from him, was his standing as a gentleman. In his son's *Memoirs*, the references to his father suggest a man grown almost pathologically touchy about his social standing. The value was passed on intact to his son, who would in his turn always believe that the image of respectability excused the reality of betrayal.

Nevertheless, Joseph Wilkinson's faith in the social advantages of being a gentleman had some justification. Although the plantation had to be sold to meet his debts, his creditors showed forebearance. His widow, Betty, was allowed to keep the Heighe land she had inherited, and some acres of Stoakley. It was not much, but in time the property gave her elder son, Joseph Wilkinson III, sufficient standing to marry Barbara Mackall. By 1783 Barbara's inheritance from her wealthy father had allowed her husband to become the owner of almost six hundred acres and a gristmill. The two Wilkinson daughters, Elizabeth and Mary, also survived, each marrying a local farmer and raising a family. It was the youngest child, the impressionable James, who found it hardest to recover from the catastrophe.

As was normal for young men of his class, he was educated by a private tutor, at the expense of his grandmother Mrs. Elizabeth Heighe. Apart from his brother, he was brought up in a household of adoring women whom he clearly learned to charm with his liveliness and energy. What must have been especially delightful to adults was his quick intelligence. His teacher, David Hunter, had the distinction of being a graduate from the highly regarded University of Glasgow in Scotland. Wilkinson's first Spanish handlers noted that he had had "a very good education," and the Latin tags and classical references that decorated his conversation, as well as the high-flown rhetorical flourishes used to disguise his true intentions, were proof of how well he had been grounded in the eighteenth-century curriculum of the classics, English literature, grammar, and rhetoric. But more far-reaching were the lessons Wilkinson learned from friends of his age. These were the sons of Maryland planters who could look forward to inheriting a plantation and the privileges that went with it. They taught each other the niceties of social distinction and etiquette and largely ignored the knowledge of their social inferiors.

Aged thirteen the boy was sent with several others, including his brother, Joseph, and John Custis, George Washington's stepson, to Baltimore, seventy miles away, to be inoculated against smallpox, an expensive precaution that was, he explained, restricted to "young gentlemen from the Southern provinces." The procedure required some pus from a smallpox victim to be rubbed into an open cut, usually made in the hand of the patient, creating a small, localized infection sufficient to create immunity. It was dangerous enough to kill one or two patients in every hundred, and Dr. Stevenson, the Irish doctor who treated Wilkinson, strictly forbade his patients to exercise for fear of spreading the infection through the blood more quickly than the body could cope with it.

With the easy disdain of his class, Wilkinson recalled, "I paid little respect to the prescribed regimen, and although my physician frequently attempted to alarm me by exclaiming, 'Young gentleman, by Jasus, you will be peppered,' I escaped with slight eruptive fever and was marked by a single pustule."

What made it impossible to lie still was the stimulation of urban life. With just 564 houses located inside its nominal limits in 1774, Baltimore was hardly a metropolis, but Wilkinson was entranced by its "bustle and excitement" compared to the isolation of a plantation life. "I thought myself transported to another region," he recalled, "[by the crowds] of men, women and children, the wagons, drays, carts, dogs and horses, and the numerous tawdry signs swinging over the street."

Serving the great wheat fields of northern Maryland and southern

Pennsylvania, Baltimore's port was already close to displacing Philadelphia for shipping grain and flour to Europe, and becoming the center for the tobacco trade. Most of the buildings were wooden, many still rough-hewn by ax, and the streets were beaten earth, but a brick-built courthouse and marketplace had been constructed alongside stone-built wharves and warehouses. The population, estimated at about thirteen thousand, had long overspilled the city boundaries. To a country boy, however aristocratic his background, the broad horizons it offered were irresistible. "Thus were the bonds of local attachment rent," he recorded in his fifties, but it was not just Baltimore that seduced him. He was developing an appetite for excitement.

Elizabeth Heighe's charity made itself felt once more when Wilkinson was sixteen, and he was sent to study at the medical school in Philadelphia. The Heighes had a high respect for medicine, and a few years later Wilkinson's young cousin James Heighe Blake, another landless young aristocrat, would also become a medical student in Philadelphia. Having qualified as a doctor, Blake's high reputation led in time to his election as mayor of Washington, where he founded the city's first school and its public health service. Wilkinson was never likely to follow that path. He enjoyed the idea of being a doctor more than the reality.

What weighed most heavily with him was the attraction of studying in Philadelphia. If Baltimore was another region, the City of Brotherly Love was a different universe. In 1774, it was the largest city in British America, with a population of forty thousand, paved streets, a university, a hospital, theaters, such public amenities as a library and firefighting service, and the sort of polite society where a young man short on money but long on charm could hope to flourish. This was where he began his real education, in which "I sought by imitating the best examples to acquire gracefulness of address and ease of manners." Girls were his motivation or, in the elaborate language he used when dressing up the naked truth, "These inclinations were seconded by my solicitude to merit the acquaintance of the most accomplished and respectable of the fair sex, whose ages corresponded with my own." His formal education took second place.

Philadelphia's medical curriculum covered anatomy and surgery, the supporting sciences of chemistry, botany, and pharmacy, as well as the critically important field known as materia medica, which included diagnosis of ills and prescription of cures. Students were expected to take three years to graduate, but Wilkinson had the added advantage of staying with an elderly relative, John Bond, who was an experienced doctor. Many eighteenth-century students learned their trade by serving as apprentices to qualified physicians, and Wilkinson undoubtedly picked up some additional skills from his host. In April 1775, after less than two years' study, he impatiently decided he was qualified to practice medicine.

He set up his practice in the distant settlement of Monocacy, Maryland, about forty miles west of Baltimore. It had been settled for barely a generation, and mostly by Germans, whose language Wilkinson did not speak. Aged seventeen, only partially trained and short of money, he was probably unable to find a more desirable area, but the drab routine of administering pills to inarticulate farmers and taking their blood was hardly likely to appeal to someone who had devoted so much energy to getting ahead in Philadelphia's high society. Before the summer was over, he had discovered a new, more exciting vocation.

On his very first day in Philadelphia, Wilkinson happened to see a military parade, with a company of artillery and four companies of infantry. The spectacle of marching redcoats, fife-and-drum bands, and horse-drawn guns thrilled him. "It appeared like enchantment," he wrote, "and my bosom throbbed with delight, and from that day I felt the strongest inclination to military life." The flames of his enchantement were fanned by Dr. Bond's reminiscences of his earlier career as a military surgeon during the French and Indian War. "Like any old soldier [he] took pleasure in recounting the details of battles, particularly Braddock's defeat near Pittsburgh and Wolfe's victory on the Plains of Abraham, and to this circumstance I ascribe my earliest military predilections."

When news of the shots fired at Lexington reached Monocacy, Wilkinson's immediate instinct was to join the fight against the British, but what drove him was the desire for battle rather than the love of liberty. "My youth had not allowed me the time or means to investigate the merits of the controversy," he conceded. So far as constitutional matters were concerned, it was enough to know that the representatives of the thirteen states assembled in congress had opted for rebellion, a choice "seconded by my feelings and supported by that predilection for arms which I had previously imbibed." His reaction was typical of the bellicose fury that swept through the colonies in response to the shedding of American blood. In the words of one Philadelphia correspondent, "The *Rage Militaire*, as the French call a passion for arms, has taken possession of the whole Continent."

A company made up of planters' sons had been assembled in Georgetown, Maryland, about forty miles away, and once a week Wilkinson rode down the Potomac Valley to drill with them. This was his first taste of soldiering, and

the patriotic excitement of preparing for war swept away his thin ambition
to be a doctor. Less than three months after setting up his practice, he had enlisted in the army. For Wilkinson, the obvious unit to join was the Maryland
militia, but no company existed in Monocacy, and to be commissioned into
the Georgetown company, he would, as an outsider, have to put his name forward to the local committee of safety. Intoxicated by the news of the battle
of Bunker Hill and by his own dreams of glory, however, he decided "not to
await the tardy procedings of committees and conventions" and in July 1775
rode straight toward the sound of gunfire in Boston.

2

CITIZENS AND SOLDIERS

THE YOUNG SUBALTERN'S TIMING could not have been better. The Continental Army, created by Congress in June 1775 with General George Washington as its commander, had just begun to send its first units to Boston to reinforce the New England militia besieging General Thomas Gage's army of redcoats. Wilkinson immediately attached himself as a volunteer to a Pennsylvania rifle company, but the new army needed officers. That September, on the basis of his short training at Georgetown, Wilkinson was appointed a captain in the recently raised Second Continental Regiment, commanded by Colonel James Reed. Put in command of a troop made up largely of frontiersmen, the *banditti* who so infuriated the planters, Wilkinson immediately encountered a problem that would dog him throughout his military career—how to reconcile the requirements of a disciplined army with the expectations of individual liberty.

The young captain was appalled by "the familiarity which prevailed among the soldiers and officers of all ranks; from the colonel to the private, I observed but little distinction, and I could not refrain from remarking to the young gentlemen with whom I had made acquaintance that the military discipline of their troops was not so conspicuous as the civil subordination of the community in which I had lived." His reaction might have been expected, given the sharp contrast between his Maryland-bred, aristocratic outlook and the democratic habits of riflemen drawn largely from New Hampshire, but it was part of a larger clash that divided both the army and Congress itself.

Within weeks of taking command of the New England militia outside Boston, George Washington came to a similar conclusion about the civilian soldiers from the north. Like his newest lieutenant, he was shocked by the "irregularities" of their behavior toward officers, their lack of discipline, and their tendency to leave camp whenever they felt they could be more useful at home. "All the General Officers agree," he reported to Congress, "that no Dependence can be put on the Militia for a continuance in Camp, or Regularity and Discipline during the short time they may stay." Washington never doubted that the Continental Army had to be made up of full-time, or at least long-serving, professional soldiers if they were to defeat the disciplined ranks and firepower of British troops. The conviction was etched into him by long years in command of the Virginia militia and experience of action with trained British forces during the French and Indian War.

Nevertheless, the New England militia had inflicted such heavy losses on their attackers in the battle of Bunker Hill that the British never again attempted to break out of Boston. "When I look to the consequences of it in the loss of so many brave Officers, I do it with horror," General William Howe reported to London after his hard-won victory. "The Success is too dearly bought." Nor did every American general agree with the commander in chief's assessment. Washington's adjutant general, Horatio Gates, who had been trained as a professional soldier in the British army, declared that he "never desired to see better soldiers than the New England men made." And Congress remained hostile to the threat of political intimidation posed by professional soldiers. "A Standing Army, however necessary it may be at some times, is always dangerous to the Liberties of the People," Samuel Adams declared. "Soldiers are apt to consider themselves as a Body distinct from the rest of the Citizens."

Thus from the start of his military career, Wilkinson was caught up in the struggle between supporters of the regulars and the militia. In military terms, the argument turned on matters of discipline, pay, and length of enlistment, but the implications of creating a professional soldiery reached beyond the army. In the minds of most independent-minded Americans, the militia represented the true spirit of the Revolution, men who took up arms, not for pay or promotion, but for sheer patriotic commitment to their country and to the ideals it reperesented.

"Our troops are animated with the Love of Freedom," New England delegates to Congress declared in February 1776. "We confess that they have not the Advantages arising from Experience and Discipline. But Facts have shewn that native Courage warmed with Patriotism is sufficient to counterbalance these Advantages."

That belief lay at the heart of the battle for liberty. Just as independent citizens were superior to obedient subjects, so soldiers fighting for democracy and freedom must prevail over those serving the dictates of a distant monarch. "We must succeed in a Cause so manifestly just," Samuel Adams insisted, "if we are Virtuous."

Washington, by contrast, held that Americans, like everyone else, fought better and for longer when they had "a prospect of Interest or some reward." With grim realism he wrote, "Men may speculate as they will, they may talk of patriotism; they may draw a few examples from ancient story, of great atchievements [*sic*] performed by its influence; but whoever builds upon it, as a sufficient Basis for conducting a long and [bloody] War, will find themselves deceived in the end." To win their liberty, Americans needed something more than idealism; they needed to create a more efficient fighting machine than the enemy's.

Wilkinson's rapid promotion in this new force would owe much to his enthusiastic support for the changes that Washington and his senior officers introduced. The Continental Army's soldiers were enlisted for a minimum of twelve months as opposed to the militia's variable terms of three to nine months. A uniform line of command was created that led up from the platoon lieutenant and company captain through the lieutenant colonel at the head of a regiment and the brigadier general commanding a brigade of several regiments to the dizzy heights of a major general in charge of a division of infantry, artillery, and cavalry units.

A revised and more severe disciplinary code, the Articles of War, was introduced, and a provost marshal was appointed to jail and, if necessary, flog offenders up to a maximum of thirty-nine lashes. The list of offenses for which soldiers could be executed was extended to include desertion and, for the first time, treason. "An Army without Order, Regularity and Discipline," Washington announced on January 1, 1776, when these changes came into effect, "is no better than a Commission'd Mob." With new powers at their back, junior officers were ordered to exert greater control over their men, a command that Wilkinson obeyed in his own fashion when he met his company for the first time in March 1776.

"The regiment was ordered for muster the day I entered on duty," he recalled, "the company was paraded, and I presented myself to take the command; but when I gave the order to shoulder firelocks the men remained motionless, and the lieutenant, stepping up to me, inquired where I was going to march the men. I answered that he should presently see but in the meantime he must consider himself in arrest for mutiny and 'March to his room,' which he did without hesitation. I then addressed myself to the company, pointed out to them my right of command and the necessity for their obedience; I informed them that I should repeat the order, and if it was not instantly obeyed, I should run the man nearest to me through the body, and would proceed on right to left, so long as they continued refractory and my strength would support me. I had no further trouble, but joined the regiment and marched to the parade of general muster."

As news of the incident spread, it became a test of the new discipline. Wilkinson's men were originally militia from New Hampshire, who had reenlisted as regulars expecting to be commanded by their popular lieutenant, Thomas Grover. In the circumstances, a court-martial decided merely to fine Grover for "insulting Capt. Wilkinson, disobeying his orders and insulting language," a verdict that astonished Washington. He wrote at once to Congress demanding the lieutenant be dismissed considering "the Enormity of his Offence & [its] dangerous and pernicious tendency." An abject apology secured Grover's pardon, but the young captain's stern attitude was noted. Soon afterward he was rewarded by being appointed an aide to General Nathanael Greene, Washington's most promising commander and an unyielding disciplinarian.

In March 1776, General Gage's redcoats were evacuated from Boston, marking the end of the first triumphant phase of the war. The nineteen-year-old Wilkinson celebrated by walking over the battleground of Bunker Hill with two of Greene's staff officers, to absorb its lessons. "Our men were more than a match for the enemy in disorderly skirmishes or behind breastworks and other impediments," Wilkinson concluded, "but when brought into regular action in open space would have been overwhelmed by their own confusion."

What the militia needed, the captain decided, was more training and discipline. This was precisely what his general believed. In Nathanael Greene, Wilkinson had found not just a commander he believed in but, as he would soon embarrassingly reveal, a man he could almost regard as a father.

SIX WEEKS AFTER that leisurely stroll across the battlefield, Wilkinson encountered the enemy for the first time, close to Montreal on the banks of the St. Lawrence River. His presence there was the result of Congress's strategy to persuade Canada to become the fourteenth colony in rebellion against the mother country. A Northern Department was created on the same day in June 1775 as the Continental Army, and an invasion force of three thousand men under General Philip Schuyler was sent to attack Quebec. The assault failed on the last day of the year, and by the early summer of 1776 disease had killed so many men in Schuyler's army that Washington had to send reinforcements north from Boston, five regiments of militia, and eight of the new Continentals.

Among the fresh arrivals was Captain Wilkinson, who led his New Hampshire company up the Hudson from New York, then by boat across Lake Champlain, and along the Richelieu River in Canada to the banks of the St. Lawrence, opposite Montreal. It was no small feat for a young southerner to lead almost eighty Yankee frontiersmen through country they must have known better than he, sweeping up a score of deserters along the way, and to deliver them all to the officer in command at Montreal, Major General Benedict Arnold.

However black his later reputation, Arnold was the first military hero of the Revolution and, next to Greene, Washington's favorite general. Nobody better epitomized the *rage militaire* that gripped Americans than this fierce, dynamic commander who hated retreat and sought to bring the British to battle at every opportunity. In May 1775, within days of the outbreak of war, he had with Ethan Allen led the surprise raid that captured the great fort of Ticonderoga guarding upstate New York and seized almost a hundred cannon and mortars to provide the Continental Army with its first artillery. During the summer, Arnold had gone on to capture a cluster of forts controlling northern New York and the entrance to the Hudson Valley. At the end of the year, he had led an independent column to attack Quebec and been shot in the leg during the assault. Undaunted, he had taken over command and maintained the siege until in April 1776 the approach of a new British army under General Sir John Burgoyne forced the besiegers to withdraw.

The appearance of Burgoyne's force was the result of the massive buildup of troops undertaken by Britain during the spring and summer of 1776 in response to the Boston defeat. The strategic plan was to encircle the rebels in New England, regarded as the source of the Revolution, in a massive pincer movement. The main army under General Sir William Howe quickly achieved the first part of the plan in August by defeating Washington on Long Island and driving him from New York. Meanwhile in the north, Burgoyne at the head of nine thousand well-trained regulars intended to clear the St. Lawrence Valley, then hook south from Canada toward the Hudson River and eventually meet up with Howe's troops. Together they would then crush New England into submission.

As the Quebec besiegers retreated up the St. Lawrence, Arnold was sent

ahead to hold Montreal, 170 miles to the west, to keep open a line of retreat to upstate New York. In this perilous situation, the arrival of a confident young officer with obvious powers of leadership must have been as
welcome as the reinforcements he brought with him. Wilkinson and his
company were immediately ordered to dig defensive positions on the banks
of the St. Lawrence against British attack.

For all his bravado in taking command, Wilkinson was only nineteen and
had seen no action. The tiny garrison of 450 men faced an enemy 1,000
strong, outlying posts had been cut off, ammunition and food were running
low, no reinforcements were available, and the British were said to be close
at hand. Understandly, on May 24, Wilkinson wanted to send a last letter,
but for reasons apparent only to him, it was addressed to General Greene.

"We are now in a sweet situation," he began bravely, and went on to describe his desperate circumstances with a British attack expected in six
hours. "The morning dawns," he ended, "—that morn big with the fate of
a few, a handful of brave fellows. I shall do my part—but remember, if I fall
I am sacrificed. May God Bless you equal to your merits. *Vale!*"

The message was delivered, and its melodramatic summary of the military position so shocked Greene that he forwarded it, minus the valedictory
ending, to Washington. Horrified by what seemed like the impending an-
nihilation of American forces in Canada, Washington promptly sent it on
to Congress with the comment that "the Intelligence from [Canada] contained in a letter from Captn Wilkinson . . . is truly alarming."

But Wilkinson had confused theater with truth, a mistake that would in
time become a habit. In reality, the nearest British troops were three days'
march away. Hobbled by indecisive leadership and internal feuding between Burgoyne and the Quebec commander, Sir Guy Carleton, they were
moving too slowly to pose any immediate threat. Besides, almost as soon as
the letter to Greene had been sent, five hundred fresh troops marched into
Arnold's camp, and in characteristically bold fashion, the general at once began to plan a counterattack against his lumbering foe. Sent to check out the
situation, General Schuyler reported to the commander in chief on June 10,
"I am happy that Captn Wilkinson's Conjectures were not realized."

By then the captain had already transferred his affections from Greene to
Arnold and, as he put it, was trying to secure "the preference of an officer,
who at that period acquired great celebrity." To belong to a general's "family," his immediate entourage of officers, was a privilege that always attracted
ambitious young subalterns. That Arnold, like Greene, should quickly have

selected Wilkinson to be his aide indicates the good impression his enthusiasm and intelligence created.

In a revealing incident, however, the young officer failed at one of the first tasks that Arnold set him. Detailed to take a platoon of soldiers to requisition supplies from the local farmers, Wilkinson abruptly lost his nerve when met by a stream of abuse from the outraged owner of a cask of Madeira he had attempted to seize. Returning almost tearfully to Arnold, he demanded to be relieved of the detail. It says much for Wilkinson's puppyish appeal that the abrasive general, who normally chewed up unsatisfactory subordinates, simply dismissed him with the comment that he was "more nice than wise." His next duty, however, revealed steelier qualities.

On June 15, Arnold sent his aide down the St. Lawrence Valley to make contact with General John Sullivan, overall commander of the Quebec army. But barely twenty miles from Montreal, the sinister sight of redcoats on the road ahead brought Wilkinson to a halt. Wheeling his horse around, he galloped back to warn Arnold, arriving at his camp shortly before dusk. Arnold quickly deduced that instead of falling back on Montreal, Sullivan must already have turned south from the St. Lawrence, leaving the garrison in danger of being cut off. Arnold ordered his own small force to evacuate Montreal and retreat back down the Richelieu River toward New York. Then he dispatched his aide to find Sullivan with an urgent request for reinforcements.

Night was falling and a storm had broken when Wilkinson came up with Sullivan's retreating army just fifteeen miles away. Although the general issued an order to the rearguard commander to send five hundred men to help Arnold, in the darkness with the rain falling in torrents, and the army confused and demoralized, the officer could not be found. Exhausted by hours of hard riding, Wilkinson fell asleep in a cabin and at daybreak learned that the man he was looking for was missing and, according to those who knew him, probably drunk and unconscious. The only one likely to be able to help was a Colonel Anthony Wayne, farther back toward the enemy. Half an hour later, Wilkinson came upon a column of disciplined soldiers on the road under an officer who appeared "as much at his ease as if he was marching to a parade of exercise."

This first meeting between two men destined to become venomous enemies could hardly have been friendlier. With the spontaneous boldness that would earn him the nickname Mad Anthony, Wayne promptly agreed to help, despite the obvious danger. He posted a guard at a bridge and forcibly enlisted every straggler who attempted to cross it until he had five hundred men, then marched them in the direction of Montreal and Arnold. They had barely covered two miles before they were intercepted by a message from Arnold to say the danger was past, but in that time Wayne grew to like Wilkinson so well that even several years later he could describe him as "a Gentleman who I have always esteemed as a friend, and who I know to be a brave and an experienced Officer."

Complacently, the British allowed their enemy to escape across Lake Champlain, confident that the continuous accumulation of resources would allow them to crush the rebels before the end of the year. The last two Americans to leave Canadian soil were Arnold, once more in command of the rear guard, and Wilkinson. They were rowed away from shore in the same boat, and it is hard to picture them far out on the waters of the lake without speculating about the nature of the capacity for treachery lying latent in each.

Physically, they were not unalike, being short and thickset, and they shared two pronounced characteristics, a crippling incompetence about money and an almost theatrical vanity—each had, for example, wanted to be the last person to leave Canada. To Wilkinson's irritation Arnold had won by taking advantage of his rank to insist on pushing off from shore with his own hand. So long as they were in the field, money became a secondary issue, and the esteem of fellow combatants kept both content. Only when they were away from the fighting, and cash and admiration were in short supply, did cracks begin to open. Yet what is striking about Arnold's career is the way that his spirit was broken by Congress's unremitting hostility to his claims for military recognition and by its persecution of him over his financial affairs. It is not too much to say that he was driven to treachery. Wilkinson's loyalty, on the other hand, was always unreliable, as Arnold himself discovered soon after their boat came to shore.

DESPITE THE HUMILIATION of the retreat, Arnold felt that he at least had nothing to be ashamed of. At the end of June, when the remains of the Canadian invasion force had retired to Crown Point, south of Lake Champlain, to lick their wounds, he took Wilkinson with him to Albany, New York, to meet the new general who had been appointed to replace the disappointing Sullivan. This was Horatio Gates, who had made his reputation as Washington's adjutant general, responsible for putting into effect the Continental Army's disciplinary structure.

Gates arrived in Albany on June 27, 1776. Congress had appointed him to command a Canadian invasion force that no longer existed, and in its absence Gates felt entitled to regard himself as the senior officer in the Northern Department. Although that position had explicitly been given to Schuyler, it became Gates's overriding priority to elbow his rival aside. In this task, he was soon to be joined by Arnold's former protégé, James Wilkinson.

3

WOOING GENERAL GATES

THERE WAS SOMETHING of the seducer in the way James Wilkinson set about winning the hearts of his generals. With all of them, as his fellow staff officers noted, he was quick, compliant, amusing, and efficient. But he could also be histrionic, as in his letter to Nathanael Greene. Or genuinely courageous, as in his efforts to safeguard Benedict Arnold. Toward General Horatio Gates, however, he exhibited an affection too intense to be pretended. The depth of feeling suggested how much he missed his real father.

At the height of their relationship, Wilkinson would write in an official, if outspoken, report, "Pardon the freedom of my language, I speak to General Gates, but in him I hope I address a friend," signing himself "my dear General's affectionate friend." Gates responded warmly, encouraging Wilkinson's extravagant opinions and judgments. As Wilkinson himself admitted, the general won him "by his indulgence of my self-love." The younger man responded by encouraging the older one's taste for intrigue. It was a dangerous exchange.

As a former major in the British army, Horatio Gates possessed a professional understanding of military organization and training. Appointed adjutant general in the Continental Army, he had begun the gargantuan task of creating a single, uniform army from the manpower of thirteen different colonies each with its own militia. Short, pudgy, and bespectacled—"an old granny looking fellow" according to one of his soldiers—Gates's kindly, conciliatory manner encouraged people to work together, and it was a considerable feat to have secured the collaboration of the colonies before they had agreed on any kind of unified constitutional government. His reputation consequently ranked high. In some people's opinion, not least his own, it rivaled that of George Washington. Nevertheless, he had never exercised independent command in combat, and his limited military experience meant that he maneuvered through the corridors of power with more confidence than he ever displayed on the battlefield.

A relationship that was to prove profoundly destructive to both Gates and Wilkinson began formally enough in early July 1776 when Gates sent Arnold with Wilkinson to Crown Point to inspect the increasingly disease-ridden survivors of the Canadian disaster. Of fifty-two hundred men, they found almost half sick with typhoid fever, smallpox, and other illnesses. Gates decided, with Schuyler's reluctant agreement, to move the stricken army farther south to the great fortress of Ticonderoga, which guarded the entrance to the head of the Hudson Valley. Arnold and Wilkinson were tasked with preparing Ticonderoga for their reception, a duty that fell largely to the junior officer after the general became embroiled in a feud over allegations of looting in Canada.

During this period when he was reporting directly to Gates, the young captain switched allegiance. It was not that Wilkinson turned against Arnold—he defended his former patron vigorously in the looting quarrel, saying, "[I] have always found Him the intrepid, generous, friendly, upright, Honest man"—rather that Gates could offer more. He was, Wilkinson declared, "a commander whom the entire army loved, feared and respected."

Gates made his appreciation known on July 20 by promoting Wilkinson to brigade major, and appointing him to the staff of his own favorite general, Arthur St. Clair. Soon afterward Wilkinson fell sick with typhoid fever himself and was sent back to the army's headquarters in Albany, where he almost died. Later he used to claim that he came so close to death he could hear the planks being sawed in the yard outside to make his coffin. Fortunately he came under the care of the army's senior medical officer, who had orders from Gates to keep the young officer alive at any cost.

By the time he was again fit for duty, St. Clair's brigade had moved south to join Washington, and so Gates attached Wilkinson to his own staff. When the general marched south in December with four regiments from Albany in response to Washington's urgent request for reinforcements, Wilkinson went with him. The next tumultuous month altered the course of many careers, not least those of the general and the new major.

HAVING DRIVEN WASHINGTON out of New York during the early fall of 1776, General William Howe had unexpectedly followed him into New

Jersey instead of going into winter quarters. Taken by surprise, with part of his force under General Charles Lee still in Westchester, New York, and many of his militia anxious to return home at the end of the year, Washington himself was in acute danger of being overwhelmed by pursuing British forces. Unsure where the commander in chief had retreated to, Gates sent his newly recovered aide ahead to find Washington.

Scouting for clues in the confusion of war, Wilkinson rode through northern New Jersey and eventually learned that Washington and most of his troops had crossed the Delaware River farther south into Pennsylvania. With swarms of British troops roaming the area, he decided to consult General Lee, Washington's second-in-command, who had moved his headquarters close to Morristown, New Jersey. Lee was a fighting general, and an exponent of small-scale warfare. During a period of his life when he'd lived as a Native American with a Seneca wife, his aggressive behavior earned him the nickname Boiling Water. He had learned his trade in the British army, then left to become a mercenary, participating in any European war he could find. As a result, he was, in Washington's estimation, "the first officer in Military knowledge and experience we have in the whole army."

At nightfall on December 12, Wilkinson found Lee at an inn outside Morristown, apparently unperturbed that the Connecticut militia guarding him had just decided to return to their homes. Not until the following morning did Lee draft a letter to Gates. Its message was unrelievedly gloomy. Lee believed that, to make best use of his untrained militia troops, Washington should be conducting a guerrilla campaign rather than trying to confront in open battle a professional army that could bring devastating firepower to bear on its enemy through parade-ground maneuvers.

"*Entre nous* a certain great man is damnably deficient," Lee told Gates. Washington's mistaken strategy had left Philadelphia defenseless and the army on the verge of defeat. "Unless something turns up which I do not expect, our cause is lost. Our counsels have been weak to the last degree." Lee intended to remain in Morristown, despite Washington's repeated requests that Lee move his forces west of the Delaware. However, Lee advised Gates to join their chief as soon as possible, with the implication that he would be needed as a replacement before long.

Lee was still eating breakfast in his dressing gown and slippers when Wilkinson heard hoofbeats on the road and looking out of the window saw a troop of British dragoons gallop up to the inn. Too late, Lee realized that he was the target of an enemy raid carried out virtually within sight of his army. He attempted to hide in the chimney, but, when Wilkinson appeared at the window, the horsemen swore they would shoot and set fire to the building unless Lee surrendered. Convinced it was not a bluff, the general gave himself up and was hustled away, still in his bedroom slippers, leaving Wilkinson to deliver his letter to Gates.

Lee was not only Gates's friend, but an authority in the area where Gates was weakest, the command of troops in battle. His message crystallized Gates's opposition to Washington. From then on, he, too, espoused the use of guerrilla warfare relying on militia forces. Following Lee's advice, however, Gates hurried to join Washington west of the Delaware River. He arrived on December 20, and with the addition of more than two thousand troops Washington at once began to plan a counterstroke against a Hessian brigade stationed across the river in Trenton, New Jersey.

Believing the attack would fail, Gates refused to take part. With the excuse that he was ill, he left for Philadelphia, intending to travel on to Baltimore, where Congress had retreated to escape the threat of British marauders. Wilkinson loyally went with him until they reached Philadelphia. There he decided he could not miss the battle. In a testimony to their friendship Gates gave him an excuse to return in the form of a letter for Washington.

On Christmas morning, Wilkinson galloped back from Philadelphia, arriving toward nightfall as the long lines of American troops were getting ready to be ferried over the icy Delaware for Washington's surprise attack. So poorly shod were the soldiers that Wilkinson later recalled the trail from their barracks to McKonky's Ferry was "easily traced, for there was a little snow on the ground which was tinged here and there with blood from the feet of the men with broken shoes." To transport them with their heavy packs across the water was a dangerous operation made more hazardous by swirling ice floes and a high wind that drove snow in the ferrymen's faces. When Wilkinson came up with Washington to deliver Gates's letter, the commander in chief was about to ride out to inspect this first, critical phase of his plan. The encounter remained etched in the young man's memory.

"What a time is this to hand me letters!" Washington exclaimed. Wilkinson replied that the dispatch was from General Gates, and Washington's response showed that he was not even aware that his senior general had gone. "Where is General Gates?" he demanded.

Wilkinson answered that Gates was in Philadelphia, to which Washington angrily asked why he had gone there.

"I understood him that he was on his way to Congress," Wilkinson replied.

"On his way to Congress!" Washington burst out, and the depth of pent-up exasperation in his voice betrayed his tension. Coupled with Lee's refusal to obey orders, Gates's blatant decision to ignore his wishes in order to lobby Congress must have made plain to Washington that after a year of defeats his authority was slipping away. His future, and that of the cause he served, depended on the surprise attack he had planned. As Wilkinson himself admitted, he was so shaken by his commander in chief's anger that he could say nothing, but "made my bow and left."

The details of Trenton, Wilkinson's first experience of battle, never faded, but he recalled with particular clarity the river crossing. A flotilla of boats had been assembled, and almost three thousand men had to be assigned, marshaled, and marched aboard in the midst of a snowstorm, an operation supervised by Henry Knox, whose "stentorian lungs and extraordinary exertions" were in Wilkinson's view essential to the proceedings. Out on the water, the difficulties only grew more severe as "the force of the current, the sharpness of the frost, the darkness of the night, the ice which made during the operation and the high wind, rendered the passage of the river extremely difficult."

In these extreme conditions the operation fell more than two hours behind schedule. Once across, however, Washington's force divided into two columns and marched south, the right column hugging the riverbank while, two miles inland, the left advanced directly into Trenton. General St. Clair's brigade was closest to the river, and as Brigade Major Wilkinson marched with them, they circled round the town to block the exit on the far side. By now the operation was so late that what had been planned as a night attack became a daylight assault, but it was still unexpected because the defenders of Trenton never imagined that the Delaware could be crossed in such a storm.

On the north side of town, cannon were placed to fire down the two main streets, preventing the highly trained Hessians from forming up to deliver the concerted volleys of shot that made them so effective. With superior numbers and firepower, the attackers quickly took control of the street battle that developed. Those who attempted to escape were shot or captured by the river column as it encircled the town. In midmorning on December 26, Wilkinson delivered a second message to Washington. This one, from St. Clair, reported that on the south side his brigade not only had Trenton surrounded, but had driven one of the three Hessian regiments in the garrison into the open where the survivors were forced to surrender. The trap had closed. From his vantage point at the north end of town, Washington had seen the other two regiments bombarded into capitulation. Wilkinson's report confirmed that the surprise attack had won a complete victory.

As he delivered St. Clair's news to Washington, Wilkinson remembered "his countenance beaming with complacency," the frustrations of the previous evening wiped away. "Major Wilkinson," Washington exclaimed, shaking the young officer's hand, "this is a glorious day for our country."

More than one thousand Germans had been captured, together with cannon, shot, and gunpowder, and another hundred had been killed. Of wider significance, the victory restored morale in the army, and as news of it rippled out through the country, it transformed the mood of despair that had begun to be felt ever more widely. "The minds of the people are much altered," Nicholas Cresswell, a Tory Virginian, admitted less than a week after the battle. "A few days ago they had given up the cause as lost. Their late successes have turned the scale and now they are all liberty-mad again."

To reinforce the impact of his victory, Washington launched a second surprise attack on the British garrison in Princeton a week later. This was a bloodier battle, with casualties of almost four hundred on the enemy side, but it ended in the rout of three battalions of regular infantry who had occupied the town. In the space of seven days, Washington's two victories had won back control of New Jersey and, as Wilkinson declared, "the American community began to feel and act like a nation determined to be free."

TRENTON ALSO OPENED UP a road that promised military glory for James Wilkinson personally. He had already risen fast in the army thanks to the patronage of his generals, but by leaving Gates to take part in the battle, he had taken a first step toward establishing his own independent career. Recognition of his qualities came in January 1777 when he was promoted to lieutenant colonel, this time on the recommendation of Washington himself, and given a commission in a new regiment. This was the ultimate proving ground for an ambitious officer, and Wilkinson had been given the opportunity when Congress had at last decided what the shape of the army should be after eighteen months of vacillation between militia and regulars.

Through the dreadful fall of 1776 when military disaster threatened to wipe out the ideals asserted in the Declaration of Independence, the case against the militia had been stated with growing force by Washington's generals. "No operation can be safely planned in which they are to take a part," Nathanael Greene declared after the retreat from New York. "I must repeat the Militia are not be depended upon," Schuyler wrote following the defeat in Canada. On the very day that he began planning the attack on Trenton, Washington found time to complain to Congress that militia troops "come in, you cannot tell how; go you cannot tell when; and act you cannot tell where; consume your provisions, exhaust your stores and leave you at last at a critical moment." The irritation of working with such undisciplined soldiers was revealed in a furious outburst from Wayne. "To say anything severe to them has just as much effect as if you were to cut up a Butcher's Chopping block with a razor," he fulminated. "By G-d, they feel nothing but down Right blows which, with the dread of being whipt thro' the Small Guts, keeps them in some Awe."

Under this weight of criticism, and with the evidence before them of Trenton, where four fifths of the troops had been Continental regulars, Congress finally accepted the need for a completely modern army. In January 1777, it recommended establishing a force of 110 infantry regiments, and with them three other components essential to fighting a late-eighteenth-century war: five regiments of artillery, a corps of engineers, and three thousand cavalry. As a sign of Congress's "perfect reliance on the wisdom, vigour, and uprightness of General Washington," their recruitment, training, and pay were to be placed under his direct control. The soldiers would serve for up to three years, or for the duration of the war.

Politically as well as militarily, Washington had won, and the newly promoted Lieutenant Colonel Wilkinson, still not twenty years old, seemed likely to be one of the brightest stars in the new Continental Army. His regiment was one of Washington's extras, and its colonel, Thomas Hartley, an efficient officer Wilkinson had known in Canada. Taking a personal interest in Wilkinson's career, the commander in chief told him he would benefit from the experience of direct command, as opposed to staff work, because it would help "to remedy his polite manners." For a young officer aspiring to behave like an aristocrat, this was useful advice, but it went unheeded. In January 1777, instead of roughing it in camp at Morristown where the new troops were beginning their training, he persuaded Hartley to send him on a recruiting drive to Pennsylvania and Maryland. It turned out to be less enjoyable than he had anticipated.

In Wilkinson's hierarchical world, it was natural for him to charm those above him, and to discipline those below him, but to persuade his fellow citizens as equals that they should join the army was impossible. After a few weeks he reacted much as he had in Canada when Arnold had sent him out to forage for supplies and simply gave up.

Instead of returning to Morristown, he stayed in Philadelphia, where many of the friends he had made as a medical student, especially among "the most accomplished and respectable of the fair sex," still lived. One girl in particular, Ann Biddle, always known as Nancy, attracted him. Her portrait, painted by Charles Willson Peale, suggests why she caught his eye. Everything about her is fashionable: her hair is piled in ringlets on her head, her eyebrows are plucked, her eyes are darkened, her lips are painted, and, compared to the settled expressions adopted by the other Philadelphia ladies who sat for Peale, her look is lively and seductive. That she was also a Quaker and should thus have been demurely dressed and modestly behaved can only have added to the excitement she aroused.

In his memoirs, Wilkinson claimed that Nancy Biddle aroused "a courting Distemper" in every young man who knew her. As an expert in the use of charm, he responded at once, recognizing in her a kindred spirit. Although his description of his "sprightly Quakeress" is too stilted to convey anything of the light, teasing, demanding character that emerges from her letters, his conduct is more eloquent. From this time on he devoted himself to winning her, and they would eventually share more than twenty years of life together. During that time, no one, not even those who charged him with the most despicable treachery to his country, ever accused him of infidelity to his Nancy.

The Biddles were an old, established family—the first of them had come to America in 1681 with the earliest wave of Quakers—and by the time the Revolution broke out they had established themselves at the heart of Philadelphia society. Nancy's parents, John and Sarah Biddle, owned the Indian King, a large, three-story hotel, one of the finest in Philadelphia, with eighteen comfortable bedrooms, each boasting plastered walls and a fireplace. One of Nancy's brothers, Owen, was chairman of Philadelphia's committee of safety; another, Clement, had enough influence to raise a regiment of volunteers; while Benjamin Franklin appointed her cousin Charles Biddle to be chief executive of Pennsylvania's supreme council.

John Biddle was in his fifties when Nancy and her younger sister, Lydia, were born, and perhaps because he was an elderly, doting father, he allowed them greater freedom than most Quaker girls enjoyed at the time. During the early months of 1777, they dressed more daringly, went to more parties, and each became attached to a man who was not a Quaker.

After Wilkinson had begun to court Nancy, his friend and fellow medical
student James Hutchinson, having returned from qualifying as a doctor in
England, followed his example by wooing Lydia. Neither had achieved his
object, however, by the time the snows melted in April and the new fighting season opened.

4

THE TRIUMPH OF SARATOGA

WITH CONFLICT LOOMING, Lieutenant Colonel James Wilkinson might have been expected to join his regiment at Morristown. Most ambitious officers would have welcomed the opportunity to command troops in battle. But his brief experience of regimental life only confirmed Wilkinson's preference for the more genteel environment of a general's staff. The chance to return to it came from his patron General Horatio Gates.

In March 1777, after a winter spent vigorously lobbying Congress, Gates was given command of the Northern Department in place of General Philip Schuyler. His appointment was a triumph for those New Englanders who, despite Washington's supremacy, still clung to their faith in the militia. Gates remained their champion.

Once more in command, the general immediately invited Wilkinson to join him as chief of staff. "My young heart leaped with joy," Wilkinson remembered, "so warmly had General Gates attached it to him, by his indulgence of my self-love." Sooner or later, most of Wilkinson's superiors recognized that his vanity, or self-love, was the key to his loyalty, but none secured it more firmly or indulged him more widely than Gates.

The decision to leave the main army for the Northern Department required the commander in chief's permission. "I would to God, gentlemen could for once know their own minds," Washington exclaimed in irritation, and although he allowed the move, he must have known that the young colonel was siding with the opposition.

The main weight of the British attack could be expected in the north. During the winter, Sir John Burgoyne had persuaded Secretary for the Colonies Lord George Germain to approve his strategy to isolate New

England with its supply of money and manpower from the rest of the colonies. Their plan required a three-pronged advance on Albany, with the main thrust from almost nine thousand blue-coated Hessians and red-coated British troops under Burgoyne himself heading south for the Hudson Valley. An inveterate gambler, Gentleman Johnny's confidence in the outcome was clear from an entry in Brooks's club wagering book: "John Burgoyne wagers Charles Fox one pony [fifty guineas] that he will be home victorious from America by Christmas Day, 1777."

To everyone, both American and British, it was obvious that the first line of defense would be the fortress of Ticonderoga, which commanded access to Lake George and the Hudson Valley. Gates, therefore, immediately sent Wilkinson to inspect its ability to withstand attack. Wilkinson's report revealed a near-derelict fortress garrisoned by twenty-five hundred men, poorly led, laid low by illness and lacking in ammunition, uniforms, and morale. He recommended that either it be evacuated or its defense be put in the charge of a senior officer such as Arthur St. Clair, his brigadier at Trenton. But any attempt to prepare the fort for either defense or evacuation was aborted by the political generalship of Congress. At the beginning of June, it abruptly decided that, after all, General Schuyler should have command of the Northern Department, with Gates as his subordinate.

Wilkinson responded furiously. "They have injured themselves, they have insulted you, and by so doing have been guilty of the foulest ingratitude," he told Gates on June 7. "The perfidy of mankind truly disgusts me with Life, and if the happiness of an amiable lady [Nancy Biddle] was not unfortunately too dependent upon my wretched existence, I should think I had lived long enough, nor would I want to breathe the air with Ingrates, assassins, and double-faced Villains."

Even before this effusive tribute to their friendship arrived, Gates had rewarded his loyal aide by appointing him deputy adjutant general for the northern army, a post that required even senior officers to obey his commands. Wilkinson was overcome. "I am this day honoured by your affectionate letter with the inclosed commission," he informed his general. "It wrung my heart and I dropped a tear upon it."

Congress's interference froze any decision about the defense of Ticonderoga until Schuyler was again in charge. Although he confirmed St. Clair's command, the weeks of inaction made certain that the fortress would fall for virtually nothing at all. In early July, British artillery occupied positions overlooking Ticonderoga, and St. Clair decided to evacuate the doomed position without further delay. Hundreds were captured on the lake and on land, but about two thousand troops escaped. With bleak ineptitude, Congress voted to court-martial both St. Clair and Schuyler for allowing the capture of a position it had rendered indefensible. By default Gates was once more put in charge of the Northern Department, the third change of command in five months.

Unaware of the vital role Congress had played in his victory, Burgoyne paused to celebrate before pushing slowly southward, "flushed with victory," Schuyler reported, "plentifully provided with provisions, cannon and every warlike store." His army of almost nine thousand professional soldiers was accompanied by more than fifty cannon and a baggage train of ammunition and food wagons, as well as officers' wives with their tents, servants, and wardrobes. This was the classic European army, a gigantic concentration of firepower designed to smash an enemy in open ground. Meanwhile, it all had to be transported through forested, often marshy terrain blocked by trees felled by the retreating Americans.

As an advocate of defensive warfare, Gates could not have hoped for more appropriate tactics from his opponent than Burgoyne's ponderous advance into unknown territory. Gates used the time well. Concentrating his demoralized force—Wilkinson reckoned desertion had reduced its numbers to about thirteen hundred militia and twenty-eight hundred regulars—at Stillwater near where the Mohawk River flowed into the Hudson, Gates set about rebuilding its confidence.

Whatever his weakness in battle, Gates's organizational skills were superb, and in six weeks of apparent inactivity he transformed the morale of his beaten army. Plentiful supplies of food and ammunition were sent from Albany, and in camp his men had time to recoup their strength. He managed his militia forces with skill, rarely insisting on strict discipline, and dispensing with the flogging that professional soldiers thought essential to discipline—"these Mortals," he once declared, "must be led and not drove." Shrewdly, he issued proclamations to remind any militia in New York and New England who still hung back that a British victory would allow the Indians accompanying Burgoyne's army to seize their land and scalp their families.

Gates's brand of generalship produced immediate results. From "a miserable state of despondency and terror, Gates' arrival raised us as if by magic," Captain Udney Hay of Vermont testified a month after the general took command. "We began to hope and then to act." Under Schuyler, the citizen-soldiers had been ineffective; under Gates, the Vermont militia delayed a diversionary attack through the Mohawk Valley until Arnold arrived with reinforcements to drive the attackers back, and in late August the New

Hampshire militia destroyed a powerful foraging party sent out to find provisions for Burgoyne's army. From then on Burgoyne would be short of food.

Meanwhile, Gates's army was reinforced by five Continental regiments sent north by Washington, including Daniel Morgan's Pennsylvania sharpshooters and Henry Dearborn's light infantry—two units ideal for harassing the enemy in the forested Hudson Valley. Eventually about twenty-one thousand troops, more than twelve thousand of them militia, would be acting either directly under Gates's command or supporting him by their harassment of British supply lines. Crucially, too, in the south General William Howe abandoned the strategy of advancing up the Hudson to meet with Burgoyne at Albany and, instead of threatening Gates from the rear, chose to direct his forces toward Philadelphia.

During this period of recuperation at Stillwater, Wilkinson's role as chief of staff grew increasingly important. In early September, the volcanic Benedict Arnold arrived at headquarters, fresh from his victory in the Mohawk Valley, and anxious to act equally aggressively against Burgoyne's main army. Gates remained reluctant to move and, confronted by a fractious subordinate and increasingly impatient commanders, found excuses either to leave to inspect militia detachments or to retreat to an inner room in the log cabin that served as his headquarters, where he was rumored to drink heavily. His effervescent young chief of staff, universally known as Wilky, had to act as go-between, smoothing relations among the generals and colonels.

"He has great merit," commented General St. Clair, one of Wilkinson's admirers, "and what is in my opinion more valuable, he has a warm, honest heart." His role was something between jester—"jocose, volatile, convivial," by his own description—and counselor. He advised Gates on what orders were necessary, then shaped, marketed, and occasionally overrode them, and where necessary filled in the gaps in his general's laid-back leadership. His charm made his behavior both forgivable and lovable.

"His conduct during that memorable campaign endeared him to me," Matthew Lyon, then a young colonel in the Vermont militia, remembered. "He seemed to be the life and soul of the head quarters of the army: he, in the capacity of Adjutant-general, governed at head quarters. He was a standing correction of the follies and irregularities, occasioned by the weakness and intemperance of the commanding general."

According to Wilkinson, he personally took out the reconnaissance party that discovered Burgoyne's slow advance down the west bank of the Hudson River. In response to his chief of staff's urging, Gates at last moved north to seize the commanding hills known as Bemis Heights that lay in Burgoyne's path. Under the direction of the Polish engineer Tadeusz Kosciuszko, trenches were dug and artillery placed so that the southern summit became a strongpoint. In mid-September the two armies finally met a few miles below Saratoga, where a great bend in the Hudson changes the river's direction from east to south. Burgoyne established his camp two miles north of the heights. On September 19, the British general led three columns of troops around the flank of the hills to attack the American position.

The crux of the battle was the part played by the light infantry and the sharpshooters on the left wing of the American army under Arnold's direct command, who were operating in the woodland that covered the ground at the foot of the hills. Threatened with being outflanked by the British right wing, they responded at about noon with an aggressive attack directed by Arnold. "Such an explosion of fire I had never any idea of before," William Digby, a British lieutenant, wrote in his journal, "and the heavy artillery joining in like great peals of thunder, assisted by the echoes of the woods, almost deafened us with the noise." Through the afternoon, Arnold continued to push more of the lightly armed men into the battle, in which they drove back the British right and center columns, but as they reached the open ground known as Freeman's Farm, they were "in turn obliged to retire," according to Gates's official dispatch, by a fierce counterattack.

To discover what was happening, Wilkinson left headquarters and at the base of the hill found apparent confusion. Scattered among the trees, commanders such as Daniel Morgan of the rifle corps and Henry Dearborn had to shout and call—Morgan used a hunter's turkey call—to keep in touch with their troops. But the forest was bushwhacker terrain, ideal for an individual soldier's sharpshooting skills. As the British attack overstretched, Morgan became aware of a gap in their line and urgently demanded fresh troops to give him the concentrated numbers to break through—concerted musket fire at close quarters was always the endgame of eighteenth-century warfare.

Promising to bring reinforcements, Wilkinson hurried back to headquarters, but could not persuade the nervous Gates to release more troops. At last Arnold, who was listening in growing exasperation, shouted, "By God I will soon put an end to it," and stormed off to lead the reserves himself. At Gates's order the chief of staff ran after him and told him to return to the log cabin. It says much for Wilkinson's personal touch that he persuaded the explosive Arnold to come back with him. As a compromise, five regiments were committed to the battle, but led by a sickly Ebenezer

Learned, they blundered into the British center and suffered numerous casualties without being able to help the riflemen.

When darkness ended the battle, both sides claimed victory. The British
had suffered heavier losses—more than five hundred dead and wounded
from a force barely seven thousand strong—but they occupied the battleground and the brunt of American casualties had fallen on the elite rifle
corps. Had Burgoyne's men been able to mount an attack the next day,
Wilkinson decided somberly, they might have secured victory. As it was, he
noted with relief, "The enemy have quietly licked their sores this day."

THERE WAS NOTHING quiet about the scenes that took place in Gates's
cabin. Convinced that outright success had been thrown away, Arnold
mutinously confronted his commander over the next few days, and his
anger took on a sharper edge after he discovered that the official report
omitted any mention of his part in the battle. Their quarrel illustrated why
Gates valued Wilkinson so highly. Conscious no doubt of his inferiority to
Arnold as a battle commander, Gates appeared unable to defend himself
until rescued by his chief of staff. "I would have given my life for him,"
Wilkinson once said of Gates, and he proved his devotion by the way he
now neatly disposed of his former patron.

Arnold's argument, he pointed out, centered on how best to exploit the
deadly effects of the rifle corps and light infantry. Because they were specialist troops, Wilkinson suggested, they would be better placed under the
direct control of the overall commander, General Horatio Gates. His general gratefully seized on this solution and, at their next meeting, informed
Arnold that he had effectively been relieved of his command. Rubbing salt
in the wound, Gates refused him permission to appeal to Congress.

This treatment produced such an explosion of anger from Arnold that
Wilkinson declared he "behaved like a madman" and must have been drunk.
"I was huffed," Arnold protested, "in such a manner as must mortify a person with less pride than I." But his former patron's distress left Wilkinson
unmoved. The real issue, he maintained, was about insubordination rather
than the conduct of the battle; the conflict was between "official superiority
on one side and an arrogant spirit and impatience of command on the
other."

History's perspective shows clearly that Arnold and Gates needed each
other's talents, and a less partisan staff officer might have found a way for
them to work together. Even at the time it hung in the air that Wilkinson
had acted like a turncoat, abandoning an old friend instead of attempting

to mediate. Richard Varick, formerly Arnold's drinking companion but now his staff officer, blamed the chief of staff for being "at the bottom of the dispute." Wilkinson's hostility to Arnold had sharpened the quarrel instead of soothing it, and he had acted like someone who was "fundamentally a Sycophant."

While the argument still raged, the outcome of the fighting at Freeman's Farm was being decided by the steady flow of militia into the American camp, and the trickle of deserters from Burgoyne's. Even with his enemy trapped, Gates still feared some unexpected move. "Perhaps [Burgoyne's] Despair may Dictate to him, to risque all upon one Throw," he confessed to a friend; "he is an old gamester & in his time has seen all chances."

On October 7, the old gamester made his last throw. A force of fifteen hundred men attempted to circle round the American position once more. They aimed at surprise, but were detected at once. On almost the same ground, almost the same battle was fought, but this time the result was different. Gates immediately sent out Morgan and the rifle corps, who had time to get beyond the British, outflanking them and picking off their officers with murderous accuracy.

At the critical moment, however, Arnold simply ignored Gates, Wilkinson, and the entire chain of command and seized control of Learned's brigade, leading it on horseback to capitalize on the confusion the riflemen had caused. "Our cannon were surrounded and taken," Lieutenant Digby wrote in his journal that night, "the men and horses were all killed—which gave [the Americans] additional spirits, and they rushed on with loud shouts . . . we drove them back a little way, [but] with so great loss to ourselves that it evidently appeared a retreat was the only thing left for us."

Among the casualties of the last British resistance was Benedict Arnold, wounded while still at the head of Learned's men. The bullet struck him on the right leg, where he had been hit at Quebec, but this time it took him high above the knee, shattering the bone and leaving him with a limp from which he never recovered. The battle of Bemis Heights was the last occasion that he led American troops in combat, and his record as a tactical commander was not surpassed until General Nathanael Greene's southern campaign in 1781.

The defeat at Bemis Heights cost Burgoyne's army the loss of another seven hundred men and sealed its fate. Two days later, he led it squelching through heavy rain toward Saratoga and found a defensive position on high ground beside the Hudson River. But it could retreat no further. New England militia to the east of the river prevented any crossing in that direction, and in the north more citizen soldiers under General Benjamin Lincoln had taken up position and were about to recapture Ticonderoga. Sharpshooters surrounded the British army. An exposed sentry was shot where he stood, and cannonballs raked through the medical officers' operating theater. Burgoyne was bottled up. The last scenes of the great victory of Saratoga concerned the terms of his surrender.

MANY YEARS LATER, Matthew Lyon told Thomas Jefferson that, having observed Wilkinson's conduct during the campaign, he had thought him "the likeliest young man I ever saw." General Horatio Gates certainly shared that opinion. Not only had his youthful chief of staff deftly stabbed Arnold in the back at a critical moment, he had proved a reliable link to the demanding and difficult subordinates, and, at least by Wilkinson's account, in the second battle at Bemis Heights he had saved the general by countermanding an order that would have sent General Poor into direct view of British artillery.

That Gates trusted his twenty-year-old protégé unreservedly was made clear on October 14 when Burgoyne sent his emissary, Major Kingston—"a well-formed, ruddy, handsome man," as Wilkinson remembered—to the American camp to request a cease-fire and ask for terms of surrender. Wilkinson met him and acted as his general's representative throughout the subsequent negotiations.

For three days, helped by an officer with legal training, William Whipple, Wilkinson hammered out the details of the surrender with two British officers, Captain James Craig and Colonel Nicholas Sutherland, in a tent pitched midway between the two armies. With news coming in that British troops from New York under General Henry Clinton were approaching Albany, Gates wanted a speedy settlement. He offered major concessions, including free passage to Britain on condition that the soldiers did not again take up arms against the United States, and authorized Wilkinson to accept minor points such as the British insistence that they be allowed to pile their weapons "on the word of command of their own officers" rather than to ground them on the orders of the Americans. What Gates required in return was agreement within twenty-four hours, meaning by two P.M. on October 15.

Hoping that the threat from Clinton might offer a way out, Burgoyne spun out talks past the deadline. In this tense situation, where more than twenty thousand soldiers continued to face each other, armed and ready, as Burgoyne put it, to "rush on the enemy, determined to take no quarter," Wilkinson's ability to create instant friendships took on unexpected significance. With Kingston he discussed the delights of the Hudson Valley, the fall colors and "the beauty of the season," and to Sutherland he talked of guns and hunting, promising he would personally look after the British officer's favorite fusee or shotgun when it had to be surrendered.

An amicable agreement among the four negotiators was eventually reached at about eight P.M. on October 15, and the articles were sent back to the generals to be signed. Before midnight, Wilkinson received a message from Sutherland saying that Burgoyne had accepted every condition, but wanted the terms of capitulation to be called a "convention" between himself and Gates. With his general's agreement, Wilkinson agreed to the change. The following morning, however, he discovered that Burgoyne wanted to back off, having heard a rumor that Clinton had reached Albany. To hold matters up, the British commander even demanded to count the size of the American army, on the grounds that it had to be four times the size of his to justify his surrender. Gates dismissed this as an absurdity and sent Wilkinson to demand "an immediate and decisive reply."

This time he went directly to Burgoyne's headquarters, where he found the gambler surrounded by his negotiators but in desperate form. Curtly Burgoyne refused Gates's ultimatum and told Wilkinson that the truce would end in one hour precisely, insisting that they both set their watches. As he marched off, Wilkinson turned to Sutherland and warned him that if fighting started again, "You will lose your fusée—and your entire baggage." Then he, too, walked away with, he admitted, "the most uncomfortable sensations," because he doubted whether a new attack could be mounted, let alone be successful: "Our troops were much scattered . . . the men had got the treaty into their heads and lost their passion for combat." Besides, the latest news of Clinton was that he had taken Fort Montgomery above West Point and now controlled the highlands close to Albany. Burgoyne was not the only one bluffing on a weak hand.

The British negotiators, Sutherland and Kingston, were less inclined to gamble. They hurried after Burgoyne and insisted that he must first consult his senior officers before rejecting the agreement. The general allowed himself to be persuaded, and Kingston ran back to catch up with Wilkinson, pleading to have the truce extended for two hours while the consultation took place. On his own intitiative, Wilkinson granted the extension, sending word back to Gates of what he had done. Just before the time was up, a disconsolate Sutherland arrived with the news that Burgoyne still refused to accept the terms of surrender. At this point, a curious kind of collusion arose from Sutherland and Wilkinson's friendship.

Wilkinson pulled out the letter in which Burgoyne had accepted the original agreement, asking only that *convention* should replace the word *capitulation*. While Sutherland listened, Wilkinson read aloud the relevant passages that showed the general's agreement to every other condition. Had Burgoyne gone back on his word? Wilkinson asked dramatically. Was this the behavior of a gentleman? It was the very argument Sutherland needed. He begged to be given the letter, promising he would use it to win Burgoyne round. While Wilkinson waited outside the British camp for a final answer, a messenger came from the impatient Gates telling him to break off negotiations at once, the extra two hours had expired and the truce was over. Refusing to give up, Wilkinson sent word back insisting on another thirty minutes. To his relief, a triumphant Sutherland appeared soon afterward with the surrender documents bearing the signature of Lieutenant General John Burgoyne.

Wilkinson's reward was to escort the British general when he came to make the formal surrender to Gates at the American camp the next day. The scene launched a thousand images printed in books, magazines, and newspapers across the young United States—Burgoyne in his gold-braided scarlet coat, General Friedrich von Riedesel, the Hessian commander in dark coat with gilded epaulets, and General Horatio Gates in his unadorned blue coat.

Everywhere to the south, British armies were establishing control, from Clinton on the bluffs outside Albany to Howe in the streets of Philadelphia. But here on the hillside above the Hudson River, a reversal of such magnitude took place that all the enemy's success was nullified, and every country in Europe from Spain to Russia was forced to take seriously the Americans' declaration of their independence. With justifiable pride, Wilkinson remembered his own position in the scene: "A youth in plain blue frock without other military insignia than a cockade and a sword, I stood in the presence of three experienced European generals, soldiers before my birth . . . , yet the consciousness of my inexperience did not shake my purpose."

It was his job to introduce the two generals, then Burgoyne doffed his hat and spoke the momentous words "The fortune of war, General Gates, has made me your prisoner." And Gates, pink and bespectacled, solemnly answered, "I shall always be ready to testify that it has not been through any fault of your excellency." An hour later, the British soldiers marched out of camp to the beat of their drums and began to pile up their muskets.

That was the public face, but privately it looked different. Burgoyne was so close to tears he could hardly speak. Marching out to surrender his weapon, a downcast Digby thought the drums "seemed almost ashamed to be heard on such an occasion." Gates never stopped beaming with pride. And the moment the surrender ceremony was over, his chief of staff collapsed from nervous exhaustion as a result of "the strong excitements produced by the important scenes in which I had been engaged."

Much of what Wilkinson did was an act, but his reaction to the long weeks of stress he had undergone was real—an agonizing attack of colic that convulsed him so painfully he thought he would die. He was taken to Albany to recuperate, where a doctor eventually relieved his agony with a heavy dose of laudanum. For someone who always wanted to appear at ease and in control, the incident offered an oddly revealing glimpse of the turmoil beneath the guise. It helps to explain the humiliating experience that was about to follow his moment of triumph.

Betraying General Gates

W HEN SIR JOHN BURGOYNE appeared before a parliamentary inquiry in London into the causes of his surrender, he claimed to have been defeated not by a militia but by a professional army. "The standing corps [i.e., the Continental Army] which I have seen are disciplined," he stated. "I do not hazard the term [use it loosely], but apply it to the great fundamental points of military institution, sobriety, subordination, regularity, and courage." This compliment to the training of the Continental soldiers, and particularly of the specialist units, was deserved, but in reality most of Gates's army had consisted of part-time soldiers. Of almost twenty-one thousand men under his command, two thirds belonged to the militia, the very troops whose "Disregard of Discipline, Confusion & Inattention" had forced their previous commander, General Schuyler, to the painful extremity of having "to Coax, to wheedle and even to Lye, to carry on the Service." Saratoga was a defeat not just for the British, but for critics of the militia.

Since its creation in 1775, the Continental Army had consumed four fifths of the revenues raised by Congress, and General Washington had insisted on ever greater control over its expenditure, not simply in battle but in military organization. Even John Adams, the Massachusetts delegate who had actually proposed Washington as commander, felt that too much power had been channeled into the hands of one man. "Now We can allow a certain Citizen to be wise, virtuous, and good," he confided to his wife, Abigail, "without thinking him a Deity or a saviour."

Saratoga revived the belief of the New Englanders in the merits of the citizen soldier, the quintessential American fighter, and their doubts about a standing army. "From a well-regulated militia we have nothing to fear,"

Boston's John Hancock insisted, "their interest is the same with that of the state . . . they do not jeopard[ize] their lives for a master who considers them only as the instruments of his ambition."

Inevitably, therefore, the generalship of Horatio Gates was compared to that of George Washington, the advocate of a professional soldiery, who had failed to prevent the capture of Philadelphia and, since Trenton, had been defeated at Brandywine and Germantown and was now preparing to retreat to winter quarters at Valley Forge, apparently incapable of inflicting harm on the enemy.

In a fan letter to Gates, the Massachusetts delegate James Lovell told him, "We want you in different places . . . We want you most near Germantown. Good God! What a Situation are we in!" Excitably, Dr. Benjamin Rush spelled out the full significance of Saratoga. "The northern army has shown us what Americans are capable of with a GENERAL at their head," he wrote. "The spirit of the southern army is no ways inferior to the spirit of the north. A Gates . . . would in a few weeks render them an irresistible body of men."

That sentiment was given practical effect by Congress within weeks of receiving the news of Saratoga. General Thomas Mifflin of Pennsylvania, once Washington's quartermaster general and close friend of his former adjutant general Horatio Gates, was authorized to select a new military Board of War to replace the original civilian version under John Adams. The board was responsible for organization of the army's entire infrastructure, its recruitment, staffing, pay, and equipment. It occupied more of Adams's time than any other activity, and its complex requirements convinced Congress that its members needed to be soldiers.

On November 28, 1777, Congress confirmed Mifflin's choice of Gates as president of the board with himself as its senior member. In early December, they appointed the newly promoted Major General Thomas Conway to the post of inspector general of the army with a duty to improve its efficiency from the newest recruit to the commander in chief. Dr. James Craik, Washington's physician and an assiduous collector of information, passed on to him the rumors flying around Congress "that the new Board of War is Composed of Such leading men as will throw such obstacles and difficulties in your way as to force you to Resign."

What became known as the Conway cabal was inseparable from the ideological conflict between the claims of the militia and the regulars. But the quarrel reached beyond military concerns. In a telling incident during the winter at Valley Forge, New Jersey troops reporting for duty initially refused to swear allegiance to the "United States of America" because, as they said,

"New Jersey is *our* country." In later years, Washington himself never doubted that the forging of a genuine Continental Army that winter represented a vital stage toward the creation of a single United States. Immense consequences hung on the move to limit his power.

Some questioned whether such an unthinkable project ever really existed—"If he *has* an Enemy, a fact which I am in doubt of," wrote Henry Laurens, Hancock's successor as president of Congress, "the whole amounts to little more than tittle tattle." But Washington was certain that "a malignant faction had been for some time forming to my prejudice" and later named its three leading members: "General Gates was to be exalted, on the ruin of my reputation and influence. This I am authorised to say, from *undeniable facts* in my own possession . . . General Mifflin, it is commonly supposed, bore the second part in the Cabal; and General Conway, I know was a very Active and malignant Partisan."

Out on the snowy hillsides of Valley Forge, with dozens of desertions reported every day, a score of officers resigning their commissions every week, Washington came close to despair on hearing of Conway's appointment. It was, he told Richard Henry Lee, "as unfortunate a measure as was ever adopted," and the despondent sentence that followed had a hint of the resignation that the cabal aimed at: "I have been a Slave to the service: I have undergone more than most Men are aware of to harmonize so many discordant parts; but it will be impossible for me to be of *any further service*, if such insuperable difficulties are thrown in my way." Watching him with growing concern, his loyal aide, Tench Tilghman, observed, "I have never seen any stroke of ill fortune affect the General in the manner that this dirty underhand dealing has done."

WHAT UNDERMINED THE PLANS of the cabal, together with the larger campaign on behalf of the militia, were the indiscretions of James Wilkinson. They were brought about by an immense storm that swept across the coast of New England on October 26, 1777. Quite suddenly a fall that had been warm and foggy, too damp to count as a real Indian summer, too still to dispel the mists and the palls of smoke that rose above battlefields from New York to Pennsylvania, gave way to high winds driving torrents of freezing rain and sleet out of the northeast.

A Brunswick officer marching his defeated troops through the Berkshires in western Massachusettts, "the American Caucasus" as he called them, recorded three nights of "rain, hail and snow" and a fierce gale "so piercing, that, no matter how warmly we wrapped ourselves in our cloaks, it penetrated to the very marrow." On the same day the extreme conditions caught up with twenty-year-old Lieutenant Colonel James Wilkinson in Reading, Pennsylvania, as he rode south carrying General Horatio Gates's official account of Saratoga to the Continental Congress. "This evening," he recorded, "it began to rain and the next day in torrents." He had set out seven days earlier. With hard riding, he might have kept ahead of the weather and have already arrived in York Town, Pennsylvania, where delegates to the Second Continental Congress desperately awaited his arrival.

Driven out of Philadelphia at the end of September by the approach of Howe's army, they had fled first to Lancaster, Pennsylvania, before crossing the broad expanse of the Susquehanna River to find refuge in York in the foothills of the Alleghenies. Doggedly, the twenty or so delegates had labored to keep alive a semblance of government, acting as executive, legislature, and constitutional assembly. Meeting in York's tiny courthouse, they issued orders to supply army commanders with food, munitions, and clothing, they assessed the financial obligations of the different states, and at the same time they haggled over the terms of a political confederation that would unite New Hampshire with Georgia and the eleven states in between.

Shrouded by fog and low-lying clouds that clung to the hillsides, York seemed cut off from the outside world, and its discomforts contributed to the delegates' depression. They were crammed into overcrowded lodging houses and inns and forced to conduct business surrounded by a sullen, largely German population. "The Prospect is chilling on every Side, gloomy, dark, melancholy and dispiriting," John Adams confessed in the privacy of his diary. "When and where will light come from?"

Symptomatic of their isolation, when rumors began to circulate in the middle of October that Washington had attacked Howe outside Philadelphia, and Gates was said to be closing in on Burgoyne at Saratoga, the delegates could not find out what was happening. The first hard news—that fog had denied Washington victory at Germantown by obscuring his view of the battlefield—was followed by the terrible storm. As the streets turned to mud, and the rain hammered on the roof of the courthouse, the delegates came closer to despair than at any other time in the Revolution. "We have been three days, soaking and poaching in the heavyest Rain that has been known for several Years," John Adams wrote on the twenty-eighth to his wife, Abigail, in Boston, "and what adds to the Gloom is the Uncertainty in which We remain to this Moment, concerning the Fate of Gates and Burgoigne. We are out of Patience. It is impossible to bear this suspence, with any Temper."

With the rain still bucketing down, Wilkinson waited another day in Reading and accepted an invitation to eat at the mess of Lord Alexander Stirling, a major general in Washington's army. Despite his title, Stirling was American born and bred. He had fought with Washington in the New York campaign, and at Trenton and Brandywine, and was convinced of the need for a professional army.

At dinner, the two men discussed the progress of the war. Wilkinson remembered that the general spent much of the evening describing in excruciating detail his experiences at the Battle of Long Island in August 1776. Notorious for his heavy drinking—Rush dismissed him as "a proud, vain, lazy, ignorant drunkard"—Stirling apparently fell asleep, leaving his guest to be entertained by his aides, James Monroe and William McWilliams, both majors but older and wiser than the young colonel. Late at night, with a drink and an attentive audience at hand, the twenty-year-old began to boast and, by his own admission, indulged in "conversation too copious and diffuse for me to have charged my memory with particulars." Otherwise all that he could recollect was that "we dined agreeably and I did not get away from his lordship before midnight, the rain continuing to pour down without intermission." However, his audience, and in particular Major McWilliams, vividly recalled that Wilkinson had betrayed a confidence that General Horatio Gates had shared with him.

OF ALL THE CONGRATULATORY LETTERS he had received, Gates was proudest of the one sent by General Conway, a veteran of the French army, who had also served under Europe's supreme military expert, Frederick II, king of Prussia. "What pity there is but one General Gates!" Conway wrote admiringly. "But the more I see of this Army the less I think it fit for general Action under its [present] Chiefs & discipline. I speak [to] you sincerely & wish I could serve under you." Not surprisingly, Gates showed this flattering tribute to his young chief of staff.

What McWilliams remembered from his convivial talk with Wilkinson was a remark criticizing Washington that the young man claimed to have read in Conway's letter: "Heaven has been determined to save your Country; or a weak General and bad Counsellers would have ruined it." As a good staff officer, McWilliams duly reported this subversive comment to General Stirling when the general had sufficiently sobered to appreciate its importance.

The next day when the rain had eased and Colonel James Wilkinson was recovered from his carousing, he continued on his way, a young man at ease with the world. His self-confidence showed in his handwriting, the letters well-formed, forward-sloping with capitals extravagantly looped. It was evident too in the casual manner he conveyed his vital message to Congress.

Having broken his journey once, he did so again, spending two days with the Biddles in Easton, Pennsylvania. Since Nancy's happpiness depended upon her Jimmy's "wretched existence," she must have been overjoyed to see him, with his dark, curly hair, bright black eyes, and amused expression, and no doubt was bewitched by his tales of valor and importance. Two days could hardly have been enough for what they had to say, and even John Adams, irritated beyond measure by the delay, acknowledged later, "Had I known that he had fallen in love with so fine a woman as his after wife really was, my rigorous heart would have somewhat relented."

Even after he finally arrived in York, Wilkinson made the exasperated delegates wait yet another day while he assembled all Gates's papers in the correct order. Impatiently Samuel Adams exclaimed that such a laggard should be presented with "a horsewhip and spurs."

Despite the irritation caused by their late arrival, the documents dispelled the delegates' gloom and despondency. Between September 19, Burgoyne's first defeat at Freeman's Farm, and the final surrender on October 17, almost nine thousand British and Hessian troops had been killed, captured, or rendered incapable of fighting. The total represented close to one quarter of all the British forces on American soil. Their weapons, 4,647 muskets, together with bayonets, cutlasses, and 72,000 rounds of ammunition, fell into American hands, as well as 42 cannon, more than 1,000 cannonballs, and dozens of barrels of gunpowder. For an army as starved of equipment as Gates's, this feast was as welcome as the 5,791 enemy who were now their prisoners. But the wider implications of the victory made the news of Saratoga even more welcome.

Within hours of receiving Gates's report, Congress sent off a summary to Benjamin Franklin and his fellow ambassadors in France saying, "We rely on your wisdom and care to make the best and most immediate use of this intelligence to depress our enemies and produce essential aid to our cause in Europe." In particular, news of the British surrender was to be employed to secure the "public acknowledgment of the Independence of these United States," and to remind France and her allies "how essential European Aid must be to the final establishment and security of American Freedom and Independence." A similar message went to American negotiators attempting to borrow money in the Netherlands.

Franklin used the information well, but so, too, did the newspapers and a flood of private letters. Once news of Burgoyne's capitulation reached Europe, neither French ministers nor Dutch bankers could mistake the fighting in North America for a short-lived rebellion. Within four months the conflict would be transformed into an international war.

To express the overwhelming significance of Saratoga, Congress called for a day of thanksgiving to be celebrated throughout the United States on December 18. "Your Name Sir," Henry Laurens assured Gates, "will be written in the breasts of the grateful Americans of the present Age & sent down to Posterity in Characters which will remain indelible when the Gold shall have changed its appearance."

In the elated atmosphere, it was impossible to deny General Gates anything. The delegates ordered a gold medal to be struck in his honor, and they passed a vote of thanks to him, to each of his two senior commanders, Benedict Arnold and Benjamin Lincoln, and to all the officers and men of his army. But one request stuck in the congressional craw, his wish to have his chief of staff, James Wilkinson, promoted to the brevet rank of brigadier general.

The idea of a twenty-year-old general was startling in itself, but it also offended the principle that promotion should take place strictly on grounds of seniority, with rare exceptions being made for outstanding bravery on the battlefield. Wilkinson was no more than a staff officer who had never actually led troops in battle, and scores of more senior colonels were desperate to be considered for the next opening as a general. Yet he had unmistakably earned Gates's admiration and trust—"I have not met with a more promising military genius," the general declared unequivocally, and Wilkinson's services were "of the [highest] importance to this army."

No one wanted to confront the Revolution's savior head-on, but the question of Wilkinson's promotion served as an excuse for Washington's supporters, primarily from the south, to criticize Gates's judgment on other matters. While they discussed the recommendation, Wilkinson was left to kick his heels in the narrow streets and crowded taverns of York. In a letter sent on November 1 to "My dear General and loved Friend," he affected to be unconcerned by the delay to his promotion—"my hearty contempt of the follies of the world will shield me from such pitiful sensations"—but the rest of his message showed how closely he had been listening to the talk in Congress. Gates had failed to inform Washington of his victory, a deliberate breach of military protocol that amounted to insubordination, and this had aroused particular resentment among southerners. And Gates had left himself vulnerable through the lenient terms of surrender that he had offered to Burgoyne. "Excuse me," Wilkinson ended, "had I loved you less, I should have been less free."

The "treaty of convention" signed by Burgoyne had not technically amounted to a surrender, and it had stipulated that his men were not to be treated as prisoners, but repatriated to Britain on condition that they did not again take up arms to fight the United States. This last requirement, releasing prisoners on parole, was common practice—hundreds of captured American soldiers had been set free on an equivalent understanding—but the sheer numbers involved at Saratoga caused consternation. Besides, once home, Burgoyne's men would be assigned duties that would release thousands of other troops for service in America. Gates seemed to have let an enemy who was at his mercy wriggle away almost unscathed. South Carolina's Henry Laurens voiced the southerners' concern by suggesting that Gates had become "a little flattered" by Burgoyne and been "too polite to make [him] and his troops prisoners."

Colonel Wilkinson was summoned to explain how this had come about and, in doing so, demonstrated why Gates thought so highly of him. With the confidence of an officer who had seen the battlefield and conducted much of the negotiation in person, the young colonel pointed out that military necessity had dictated the terms offered by General Gates. Burgoyne's forces were well entrenched in a strong defensive position, and another British army, four thousand strong, was approaching up the Hudson River threatening Gates's supply lines. The situation made it essential to negotiate a quick surrender or to assault Burgoyne's position. "Had an Attack been carried against Lt. General Burgoyne," Wilkinson explained, "the dismemberment of our army must necessarily have been such as would have incapacitated it for further action [in] this Campaign. With our armies in Health, Vigour and Spirits, General Gates now awaits the commands of the Honourable Congress."

The New Englanders seized on Wilkinson's masterly presentation. Not only did it clear Gates of incompetence and show him instead to be the master of a dangerous military situation, it offered Congress a way of circumventing his promise to repatriate British troops. Since Gates was not acting freely but under pressure from British attack, the United States need not feel honorbound to abide by the spirit of the agreement. Once the letter of convention was examined, the lawyers in Congress easily picked it apart to prevent repatriation.

The next day, November 6, 1777, on the recommendation of the Board of War, the Continental Congress resolved, "That Colonel James Wilkinson, adjutant general in the northern army, in consideration of his services in that department, and being strongly recommended by General Gates as a gallant officer, and a promising military genius, and having brought the despatches to Congress giving an account of the surrender of Lieutenant General Burgoyne and his army on the 17 day of October last, be continued in his present employment, with a brevet of brigadier-general in the army of the United States."

Thus, at the age of twenty, James Wilkinson became a general. Brevet rank was temporary and confined to a particular campaign, but for the moment he was the youngest American-born general in the Continental Army. The opportunities that awaited him were almost unlimited.

BY HORRIBLE SYMMETRY, on the very day James Wilkinson was made a general, Stirling passed on to the commander in chief an account of Wilkinson's dinner-table boasting on the night of the great storm. Three days later, on November 4, General Washington wrote a terse note to Thomas Conway with the information that he knew of Conway's comment to Gates about the country being ruined by "a weak General or bad Counsellors."

The new inspector general replied denying he had used the phrase, although the real one about the army not being "fit for general Action under its [present] Chiefs" was no better. Then with breathtaking arrogance, Conway observed patronizingly to Washington, "Your modesty is such that although your advice is *commonly* sound and proper, you have often been influenced by men who were not equal to you." What might have remained a private quarrel became public when Conway sent Henry Laurens, president of Congress, both the original letter to Gates and this exchange with Washington.

Alarmed by news that the Conway letter had been leaked to Washington, Mifflin begged Gates to keep his correspondence and the links between them secret, otherwise "your generosity and frank disposition . . . may injure your best friends." Gates immediately began a furious search for the culprit—"No punishment is too severe for the wretch who betrayed me," he declared, and subjected every member of his staff to questioning. Wilkinson had been delayed on his return from York by the need to see Nancy Biddle again, but in early December he was put through the same procedure. Wilkinson might have confessed at that point—Gates, he acknowledged, forgave people easily—but instead he professed utter outrage at the mere imputation of guilt.

"[The situation] makes me the more unhappy," an embarrassed Gates confided to Mifflin, "as a very valuable and polite officer was thrown into a situation which must increase his disgust." But Wilkinson was not simply disgusted. To divert suspicions, he pointed the blame elsewhere. The bearer of Conway's incriminating letter was Gates's aide Lieutenant Colonel Robert Troup, and soon after it was delivered, Alexander Hamilton, Washington's aide, had visited Gates's camp. During this visit, Wilkinson suggested, Troup "might have incautiously conversed on the substance of General Conway's letter with Colonel Hamilton."

Gates's fatal mistake was to believe Wilkinson. In high indignation, he at once wrote to Washington to remonstrate with him for having acquired access to Gates's private correspondence illicitly. "Those letters have been stealingly copied," he protested, "but, which of them, when, or by whom, is to me, as yet, an unfathomable Secret." To underline the seriousness of the charge, he declared that he intended to forward his letter to Congress so that with Washington's help its members could discover the person responsible. "Crimes of that Magnitude ought not to remain unpunished," he concluded sententiously.

Everything about this communication was calamitous for Gates. The plural "letters" told Washington, who had not realized it till then, that Conway had been in contact with Gates more than once. The demand for help in tracking down the perpetrator revealed that he did not know who was really responsible for leaking the "weak General" sentence, while Washington did. Worst of all, Gates's decision to involve Congress required Washington to do the same—"I am under the disagreeable necessity of returning my answer through the same channel"—so making public the connection between Gates and Conway. Neither then nor forty years later when he came to write his *Memoirs* did Wilkinson ever admit that he had done anything wrong. Instead he argued that he was justified in attempting to throw the blame elsewhere because Gates had "read [Conway's] letter publicly in my presence." Thus it was technically possible for either Troup or Hamilton to have overheard its contents.

Washington's reply must have come as a cold shock to Gates. No one had stolen the material, Washington wrote, it had been "communicated by Colonl. Wilkinson to Major McWilliams." Furthermore, Wilkinson had passed it on so openly that "I considered the information as coming from yourself; and given with a friendly view to forewarn, and consequently forearm me, against a secret enemy [General Conway]. But in this, as in other matters of late, I found myself mistaken."

This devastating letter did not arrive in Albany until January 22, 1778, but from the moment Gates caught his commander in chief's tone of mockery, he must have guessed the cabal had lost any remote chance of achieving its object. The Washington who had come close to despair in December after learning of Conway's appointment might have been hassled into resignation. The Washington with morale high enough to make fun of his challenger was not going to be moved.

The change was apparent from the groveling tone of Gates's reply. He denied any friendship with Conway—"I never had any sort of intimacy, nor hardly the smallest acquaintance with him"; he claimed the "weak General" passage was "a wicked forgery . . . fabricated to answer the most selfish and wicked purposes"; and finally he declared that James Wilkinson was personally responsible for "sowing dissensions among the principal officers of the army, and rendering them odious to each other by false suggestions and forgeries." It amounted, in Gates's opinion, to "positive treason"—the first time the charge had been laid against Wilkinson, and unique in being the only occasion it was wholly unjustified.

Sensibly, Wilkinson found it necessary to spend January 1778 inspecting fortresses in the western hills of New York. On his return to Albany at the end of the month, he learned that Gates had left to take up his post as president of the Board of War in York Town, and that he himself had been appointed, early in January, secretary to the board. There was also a letter from Stirling asking him to confirm the "weak General" quotation, since Conway had denied using it. Realizing at last that he had been outed, Wilkinson replied, acknowledging, "It is possible in the warmth of social intercourse, when the mind is relaxed and the heart unguarded, that obsevations may have elapsed which had not since occurred to me."

With what must have been a sense of foreboding, he then set off toward York, along the same path he had traveled in such glory in October. He reached York in the last week of February, and by then the Conway cabal was at an end—almost entirely as a result of Wilkinson's disreputable behavior.

By definition, a cabal is a secret intrigue, and when the bitter exchanges of Washington, Gates, and Conway were made public, most members of Congress were shocked by the maneuverings and hostility that had gone on behind the scenes. "I always before heard [General Conway] mentioned as having great Military Abilities, and this was all I had ever heard concerning him," Abraham Clark, a New Jersey delegate, confessed. "The kind of Correspondence he carried on with General G[ates] was not known at the Time of his promotion. His Letters to General Washington is of late date. Was the business now to be done Congress would probably Act otherwise."

The Marquis de Lafayette liked to boast that at dinner on January 31 he had broken up the plot by forcing Gates and Mifflin to drink to Washington's health, but in reality the publication of their letters in December and early January sealed their fate. Whatever their arguments about the effectiveness of the militia and the dangers of a standing army, the delegates all accepted that "dissention among the principle Officers of the Army must be very injurious to the Publick interest." Combined with the protests delivered to Congress from nine generals against Conway's promotion and from forty-seven colonels against Wilkinson's, it rapidly destroyed all confidence in the ability of the cabal's triumvirate to run the army.

By mid-February, when Dr. William Gordon asked whether he had ever contemplated resignation, Washington felt able to brush the suggestion away, denying that anyone had "ever heard me drop an expression that had a tendency to resignation." Soon afterward, Gates hauled up the white flag. "I earnestly hope no more of that time, so precious to the public, may be lost upon the subject of General Conway's letter," he wrote on February 19. "I solemnly declare that I am of no faction." To which Washington replied magnanimously, "I am as averse to controversy as any Man," and promised to bury the attempted coup "in silence and, as far as future events will permit, oblivion."

So FAR AS General James Wilkinson was concerned, however, to forget what had happened was impossible. News of his indiscretion was spreading through the army. On the whole, his friends were forgiving. General Wayne mentioned something about "the very improper steps my old friend Wilkinson had made use of," and a fellow staff officer, Walter Stewart, wrote to Gates, "I ever was sensible of Wilky's volatility and open heartedness, and feared he might in an unguarded moment mention something of the affair to a person he looked upon as a friend . . . but his heart is truly good."

But as Wilkinson rode toward York, he received a bitter note from Colonel Troup that read, "Your generous Conduct at Albany, in indeavouring to fix Genl. Gates's Suspicions on me, will be duly remembered." By rights Wilkinson should have felt contrite not just for ruining his patron's plans but for falsely accusing his aide. His reaction was quite different. The imputation he drew from the letter was that he had deliberately leaked the contents of Conway's letter. It enraged him to think "that General Gates had denounced me [to Troup] as the betrayer of Conway's letter, and spoke of me in the grossest manner." From Lancaster, Wilkinson dispatched a furious

letter to Gates issuing a challenge to a duel—"in spite of every consideration, you have wounded my honor, and must make acknowledgement or
satisfaction for the injury."

His murderous reaction was so extreme as to require some explanation.
In his *Memoirs*, he justified it in terms of emotional betrayal: "I was ready to
have laid down my life for him, yet he had condemned me unheard for an
act of which I was perfectly innocent." Almost self-pityingly he pictured
himself as "a boy of twenty without experience, without patronage . . .
whose character remained to be established." However unsure of what he
should do, the imputation of deliberate betrayal left him with no choice.
"Although my feelings and affections were outraged, my resolution was not
appalled. I remembered the injunction of a dying father, I worshipped honor
as the jewel of my soul."

Already beaten down by Washington, Gates appeared crushed by this
new attack. Feebly he pointed out that Wilkinson really had leaked the
"weak General" passage, then deliberately misled him about the culprit.
"I am astonished if you really gave McWilliams such information," he
protested, "how you could intimate to me, that it was possible Colonel
Troup had conversed with Colonel Hamilton upon the subject of General
Conway's letter."

Wilkinson brushed the objection aside. What mattered now was Gates's
failure to apologize for the original insult. No sooner had Wilkinson arrived in York than he sent a fellow officer to Gates with the challenge "Sir,
I have discharged my duty to you and my conscience; meet me tomorrow
morning behind the English church, and I will there stipulate the satisfaction which you have promised to grant."

What happened next was described only by Wilkinson. At eight the next
morning, he and Gates met as arranged. Pistols were the chosen weapon,
but, as the seconds were loading them, Gates asked for a few words alone
with his former friend. Then he clasped Wilkinson's hand and burst into
tears, exclaiming, "*I* injure you! It is impossible. I should as soon think of in-
juring my own child." There was, Gates said, no need for a duel because
Conway himself had acknowledged writing the letter and "has since said
much harder things to Washington's face." Any suggestion that Wilkinson
was responsible for stirring up dissension must therefore be without foundation. According to Wilkinson, this barely credible recital "left me nothing to require, it was satisfactory beyond explanation and rendered me more
than content. I was flattered and pleased." Wilkinson in turn promised Gates
that he had never "done any thing with design to injure him."

Some sort of reconciliation on these grounds undoubtedly took place because the duel was canceled and Wilkinson agreed to take up his position as secretary to the Board of War with Gates as president. Yet the account of how it occurred must have been embellished. Wilkinson's triumph was too complete to be convincing, and Gates soon showed that he was quite prepared to injure his "child."

As THOUGH A DUEL with one major general were not enough, Wilkinson at once prepared to challenge another, General Stirling, in whose house he had originally blabbed about Conway's letter. The supposed insult was again the suggestion that he had deliberately betrayed a secret—"My Lord shall bleed for his conduct," he declared vaingloriously—but the quarrel lacked the emotional intensity of his challenge to Gates. In March he traveled to Valley Forge to exact revenge, but allowed himself to be distracted on the way by another visit with the delectable Nancy Biddle in Reading that lasted for a blissful fortnight, although in memory it "flitted away like a vision of the morn."

On his arrival, he allowed Clement Biddle, her elder brother and one of Washington's staff officers, to persuade him that the wiser course was to ask Stirling for a declaration that the reference to Conway's letter had been "passed in a private company during a convivial Hour." A letter from Stirling duly provided this assurance, with the qualification that Wilkinson had spoken "under no injunction of secrecy," so that McWilliams was justified in passing on what he had said. With that, everyone should have been content, and Wilkinson should have gone back to his onerous and essential duty at the Board of War in equipping the army for another summer of fighting.

However, once Gates had ceased to be his patron, Wilkinson was left with only one general higher in rank to charm, and almost as a reflex he began to try to win over the unbending figure of George Washington. Although obviously a member of Gates's entourage, Wilkinson took steps to show his loyalty to the commander in chief. In agreeing to resolve his quarrel with Stirling, he let Clement Biddle know that he was guided by Washington's public disapproval of dueling among his officers. Then on March 3, he publicly renounced the promotion to brigadier general that Gates had procured for him.

His reward was to be summoned to an interview with the commander in chief, where he was able to demonstrate that, as Washington himself had believed, he "was rather doing an act of justice than committing an act of infidelity" in quoting from Conway's letter. The difficulty was that he had not quoted it accurately. To demonstrate the point, Washington showed Wilkinson the entire file of correspondence concerning the cabal, including Gates's letter accusing Wilkinson of "a wicked forgery" and demanding that he be "exemplarily punished" for a crime that amounted to "positive treason."

"He seemed a good deal surprized at G[ate]s's Letters," Washington commented laconically to Stirling, "& was not at all sparing in his abuse of him & C[onwa]y."

In fact, the discovery that Gates had turned so viciously against him overwhelmed Wilkinson. He hurried back to Reading to be consoled by Nancy and, while there, came to a momentous decision about his military career. In a short, cold letter sent from the Biddles' house on March 29 to Henry Laurens, president of Congress, he peremptorily resigned from the Board of War, declaring, "After the act of *treachery* and *falsehood* in which I have detected Major General Gates, president of that board, it is impossible for me to reconcile it to my honor to serve with him." Coolly, Laurens advised Congress to accept the resignation, but returned the letter as "improper to remain on the files of Congress."

Had that been the end of the relationship, it would at least have been a clean break. But almost four months later, Wilkinson inadvertently encountered Gates as both men arrived in White Plains, New York, to give testimony on behalf of General Arthur St. Clair at his court-martial for the loss of Ticonderoga. The sight of the man who had termed him a forger ignited Wilkinson's smoldering fury, and again his dying father's words about honor sprang to mind. This time Gates accepted the challenge and fought the duel. Each was to fire three times, but when Gates's pistol twice flashed in the pan and misfired, Wilkinson shot in the air, an action that should have satisfied honor on both sides. Gates refused to fire a third time and duly declared that Wilkinson had "behaved as a gentleman."

By the conventions of dueling that was sufficient to satisfy honor, but Wilkinson wanted more. He demanded to have the declaration in writing, and when it was given, refused to provide a similar certificate for Gates. Next day, both men with their seconds, the engineer Tadeusz Kosciuszko for Gates and John Barker Church for Wilkinson, assembled in the courthouse to settle the matter, and at that point Wilkinson exploded. To provide such a certificate, he shouted, would be "to prostitute my honor" because Gates was no better than "a rascal and a coward," and in a frenzy of indignation he challenged the general to yet another duel.

Gates walked away from a man so clearly out of control, but now the seconds began to argue over the certificate and the quarrel rapidly descended
into farce. Kosciuszko and Church were also supposed to appear for St. Clair's
defense, but pushed each other aside trying to enter the courtroom at the
same time. In their fury they drew their swords and began to fight until
driven off by guards. Despite the absence of his homicidal witnesses, St. Clair
was cleared of all charges against him.

There was an edge of hysteria in James Wilkinson's uncontrollable rage,
as though what Gates had done to him was so unbearable he had to be
blotted out. But the urge to destroy Gates had only succeeded in destroying
his own desire for military glory. When he finally recovered his composure, his career as an officer in the Revolutionary War was at an end. He
had neither command nor patron, and too much pride to seek either again.
He had trusted Gates and, in his own mind, been betrayed, and the experience had erased a small but curiously childlike innocence.

LOVE AND INDEPENDENCE

O N NOVEMBER 12, 1778, Colonel James Wilkinson married Miss Ann Biddle at an Episcopalian ceremony in Christ Church, Philadelphia's most fashionable church. The place and the denomination signified that Nancy Biddle was prepared to be expelled from the Society of Friends for breaking its rule against marrying one of "the world's people" rather than a Friend. Her brothers, Clement and Owen, both military officers, had suffered the same fate for flouting the Quaker doctrine of pacifism. Nevertheless, it cannot have been an easy decision for someone who, for all her high spirits, needed to be surrounded by familiar faces and close friends. Her parents and two sisters remained Quakers, while Owen secured readmission after the war. For years Nancy retained her Quaker speech with its *thee* and *thy*, even after she had left Philadelphia. But being married to "my beloved Jimmy" ensured a lifelong exile from the calm and quiet in which she had been reared.

The wedding also forced her nominally Episcopalian husband to enter a different world. Hitherto he had had to follow the spartan lifestyle of a U.S. army officer, and, before that, of the son of a near-bankrupt. By marrying into the Biddle family, James Wilkinson exchanged this pinched existence for a world of mouthwatering financial prospects.

The decision of the British general William Howe to withdraw from Philadelphia in June 1778 allowed the wedding to take place in the city. The British retreat also enabled John Biddle to regain ownership of his house and other enterprises in the city, including the badly damaged Indian King, renamed by the invaders the British Tavern. One of Wilkinson's first civilian jobs was to help his father-in-law take control of his business once more. But the scope for making real money came from the fierce turf war that was fought for political control of the evacuated city.

It was won by the Constitutionalists, an egalitarian alliance of Presbyterians from western Pennsylvania and radical Whigs, who earned their name by their ideological commitment to the state's one-man, one-vote constitution. Having spent the months of British occupation in hungry exile while others remained in the city and grew rich under enemy protection, the Constitutionalists returned to Philadelphia determined on both democracy and restitution. The program had broad appeal, not just to frontier farmers and politicians, but to mainstream families such as the Biddles, and to young professionals such as Wilkinson's medical friend Dr. James Hutchinson.

The Constitutionalists' leader, Joseph Reed, was elected president of the Pennsylvania supreme executive council in December. At once he began to hunt out Tory sympathizers, both among the large Loyalist population who had actively collaborated with the British, and among pacifist Quakers and moderate patriots who had simply accepted occupation. Acts of attainder were issued against almost five hundred people suspected of helping the British, requiring them to stand trial or risk confiscation of their property, and everyone holding public office was ordered to take an oath of loyalty to the Pennsylvania constitution.

There were dangers to this divisive strategy. Philadelphia's powerful business community had numerous contacts with the British who controlled the coastline. To trade or do business on any scale was virtually impossible without negotiating some mutually beneficial arrangement with the enemy. Vulnerable to the Constitutionalists' attack, Philadelphia's merchants formed a rival party called the Republicans in March 1779, to fight for "the Happiness and Liberty of Pennsylvania" under the leadership of the financier Robert Morris and the lawyer James Wilson. They soon accused Reed himself of having contacts with the British and asked pointedly why it was that the most valuable estates confiscated from the Loyalists seemed to end up in the hands of prominent Constitutionalists. Among those favored in this fashion was Colonel Wilkinson. He owed his good fortune to the Biddle connection.

The family had not only suffered grieveously from the British occupation—the Indian King never recovered its former opulence—but were friends of both Joseph Reed and his first wife, Esther. Reed and Clement Biddle were fellow officers on Washington's staff, and the ties grew stronger when after Esther's death Reed began courting Sarah, the eldest Biddle sister.

In May 1779, Wilkinson was given the chance to buy Trevose, the finest estate to be confiscated from any Tory in Pennsylvania. It comprised a distinguished one-hundred-year-old mansion, large stables, a substantial farmhouse and barns, and five thousand well-cultivated acres spread across Bucks County. According to Benjamin Franklin, writing barely three years later, land in Pennsylvania "could be sold for three pounds an acre [about $13.50]," suggesting that the Trevose farmland alone was worth at least fifteen thousand pounds, but Wilkinson was able to buy the entire property, once owned by Joseph Galloway, a president of the colonial assembly who had thrown in his lot with the British, for just forty-six hundred pounds. As a further concession, the price was payable in installments and with paper money rather than coins. This reduced Wilkinson's outlay by more than one third because the reckless printing of bills by both state and central governments had drastically cut the value of paper money compared with that of silver and gold.

Such generosity had to be earned. Wilkinson's contribution was to deliver a vicious attack on General Benedict Arnold, his old patron and army companion but now Reed's adversary. Appointed military governor of Philadelphia by Congress on the recommendation of Washington, Arnold was expressly instructed to "take every prudent step in your power, to preserve tranquility and order in the city and give security to individuals of every class and description." He interpreted this to mean extending military protection to those on the Constitutionalists' hit list and made no secret of his intentions. He hosted a public dinner to which Quaker and Loyalist guests were invited; sent his carriage to help Grace Galloway, Joseph's wife, when she was evicted from Trevose; and was soon seen in the company of Peggy Shippen, daughter of a judge strongly suspected of being a Loyalist.

The Constitutionalists responded by charging him in February 1779 with using army resources to aid his own business interests. Soon afterward Wilkinson weighed in with the specific and damaging accusation that Arnold had "borrowed a sum of money of the Commissaries [responsible for buying the army's food], which was afterwards discounted on a Contract for Rum," in other words, that the commissaries had advanced him money to buy rum at a price higher than the amount Arnold actually paid, and that he had pocketed the difference. Whether it was this blow that finally cracked him, or the influence of his newly married wife, Peggy, that April Arnold let it be known to the British through a Loyalist intermediary that he was open to offers.

"If your Excellency thinks me criminal," he wrote Washington on May 5, "for heaven's sake let me be immediately tried and, if found guilty, executed." It was a curiously extreme reaction to the allegations of Reed and Wilkinson: their charges were, with one exception, eventually thrown out and might at worst have warranted his forcible retirement. But, as an unconscious warning of what he was contemplating, the reaction was not out of place. All the impulses to treachery were referred to in his letter. He was in debt, had not been paid for more than a year, and was alleged by Congress to owe the government three thousand dollars. He was under constant attack by the "artful and unprincipled men" who followed Reed. And he was in pain from his barely healed Saratoga wound that had left one leg two inches shorter than the other. "I have made every sacrifice of fortune and blood," he wrote, "and become a cripple in the service of my country . . . I little expected to meet the ungrateful returns I have received from my countrymen." Five days later he made direct contact with the British general Sir Henry Clinton.

As ARNOLD HEADED TOWARD the act that defined his place in history, Wilkinson set out to live the life of a country gentleman, the beginning as it turned out of a more circuitous route to a similar destination. The Galloways' mansion needed a dozen servants to run it; the stables held a score of horses with grooms to look after them; there was a distillery worked by stillmen; shepherds and cattlemen to care for the livestock; and farmhands to sow and harvest the wheat. Trevose was a small kingdom.

Wilkinson reveled in its possibilities. He and Nancy organized balls elegant enough to be reported in the Philadelphia press and visited neighbors in a carriage drawn by four horses with two footmen at the back. He took an interest in farming, admired his cattle, gave lavishly to charity, and joined the Freemasons. All this was expensive, and the Biddle family fortune was not unlimited. But, according to the shrewdest advice, Trevose could hardly fail to be a good investment. As the population increased, the value of land would rise, too. Even a financier as astute as Silas Deane, whose deals were too sharp for conventional tastes, agreed that land was the best investment. "If we review the rise and progress of private fortunes in America," he wrote in 1781, "we shall find that a very small proportion of them has arisen or been acquired by commerce, compared with those made by prudent purchases and management of lands."

Lacking capital of his own, Wilkinson had paid the deposit of £1,160 on Trevose with Nancy's money, and it was owned in both their names.

But he needed an income to pay the remainder of the purchase price, so on July 29, 1779, he accepted Congress's offer of the post of clothier general to the army at a salary of $5,000 a year.

It might lack the glory of Saratoga, but next to food and weapons no item was more crucial to Washington's Continental Army than the supply of uniforms. Only the clothier general could prevent a repetition of the scenes at Valley Forge—"Men without Cloathes to cover their nakedness, without Blankets to lay on, without Shoes, by which their Marches might be traced by the Blood from their feet," in Washington's vivid words. Between the purchase of blankets, clothes, and shoes and their issue to the troops stood a system of paralyzing complexity.

Most clothing was imported from Europe through Boston with up to a year's delay between order and delivery, although shoes and blankets were produced in the United States. They were paid for by Congress, but responsibility for their purchase and allocation was divided between the Continental Army and the thirteen individual states. The clothier general's specific duty was to procure and distribute clothes, shoes, and blankets for the Continental Army, but he was answerable not to the commander in chief but to the Board of War, and the board kept him permanently short of money and wagons.

"The clothing department has occasioned more trouble to me and has given more distrust to the officers than [any] one thing in the army," Washington testified to Congress, admitting that he had been forced to act as his own clothier general even to the point of sending out officers on house-to-house searches for garments to wear. A year after Valley Forge, with the morale of the 25,000-strong Continental Army hardened by its experience, and its drill and training molded by Friedrich von Steuben's Blue Book of discipline, Washington deemed uniforms more essential than ever to reflect the soldiers' new professionalism. Lack of them created "an ill Appearance" and made good order harder to maintain, Washington explained to the civilians in Congress. "For when a Soldier is convinced that it will be known by his dress to what Corps he belongs, he is hindered from committing many faults for fear of detection."

Washington's one expectation of Wilkinson was that, to sort out problems as they occurred, "you will employ as much of your time with the Army as will be consistent with the great Objects of your appointment." In this, he was persistently disappointed.

Within two months of Wilkinson's appointment, the commander in chief was wearily writing to Congress, "I am again reduced to the necessity of acting the part of Clothier General." During the next year, the tone of his requests for Wilkinson's presence at headquarters grew steadily more acerbic as the official clothier general repeatedly found excuses to remain in Philadelphia, or to be absent on duties elsewhere. Even a direct order from Washington in October 1780—"I shall expect to see you with the army immediately after receipt of this letter"—was ignored for ten days before he received the casual reply "I expect this day to borrow a sufficient fund to carry me to your excellency's quarters, and propose setting out tomorrow or the next day."

Initially Wilkinson attempted to make an inefficient clothing system work, but lack of funds exacerbated its shortcomings. By early 1780, he had established three supply depots in Massachusetts, New York, and Pennsylvania, but in June, when the depot in Massachusetts held "thirty-five waggons load of Summer Clothing that the army are most distressed for," he had no means of transporting it to Pennsylvania where it was needed. In the fall of 1780, he warned that "the very scanty stock of clothing on hand" made winter shortages inevitable, but although material had been purchased in Boston, the Board of War was unable to have it made into uniforms, "for want of money to pay the workmen." In October 1780, Wilkinson presented Congress with a plan to centralize both the procurement and issue of uniforms and blankets under his office, rather than continuing to have fourteen different departments—the thirteen states plus the clothier general—bid against each other for the same clothing, each working on commission and spending money provided by Congress. Nothing came of this seemingly rational proposal, however, because it depended on a central government with sufficient power to impose its wishes on the states that brought it into being.

A more energetic clothier general might have forced through the practical improvements that eventually came in 1782 or at least have shaken the system into greater effectiveness. But what Wilkinson required was glory or at least public approval, and without it he simply lost interest. By March 1781, Washington confessed to such frustration—"I have so repeatedly without effect called upon you to attend to the business of your Department near Headquarters"—that he was forced to appeal to Congress to intervene: "I know not how necessary Mr. Wilkinson's almost constant residence in Philadelphia may be, but should it not be deemed essential, I could wish that Congress would interpose their authority since mine has been ineffectual."

According to the newspapers, Wilkinson had been distracted by social pleasures such as his noisy participation in a fashionable evening at Hart's Tavern in Philadelphia, where he organized dances with names like Burgoyne's Surrender and Clinton's Retreat. At the same time, financial pressure diverted his energies into maximizing the income from Trevose. He placed advertisements offering the pasture for rent at "seven shillings and sixpence [about $1.25] per week"; he bred horses for sale in the markets at Philadelphia and Trenton and promoted the services of the stallions at his Godolphin stable for "four guineas the season." He also contacted his old Maryland acquaintances and accepted a commission to sell their tobacco to French buyers. He even undertook to act as clothing agent for Maryland, effectively competing with himself as clothier general, and with apparent success if the 1780 report of the state's congressmen is to be believed. They castigated the Board of War for its inability to provide enough uniforms for Maryland's troops, but Wilkinson was lauded as "a native of Maryland a man of Honor and a good officer," who could be relied on to look after the state's interests.

Yet he was not alone in neglecting the needs of the Continental Army during this period. From early spring in 1778 when news began to spread that France and the United States had signed a treaty of alliance on February 6—the direct result of Saratoga—an irrational overconfidence seemed to grip the civilian population. When the British evacuated Philadelphia fearing that a French fleet might blockade them, gamblers in Lancaster offered bets at five to one on the war being over in six months. In October, Pennsylvania's supreme executive council decided it would no longer pay a bounty for recruits because "the war would be shortly finished, and there was no need for throwing the State to farther expence."

By 1779 Spain had also declared war against Britain, and the following year the fabulously wealthy Netherlands joined the alliance. The Revolution had become international, Britain was isolated, and independence appeared a foregone conclusion. Other state legislatures behaved like Pennsylvania's, growing reluctant to help in the recruitment, feeding, and clothing of the Continental Army and thus making their own contribution to the mutinies in the winter of 1779–80. By the spring of 1780 General Jedidiah Huntington felt compelled to ask, "Is it not a possible Thing to revive the feelings which pervaded every Breast in the Commencement of the War, when every Man considered the Fate of his Country as depending on his own exertion?"

The mood of complacency was exploded in May 1780 when Henry

Clinton's army, shipped south from New York in December, besieged General Benjamin Lincoln in Charleston and forced an army of thirty-three hundred men to surrender. It was the most severe loss of the war, and two more hammer blows followed. In August, Horatio Gates fled in panic from the bloody defeat at Camden, South Carolina, where more than one thousand Americans were killed or wounded; then in September came the most pulverizing blow of all, Benedict Arnold's treachery.

The Marquis de Lafayette was with Washington in an upstairs room at West Point when he opened a packet of letters taken from Major John André and realized that Arnold had planned not only to hand over West Point and with it control of the Hudson Valley to the British, but to let them capture the commander in chief. The enormity of the treachery—perhaps enough to defeat the Revolution at a stroke—physically shocked Washington. Lafayette noted that Washington's head was down, and the papers in his hand trembled. "Arnold has betrayed me," he whispered. "Whom can we trust now?"

A sense of horror rippled through the nation. In Philadelphia and Bucks County, Wilkinson drew up lists of suspected Loyalists, then called on patriotic Americans to boycott their homes and businesses. "Wilkinson is ready to burst with Indignation," one of Joseph Reed's friends reported. "[He] is drawing up Associations against any Intercourse with Tory & Suspicious Characters." No one was immune from the wave of bitter recrimination. "We were all astonishment, each peeping at his next neighbor to see if any treason was hanging about him," Alexander Scammell, Washington's adjutant general remembered. "Nay, we even descended to a critical examination of ourselves."

Reed himself, Pennsylvania's chief executive, was targeted as a turncoat by Republicans, who alleged that contacts he had made with the British were preliminaries to his own switch of loyalties. In his new role of loyalty judge, Wilkinson drew up a flowery-worded "Address of Confidence" to Reed and cajoled his wide circle of military and fashionable friends to sign it. Although it did not silence the rumors, his action earned Reed's gratitude.

This volatile environment gave birth to two astonishing developments. Congress at last yielded entirely to Washington's demand for a professional army completely centralized in its structure, training, and supply. The states' militia should be used simply "as light Troops to be scattered in the woods and plague rather than do serious injury to the Enemy," he told Congress in September 1780. "The firmness requisite for the real business of fighting is only to be attained by a constant course of discipline and service." In the last year of the war, General Greene's southern army of Continentals and militia bore some resemblance to this model, but Washington's vision of a fully professional force may ultimately have been beyond the resources of a near-bankrupt Congress.

Nevertheless, in the wake of Arnold's treachery, the need to finance such an army gave rise to a still more surprising demand by the New York legislature in October 1780. It called for every state to be made to pay the requisition made upon it by Congress, and in the event of a default Congress should "Direct the Commander-in Chief . . . to march the Army . . . into such a state: and by a Military Force, compel it to furnish its deficiency." This was the nightmare predicted by every opponent of a standing army, that it would be used by the government to coerce its own citizens. Yet so widespread was the panic that Rhode Island, New Hampshire, and Connecticut adopted the same resolution in November.

In the event, no action was taken on their demand, and the surrender of General Cornwallis at Yorktown a year later made further army reform irrelevant, but both initiatives threw long shadows down the years that followed. When peace came, no one was prepared to argue for more than the smallest possible military force to defend the United States.

ON MARCH 27, 1781, Wilkinson resigned as clothier general, citing with uncharacteristic honesty a lack of aptitude for the job. "I should be wanting in Personal Candour and in Public Justice," he wrote in his letter of resgination, "if I did not profess that I find my Mercantile knowledge, on thorough examination, inadequate to the just Conduct of the Clothing Department, under the proposed establishment." Behind this truth was another more compelling one. Washington's criticism of Wilkinson's incompetence had led Congress to cut his salary by half, and as Wilkinson belatedly recognized, he had no possibility of appealing against Washington's judgment. Even to question it "would be esteemed a sort of impiety." Still encumbered by loans taken out to pay for Trevose, he could not afford the loss of half his salary, and it was urgent to find some other way of earning a living.

In October 1781, Reed repaid a favor by appointing Wilkinson a general in the Pennsylvania militia and helping him win election to the Pennsylvania assembly representing Bucks County. Such influential positions should have been profitable, but in the wake of Cornwallis's surrender on October 19, 1781, the wartime economy began winding down, and Wilkinson's lack of "mercantile knowledge" was a handicap in making money in a falling market.

Through the remaining months of the war, he cobbled together earnings from Trevose with what he made from Maryland's tobacco deals and uniforms, but the income was not enough to meet his needs. Shortly before Yorktown, his natural optimism abruptly gave way to deep gloom that expressed itself in forebodings about the war. Since General Nathanael Greene had won a series of victories in the early part of 1781, helping to drive Cornwallis back to the coast, there was little justification for his dark mood. "I think General Wilkinson too desponding," Reed protested with a hint of exasperation. Yet, the very success of his old patron may have contributed to Wilkinson's despondency.

By chance he had visited Greene in June 1780 at his then headquarters in Springfield, New Jersey, arriving as a British and Hessian column from Staten Island was advancing into the New Jersey hills to threaten the American position. Wilkinson at once led out a vigorous reconnaissance patrol that provided Greene with intelligence about enemy movements, and in the aftermath of the victorious skirmish that turned back the British force, the general wrote appreciatively to Clement Biddle, "General Wilkinson was with me the other day in the action of Springfield; and was very active in discovering the enemy's motions. It is a pity so good an officer is lost to the service." Whatever Wilkinson's other shortcomings, none of his generals doubted his tactical sense and energy. At least part of the twenty-four-year-old's dark mood must have sprung from the realization that he had thrown away a career for which he possessed a natural talent.

In the months following Yorktown, it became clear that the conflict was effectively over, and diplomatic contacts began to move toward peace negotiations. By the end of 1782, Wilkinson was by his own account without "cash or credit," and, with the birth of his first child, John, faced the added expense of fatherhood. Ownership of Trevose had become a burden, but it created an ambition that never left him of making a fortune from land speculation. As he aged, his hunger for it grew larger until he dreamed of possessing an empire comprising much of Texas. The ambition gave shape to the rest of his career and to his treachery. And before the war was over, he took the first step to achieving it.

In the spring of 1783, he sold Trevose, and Nancy moved with one-year-old

John, and his newborn brother, James, into her father's house. By September 3, 1783, when the Treaty of Paris was signed, James Wilkinson had crossed the Appalachians to join the flood of Americans hoping to buy cheap land on the western frontier.

THE KENTUCKY PIONEER

KENTUCKY WAS DESTINED to be bought. So thought the first Europeans who found a way through the mountains and were stunned by the natural wonderland on the other side. "The vallies are of the richest soil, equal to manure itself, impossible in appearance ever to wear out," the Dutch-born, South Carolina–based explorer John William de Brahm reported in 1756. "This country seems longing for the hands of industry to receive its hidden treasures, which nature has been collecting and toiling since the beginning ready to deliver them up." Watered by innumerable clear streams, forested with gigantic trees that three men with outstretched arms could not circle, its woodland provided a haven to "innumerable deer," elk, and beaver, and the grasslands fed buffalo that arrived at salt licks in their thousands and stood belly deep in the blue grass "more frequent than I have seen cattle in the settlements," according to Daniel Boone, "browzing on the leaves of the cane, cropping the herbage on those extensive plains."

In 1775 Judge Richard Henderson of North Carolina gave voice to the inner dream that Kentucky inspired. "The country might invite a prince from his palace merely for the pleasure of contemplating its beauty and excellence," he declared, "but only add the rapturous idea of property and what allurements can the world offer for the loss of so glorious a prospect?" Most of the land was owned and occupied by the Cherokees, but Henderson's Transylvania Land Company had purchased twenty million acres— reduced to two hundred thousand acres by the Virginia assembly, which reserved to itself the right to buy land from Native Americans—and he was ready to offer the rapture of property to anyone determined enough to take a train of horses through the Cumberland Gap or ride a flatboat down the Ohio River. During the next eight years, while the war of independence was being fought, thirty thousand settlers heeded his advice and crossed the mountains to buy land in the west.

Among this first wave of pioneers, James Wilkinson stood out. His exceptional war record, his political contacts in Philadelphia, his medical knowledge, and his outgoing personality, all counted in the turbulent, egalitarian society of Kentucky's frontier. In staccato style, a fellow settler, Humphrey Marshall, noted the impact of Wilkinson's physical presence, energy, and wit: "A person not quite tall enough to be perfectly elegant, compensated by symmetry and appearance of health and strength; a countenance open, mild, capacious, and beaming with intelligence; a gait firm, manly, and facile; manners bland, accommodating and popular; and address easy, polite and gracious, invited approach, gave access, assured attention, cordiality and ease. By these fair terms, he conciliated; by these he captivated."

This pleasing impression was reinforced by the evidence of his wealth, or at least of wealthy backers. Despite having limited funds at his disposal, within three months Wilkinson had bought 12,550 acres on the Kentucky River and filed claims for another 18,000 acres at the Falls of the Ohio, the future Louisville, and farther east on the Licking River where the land was cheaper. Following old frontier advice that "the best method of getting first-rate lands . . . is by way of goods," he set up a store in Lexington, a strategic point at the end of a good trail from Virginia. The settlement amounted to no more than thirty log cabins and a stockade on either side of a dusty track, but from here new arrivals might move northwest to the Ohio or southwest into the grassy "wilderness."

The money for buying land came from wealthy friends in Philadelphia, such as Dr. Hugh Shiell, a Scots land speculator, and his brothers-in-law, James Hutchinson and Clement Biddle, while the Lexington store was set up with two partners he had known from his days on Horatio Gates's staff, Isaac Dunn and James Armstrong. Even the goods it sold, lengths of calico, corduroy, chintz, and Marseilles lace suitable for petticoats, as well as shoes, beads, "trinkets and gewgaws," were supplied on easy terms courtesy of another friend, John Moylan, whose business, Moylan, Barclay & Company, was one of the largest in Philadelphia.

Within Kentucky itself, the warmth of Wilkinson's personality quickly enabled him to build up a network of useful friends. At its heart was his lawyer, Harry Innes, the newly appointed attorney general for Kentucky district, who handled all Wilkinson's land deals and increasingly complex financial arrangements. Another was Humphrey Marshall, who, seduced by the newcomer's winning personality, promised to join forces with Wilkinson in the search for suitable land, a pledge that in time developed into lawsuits and a rancorous hatred.

In his early days on the frontier, however, Wilkinson's charm was literally as bankable as cash. Half a century later, William Leavy, whose father arrived in Lexington in 1785, could still remember Wilkinson's "wonderful address" in dealing with awkward financial affairs. "A friend living in the neighborhood of Lexington had loaned Wilkinson money," Leavy recorded, "which, on making a special call at his house to ask its return—he was so graciously received by him—having him to dine, &c.—that in place of urging its return he was before he left the house induced to increase the loan."

Frontier life also required a rugged determination that Philadelphia society rarely demanded. In Wilkinson's first winter, the cold was so intense that the Ohio River became blocked by slabs of ice as early as November, trapping a boatload of goods destined for the Lexington store, and the snow lay so deep it took the train of packhorses sent to rescue the cargo seven days to reach the river. Wilkinson boasted that he spent so many days on horseback exploring the wilderness that he knew it "better than any Christian in America." He used to lead a mule loaded with goods to sell, and bacon and biscuit for his food to save the expense of "damn'd Tavern Keepers," but wherever he went, his eyes were always open for good land to buy, both for himself and for his eastern backers. In July 1784, he signed a contract with John Lewis, a Philadelphia financier, to find and acquire eleven thousand acres, in return for which Lewis promised to give Wilkinson half of all the land he located.

The return on real estate was slow, however, and the store paid the bills. In his first year of business, bags of salt, essential for curing pork and preserving other food, were added to the goods for sale, and in July Wilkinson set up a partnership with Lewis to trade with Shawnee townships, giving cloth in exchange for beaver pelts and other furs. Probably the Lexington store also sold seeds and medicines, because writing to another military acquaintance, General Charles Scott, Wilkinson lamented the difficulty of getting vegetables suitable for the Atlantic coast to grow in Kentucky. "Be sure you bring a double stock of great variety," he advised Scott, "and try to make out more with Turnips and Potatoes—get a snug little assortment of medicine; don't forget Blistering Plaister, a plenty of Salts, Tart-Bark [for malaria], Laudinum [for pain relief]." In 1786, Wilkinson also built a tobacco warehouse, and in Virginia's tobacco economy, this was equivalent to setting up a bank, because the receipts he issued at three dollars per hundredweight of leaf could be exchanged as legal tender. Within three years, he had become a leading figure in Kentucky's growing community.

His letters to friends in the east made no mention of political difficulties and became prolonged invitations to come and settle. "Our country is now a continued Flower Bed," he told Charles Scott in 1785, "and the whole aire breathes the richest fragrance . . . The Indians are peaceable, and [the price of] corn and Bacon is on the fall."

In September 1784, Nancy and the two boys succumbed to his entreaties and left Philadelphia for life on the frontier. Unlike her husband, Nancy hated the harshness of the wilderness. Even three years later, she still bitterly missed her family and the conversation and comforts of city life. "It is impossible for me to describe the torture my mind endures," she wrote to her father, "not [being] blessed with the Sight of a relation this ten months, & Surrounded by People that has been brought up so differently from myself, that when Sick & Low spirited, there Company only disgusts—O what would I not give to be blessed with a sensible agreeable woman for a Neighbour that had been brought up tenderly as I have myself."

Quick-witted, gentle, and funny, she had the qualities of a city girl rather than the hard endurance needed by a frontier wife. The affectionate messages to her that Wilkinson's friends always included in their letters show how much she was liked, and according to rumor, Lexington's inhabitants much preferred her to her self-promoting husband. But for Nancy, Wilkinson was the only thing that made Kentucky bearable. With months of her arrival in Kentucky she was pregnant once more, and when he was away, she confessed to her father, "I feel so Stupid I Can scarce hear my Children when they speak to me; my Jimmys [sic] Presence would soon make me well." However, soon it was not only business and land-hunting that drew him from her side. Wilkinson had become involved in Kentucky politics.

ALTHOUGH THE MYTH of frontier life promised an escape from government and the constraints of the law, the reality made it impossible to avoid either. The first guide to Kentucky life, John Filson's *The Discovery, Settlement and Present State of Kentucké*, published in 1784, illustrated why. The myth was catered to in the appendix. This contained the story of Daniel Boone, the archetype of the frontier hero, who enjoyed danger and solitude, and who climbed to "the summit of a commanding ridge" simply for the pleasure of viewing "the ample plains, the beauteous tracts below [stretching to] the famous river Ohio that rolled in silent dignity, marking the western boundary of Kentucke with inconceivable grandeur." Speaking the language of the romantics, Boone concluded, "No populous city, with all the varieties of commerce and stately structures, could afford so much pleasure to my mind, as the beauties of nature I found here."

Filson's main text, however, amounted to an advertisement for Kentucky real estate. He described a fabulous land where a hundred bushels of corn per acre could be grown without the need for irrigation or fertilizer, along with sugar, coffee, cherries, and cucumbers, where the existing settlers were "polite, humane, hospitable and complaisant," where scores more arrived every day so that "the country will be exceedingly populous in a short time," and where property could be bought simply and safely because Kentucké belonged to the state of Virginia and was "governed by her wholesome laws, which are virtuously executed, and with excellent decorum."

Yet the failure of Virginia's government to operate either virtuously or decorously was precisely what infuriated Kentucky settlers. The most serious failing was the absence of protection against Indian attacks, principally by the Shawnees, who claimed hunting rights and saw their game increasingly frightened off by European settlers. Located two or three weeks away across the Allegheny Mountains, the Virginia legislature could not call out the militia in time, and left to their own defenses, more than one third of the two hundred pioneers round Lexington had been killed in a single Shawnee attack in 1782.

Less dangerous, but more toxic to the hopes of new settlers, was the confusion over land titles. To convert the wilderness into rapturous property, the land had to be surveyed, then the claim had to be registered and title to the property patented, both in Richmond. Even without counterclaims, a minimum of ten months was required. And Virginia's decision to mortgage much of Kentucky to fund its wartime expenditure made counterclaims inevitable.

The state printed paper money with a face value of more than sixty million dollars during the war, much of it backed by land in the west. By 1783, wealthy speculators in the east owned huge quantities of treasury bills and certificates, bought cheaply when their value dropped to one tenth of a cent in the dollar, that entitled them to ownership of up to one third of all Kentucky. Poorer settlers who came west to claim their land in person discovered that they were debarred from the best ground, or that farms they were working really belonged to a stranger far away in Richmond or Philadelphia. In 1785, the traveler Michael Austin passed more than seven hundred pioneers on the Wilderness Road heading for Filson's dream country. "And when arrivd at this Heaven in idea," he warned, "what do they find? a goodly land I will allow, but to them forbidden Land."

Caught in the morass of competing claims and dogged by fraud and widespread corruption, Kentucky's property market would become so notorious for the uncertainty of its land titles that within a generation one expert predicted accurately, "The titles in Kentucky w[ill] be Disputed for a Century to Come yet, when it's an old Settled Country." For many Kentuckians, the only possible solution was to cut themselves free from Virginia. Beginning in 1784, a series of settlers' conventions took place in the eastern town of Danville to consider proposals for separation from Virginia.

It was always likely that Wilkinson's volatile temperament, so quick to resent direction from above, would drive him to join the anti-Virginian movement. But he had other more pressing motives. He had made large purchases of land, then used some as collateral on loans, usually from his partners, and Wilkinson's tendency to extravagance meant that most of his partnerships ended in quarrels and litigation. He made the problem worse by running up lines of credit with friends to raise ready cash for urgent purchases. "I find I shall be under the necessity of employing about £40 of your cash to discharge sundry engagements incurred on Acct. of the old cargo," he wrote his associate Hugh Shiell late in 1784, "for which I will give you a bill at 30 Days on Col. [Clement] Biddle." Either because of this transaction or another soon afterward, Shiell broke off their association. He was replaced by Peyton Short, son-in-law of the wealthy John Cleves Symmes, who had bribed his way to ownership of more than a million acres of government land north of the Ohio River. That partnership also eventually broke down. In each case, land had to be sold hastily to pay the debt before Wilkinson had time to benefit from the rise in its value.

As he admitted in his *Memoirs*, he was "far from affluent [and] my expectations were damped by the obstructions which the Spaniards opposed to the free navigation of the Mississippi." In colonial times and for most of the war, the river had been under the loose control of the British, who had allowed settlers to ship their tobacco, flour, and whiskey down the river to New Orleans. But in a lightning campaign in 1781, Spanish forces had taken control of the Gulf Coast and the river, and since 1783 the Mississippi had been closed to American traders. Nothing would do more to increase the prosperity of Kentucky, and of Wilkinson, than opening the Mississippi to navigation by American vessels.

Wilkinson missed the first two Danville conventions, but was elected to the third in August 1785, where a formal petition calling for Kentucky's independence was sent to Richmond. By then his social influence equaled his personal ambition, and his fellow delegates appointed him to write "in the plain, manly and unadorned language of independence," as he described his flowery style, the actual petition to the Virginia assembly that called for legislation "declaring and acknowledging the independence of the District of Kentucky." In the excitement, the resolution passed by the convention merely called for Kentucky's independence but said nothing of seeking admission to the Union.

This was not entirely a mistake. Kentucky's assertive settlers had no particular loyalty to the United States. As Washington himself admitted to Richard Henry Lee in August 1785, "There is nothing which binds one country or one State to another but interest. Without this cement the Western inhabitants can have no predilection for us." One powerful interest did tie Kentucky to the United States, however: the need for help in opening the Mississippi River so that settlers could ship their produce to the great port of New Orleans. Because Spanish galleys and forts dominated the river as far north as the mouth of the Ohio, Kentucky's farmers wanted the American government to bring diplomatic pressure to bear in Madrid. If they did not get what they wanted, Wilkinson assured his brother-in-law James Hutchinson that year, "The People of Kentucky alone, unaided by Congress . . . could dislodge every Garrison the Spaniards have on or in the Neighborhood of the Mississippi." The Danville delegates certainly knew of Wilkinson's outlook, and suspicious of a Congress influenced by New England representatives with little interest in opening up the Mississippi, most welcomed his call for Kentucky to take unilateral action.

In January 1786 Virginia's legislature responded cooperatively by passing an enabling act that allowed Kentucky to separate on three conditions—a convention formally voted for it, a suitable constitution was adopted, and Congress voted for the state's admission to the Union. The convention that met at Danville in September 1786 was intended to be the first step along this path. Wilkinson, representing Fayette County, arrived there in his guise as landowner, storekeeper, tobacco banker, and leading citizen. Continuing his theme from the previous convention, he argued for total independence from both Virginia and the United States. He made his case in a speech that marked his arrival as one of the dominant figures in Kentucky politics, a place he continued to occupy for the next fifteen years.

"I pleased myself," he boasted to James Hutchinson after his triumph, "&, what was more consequential, every Body else, except my dead opponents— these I with great facility turned into subjects of ridicule and derision." He had planned to speak for no more than ninety minutes but found to his surprise that he had been on his feet for three and a half hours. Life in Kentucky, he concluded, had altered him. "I have experienced a great change since I held a seat in the Pennsylvania Assembly," he confided to Hutchinson. "I find myself much more easy, prompt, & eloquent in a public debate, than I ever was in private conversation, under the greatest flow of spirits."

Yet it was not so much Wilkinson's eloquence as the behavior of Congress that drove the movement for Kentucky's total independence. Throughout the critical year of 1786, the United States, represented by the secretary for foreign affairs, John Jay, had been negotiating with Don Diego de Gardoqui, the Spanish minister in Philadelphia, to find a way of continuing the alliance that had begun during the war with Britain. The diplomats agreed that difficulties over the frontier they shared along the Mississippi had to be balanced against the mutual advantages of increasing trade. Scenting mischief, Wilkinson had warned as early as April 1786 that Jay was secretly prepared to sacrifice Kentucky's need to have access to the Mississippi. He swore to make it his mission to alert every settler in the district: "They shall be Informed or I will wear out all the Stirrups at every Station."

Despite the myth, the frontier grew around communities rather than individuals. Public buildings were invariably constructed, a stockade, a church, a courthouse, a tavern, where people met to share past experiences and future forebodings. At these places and at social events such as turkey shoots and militia musters, a stranger with the gift of the gab could be sure that he would have an audience, and that his news and views would noisily be chewed over by outspoken frontier folk.

During 1786, his third year in the west, Wilkinson made his name widely known. When the convention met in Danville, independence for Kentucky was no longer an extreme view but close to a majority opinion. It was generally known that Jay had concluded an agreement with Gardoqui accepting the closure of the Mississippi in exchange for allowing shippers and businessmen on the Atlantic coast access to Spanish ports. In Congress, a bare majority of the states voted to accept Jay's agreement. Since nine of the thirteen were required to approve a treaty, Jay's agreement failed to become law, but, according to James Monroe, the barefaced betrayal of Kentucky's interests was deliberate. The northern states intended "to separate those people, I mean all those westward of mountains, from the federal government, perhaps throw them into the hands eventually of a foreign power."

Even Kentucky's attorney general, Harry Innes, was convinced that "this country will in a few years Revolt from the Union and endeavor to erect an Independent Government." His belief was loudly endorsed by his client James Wilkinson. But before the convention could discuss the matter, a new Indian attack across the Ohio called away so many delegates to join in the defense of their homes that proceedings had to be abandoned, leaving the great question unanswered for another year.

Most delegates felt frustrated, but Wilkinson reacted differently. Late in 1786 he asked John Marshall, Humphrey's cousin, then a member of the Virginia assembly, to persuade the governor, Edmund Randolph, to issue him a passport to visit New Orleans. When Randolph refused, Wilkinson approached the Spanish minister, Gardoqui, again with no success. His purpose became clear in December when he wrote for a third time, now addressing Francisco Cruzat, commandant of the Spanish fort at St. Louis.

The tone of his message was strikingly different from that of his public speeches. It contained no hint of dislodging Spanish garrisons, but instead offered regrets for the behavior of General George Rogers Clark, who had destroyed three Spanish boats earlier in the year in retaliation for the confiscation of two Kentucky flatboats carrying flour. Clark's action was "an outrage . . . generally disavowed here," Wilkinson assured Cruzat, and as evidence of his good intentions he added a warning that "a certain Colonel Green and other desperate adventurers are meditating an attack of the posts of his most Catholic Majesty at Natchez." Wilkinson concluded by promising that he would "do eveything in our power here to foil this band." Almost as an afterthought, he added the hope that his warning could be passed on to Don Esteban Miró, governor of Louisiana.

By the beginning of 1787, while ice still blocked the Ohio River, his intentions were generally known in Kentucky. He advertised for consignments of ham, tobacco, and butter to be carrried down the Mississippi for sale in New Orleans. Spain might not be prepared to open up the river to Kentucky traders, and the United States might be reluctant to intervene, but James Wilkinson was proposing to defy both sides and strike a blow "for the rights of navigation and free trade." That was authentic frontier behavior, to do what seemed right regardless of what the authorities wanted.

When his fifty-foot-long flatboat with its cargo of Kentucky goods floated away from the dock at the Falls of the Ohio in April 1787, Humphrey Marshall recorded that Wilkinson left behind crowds of Kentucky settlers "enraptured with his spirit of free enterprise and liberality, not less than his unbounded patriotism."

8

SPANISH TEMPTATION

A T THE AGE OF THIRTY, James Wilkinson was no longer the young genius
whose boundless enthusiasm won the hearts of susceptible generals.
Yet his plans still crucially depended on the impact of his personal appeal.
The first test came when he and his twenty-strong crew came within range
of the cannon in the Spanish fort of St. Louis. They were clearly breaking
the ban imposed in 1783 on all vessels except those flying the Spanish flag.
The fort's commander had the power to confiscate their cargo and their
boat, a potential loss of about five thousand dollars, and the two Kentucky
flatboats had been seized in these very circumstances the previous year. But
the chief danger was to Wilkinson's dreams. For him, this voyage was only
the first step toward making his fortune. What he hoped to gain was "the
privilege of furnishing a considerable annual supply of tobacco to the Mexican market which would have secured immense fortunes for me and my
friends."

Within the bureaucratic structure of Spain's colonial service, the status
of Francisco Cruzat, who commanded the fort and its galleys, could hardly
have been lower. It was dictated by the remote location of St. Louis on the
uttermost edge of the empire. His immediate superior was Carlos de
Grand-Pré, the commander of the Natchez region, comprising modern
Alabama and Mississippi, who was himself subject to the orders of Esteban
Miró in New Orleans, governor of Louisiana and West Florida. He in turn
fell under the supervision of Luis Las Casas, the captain general in Havana,
Cuba, who ranked alongside the viceroy of Mexico as one of the two great-
est officials north of the equator in the mightiest power west of the Atlantic.
Above the captain general existed only the royal council in Madrid, and in

particular the minister for the Indies, under the direction of His Catholic Majesty Carlos III.

The gigantic extent of the Spanish empire, already stretching from Tierra del Fuego at the southern tip of South America to the Great Lakes and Canada in the north, had been swollen still farther by its participation in the war of American independence. Indeed, apart from the United States, no country gained more from the conflict. In 1781 Spanish forces seized British forts along the Gulf Coast and up the Mississippi Valley, and as part of the peace negotiations, Britain ceded to Spain modern Florida and the Gulf Coast—then known as East and West Florida. The border with the United States was ill-defined—in 1782 a Spanish diplomat insisted it ran just west of the Appalachians as far as the Ohio River, "thence round the western shores of Lakes Erie and Huron and thence round Lake Michigan." The exact details might be open to dispute, but no one doubted that both banks of the Mississippi and the river itself lay under Spanish control. When Wilkinson's crew poled the flatboat to shore at St. Louis in May 1787, the colossus was at the peak of its power and, in North America alone, claimed an area three times that of the United States.

Despite his inferior position, Cruzat was also the gatekeeper to this mighty empire. He had decided Wilkinson's letter deploring the seizure of Spanish vessels was significant enough to send on to Natchez, and thus he was prepared to let its writer land at St. Louis. The good impression created by the letter, however, was nothing compared to the effect of the present Wilkinson brought with him, two Virginia thoroughbred horses. And if the American's ease and polished manners had the same effect on the lowly commander as they did on his superiors, Cruzat must have been overwhelmed. Certainly he provided Wilkinson with an official passport as far as Natchez, together with an effusive letter of recommendation to its commandant, Grand-Pré. Once inside the empire, Wilkinson's preparations and personality became irresistible. At Natchez, Grand-Pré was especially grateful for the warning against Thomas Green, who claimed that the settlement was really part of Georgia. When Wilkinson arrived armed with Cruzat's recommendation, Grand-Pré not only received him warmly but sent him on to New Orleans with an even more supportive document addressed directly to Miró. By the time his cargo reached the dockside there on the last day of June, a cascade of approval ensured that Wilkinson would at least be listened to by the man who controlled the Mississippi.

He was escorted to Government House by the corporal of the guard and presented to Esteban Miró and his intendant, or chief financial officer,

Martín Navarro. Both were men of exceptional quality. Each had risen through the service on merit alone—Miró as a soldier and Navarro as an accountant—and together were engaged in a concerted drive to change Spain's existing strategy of limiting the movement of goods and people in North America.

What drove Spanish policy was the need to protect Mexico's rich silver mines in Zacatecas and the northern province of Nueva Vizcaya. Their output was worth as much as seventeen million dollars a year, according to the German explorer Alexander von Humboldt, the largest source of silver in the world and almost half the total value of the empire's exports. The only purpose of Louisiana, along with Texas and New Mexico, was to provide a barrier against any threat to Mexico from the north. Consequently, entry had been denied to all but approved immigrants, and trade was restricted to what was required by the direction of the captain general in Havana. It cost about five hundred thousand dollars a year to maintain Louisiana, a colony that had fewer than thirty thousand inhabitants, but the silver justified the outlay.

Until 1783, the only attacks came from marauding Comanches, and the occasional incursion by British smugglers and adventurers, but American independence and the flood of migrants across the Appalachians changed the equation. Within five years, an estimated fifty thousand settlers had poured into the Ohio Valley and the western lands, and Spain's near empty colony was no longer a protection but an incitement to land-hungry pioneers.

Navarro, the older of the two Spaniards and, according to his colleague, "a man of talent, active, disinterested and popular," took the lead. Not only was he one of the wealthiest merchants in New Orleans, he was the originator of a policy of free trade and relaxed immigration for Louisiana put forward in a pamphlet as early as 1780. Under "a sovereign whose laws were not opposed to a system of free trade," he wrote, Louisiana would develop "a numerous population and large commerce [and become] one of the most useful and best established provinces in America." As the tide of American settlers swept over the Blue Ridge and Allegheny mountains, it became increasingly urgent for Louisiana to match them in wealth and population.

In February 1787, months before Wilkinson's arrival, Navarro had bluntly repeated his message to Madrid: "The only way to check them [the Americans] is with a proportionate population, and it is not by imposing commercial restrictions that this population is to be acquired, but by granting a prudent expansion and freedom of trade." For someone as alert as Wilkinson, it would not have been hard to sense the drift of Navarro's ideas, since it harmonized so closely with his own.

Nevertheless, the important bond he formed was with his fellow soldier Miró, who had joined the army at the age of sixteen and invariably addressed the American as "brigadier." The title emphasized their similarities and pleased Wilkinson, who even as a trader never ceased to see himself as a soldier. In subsequent reports, he would address Miró as "my dear friend" and, as he had in writing to Gates, ask to be excused his bluntness on the grounds that he wrote "out of friendship." It had taken Miró thirty-five years to reach the rank of brigadier, but he would eventually end his career as a field marshal, the highest rank in the Spanish army, having worked his way to the top by unremitting energy and competence. Although the senior as governor, he and Navarro worked as equals. They were in complete harmony about the need to strengthen Louisiana by encouraging immigration and promoting trade.

In their joint report to Madrid, the two Spaniards recorded their favorable impressions of the American: "He is a young man of about thirty-three years of age, although he looks older; of exceedingly agreeable appearance, married, with three small children. In his manners and address, he shows that he has had a very good education which his uncommon talents have taken advantage of." In an epoch when years and seniority were synonymous, the mistake about his age evidently arose from his air of authority, and nothing that they learned from him over a long, hot summer shook their confidence in his ability to give a lead to Kentucky opinion.

After their first meeting, they had other interviews, often with interpreters, occasionally by themselves, since Navarro spoke excellent English and Miró a little. Ostensibly they were discussing Wilkinson's wish to sell the goods he had brought with him to New Orleans. In the long term, the American made it clear, he wanted to extend the list to include "Negroes, live Stock, tobacco, Flour, Bacon, Lard, Butter, Cheese, tallow, Apples, to the amount of fifty or sixty thousand Dollars." But once each side discovered the overlap in their interests, their discussions took on a different dimension.

According to Miró and Navarro, after ten or twelve days Wilkinson announced that he had a "project of great importance to propose," and having heard what he had in mind, they asked him to write it down. By then, all three must have clearly understood what each wanted. On August 8, Miró signaled their good intentions by granting a permit to "the American Brigadier Don James Wilkinson . . . to direct or cause to be brought into this country by inhabitants of Kentucky one or more launches belonging to him, with cargoes of the productions *of* that country." Since only Madrid could authorize an exception to the ban on trade, this meant less than it appeared, but with the governor's backing it could become reality, giving Wilkinson a monopoly of trade into New Orleans, worth tens of thousands of dollars. In return, Wilkinson delivered on August 21 a 7,500-word report that became known as his "First Memorial."

The memorial presented a program for their mutual advantage. Its first part concerned the political future of the western settlers. Wilkinson had come to New Orleans, he said, at the request of "the notables of Kentucky" to discover whether Spain might be interested in opening negotiations "to admit us under its protection as vassals."

The key to the loyalty of the Kentuckians, he explained, was access to the Mississippi, "the object on which all their hopes of temporal happiness rest, and without which misery and wretchedness is their certain portion." To gain it, their present inclination was to ally themselves to Spain, but if that failed, they would turn to Britain for help. To decide the issue, Spain needed to act immediately. Wilkinson recommended that it should begin by "peremptorily and absolutely [refusing] to the Congress the Navigation of the Mississippi" in order to force the settlers to look to "the power which secures them this most precious privilege."

This was the heart of what became known as the Spanish Conspiracy: to induce the Kentuckians, by offering the reward of free trade on the Mississippi, to leave the Union and become part of the Spanish empire. As its instigator, Wilkinson promised to employ "all my faculties to compass this desireable event."

Although his recommended tactic of shutting the river to American traffic was the reverse of the policy that made him popular in Kentucky, he insisted that "a man of great popularity and political talents will be able to alienate the Western Americans from the United States, destroy the insidious designs of Great Britain and throw [the Kentuckians] into the arms of Spain." Such a person would need to be rewarded. It would be advisable, therefore, "to offer indulgence to men of real influence" by allowing them to ship goods to New Orleans free of charge.

Independently of this policy, he also recommended that the Spaniards construct a strong defensive post near the settlement of New Madrid, just below the junction of the Ohio River with the Mississippi. This was needed because in any negotiations between Spain and the United States "the more respectable and independent the military stength of the former, the greater will be the concessions she will receive from the latter." Once the post was constructed, immigrants should be encouraged to settle below the fort with the inducements of free land, religious toleration, and free trade on the Mississippi. Americans would flood in and "this Province would then rise into immediate Wealth, Strength and National Importance."

In his *Memoirs* Wilkinson denied that he had done anything more than offer empty promises in return for the commercial advantage of importing tobacco and other products to New Orleans. "The idea of alienating Kentucky from the United States, while a prospect of national protection remained, would have been as absurd as the idea of reducing them to the vassallage of Spain," he declared, knowing that he had advocated both.

A few years later he certainly urged an associate, Hugh McIlvain, to follow his example. "When you get to Natchez, put on your best bib and tucker," he advised. Smartly attired, McIlvain should flatter Miró, take an oath of allegiance, and "to his enquires respecting Kentucky, say nothing that is not flattering and favourable to Luisiana." The purpose was simply to get permission to sell tobacco in New Orleans.

Yet if his "Memorial" was designed to secure valuable trading rights, it could achieve that end only by being a serious proposition. Both Miró and Navarro were realistic enough to understand that Wilkinson was less committed than he pretended, but they were also shrewd enough to guess that he could be persuaded to perform more than he intended. To secure his loyalty, they were prepared to offer not just financial inducements, but their esteem and respect. To someone as economically careless and emotionally hungry as Wilkinson, that exchange would come to seem like an irresistible bargain.

The next day, August 22, he signed a formal document "transferring my allegiance from the United States to his Catholic Majesty." For McIlvain and many other Americans who later made similar declarations when they sought Spanish trading privileges, this amounted to no more than a formula. But Wilkinson went on to defend what he had done in words clearly intended to carry weight with the two men he wanted to impress.

Echoing Washington's own dictum, he asserted, "[Self]-interest regulates the passions of Nations, as also those of individuals, and he who attributes a different motive to human affairs deceives himself or seeks to deceive others: although I sustain this great truth, I will not, however, deny that every man owes something to the land of his birth." To explain how his interests had come to diverge from those of his country, he reverted to a familiar theme—blaming his behavior on the failings of someone, or in this case some country, he had trusted.

"Born and educated in America, I embraced its cause in the last revolution, and remained throughout faithful to its interest, until its triumph over its enemies," he declared. "This occurrence has now . . . left me at liberty, having fought for her happiness, to seek my own. [But] circumstances and the policies of the United States having made it impossible for me to obtain this desired end under its Government, I am resolved to seek it in Spain."

Defiantly, he declared that no one could accuse him of having "broken any of the laws of nature or of nations, nor of honor and conscience" in changing his allegiance, but the conclusion of his "Memorial" made his unease explicit: "Gentlemen, I have committed secrets of an important nature, such as would, were they divulged, destroy my Fame and Fortune forever." Should their plans not work out, he relied on Miró and Navarro "to bury these communications in eternal oblivion."

SEEN ACROSS MORE THAN TWO CENTURIES, the Spanish Conspiracy might appear doomed to failure, but Americans living in the years immediately after the Revolution saw it in a different context. To them the ramshackle constitution created by the Articles of Confederation seemed more likely to destroy the Union than hold it together. A bankrupt Congress, dependent on revenue from the states, could do nothing to prevent the different economic interests within the United States from pulling it apart.

Democratic, commercially minded New Englanders had little in common with aristocratic, rural southerners. Fiscally conservative southerners were infuriated by the north's readiness to print paper money to pay its debts, and shocked by the lawlessness that erupted into tax revolts such as Shays's Rebellion in 1786. The decision of northern states to follow Pennsylvania and Massachusetts in abolishing slavery alienated southern plantation owners, who felt their human property under threat. The catalyst for these divisions came in November 1786, when Henry Knox assured his former commander in chief that up to fifteen thousand New Englanders were ready to rebel rather than pay more tax. A shaken Washington stared into the abyss. The United States, he told Knox, was "fulfilling the prediction of our transatlantic foe! 'leave them to themselves, and their government will soon dissolve.'"

Their fear that the Union really would fall apart was what drove James Madison and George Washington to push for a new constitution and the creation of a stronger federal government. It was no coincidence that James Wilkinson's negotiations with Miró and Navarro in the summer of 1787 coincided with the proceedings of the Constitutional Convention in

Philadelphia. One set of negotiations was aimed at partition, the other at union, but each arose from the same divergent tendencies within the United States.

Until a new central government showed it could protect the western settlers' interests, Wilkinson's proposals would continue to provide the largely hidden agenda of Kentucky politics. They would also become the last, best hope for the survival of the Spanish empire in North America.

ON SEPTEMBER 19, 1787, James Wilkinson left New Orleans by ship bound for Charleston, South Carolina. Miró and Navarro reported that before sailing he had set up "one of the most complex ciphers to give us the news which this delicate subject may call forth." Although often taken to be suspicious in itself, the use of a cipher was common in an era when letters were frequently opened by inquisitive postmasters, political opponents, and commercial competitors. What made Wilkinson's ciphering exceptional was that he took to its use so readily. Whole swaths of his massive correspondence—a single communication might be thirty pages long—would eventually consist of numbers, symbols, or seemingly randomly selected letters. (See appendix.) He expected congressional allies and friends such as Aaron Burr to decipher these, as well as his Spanish handlers.

Since he wrote in English, his reports not only had to be transcribed, but translated into Spanish. Replies went through the same process in reverse. Miró never doubted that Wilkinson was worth the trouble. The Spanish cipher, using as its key an English-Spanish dictionary, was known within Spain's colonial service as Number 13. Over time, and to preserve his anonymity, Miró and Navarro came to ascribe the name to Wilkinson himself, Agent 13. Eventually he insisted on being known by that pseudonym alone.

Miró and Navarro's satisfaction in the outcome of that climactic summer was reflected in their recommendation to Madrid that as well as his commercial monopoly the American brigadier "be rewarded generously for his services if he succeeds in the first and principal object [Kentucky's admission into the Spanish empire] or brings all his influence to bear in the accomplishment of the second [bringing American settlers to Louisiana]." They had exceeded their authority by allowing him to break the ban on American traders using the Mississippi, but promised that the value of imported goods would be capped at about thirty-five thousand dollars, and that the money would remain in New Orleans until Madrid had given its approval. From their point of view, it represented an important first step toward free trade. For Wilkinson, the move possessed far greater significance. Up to this point, his betrayals had been small and personal. The agreement with Miró and Navarro had a different quality. It was the first tentative step toward leading a double life.

NOT UNTIL FEBRUARY 1788 did Wilkinson get home, and his delay in completing the last part of his journey after so long away almost broke Nancy's nerves. "I have look'd for my Wilkinson this several Months with the utmost impatience, & now know not where he is," she wrote her father. "The last letter I had from my Belov'd Wilkinson was dated at Richmond. In that he assures me he will be Home by the 15th or 20th of Jan., & now it is the middle of Feb. I am sorry to express the feelings of my Heart so much—but indeed I am too wretched at the Long Absence of a *dear Husband to feign a composure I do not feel at Present*. I am almost distracted."

Their son Joseph had been born in December 1785, her third child in three years. To add to the pressure of looking after three boys under the age of seven, just before her husband left for New Orleans, he had moved the family from the relative comfort of the frame house in Lexington that was also the store and taken them to land he owned in the wilderness of Frankfort. Although strategically placed near the center of the state, on the Kentucky River and at the edge of the bluegrass prairie, the isolated location had nothing to distinguish it from the rest of the empty, rolling landscape, except that in October 1786 the Virginia assembly had given Wilkinson permission to lay out a town on his property and operate a ferry across the river. To attract more inhabitants, he had a large, two-story house built in Frankfort and went to live there with his family.

While he was in New Orleans, however, Nancy was effectively marooned with her three small children, deprived of company and the comforts that were a necessity to her. Her eighty-one-year-old father sent her blankets and a barrel of sugar, whose sweetness she and the children adored, but she also needed new shoes for them and herself, scrubbing brushes, brooms, china cups, two hundred black sewing pins, and "a Pattern of a Black Sattin Cloak as I must make me one & wish to have it fashionable & let me know how they trim them [back in Philadelphia]." Most of all she yearned for contact with people who loved her, with her family—"It is impossible to say how much good perusing thy dear letter does me," she ended one letter to her father—and with her absent husband.

Her emotional hunger matched his, and in the absence of Wilkinson's letters to her, it must be presumed that this neediness was important to the

warmth of their marriage. They were like each other, too, in the delight
they took in clothes and luxuries, and in their lively talk and sociability. Usually their homes were filled with friends, and when Wilkinson had a regular
income, the parties she gave were locally famous—and in the sparse society
of the frontier that counted for much. But neither possessed the sort of
practical skills to make the most of their demanding environment and between them were unable to cook, preserve, make do, add accounts, or save.
Thus shortage of money to satisfy their wants constantly drove Wilkinson
to ever more dubious ways of making it.

HIS GROWING POLITICAL STATUS had delayed his return to Frankfort. In his
absence, the convention in Philadelphia had agreed on a constitution for a
new federal government that the states now had to ratify. In Virginia, the
outcome was close enough to make the votes of western settlers vital, and
from Charleston, where he landed, through Philadelphia, Wilkinson's views
were sought and listened to by politicians at every level. Even Washington
showed himself ready to set aside memories of Wilkinson's behavior as
clothier general and wrote expressing regret that "your business was so
pressing as to deprive me of the pleasure of seeing you at this place."

Back in Kentucky, his daring voyage and successful commercial arrangement with New Orleans marked him as a hero. Within weeks of his return,
he had assembled a fleet of twenty-five large flatboats to take unprecedented
quantities of tobacco, flour, and ham down the Mississippi. That summer,
tobacco worth $2 a hundredweight in Kentucky sold for $9.50 in New Orleans; flour went for $7 a barrel, three times the price in Kentucky. Because
the demand from New Orleans pushed up prices for those products across
Kentucky, all growers benefited, small farmers and large-plantation owners
alike.

The fleet was sent away under the direction of Wilkinson's partner in
the Lexington store, Isaac Dunn, and a young, high-spirited assistant, Philip
Nolan. They traveled with letters of recommendation to Miró whose
affectionate tone—Miró was "my dear friend" and "the friend of my
bosom"—suggests that Wilkinson felt, or pretended to feel, the sort of affection that he had lavished on Gates. The salutation of a letter sent to
Miró in February 1789 echoed the warmest of those he addressed to his
general: "My much esteemed and honored friend, having written to you
on the 12th instant, with all the formality and respect due to the Governor
of Louisiana as the representative of his Sovereign, I will now address the
man I love and the friend I can trust, without ceremony or reserve."

With the seventeen-year-old Nolan, who worked as a bookkeeper in the Lexington store, the roles were reversed. Wilkinson was the patron, and the object of the younger man's devotion. Indeed, Nolan must have reminded Wilkinson of himself at the same age—he commended the youth to Miró as "a child of my own raising"—although, as events were to prove, Nolan would turn out even wilder, more carefree, and less moral than his mentor.

That spring of 1788 New Orleans suffered the worst disaster in its history when fire swept across the city, destroying almost nine hundred buildings, and transforming three quarters of the city "into an arid and horrible desert," as Miró's official report put it. But a measure of his and Navarro's efficiency was that they immediately provided public funds, organized building materials, and offered tax breaks to owners who rebuilt, so that by June when the Kentucky goods arrived, the vigorous rebirth of the city was under way. Navarro had retired in May, leaving the double burden of finance and government on Miró's shoulders. Yet he seemed to thrive under the pressure, and Madrid rewarded him with promotion to the rank of brigadier "in testimony of the Royal satisfaction in his zeal."

From New Orleans, Isaac Dunn sent word of their warm reception. The goods were not only admitted free of the 25 percent tax that other importers had to pay, they were stored in the royal warehouse, an added favor, although it came at a cost—"you cannot be at a loss to know where a participation of Profits is expected, & where it is due," Dunn wrote discreetly, referring to Miró's rake-off. But Wilkinson was accustomed to sharing profits with his partners. The only cloud over the enterprise concerned the quality of the tobacco: a quarter was deemed unsatisfactory, and another quarter was rotten enough to be destroyed. Nevertheless, his own share of the profits amounted to $9,830.50, a sum held for him by Daniel Clark, an Irish-born merchant in New Orleans.

Intoxicated by this return on his agreement with Miró, Wilkinson decided to back another trading scheme, heavily financed by Clark and approved by Miró, which was designed to tie Kentucky more closely into the New Orleans economy. In August 1788, with Dunn as a third investor, Wilkinson and Clark spent almost twenty thousand dollars on a cargo of luxury goods including sugar, linen, wine, and brass candlesticks to be exported back up the Mississippi to Kentucky. "It is exceedingly important," Miró explained to Madrid, "that the Western people should see, before declaring themselves for a change of domination, that the true channel through which they are to be supplied with the objects of their wants, in exchange for their own productions, is the Mississippi."

By the time he came to write his *Memoirs*, bitter experience had taught Wilkinson a lesson: "I am not by education, habit or disposition, fitted for a dealer or trader." But in the summer of 1788, it seemed that whether as importer or exporter, he could not fail to make the "immense fortunes" that he had dreamed of when he set sail for New Orleans the year before.

9

CASH AND CONSPIRACY

T HE EXPEDITION TO NEW ORLEANS cemented James Wilkinson's reputation among Kentucky's settlers. Its spectacular effect on prices was
seen as confirmation of his political message that the settlers' interests lay
not on the Atlantic but westward with Spain. In June 1788, Miró advised
Madrid that, such was Wilkinson's influence among Kentucky's swelling
army of settlers, Miró had decided to accept the American's demand for
three thousand dollars in expenses rather than risk "the mischief that might
arise from vexing him, and the impediments that the lack of Income would
doubtless put in the way of his operations."

The rapid progress of the conspiracy suggested it was a wise decision. On
his return, Wilkinson had cautiously shared at least part of his plan for joining the Spanish empire with the "Kentucky notables" he trusted most. His
first contact was with his lawyer, Harry Innes, by now impatient for independence from Virginia and willing to consider all options. His outlook was
shared, though less enthusiastically, by judges Alexander Bullit and Caleb
Wallace, and by other leading figures such as John Brown, the district's representative in the Continental Congress, and a lawyer, Benjamin Sebastian.
Only Innes and Bullit were trusted with the naked proposal that Kentucky
should become part of the Spanish empire, and both recoiled. Wilkinson
promptly toned down the plan to one of an alliance between Spain and the
sovereign state of Kentucky. It was a small setback, but that summer 90 percent of the frontier votes went against ratifying the new, federal Constitution
that had emerged from the convention. In Fayette County an overwhelming
majority chose Wilkinson yet again to represent them at the next Danville
convention, the sixth, to decide Kentucky's future.

In July the latest convention again failed to resolve Kentucky's future, but it was remarkable for the speeches of Innes, Wallace, and Sebastian demanding an immediate separation from Virginia without waiting for prior approval from Congress. "The consequences of depending on a body [the Virginia legislature] whose interests were opposed to ours were depicted in the most vivid colors," Wilkinson reported to Miró, "and the strongest motives were set forth to justify the separation." The convention agreed that at its next meeting, it would draw up a constitution and negotiate its independence from Virginia. Seen from New Orleans, the current of opinion was clearly flowing in the right direction.

In the summer of 1788, the current accelerated when Kentucky's petition to become part of the United States was rejected by the Continental Congress on the grounds that no additional state should be admitted before the new federal government took office in 1789. The decision played directly into the conspirators' hands. When the next convention, due in November, voted for independence from Virginia, it would also inevitably be voting for independence from the United States. To gauge Spain's response, Kentucky's representative in Congress, John Brown, made contact with Gardoqui, the Spanish ambassador, and was promised that concessions would be made to Kentucky for use of the Mississippi "if she will erect herself into an independent government. [But] they can never be yielded to her by Spain as long as she remains a member of the Union."

In New Orleans, the normally cautious Miró looked forward to Kentucky's November convention and confessed to Antonio Valdes, the minister for the Indies and his political master in Madrid, "This affair progresses more rapidly than I had anticipated." In his frustration Brown had told a friend, who passed the news on to Miró, that he intended "to call for a general assembly of his fellow citizens, in order to proceed immediately to declare themselves independent, and to propose to Spain the opening of a commercial intercourse with reciprocal advantages." In the spring, Miró predicted, "I shall have to receive a delegation [from Kentucky] appointed in due form," and asked Valdes how he should respond.

A small but significant setback occurred before the convention opened. Brown mentioned Gardoqui's offer to George Muter, who was in favor of splitting from Virginia but not from the Union. Muter immediately leaked the letter to the *Kentucké Gazette*. It crystallized opposition among the "country party," composed of large-plantation owners whose property titles, often acquired with Virginia's paper money, might be questioned should Kentucky become a sovereign power. Undeterred, Wilkinson delivered a speech on the opening day that outlined the steps needed to achieve the goal that all Kentuckians wanted, the freedom to carry their goods down the Mississippi. "The way to obtain it," he argued, "has been indicated in the former convention, and every gentleman present will connect it with a declaration of independence, the formation of a [Kentucky] constitution and the organization of a new State, which may safely be left to find its own way into the Union on terms advantageous to its own interests."

According to Edward Butler, who wrote his *History of Kentucky* in 1834 while the convention was still within living memory, Wilkinson dominated the proceedings: "This gifted man drew all eyes upon him and was looked up to as a leader and a chief." But opposition to the idea of independence was already growing from the country party, led by Muter and Humphrey Marshall. Looking for allies, Wilkinson turned to his fellow conspirator John Brown, expecting him to cite Gardoqui's offer as evidence of the advantages of independence. But Brown had been worked on by Muter. At the crucial moment he lost his nerve and called instead for unanimity in whatever they decided. "He is a young man of respectable talents, but timid, without political experience, and with very little knowledge of the world," Wilkinson reported in disappointment to New Orleans. "Nevertheless, he firmly perseveres in his adherence to our interests."

The next day Wilkinson adopted a bold strategy. He read a long paper to delegates modeled closely on his New Orleans memorial, but crucially omitting any reference to becoming "vassals" of his Catholic Majesty. No vote was taken on its proposals for independence and a Spanish alliance, but the convention voted to thank him for his address, while it tabled Brown's motion for joining the Union. Delegates might sympathize with Wilkinson's aims, but for most the double leap that independence required— defiance of Virginia and rejection of the United States—was too much. The only action they could agree on was to call for an eighth convention after the new federal government was elected.

Politically the November convention was a failure, but in the slow development of Wilkinson's double personality it became an important milestone. In February 1789, he sent Miró a long account of his performance at Danville that was almost entirely deceptive. Despite the opposition of the country party, he claimed "our cause has acquired considerable force." Relying on the lack of good communication between Kentucky and New Orleans, he assured Miró that "in order to elicit an unequivocal proof of the opinion of that assembly, I submitted to its examination my memorial, and the joint answer of yourself and Navarro." To confirm that he was telling the truth, he enclosed newspaper cuttings with reports of his speech, together with the convention's expression of gratitude and its rejection of Brown's resolution.

Sending the letter and the newspapers on to Madrid, Miró added his own balanced view of what had happened. "You will find an account of the bold act which General Wilkinson has ventured upon, in presenting his first memorial in a public convention," he told Valdes. "In so doing, he has so completely bound himself [to us], that, should he not be able to obtain the separation of Kentucky from the United States, it has become impossible for him to live in it, unless he has suppressed, which is possible, certain passages which might injure him."

That delicate cocktail of hope and distrust became the hallmark of Wilkinson and Miró's relationship. Each liked, exploited, and was compelled by political and financial necessity to forgive the other. "I am aware that it may be possible that his intention is to enrich himself at our expense, by inflating us with hopes and promises which he knows to be vain," Miró acknowledged to Valdes. "Nevertheless, I have determined to humor him."

On his side, Wilkinson always assumed that his efforts to deceive were no more than those practiced on him by the governor and Navarro. Or as he put it in his autobiography, "It is but reasonable to presume, that they had duties and obligations to consult as well as myself; and . . . it was fair that they should play back upon me my own game, to the best advantage." In fact, apart from taking a cut of Wilkinson's profits, Miró handled Wilkinson with remarkable integrity, noting his failures and weaknesses, but never cheating or blackmailing him. From this uneven base grew an astonishingly firm friendship, the most enduring of Wilkinson's oddly dependent relationships, and one that seamlessly evolved into that between spy and handler.

UNDER THE LAYERS OF DECEPTION that Wilkinson was beginning to practice with growing ease lay unavoidable truths. The first was his financial extravagance. The second was the realization that his one hope of economic rescue lay in New Orleans. The third was that others wanted to take his place in Spanish affections. All these were thrown into sharp focus by the response of the royal council in Madrid to his memorial.

No direct comment was sent to Miró, but in May 1788, Spain's chief minister, José, Count of Floridablanca, had instructed the Spanish minister in Philadelphia, Diego de Gardoqui, of a change in official strategy. The Mississippi would remain closed, but Spain should boost the population of its North American colonies by trying "to attract to our side the inhabi-

tants of the Ohio and Mississippi." In response, Gardoqui became an enthusiast for inducing Americans to migrate to Louisiana and Natchez by offering them free land, access to the river, and religious toleration.

All at once Wilkinson's privileged position was threatened by the readiness of other prominent Americans to take advantage of Gardoqui's offer.
George Rogers Clark, the hero of the capture of Vincennes from the British,
asked for permission to settle in Louisiana, as did Friedrich von Steuben
and Daniel Boone, while John Sevier, victor of Kings Mountain in the
south and founder of the short-lived Franklin colony, assured Gardoqui
that the settlers in eastern Tennessee were "unanimous in their vehement
desire to form an alliance and treaty of commerce with Spain, and put
themselves under her protection." In December 1788, Wilkinson's own
partner Isaac Dunn hurried into Frankfort with news that Gardoqui had approved a proposal by Colonel George Morgan to settle one hundred thousand people on several million acres in Louisiana. His project had already
reached the stage of receiving permission to create a town on the Mississippi
that its owner called New Madrid.

As a result, every word of Wilkinson's letter to Miró in February
1789—and the lies about the convention made up only a small part—was
designed to demonstrate his unique usefulness and loyalty to Spain's interests. Bundled up with his writing was a letter from his old commanding
officer, General Arthur St. Clair. It had been sent to Dunn and described St.
Clair's distress at hearing that "our friend Wilkinson" was a leader of the
Kentucky secessionists, whose goal "would completely ruin this country."
Unaware that Dunn was part of the conspiracy, St. Clair pleaded, "Should
there be any foundation for these reports, for God's sake, make use of your
influence to detach Wilkinson from that party." This was proof, Wilkinson
confided to Miró, "that the part which I play in our great enterprise, and
the dangers to which I am exposed for the service of his Catholic Majesty,
are [publicly] known."

As though this were not enough, Wilkinson also told the Spanish governor that in November 1788 he had been contacted by John Connolly,
a British spy sent to investigate the loyalties of western settlers by Lord
Dorchester, governor of Canada. Connolly's cover was the pretense of trying to recover Kentucky properties confiscated during the war, but it was
blown as soon as he entered the newly established Northwest Territory beyond the Ohio River. "My Information is, that he is sent to tamper with
the People of Kentuckey and induce them to throw themselves into the
Arms of Great Britain," St. Clair, the territorial governor, informed John

Jay in Philadelphia, ". . . [and] if that cannot be brought about, to stimulate them to Hostilities against the Spaniards, and at [any] rate to detach them from the united States."

Connolly had visited Wilkinson expecting him to be sympathetic and promised British money, ammunition, and ships to help the Kentuckians "open the navigation of the Mississippi." But by Wilkinson's account, instead of welcoming an insurrection that was both anti-Spanish and anti-American, he made Connolly the victim of an audacious sting. "I employed a hunter, who feigned attempting his life," Wilkinson boasted to Miró. "As I hold the commission of a Civil Judge, it was, of course, to be my duty to protect him against the pretended murderer, whom I caused to be arrested and held in custody. I availed myself of this circumstance to communicate to Connelly [*sic*] my fear of not being able to answer for the security of his person, and I expressed my doubts whether he could escape with his life. It alarmed him so much, that he begged me to give him an escort to conduct him out of our territory, which I readily assented to." In return, Connolly supposedly promised to keep Wilkinson informed of British plots against Louisiana.

The story is not entirely credible, and no evidence suggests that Miró took at face value, even though Wilkinson promised that he wrote "as a good Spaniard." But the reminder that Spain could not afford to ignore Kentucky's disaffected settlers served Miró's purpose. Convinced that the threat they posed to Louisiana had to be neutralized, he regarded Gardoqui's intervention as a piecemeal solution. His preferred strategy remained that put forward in Wilkinson's memorial. That plan was Miró's plan, just as Wilkinson was Miró's man, and the Louisiana governor still pressed Madrid for a favorable response.

ADDING URGENCY TO Wilkinson's appeal was a misfortune that had blasted his first hopes of growing rich from trade. In September 1788, the *Speedwell*, the ship carrying the cargo of luxuries that Clark, Dunn, and Wilkinson intended to sell to Kentuckians, left New Orleans. Its voyage upriver was slow, and she had only just entered the Ohio River in November. There she was caught by ice that formed unseasonably early that winter. Before her precious cargo could be off-loaded, the hull was crushed, and she sank to the bottom with Wilkinson's investment of more than $6,000.

To recoup the expense, he assembled another, larger fleet to take goods down the Mississippi. Short of funds, he was forced to borrow from wealthy speculators such as John Lewis of Louisville, and the boats were sent south as soon as the ice began to break in the spring of 1789. When they arrived in New Orleans, the governor of Louisiana—"the man I love and the friend I can trust"—immediately agreed to buy 235,000 pounds of Wilkinson's tobacco, "on the grounds" as Miró informed Madrid, "that it was important to keep the General contented."

To calm Wilkinson's fears that he was being displaced, Miró also found time in his fourteen-hour working day to write and assure him "that I still continue to hold you as the principal actor in our favor," and to submit for his consideration Sevier's proposal that the settlers in Tennessee should become Spanish subjects. "I hope that, gathering all the information which you may deem necessary," Miró continued, "you will give me your opinion on this affair, in order that I may shape my course accordingly." He signed himself "your most affectionate friend."

Despite this reassurance, Wilkinson felt it necessary to see Miró in person and in June 1789 followed his boats down to New Orleans. He arrived to discover that his trading ambitions had suffered a second devastating blow. His partner, Isaac Dunn, had killed himself days earlier from despair at his wife's infidelity and his own debts. Later, Wilkinson estimated his losses from the tragedy to have amounted to ten thousand dollars. He may have exaggerated, but not by much. At the end of the 1789 season, when Joseph Ballinger, a courier from New Orleans, arrived with two barrels of silver to pay the farmers of Lincoln County for the tobacco they had entrusted to Wilkinson, there was not enough to cover what was owed them. Their anger and abuse began the erosion of Wilkinson's popularity in Kentucky.

The financial loss made him still more dependent on Miró's goodwill, but to his alarm the royal council in Spain showed itself hostile to his secessionist plans. Its first direct reaction to his memorial was only delivered to New Orleans early in 1789. Both the eighteen-month delay and the woolly quality of the response help to explain Spain's inability to deal with the swiftly changing events in the Mississippi basin. Demonstrating its failure to understand the central point of Wilkinson and Miró's strategy, that access to the river was the key to political influence in the region, the council declared that the Mississippi should be opened to American trade, subject to a mere 15 percent duty on goods sold. Although this eliminated much of the settlers' incentive to put themselves under Spanish rule, the council also declared that migration to Louisiana was to be encouraged. Finally, in a direct rebuff to Wilkinson and Miró, a ban was placed on any help being given to Kentucky's secessionist movement.

The need to counter the damage of this new policy kept Wilkinson in

New Orleans during the summer of 1789. Amid efforts to disentangle the legal mess left by Dunn's suicide, he and Miró spent three months discussing the proper strategy for Spain to follow. The outcome was a second memorial, written in September. That it was a joint collaboration, not just with Miró but with the free-trade philosophy of Navarro, was apparent from a striking passage extolling free enterprise over Spain's mercantile economy that restricted trade to its own colonies and ships: "Our navigation being confined at present to Spanish vessels, and our commerce to a few Spanish ports and islands, rivalry [i.e., competition], which is the vital principle of commerce, is dead, and the immediate consequences follow; our merchandise in dry goods [i.e., textiles and clothing] is now sold at from 75 per cent. to 150 per cent. more than in North America, and the freightage of one cask of tobacco from New Orleans to any part of Europe costs as much as four casks from any part of the United States to the same place."

Their solution was to urge the council to make New Orleans a free port open to all trade from the sea, although river traffic would still be restricted. But by now the United States had both free enterprise, and, since the inauguration of George Washington as president in April, a democratic, federal government that "although untried and of doubtful success," as Wilkinson grudgingly put it, "has inspired the people in general with the loftiest hopes." Nevertheless, he believed a window of opportunity existed before this new, formidable entity could unify the conflicting ambitions of east and west. "To seize this interval," he declared, "and to take advantage of the occasion are certainly the true policy of Spain, are my longings, are my desire."

Some requirements remained unchanged—the Mississippi had to be closed, immigration encouraged, influential men given commercial advantages to illustrate the advantage of Spain's protection—but the secessionist cause now had to overcome the effects of U.S. patronage. Many of Kentucky's "notables," once loudly in favor of independence, had fallen silent after being appointed as federal judges, revenue officers, or tax officials, so Spain should be ready to buy their loyalty back and pay them "to accomplish the above-mentioned separation and independence from the United States." For a cost of twenty thousand dollars a year, Wilkinson estimated, Spain could procure the support of the most influential men in Kentucky. The alternative, as he bluntly predicted, was that "instead of forming a barrier for Louisiana and Mexico, [the settlers] will busy themselves in conquering the one and attacking the other."

In a separate document, he provided a list of twenty-two people who should be offered bribes. Nearly all were either friends, such as Harry Innes, who, although a federal judge, "would much prefer to receive a pension from New Orleans than one from New York," or enemies he wanted to buy off, such as Humphrey Marshall, once his partner but now suing him over a failed land deal, and thus "a villain without principles, very artful and could be very troublesome." As though conscious that he was serving his own purposes, Wilkinson stressed his zeal and loyalty to Spain's interest. In one passage, he suggested openly switching sides and asked Madrid to grant him "a military commission, because I know that the force of my genius inclines to the science of war, and that in this capacity I can afford the strongest proofs of fidelity, loyalty, and zeal."

Again the royal council failed to provide a speedy response. To its members, it must have seemed clear that the bribery proposal was designed for Wilkinson's own benefit, an inference reinforced by his request for a loan of seven thousand dollars. But as a soldier, Miró would have understood the significance of Wilkinson's request for a Spanish commission. Armies required oaths of loyalty. There were no gray areas about service in a foreign force. It was not like politics. His friend had crossed a line. He was prepared for treachery.

James Wilkinson's long absence in New Orleans left Nancy distraught once more. "My anxiety about him is so great that I scarce have Composure enough to write," she told her elderly father that fall, "not a foot steps quick into the House but agitates me, his Continual absence keeps my Mind on the rack." In 1788 the family had moved from the wilderness back to the comparative civilization of Lexington, whose population was 834 in the 1790 census. "I like living in Lexington far better than in the Country," she wrote soon after the move. "The Society is much better." Being close to the store made it easier to receive the bags of tea, coffee, and sugar that were sent from Philadelphia—"I really think I could do better without my dinner than my Tea & Coffee," she declared—and goods such as earthenware cups and saucers could be bought to replace all the ones the family broke, although she still had to ask her father to send the delicate chinaware that she preferred.

Yet the taste of these comforts only made her hungrier to see her family in Pennsylvania again. "I can't help wishing more and more every day to Visit you, & my dear children seem to join me most ardently in my wish." Loyal to her husband, she did not allow herself to write of her deepest feelings about life on the frontier, but her children became her mouthpiece. In revealing asides, she wrote of her eldest son, John, exclaiming that "if he ever gets out of Kentucky he never will return if he can prevent it," and of two-year-old Joseph crying bitterly for the grandfather he had never seen.

Her health remained delicate. A baby had been stillborn in early 1789 while Wilkinson was absent in Frankfort loading tobacco in the boats, and Nancy was slow to recover. A doctor had suggested that the fresher river air by the Ohio might do her good, and just before he departed for New Orleans, Wilkinson bought a half-acre lot in Louisville from an unreliable French-born speculator named Michael La Cassagne. Louisville was only a quarter of the size of Lexington, but from Nancy's point of view it had the advantage of being on the Ohio, the main line of communication with the east. But like her hopes of seeing her family back in Philadelphia, the move would happen only if they had the money. In September 1789 when she began to expect her husband back, she wrote optimistically, "I think it Probable we shall spend Part of this Winter at the falls [Louisville], however it will depend greatly on My Jimmy's Business."

When Wilkinson returned at the end of October, they did indeed move to Louisville, but not because his business was thriving. Much of his most valuable real estate was put up for sale, "a valuable tract of land of 10,000 acres, together or in small parcels," along with the livestock he kept on it, and "several houses and lots in this town [Lexington]," including the store. It was not quite a fire sale, but all of it was "to be sold for cash or exchanged for merchandise" as soon as possible.

ENSHACKLED BY DEBT

J AMES WILKINSON HAD TWO WEAKNESSES as a businessman—his readiness
to mistake his gross profit for net gain, and his reluctance to prepare for
the worst. On his 1787 voyage, when he had stayed so long in New Orleans, expenses ate up all but $377 of the $10,185 his cargo earned. The
following year, tobacco sales brought in $16,372, but expenses, including
almost $1,000 for boatmen's wages, left only $6,251 in silver Mexican dollars for Abner Dunn, brother of his partner, to bring north.

In 1789, Wilkinson sent down 342 hogsheads of tobacco, and although
almost one third was found to be so rotten it could not be brought to market, the remainder sold for $18,131. Yet once Clark, an investor in the
cargo, had been paid his share, Miró had taken his $3,000 cut, and Nolan
had paid out other sums, just $49 was left in the Wilkinson and Dunn ac-
count. There was nothing to invest in next season's trade. Whatever credit
Wilkinson still had in Kentucky absolutely depended on the goodwill of
New Orleans. Without Miró he could not survive.

Recognizing the situation, Miró had immediately authorized the seven-
thousand-dollar loan without waiting for Madrid's approval, even though
both he and Wilkinson were aware that the drive had gone out of the separatist movement. "On my arrival here," Wilkinson wrote from Louisville
in early 1790, "I discovered a great change in those who had been so far
our warmest friends. Many, who loudly repudiated all connection with the
Union, now remain silent . . . At present, all our politicians seem to have
fallen asleep. Buoyed up by the privilege of trade which has been granted
to them on the Mississippi, the people think of nothing else than cultivat-
ing their lands and increasing their plantations."

With the cool insight that characterized his dealings with Wilkinson, Miró commented to Valdes that while secession had certainly lost its impetus, the real problem was with Wilkinson. Faced with growing hostility to his views, he had simply backed down or avoided the subject. "The great falling off which I observe in his last letter," Miró wrote, "induces me to believe that, full of good will and zeal, and persuaded, from the experience of past years, that he could bring round to his own opinions the chief men of Kentucky, he declared in anticipation that he had won over many of them, when he had never approached them on the main question."

Under acute financial strain, with his popularity draining away, Wilkinson had in fact lost his political nerve. "I am justified in saying that Congress strongly suspects my connection with you," he told Miró in February 1790, "and that it spies my movements in this section of the country . . . I am narrowly watched by the servants of General Washington." When Manuel Gayoso de Lemos replaced Grand-Pré as governor of Natchez in 1789, Wilkinson at once sent him two dictionaries, so that he and "our Friend below," meaning Miró, could communicate more safely; "I dare not hazard a word on politics but in Cypher."

Looking for a way out of the mountain of debt that threatened to engulf him, Wilkinson reverted to the idea that had surfaced in his second memorial, of openly declaring his change of loyalties. "My situation is mortally painful," he told Miró, "because, whilst I abhor all duplicity, I am obliged to dissemble. This makes me extremely desirous of resorting to some contrivance that will put me in a position, in which I flatter myself to be able to profess myself publicly the vassal of his Catholic Majesty, and therefore to claim his protection, in whatever public or private measures I may devise to promote the interest of the Crown."

This posed a potentially awkward question: what should Spain do with a client politician who had lost his confidence, who no longer dared advocate secession, and who wanted to come clean about his past? Miró's reply in April 1790 showed how well he understood his friend's instinct for duplicity. "I much regret that General Washington and Congress suspect your connection with me," he wrote coolly, "but it does not appear to me opportune that you declare yourself a Spaniard for the reasons which you state. I am of opinion that this idea of yours is not convenient, and that, on the contrary, it might have prejudicial results. Therefore, continue to dissemble . . ."

Three weeks later, Miró sent a message to Valdes urging him to put this talent for dissembling on a professional basis: "I am of opinion that said brigadier-general ought to be retained in the service of his Majesty, with an annual pension of two thousand dollars, because the inhabitants of Kentucky, and of the other establishments on the Ohio, will not be able to undertake anything against this province, without his communicating it to us, and without his making at the same time all possible efforts to dissuade them from any bad designs against us, as he has already done repeatedly."

Don Esteban Miró had been appointed governor of Louisiana and West Florida in 1782, immediately after the Gulf Coast and the Mississippi River had been seized from the British. When he arrived, the colonies were racked by racial tensions between French and Spanish, the economy was moribund, and the land empty enough to be called "a desert." By the time he was recalled to Spain at the end of 1791, Louisiana was calm, growing in prosperity, and its population had more than doubled to about fifty thousand.

Yet of all the advantages he bequeathed, no single one was more useful than his success in recruiting James Wilkinson as a spy. As a civilian, his friend might only be able to pass on information, but before the year was out, the onetime brigadier general would be on the way back to his old profession.

IN BUSINESS AS IN WAR, a chief executive needs luck. Wilkinson was both careless and unlucky. The shipwreck and suicide that ate up the profits of 1789 were followed in 1790 by the loss of two thirds of his cargo. Since speed was essential to get the best prices in New Orleans, the adventurous Philip Nolan had volunteered to take Wilkinson's flatboats boats down the snow-swollen Kentucky River in spring. With navigation marks obscured, he ran three of them onto sandbanks, where the receding water left them stranded through much of the summer. A fourth sprang a leak in the turbulent current, ruining part of its cargo.

Growing competition had made the gamble necessary. Wilkinson's pioneering voyages had shown other settlers the profits that could be made, even paying 15 percent duty. Those living closer to the Ohio or on the Mississippi itself were able to get to market quicker than he, and many found that bribery and forged papers allowed them to escape the duty.

"Let me conjure you to be rigid in exacting the duty [and] every other charge," Wilkinson begged Miró in February 1790. And just before Nolan left with the boats, Wilkinson wrote again with greater desperation, "For God's sake cut off the commercial intercourse with this country [Kentucky], it utterly destroys all our plans & views, & if not immediately checked may eventually ruin Louisiana."

That year Wilkinson secured a new partner, Peyton Short, son-in-law of the wealthy land speculator John Cleves Symmes. But even with his help, Wilkinson had had to borrow money to assemble the flotilla, and lack of capital forced him to act as broker for other merchants, taking a percentage on their profits. Nolan's shipwreck forced Wilkinson to appeal to his creditors in January 1791 for an extension on his loans.

Writing to his most insistent lender, he admitted that half the expected amount of tobacco had been sold in 1790, and instead of a profit of ten thousand dollars he had lost six thousand dollars on the season. His despair at defaulting on his loans was unmistakable even through his habitually high-flown language. The prospect, he said "appalled my Spirit, and filled my mind with an horror not easily to be subdued. The conflict now is over, my spirit is broken, and I kiss the rod of humiliation." As security, he could offer only the profit he expected to make on marketing a hundred hogsheads of tobacco in 1791. "I have but one stake left," he pleaded, "if I give that out of my hands, my race is run, and all my prospects in life must speedily be terminated."

Unfortunately for him, the creditor he addressed was the flint-hearted La Cassagne, who had sold the Wilkinsons their Louisville house. Although professing to be deeply moved by the plea—"not only because my own interests are materially affected, but because you must thereby be subject to innumerable pangs—which must destroy in a great measure that peace of mind which you have long laboured to secure"—La Cassagne behaved like a shark. The loan would be extended only if it was guaranteed by the wealthy Peyton Short, and the terms would include charging interest not just on the principal but on the interest already accrued. Together with other loans he had backed, Short was left liable for nine thousand dollars, and Wilkinson's next three largest creditors were owed another thirteen thousand dollars. Even with this burden hanging over him, he might have carried on trading.

Secretly Wilkinson sent Hugh McIlvain, who was owed five thousand dollars, to New Orleans with two hundred hogsheads of tobacco, equivalent to roughly two hundred thousand pounds. But this sale also failed. Not only was much of the cargo in poor condition, but in 1791 Madrid arbitrarily capped sales of tobacco in New Orleans at forty thousand pounds. Wilkinson's days as a trader were over. The former brigadier general was equipped for only one other profession. Showing an uncharacteristic practicality, he had already made preparations to return to a way of life for which he was better suited.

IN LATE OCTOBER 1790, the torrent of settlers spreading into the Ohio Valley provoked a backlash. Under the outstanding fighter Little Turtle, a 1,500-strong army was assembled from Native American tribes in the area south of Lake Erie, and in a series of ambushes and skirmishes it destroyed a U.S. column of 320 regular soldiers and more than 1,000 militia under General Josiah Harmar. Although the defeat occurred far to the northwest of Cincinnati, it posed a clear threat to Kentucky's settlers, and Wilkinson immediately volunteered to lead a column of volunteers in a retaliatory attack.

"The voice of all ranks called me," he told Miró, always his faithful confidant. Although winter was coming, he promised to lead them through "all obstacles arising from the inclemency of the season, from Frost, from Ice & Snow, from deep and Rapid Rivers." He had, however, overestimated his popularity. Not until the spring of 1791 did the Kentucky committee, the embryonic state's governing body, authorize a punitive raid, and the command was given to General Charles Scott, with Wilkinson only second-in-command.

The raiders consisted of about eight hundred horsemen, and in six weeks they destroyed dozens of villages, killed scores of Indians, and burned hundreds of acres of young corn. Wilkinson took independent command of a party responsible for torching several habitations, taking thirty-two lives and seizing fifty-four captives. Back in Kentucky, the raid was counted such a success that a second was called for before the summer was over. This time the Kentucky committee put Wilkinson in command. About five hundred volunteers followed him on a daring expedition deep into Indian territory as far as the Wabash and Eel rivers, near modern Logansport, Indiana. There they burned the Kickapoo village of Anguile and surrounding cornfields and killed or captured forty-two Indians. Reporting to the president, Henry Knox, the secretary of war, commented approvingly, "The consternation arising from the demonstration of their being within our reach must all tend to the great object, the establishment of peace." He also alluded to Wilkinson's letter sent on August 26 expressing a desire "to enter the military service of the United States."

Wilkinson was never wholly honest about his motives for any major decision, and the guise that he presented to Knox was that of a patriotic frontiersman anxious to serve his country. "During a residence of more than seven years in these woods, I have spared no pains, nor no expence to make myself acquainted, with the extensive regions watered by the Mississippi, and its tributary streams," he wrote. "I have personally explored much of this extensive tract, have acquired an exact knowledge of a great part and a general knowledge of the whole— It is my wish to be employed in some station in which I may be able to employ and apply my information, and my small abilities to the public advantage, and my own honor." The station he had in mind was command of the new regiment that Congress authorized to be raised in response to Harmar's defeat.

Replying almost at once, Knox sent a congratulatory message "in the name of the President of the United States, for the zeal, perseverance and good conduct manifested by you in the Command of the expedition, and for the humanity observed towards the prisoners whom you captured; and also to thank the officers and privates of volunteers, for their activity and bravery while under your command."

With such an endorsement and his record in the Revolutionary War in his favor, Wilkinson's suitability to command the new regiment should not have been in doubt. Against him, however, was a letter sent by Thomas Marshall, father of John and uncle of Humphrey, to George Washington in October 1789 in which he sketched the outline of the Spanish conspiracy "to effect a violent seperation from the United States." The accusation was largely based on Marshall's memory—"not very accurate," he admitted—of the proposals for independence Wilkinson had put before the 1788 Danville convention. Although these were not secret, Marshall insisted he had seen a letter from Miró promising to place Wilkinson's ideas "before the king of Spain." To this message, Washington had replied, "I was greatly alarmed at the nature of the transactions mentioned in it . . . It is true I had previously received some verbal and written information on the subject of a similar tenor; but none which placed the affair in such an alarming point of view." He begged Marshall to keep him informed of Wilkinson's actions.

Two years later, the president had heard no more from Marshall, but further allegations had come from another, less reliable source. James O'Fallon acted as agent to the South Carolina land company that was attempting to bribe the Georgia legislature into selling it twenty million acres of land on the Yazoo River. In September 1790 he warned the president, among others, that "an influential American has been engaged in trade to New Orleans and now acts the part of secret Agent for Spain in Kentucky." Although there could be no doubt about the agent's identity, Washington made no public comment. Presumably, he suspected the motives of a notoriously unreliable source. Nevertheless, he had now heard two specific charges about Wilkinson's collusion with Spain.

Weighing the allegations against the clear evidence of Wilkinson's ability, the president came to a fateful decision. Writing to Alexander Hamilton, always his closest confidant in military matters, he stated his belief that Wilkinson had behaved foolishly, but not illegally. Demonstrating a sound grasp of human psychology, Washington explained that it was "expedient" to give him command of the regiment: "To hold a post of such responsibility would feed his ambition, soothe his vanity, and by arresting discontent produce a good effect." All this was true, but lacking Miró's intimacy with the man, he did not appreciate that Wilkinson's true life took place at a different level.

What had begun four years earlier as an expression of loyalty to Spain designed to finesse lucrative privileges from its uncertain empire had imperceptibly become a reality. "Some men are sordid, some vain, some ambitious," he had declared in his 1787 memorial. "To detect the predominant passion, to lay hold and to make the most of it is the most profound secret of political science." In this case, it was Miró who had found the secret. Trapped by economic need and emotional attachment, James Wilkinson had become Spain's man. No matter what encouragement he was given by the president, the new lieutenant colonel would still dissemble.

THE ARMY THAT General James Wilkinson had left in 1781 came to an end on December 23, 1783, in the delicate blue-and-white symmetry of Maryland's Senate chamber in Annapolis. Shortly after midday, its commander in chief bowed to the members of Congress, who were his political masters, and announced in balanced phrases suitable to his surroundings that he was laying down his command: "Happy in the confirmation of our Independence and Sovereignty, and pleased with the oppertunity afforded the United States of becoming a respectable Nation, I resign with satisfaction the Appointment I accepted with diffidence."

It was the last act in the slow dissolution of the great force created to win independence that at its peak had a nominal strength of thirty-five thousand men, though closer to twenty-five thousand in practice. From the beginning of 1783, recruiting had gradually ceased, soldiers on two- and three-year terms did not have their enlistments extended, and men sent home on furlough were no longer expected to report back. Constantly pushed to make greater economies by a virtually bankrupt Congress, the army reduced regiments to companies, amalgamated five or six companies to make a new regiment, then demobilized that, too.

The approaching end was so obvious in March 1783 that officers grew anxious they were about to be returned to civilian life before Congress had fulfilled its promise to make up pay arrears or guarantee a pension for their service. In their main camp at Newburgh, New York, a document was circulated that urged them to threaten a strike unless their demands were met—"[Tell Congress] that though despair itself can never drive you into dishonour, it may drive you from the field." For a brief ten days the heroic defenders of liberty took on the hideous mask of a standing army that could bully a democratic government into doing its will.

The threat was defused by a moment of pathos—Washington strained to read a speech of reproof to the assembled officers, then remarked as he put on a pair of spectacles that he had grown gray in service of the Revolution and was now going blind as well. The sight of their unshakable commander's frailty took the sting from his listeners' resentment, and when Congress belatedly agreed to pay them five years' salary in place of a pension, the mutiny collapsed. But the Newburgh address's call to officers to play upon "the *fears* of government" continued to haunt Congress.

Vainly Washington pleaded for a peacetime army of four professional regiments, supported by a militia trained to a uniform standard of discipline. Congress promised nothing. Even with the army reduced to the small number of men whose terms of enlistment ran into 1784, no move was made to authorize any kind of replacement. Attention focused on the historic drama of Washington's closing words in the Maryland Senate chamber—"bidding an Affectionate farewell to this August body under whose orders I have so long acted, I here offer my Commission, and take my leave of all the employments of public life"—but in reality his army had already ceased to exist.

Repeated attempts to revive it failed. A proposed force of 900 men was rejected by Congress; one of 350 men suffered the same fate; the lowest point came on June 2, 1784, when Congress dismissed all but 55 artillerymen in West Point and another 25 in Fort Pitt, declaring, "Standing armies in time of peace are inconsistent with the principles of republican government, dangerous to the liberties of a free people, and generally converted into destructive engines for establishing despotism."

This fear of a professional army extended beyond its physical power to the pervasive influence it exerted. When Jefferson criticized the retired officers' association, the Society of Cincinnati, for being hierarchical, undemocratic, and creating "a distinction . . . between the civil & military, which it is for the happiness of both to obliterate," he was also criticizing the values encouraged by the army in general.

Yet the institution could not help being political. In his farewell to his soldiers, Washington had dwelled on the army's surprising power as a unifying force. "Who, that was not a witness, could imagine," he asked, "that Men who came from the different parts of the Continent, strongly disposed, by the habits of education, to despise and quarrel with each other, would instantly become but one patriotic band of Brothers?" Under his command, the Continental Army had been the Union in action, a single force, a model of what the loose association of states whose representatives gathered in Congress could become if they really wanted to unite into a single nation. Since most states recoiled from such a goal, the army that Congress finally brought into being on June 3, 1784, was as small as it could be—a force of just seven hundred men enlisted for one year, drawn from the four middle states, and formally designated the First American Regiment.

This in effect was the army that Wilkinson rejoined in 1791. The only change had been made in response to Little Turtle's victory. Echoing the Continental Army's old complaints against citizen-soldiers, Harmar blamed the headlong flight of his troops on "the ignorance, imbecility, insubordination and want of equipment of the militia." This presented an uncomfortable challenge to Congress's stubborn belief that the nation could be defended by a well-regulated militia. But the commander of the Continental Army was now president, and western settlers were demanding adequate protection. Ideology had to give way to reality. Reluctantly Congress voted to raise a second regiment of professionals, thus creating the opening for a new lieutenant colonel to command it.

On November 7, the Senate confirmed Washington's appointment of Wilkinson to command the Second American Regiment. His relief at being able "to resume the sword of my country" was unmistakable. "Ignorance of commerce" had brought nothing but disappointment and misfortune, he told friends in Philadelphia, but he knew about soldiering, and the rewards it could bring. "My views in entering the Military Line are 'Bread & Fame,'" he confided with a flash of his old optimism, "uncertain of either I shall deserve both."

Later that day, he duly took the oath of loyalty required of every American soldier, "to bear true allegiance to the United States of America, and to serve them honestly and faithfully, against all their enemies or opposers whomsoever." Spain might not be an enemy, but she was an opposer. From now on, he was forsworn whichever course he followed. He had pledged allegiance to Spain, offered to serve in her army, and was now drawing her wage. He could continue to aid her—or he could abide by his oath to the United States. Either way, he would betray one of them.

A General Again

I N THE FALL OF 1791, General Arthur St. Clair, governor of the North-west Territory, led an army fourteen hundred strong northward out of Fort Washington, the gigantic red-walled fortress that protected Cincin-nati's thriving settlement. The intention was to construct a chain of forts from the Ohio River across the low, rolling land hunted over by the Miami and other western confederation tribes, to extend as far as modern Fort Wayne, Indiana. About four hundred regulars, including a company of ar-tillery with eight guns, made up the core of the force, but the remainder were Kentucky militia, accompanied by almost six hundred wives, children, and camp followers. It was hoped that this slow-moving but overwhelming display of force, whose peaceful intentions were made plain by the families traveling with the soldiers, would convince the Indians to make a treaty that would establish new boundaries for their territory.

Although two forts, Hamilton and Jefferson, were constructed and gar-risoned about twenty and forty miles from Cincinnati, the lack of aggres-sion infuriated the Kentucky militia. They resented the discipline imposed on them and were, in the words of Congressman John Brown, "extremely averse to a co-operation with the regulars." The division made itself felt on the night of November 3. When the army camped close to their final des-tination near the Wabash River, the militia chose to pitch their tents across a creek some distance from St. Clair and the regulars of the First and Second American regiments.

During the night, they were surrounded by about one thousand men of the Miami, Shawnee, Kickapoo, and other tribes of the western con-federation led by Little Turtle of the Miami, and the Shawnee Blue Jacket.

Although warned by Washington to be wary of ambush, St. Clair had had no fortifications erected, and when the first shot was fired before dawn, the surprise was total.

"The [regular] Troops were instantly formed to Receive them," William Darke of the First Regiment reported to Washington, "and the pannack Struck [*sic*] Militia Soon broke in to the Center of our incampment; in a few Minutes our Guards were drove in and our whole Camp Surrounded by Savages advancing up there to our Lines, and Made, from behind trees Logs etc., Grate Havok with our Men." Courageously Darke rallied his troops and with two charges drove off the Indians in front, but behind them others got into the camp and scalped its defenders. Then confusion took over, and in Darke's words "the whole Army Ran together like a mob at a fair, and had it not been for the Gratest Exertions of the officers would have Stood there til all killed."

Small groups formed up and with bayonets fixed kept the enemy at bay. But as Major Ebenezer Denny noted in his journal, "[The Indians] could skip out of reach of bayonet and return, as they pleased. The ground was literally covered with the dead . . . It appeared as if the officers had been singled out, as a very great proportion fell." Surrounded on all sides, the resistance grew weaker until St. Clair ordered a retreat to Fort Jefferson that might have become a massacre had Little Turtle's army not been distracted by the huge booty of arms, artillery, and equipment they had captured. Everything was abandoned, including more than a hundred wives and children, nearly half of whom were slaughtered.

Almost six hundred of the fourteen hundred soldiers in St. Clair's force were killed, including his second-in-command, Brigadier General Richard Butler, and thirty-seven other officers, while wounds accounted for as many more. It was the bloodiest defeat Native Americans ever inflicted on the U.S. army. The shock felt throughout the nation was epitomized by the reaction of the president when he read St. Clair's dispatch with the news. Having waited until the room was cleared of strangers, Washington burst out to his secretary Tobias Lear, "To suffer that army to be cut to pieces—hacked, butchered, tomahawked—by a surprise—the very thing I guarded him [St. Clair] against! O God, O God, he's worse than a murderer! How can he answer for it to his country! The blood of the slain is upon him—the curse of widows and orphans—the curse of Heaven!"

Yet amid the chaos and terror, the resistance of the trained soldiers, who had withstood the initial onslaught and held their ground for some hours, stood out. When the national horror had subsided, it left a clear determination to create a professional army that would be large enough to inflict decisive military defeat on the Indians. In December 1791, Henry Knox, Washington's secretary of war, proposed that its strength should be 5,120 men, the same number as that of a Roman legion. Three months later, in March 1792, Congress conquered its doubts about professional soldiers and not only voted the necessary funds but left it to Washington to determine the exact composition of the new army that was soon to be termed the Legion of the United States. He was also to appoint its commander.

COLONEL JAMES WILKINSON assumed that position would fall to him. Early in December 1791, he wrote to Miró, primarily to explain why he had joined the army—"my private interest, the Duty which I owe to the Country I live in, & the aggrandizement of my family"—but he predicted that with the death of General Butler and expected dismissal of General St. Clair, "it is most probable that I shall be promoted [to] the chief command."

To underline his credentials, he embarked on a whirlwind campaign designed to display his energy and unswerving adherence to the virtues of discipline and obedience. In January 1792, he arrived at the army's western headquarters, Fort Washington. This massive defensive post, two stories high with a blockhouse at each corner, was, according to Harmar's report, "one of the most solid substantial wooden fortresses . . . of any in the Western Territory." It was home to almost three hundred soldiers, roughly the same number as the inhabitants of Cincinnati.

Pausing only to organize a covering party of militia cavalry, Wilkinson led out a column of 150 men on January 24, "whilst the snow is on the ground," as he informed Knox, to follow the route taken by General St. Clair's army. He resupplied the defenses at Forts Hamilton and Jefferson, the first two links in a chain of forts that would eventually stretch north from the Ohio. From Hamilton he sent an urgent message back to Samuel Hodgdon, in charge of supplies at headquarters, demanding that a depot be established at Fort Jefferson. "The depth of the snow and the hardness of the Roads makes [sic] it almost impossible for the Corn to be got on," he admitted, "but it is an object of such great Moment that no effort should be left untried. The moment the season breaks, you are to get the business done."

At the scene of St. Clair's defeat, they found, in the words of one officer, "upwards of six hundred bodies, horribly mangled with tomahawks and scalping knives and by wild beasts." Although blackened by frost, the corpses had been preserved through the winter, and the scene was "too horrible for description." While some men were detailed to dig pits for burial of the bodies, Wilkinson ordered others to scour the battlefield, where they recovered a cannon and several hundred muskets. On the way home, he set the men to building another fort, which he named St. Clair, midway between Hamilton and Jefferson, boasting that although put up in just six days, it was as "handsome, stronger & as extensive" as its neighbors. Early in March, he sent an order for "60 good felling axes, 2 cross-cut saw, 4 whipsaws" and two carpenters to help in the construction of the new fort. It was followed soon afterward by a demand for mattocks, shovels, spades, ropes, and chains.

When the exhausted column returned to Fort Washington at the end of the month, the colonel turned his unrelenting energy to the task of restoring discipline in the garrison. Despite St. Clair's devastating defeat, and the scalping of an army blacksmith within sight of the wooden walls, the fort was laxly defended, and Wilkinson was appalled by the disorderly atmosphere and by the sight of brawling soldiers in the town.

"A drunken Garrison and a Guard house full of prisoners appears to be the result of a relaxation in [discipline]," he stormed in a general order following his inspection. "Any private, therefore, who may henceforward be discovered drunk beyond the Walls of the Garrison Shall receive fifty lashes on the spot where he may be detected." To enforce his order, he instituted daily patrols to pick up defaulters and established a routine of drill and exercise culled from Steuben's Blue Book "to check and restrain the licentious habits which have infested the troops."

Deeply impressed, the garrison chaplain, the Reverend William Hurt, assured Washington, "General Wilkinson is the prominant character in this country, & is thought by many will have the Chief command in the next expedition, & I really believe he has abilities equal to it; & far superior to what his enemies, or even friends, are aware of." From Philadelphia, Wilkinson received a letter of congratulations from Henry Knox. "The Zeal and promptitude with which you execute the wishes of the executive are noted with pleasure," Knox wrote, "and will not fail of receiving the approbation of the President."

ON MARCH 9, the president brought together his innermost cabinet of Thomas Jefferson, Alexander Hamilton, and Henry Knox to consider the candidates for command of the Legion. Washington ran through the qualities of each, and even in the official version of their discussions his verdicts sound uncompromising. Of the nine major generals from the Revolutionary War, most were ruled out by age, drink, or reluctance to serve. The fifth was Anthony Wayne. "More active & enterprizing than judicious & cautious," Washington decided. "No œconomist it is feared. Open to flattery—vain—easily imposed upon—and liable to be drawn into scrapes. Too indulgent (the effect perhaps of some of the causes just mentioned) to his Officers & men. Whether sober—or a little addicted to the bottle, I know not."

Wilkinson came at the head of the brigadier generals—his brevet rank dating from November 1777 gave him seniority over those promoted later—and the president's opinion was curiously brief: "As he was but a short time in Service, little can be said of his abilities as an Officer. He is lively, sensible, pompous and ambitious; but whether sober, or not, is unknown to me." In public at least, not a word was said of his failings as clothier general, or of the allegations of conspiracy leveled at him. But from Jefferson, who jotted private notes of cabinet meetings, came the suggestion of a deeper discussion of his background. Wilkinson was deemed to be "brave, enterprising to excess, but many unapprovable points in his character." Among those points were presumably the doubts aroused by his Spanish connections.

At the end of March, while Wilkinson was still waiting to hear the results of the president's deliberations, Nancy and the boys joined him at Fort Washington, and the *Kentucky Gazette* soon reported that in the colonel's "schemes for adornment and social pleasure he was ably and cordially seconded by his wife." There was not much to choose between Louisville and Cincinnati in terms of population, but Nancy's preference was always to be with her husband. And for the first time since they came out to the frontier, his regular salary and access to government transport opened up the long-deferred chance to see her family in Philadelphia again.

In the winter of 1789, her beloved father had died, but anxiety about the future of her children still made her long to return east. In one of her last letters to John Biddle, she had confessed, "I regret much, indeed it grieves me, that they have not an Opportunity of going to a good School. However I pay every attention to there Learning that my Domestic affairs will admit off; John Reads Prettily, James Spells, but he is so heedless that it is with difficulty I can prevail on him to say a lesson."

In Kentucky, she had to make do with what they could learn from "a Poor Simple looking Simon who told me he was taught [in Philadelphia] which prejudiced me in his favor & I concluded he could not learn them bad Pronunciation; at any rate it was better than running about the Streets." The schooling available in Philadelphia, however, would smooth away the frontier roughness she fought against. In July, before the river dropped and cut off access to the east, she and the boys boarded an army boat and headed upstream to civilization. Looking after them was Lieutenant William H. Harrison, later president of the United States, who had been detailed "to accompany Mrs Wilkinson to Philadelphia" by the new commander in chief of the Legion, Major General Anthony Wayne.

The president had made the appointment on April 9. On the same day Wilkinson received a consolation prize of promotion to brigadier general, and with it the assurance that he would be second-in-command. Later in the summer, Knox sent the president a note: "Brigadier Wilkinson's attention to all parts of his duty and his activity render him a great acquisition to the public." To this Washington immediately replied, "General Wilkinson has displayed great zeal & ability for the public weal since he came into Service—His conduct carries strong marks of attention, activity, & Spirit, & I wish him to know the favorable light in which it is viewed." The compliment was deserved, but it was also intended to soothe Wilkinson's wounded vanity.

IN DECEMBER 1791, Esteban Miró sailed for home, handing over the governorship of Louisiana to Baron Hector de Carondelet. Like Miró, Carondelet had been a soldier before joining the colonial service, but, Flemish-born and something of an outsider, he lacked his long-serving predecessor's confident judgment. Small, portly, and fussy, he compensated by paying close attention to administrative detail—his modernization of the municipal government of New Orleans, and the introduction of street lighting and waste collection, left it a better-run and cleaner place. It was also more expensive for, as an anonymous official in Madrid sharply noted, "He has always shown a great predilection for new projects . . . without ever thinking of the funds or expenditures that such Projects naturally will cost." During his administration the expense of running Louisiana rose to over $800,000 a year, while its revenues never amounted to more than $75,000, a disparity that would eventually force Madrid to look for cheaper ways of defending its silver-cored empire.

The flair in Carondelet's administration came from the governor of Natchez district, Manuel Gayoso de Lemos. Miró, who was rarely deceived about character, judged that Gayoso "distinguished himself through his talent, knowledge of various languages and excellent conduct." He was also artistic, emotional, and devoted to his family. Educated in England and twice married to American women, he had a cosmopolitan background that helped in the government of a fast-growing, volatile population of

American, British, French, and Spanish settlers. Although most were concentrated around Natchez, others were scattered across much of modern Alabama and Mississippi, and Gayoso's responsibilities included command of all the forts that stretched north along the Mississippi.

On July 5, 1792, he provided Carondelet with a report on the province he now governed, entitled "Political Conditions of the Province of Louisiana." Ranging widely over the challenges presented by American settlers, British imperialists, and French revolutionaries, Gayoso picked out one unjustly neglected asset: "In Kentucky we have had Don Jaime Wilkinson well affected to our side. He is a person of great talent and influence, who has twice come down to this province and presented several memorials. In his own country he has performed several important services to this province. Yet although he was recommended by Don Esteban Miró for a pension and other help, the resolution was so long delayed because of the distance that separates us from the court [in Madrid] that in the meanwhile he lost his credit in Kentucky for lack of means to maintain it." To retrieve his fortunes, Gayoso explained, Wilkinson had joined the U.S. army, but since his enlistment he had "suspended his correspondence with the governor at New Orleans and with me."

Like many colonial reports, Gayoso's was designed for reading back in Madrid as well as in New Orleans. In fact, as he knew well, Wilkinson was one of Carondelet's top priorities. In February 1792, the new governor of Louisiana had sent the American a message informing him that the pension of two thousand dollars a year suggested by Miró had at last received royal approval, and that it was to be backdated to January 1, 1789. Should Wilkinson wish to resume his connection with New Orleans, Carondelet could promise that the sum of four thousand dollars was immediately available. Gayoso was still drawing up his report when, as he noted, a messenger, Michael La Cassagne, passed through Natchez on his way to New Orleans with a sealed letter from Don Jaime. Although he had not read its contents, Gayoso expressed his confidence that by the time his report was delivered, the governor of Louisiana would know whether Miró's spy had been reactivated.

OF ALL THE CREDITORS pressing Wilkinson for money, La Cassagne was the most insistent. Having converted Wilkinson's original loan to one involving his partner Peyton Short, the Frenchman had begun to squeeze both for payment. As La Cassagne's vise closed, Short's pleas for help from his partner became ever more desperate.

In December 1791, just before leaving for Fort Washington, Wilkinson put up his most valuable asset for sale, the town of Frankfort, with its strategic location, fine house, and ferry. His haggling over the price offered by Andrew Holmes, another Lexington storekeeper, brought a cry of pure anguish from Short. "To save me in this hour of extreme distress," he wrote, "I now call upon you by every principle that ever warmed an honest heart. Both God and man can witness that you now have it in your power. I beg, entreat, and conjure you to avail yourself of the happy occasion—embrace the offer made you by Mr. Holmes." To his relief, Wilkinson finally accepted Holmes's price, three hundred thousand pounds of tobacco, in January 1792. Less than twelve months later, Kentucky's legislature chose Frankfort as the site of the newly independent state's capital. Land values quickly rose, and the fortune that Wilkinson always dreamed of passed instead to Holmes, and soon afterward to his creditors.

Still outstanding were a further fourteen hundred dollars due to La Cassagne and other debts amounting to more than fifteen thousand dollars, about twelve times his military salary. In the first four months of his career in the army, he sent his friend and legal adviser in Lexington, Judge Harry Innes, $180 from his meager pay of $104 a month to satisfy the most urgent demands and asked him to stave off the rest. "I pray you, my friend, to say that I have left (if you think as I do) sufficient property to discharge my debts and that I am determined to do this at any sacrifice," Wilkinson told Innes. "There is much confusion in my books and papers, but yet under such an explanation as I can give, justice may be done."

He had a few remaining assets—the house in Louisville, and a partial interest in up to seventy-five thousand acres elsewhere in Kentucky, although their real ownership was in dispute. These doubts about property titles were the legacy of Virginia's confused and corrupt land-sales policy. To establish ownership entailed complex legal battles pitting wealthy outsiders against homegrown occupiers, and that destroyed the market for land in Kentucky.

In April 1792, Wilkinson wrote again to Innes, offering to transfer all his assets and give him "uncontrolled power over my whole property in your own language." He wanted above all else to "remove the shackles [of debt] which oppress my spirit and sit heavy on my soul." The heaviest shackle on his soul was the penal interest on what he owed La Cassagne—within two years the charges increased an original loan of one thousand dollars by almost half. In this desperate state, Carondelet's offer of four thousand dollars must have appeared as a lifeline. Yet Wilkinson took five months to respond. So long as he had a chance of being made commander of the Legion, he appears to have resisted the lure.

The decision to send La Cassagne to pick up Wilkinson's back pay as a Spanish agent demonstrated not only that he had made an irrevocable, life-changing decision but, more mundanely, that his credit had finally run out. The Frenchman spent three months in New Orleans developing contacts in the city—he later settled there and made another fortune as a slave dealer—but when he arrived back in Louisville in November, he passed on only twenty-six hundred dollars to Wilkinson. The rest was retained to pay off the loan. In December 1792, Wilkinson sent Carondelet the first report for which he had been paid as a spy.

IN HIS OTHER LIFE, he was the energetic, extrovert officer praised by Washington and Knox. No hint appeared of the inner struggle caused by the temptation of treachery and the threat of bankruptcy. With the warmer weather in 1792, he sent out construction, foraging, and haymaking parties to each of the new forts. And at Fort Washington, he also demonstrated a gift, learned perhaps from his mentor Horatio Gates, for raising the morale of defeated troops.

Although its professional core had been strengthened, the army still relied heavily on the militia, especially for cavalry duties, and unlike most of his colleagues Wilkinson understood that the militia had to be cajoled rather than ordered. He made a habit of detaching them as guards and scouts so that they did not have to come under the army's direct command. At the same time, he paid proper attention to the full-time soldiers' fundamental need for regular food, pay, and clothing, and a barrage of dispatches hurtled up the Ohio and on to Philadelphia if supplies were lacking. By the summer, Knox could assure Washington, "The Vice of drunkenness is no more among the Officers who fall under his personal observation—and the Troops are in a great degree reformed."

Another sign of his influence was apparent in the increasingly stylish language of his subordinates. One major smoothly alluded to a failed Indian attack as "an attempt at mischief," another termed the ambush of Indian cattle thieves as an effort "to baffle their intentions," and a letter of gratitude to Mrs. Wilkinson for a gift allowed a third major to offer a dizzying example of gentlemanly eloquence: "Be pleased therefore, Madam, to accept the thanks of my family, *alias the mess*, for your polite attention in sending us garden seeds, etc., and should we be honored by a visit from the donor, the flowers shall be taught to smile at her approach, and droop as she retires."

Aping Wilkinson's flamboyant manner was a sure indication of a desire to follow his lead.

The military theater of parades and ceremonial that he devised served a similar purpose, allowing everyone from privates to colonels the chance to show off. On May 1, 1792, General Wilkinson put on a frontier version of St. Tammany's Day, the Pennsylvania spring celebration that was turning into a national holiday. A wigwam was erected beside the Ohio River close to the red-painted walls of Fort Washington, and there influential civilians such as Winthrop Sargent, secretary of the Northwest Territory, John Cleves Symmes, who owned a million of its acres, various judges, and Cincinnati's "most respectable citizens," according to the *Kentucky Gazette*, together with Wilkinson's senior officers, "sat down to a most sumptuous dinner at 3 o'clock, where the following toasts were drank [*sic*] under the discharge of many cannon. (1) North American Nation; (2) Washington; (3) The Congress; (4) The Atlantic States; (5) The Western Settlements; and eleven others of a similar nature, 16 in all." Later Wilkinson mustered his troops on the edge of the nearby forest and reviewed them, clad, according to the *Gazette*, in "hunting shirt, mocassins, belt, knife and tomahawk—a real woodman's dress," then ended the day with "an excellent and eloquent appeal to the feelings of his men." Whatever the private thoughts of the soldiers, they must at least have been a long way from the horrific scenes of St. Clair's defeat.

Symmes, who had seen Wilkinson in action, noted that "his familiar address and politeness render him very pleasing to the militia of Kentucky by whom he is much respected and loved." The *Gazette*'s fawning reporter went further. The general, he declared, was "a gentleman and a scholar who delighted in surroundings of beauty and refinement." None of them could have imagined that such a flamboyant, charismatic figure was secretly intending to accept Spain's offer of four thousand dollars to become a spy.

AT THE PROSPECT of being freed from his debts, James Wilkinson's mercurial spirits soared. His mood was reflected in the first report he sent in December 1792 to his new handler. It was imaginative, lively, and permeated with untruth. He claimed to be in command of "2000 select troops composed of Musketeers, Chasseurs, Light, and Artillery," and to be paid "independent of prerogatives and facilities 3000 dollars a year." Despite this, he pretended to be so disillusioned by having to soldier under "an incompetent Secretary of War and an ignorant Commander-in-Chief" that he wished to be given a commission in the Spanish army where his passion for "military fame" could be gratified. But he was ready to let Carondelet decide "whether I am to continue in this quarter or descend the Mississippi to New Orleans."

All this—the inflation of his powers and pay scale, as well as the feigned indifference to his career—was designed to make Carondelet realize how much Wilkinson was worth. The clear implication was that the Spaniard should think of paying the general more to keep him from resigning. By way of encouragement Wilkinson also promised, "I have not abandoned those views, principles and attachments which I professed to Miró." As evidence of his commitment, he pressed Carondelet to strengthen Spanish defenses on the Mississippi, a tactical hint that prompted the governor to authorize additional galleys on the river and garrisons for the forts at Walnut Hill and New Madrid. Militarily, Wilkinson promised his paymaster that the Spanish empire had little to fear from its neighbor, owing to the "intestinal discord" between New England and the south and between the Atlantic states and the west. The conflict, he concluded, "renders the whole [nation] weak and contemptible, the occasion is favorable to Spain and you know how to improve it."

The deep relationship with Miró, the change of allegiance, and the repeated pledges of loyalty to Spain's interests must have made this final momentous transition seem like a small step. But by reporting to the Spanish governor in return for payment while he held the rank of brigadier general in the U.S. army, Wilkinson had crossed a Rubicon. He was no longer a private citizen, and his actions had moved beyond moral flexibility or political grandstanding. A soldier who aided a foreign power broke his military oath and was liable to court-martial. If it could be proved that he had attempted to suborn others from their loyalty to the United States, Wilkinson would face the death penalty for treason.

DISCIPLINE AND DECEIT

THE CREATION OF THE LEGION of the United States remains a high
point of military innovation in the country's history. This force was
designed for the particular needs of fighting on the North American continent, but organized according to the most sophisticated European thinking on how best to use the three different arms of infantry, artillery, and
cavalry. Henry Knox, bookseller, general, and secretary of war, was largely
responsible for the concept, and in recommending the Legion to the president, he cited both classical authorities, such as the historian Polybius on
the Roman legion, and eighteenth-century experts such as Marshal Maurice de Saxe, author of *My Reveries on the Art of War*. But George Washington, adamantly conservative on the shape of the army he wanted for
fighting the British, turned Knox's radical ideas into reality.

What made a disciplined army essential was not just the defense of settlers, but the implementation of the president's ambitious policy toward
Native Americans. From the Kentucky settlers' point of view, Indian attacks
required the sort of punishment inflicted by Wilkinson in 1791 that would
clear the land of its original inhabitants. In Philadelphia, however, the president was determined to find a place for Native Americans within the
Union, an approach warmly endorsed by Henry Knox.

"It is painful to consider that all the Indian Tribes once existing in those
States, now the best cultivated and most populous, have become extinct,"
Knox had written Washington in July 1789. "If the same causes continue,
the same effects will happen, and in a Short period the Idea of an Indian
on this side of the Mississippi will only be found in the page of the historian." Knox proposed that "instead of exterminating a part of the human

race by our modes of population," the United States should impart "our Knowledge of cultivation, and the arts, to the Aboriginals of the Country by which the Source of future life and happiness [might be] preserved and extended."

It would be difficult and expensive, he acknowledged. In the long term, the Indians would have to learn how to farm and to develop "a love for exclusive property," and in the short term, the boundaries of their lands needed to be defined and protected from unscrupulous settlers. But the policy was cheap compared to war. To overawe the Indians and restrain the settlers, an army of at least five thousand would be needed.

Knox's plan underpinned the administration's first formal treaty, signed in August 1790 with Alexander McGillivray, the half-Scots leader of the Creeks. Later that year, in December, Washington gave a similar guarantee of inviolable boundaries and protection by the federal government to Cornplanter, the Seneca chief: "No State nor person can purchase your lands, unless at some public treaty held under the authority of the United States. The general Government will . . . protect you in all your just rights."

This policy of inclusion was damaged in the south by Georgia's hunger for Creek land, and destroyed in the north by New York and Pennsylvania's program to expel the Six Nations from their rich lands below Lakes Ontario and Erie. The Northwest Territory, covering modern Ohio, Indiana, and Illinois, belonged to the federal government, however, and there Knox and Washington were determined to make their ideas a reality. In the long term, the chain of forts stretching north from the Ohio would keep both Indians and settlers pacified. In the short term, the Legion had to regain control of the area.

The Legion's salient characteristic was the integration of guns, horses, rifles, and bayonets within a single unit. Traditionally, each was accustomed to train and act separately: the artillery found a strategic position and fired; the cavalry waited for a weakness, then charged; the riflemen sniped and scouted ahead of the infantry; and the infantry formed a line or column with the sole purpose of concentrating the impact of a volley and a charge regardless of what was happening around them.

Large armies fighting static battles could afford such specialization, but in the wilderness of North America, Native American warfare had demonstrated the superiority of small forces and rapid movement. According to Knox, the smallest feasible unit numbered exactly 1,280, excluding officers, and was made up of about 720 infantrymen and 400 riflemen, with the remainder divided between artillery and cavalry. The Legion of the United

States consisted of four such self-contained, miniature armies, together with officers and staff. But for these sub-legions to be effective, each arm had to train both separately and in unison. From the moment he was appointed in April 1792, General Wayne's goal was to prepare his soldiers to fight in this new way. It required longer training and more intense discipline than the old model. But intensity was Wayne's dominant characteristic.

The high point of his service in the Revolutionary War was a savagely violent bayonet attack at night that he personally led on a British position at Stony Point, New York, in 1779. Reviewing his record, Washington noted that he was too impetuous, but decided it was a fault in the right direction, and at the end of the war approved his promotion to major general. By then his single-minded, almost autistic focus had earned him a telling nickname, Mad Anthony, and Jefferson's note of the 1792 cabinet discussion about the general's qualities pointed in the same direction. Wayne was thought to be "brave & nothing else," with the danger he would "run his head ag[ains]t a wall where success was both impossible & useless."

True to character, Wayne attacked the problem of creating virtually a new army from scratch as though it were an enemy position. All but a handful of the enlisted men came from New England and the middle states. They lived far from the territory they were to defend and lacked any obvious motive for hostility to Indians. Except for a large contingent of Connecticut farm-workers, most were town dwellers from Baltimore, Philadelphia, and New York, more than half were foreign-born, and almost 40 percent were illiterate. Although patriotism motivated some, and as many as one in five had served in the Revolutionary War, the majority enlisted to escape whatever civilian life had to offer—debts, prison, or boredom—and a large minority signed up because the recruiters made them drunk. Even with the threat of hanging if caught and a ten-dollar bounty for bringing back a deserter, the annual rate for desertion rarely dropped below 10 percent.

Wayne established a training camp for these new recruits at Fort Fayette outside Pittsburgh, but immediately encountered a new handicap. Almost one quarter of the army's officers, those with experience who should have been the Legion's instructors, had been killed in St. Clair's defeat—a horrifying ratio equal to that of the bloodiest battles of the Civil War. To overcome the almost insuperable difficulties, Wayne instituted a regime of legendary severity.

"Every thing depends on discipline," Knox had told him. "The public interest, the national Character and your personal reputation." Wayne needed no encouragement. The guardroom and whipping were for minor offenses. Drunkenness, sleeping on guard duty, and desertion made a soldier liable to flogging with up to one hundred lashes, and one in ten of those found guilty of such offenses were condemned to death by hanging or firing squad. For drill he relied on the close-quarter maneuvers of Steuben's Blue Book, but the training included marksmanship, maneuvers with cavalry and artillery, and incessant digging of entrenchments and fortifications. Whatever happened, they were never again to be surprised by a dawn attack.

So long as Major General Anthony Wayne remained out of view, Brigadier General James Wilkinson could live with the humiliation of seeing command of the Legion exercised by a man he despised. In character, behavior, and outlook, Wayne was his antithesis. Despite a reputation as a philanderer, Mad Anthony lacked charm. While his second-in-command went to great lengths to be liked, Wayne was largely indifferent to what men thought of him. Confronted by an angry Canadian farmer or hostile Kentucky representatives, Wilkinson backed off, but Wayne rode roughshod over those in his way.

Professionally, however, they were at one in their belief that the army needed more training and discipline. In a curiously self-righteous judgment, Wilkinson assured his superiors in November 1792 that the officers of the First American Regiment "had contracted Ideas of speculation incompatible with the principles of [a] Soldier of Honor; some were pedlars, some drunkards, almost all fools." Wayne agreed that the task facing them was "to make an army from the rawest heterogeneity of materials, that were ever collected together." The force that they would create, he told Wilkinson, must "produce a conviction not only to the Indians but to the World that the United States of America are not to be insulted with impunity."

For almost a year, Wilkinson was able to exercise a nearly independent command from Fort Washington while Wayne was occupied with training his new recruits at Fort Fayette. The arrangement allowed Wilkinson to devote himself without interruption to his twin careers as general and as spy. In his military role, he flogged drunkards, kept the chain of forts under his command supplied and defended, and set himself to map and acquire intelligence about the territory north of the Ohio Valley where war could be expected. Seen from New Orleans, however, nothing compared to the value of his secret activities. Indeed when the convulsive effects of the French Revolution came rolling across the Atlantic like a tsunami, it seemed to the governor of Louisiana that he alone could protect Spain's North American empire against this unexpected threat.

It began with the execution of Louis XVI in January 1793, an event that provoked his brother monarch, Charles IV of Spain, to declare war on republican France. Consequently, when the headstrong, short-tempered Edmond Charles Genêt arrived in the United States as France's ambassador in March that year, he came determined to attack Spanish interests in the west.

Within months of Citizen Genêt's arrival, his Spanish counterpart, Josef de Jaudenes, sent Carondelet the alarming news that Genêt "is engaged in secretly seducing and recruiting by every means that presents itself all the Frenchmen, and others as well, to form an expedition against Louisiana." Genêt's fellow countrymen in New Orleans responded with nightly performances of the "Marseillaise" in the theater until Carondelet banned the tune, and more than one hundred French residents signed a petition asking for their government to intervene in Louisiana. Meanwhile, George Rogers Clark promised to lead a force that Genêt named "the French Revolutionary Legions on the Mississippi" and do for France what Wilkinson planned for Spain, give her control of the Mississippi basin by seizing New Orleans. "The possession of New Orleans will secure to France the whole Fur, Tobacco and Flour trade of this western world," Clark predicted.

In alarm, Carondelet demanded that Gayoso should "send as soon as possible a canoe to New Madrid with a letter for General W[ilkinson] asking him to advise us properly . . . of whatever maybe concocted, either in Kentucky or in Cumberland [modern Alabama and middle Tennessee] contrary to the interests of Spain."

Carondelet's plea arrived at a convenient moment for Wilkinson— several Kentucky creditors, among them Humphrey Marshall and Peyton Short, were pressing for payment on old debts. It was apparent from his reply to Carondelet's plea that Wilkinson saw the chance of an unexpected windfall. He conjured up a nightmare variant of the original Spanish Conspiracy—Kentucky might still detach itself from the United States, but this time as an ally of France. In graphic terms, he warned Carondelet of the dangers of "the projected attack against Louisiana by the people of Kentucky at the instigation of the French minister." Having played on the governor's all too susceptible fears, Wilkinson characteristically offered to remove them. An informant had already been recruited from Clark's inner circle, and Wilkinson promised that no expense would be spared in persuading Kentucky's leading citizens to turn against the adventure. Finally he could also guarantee that the army would prevent any supplies from being shipped down the Ohio to Clark's French Legions.

The value of Wilkinson to Carondelet was made starkly clear in a secret warning that the governor sent to the royal council that October. To defend the forts on the Mississippi between St. Louis and Vicksburg, a distance of five hundred miles, the governor could muster only ninety regular troops and two hundred militia. Should Clark's forces reach Natchez, he predicted, "It is evident that all Louisiana will fall into their hands with the greatest rapidity and ease." From his point of view, everything depended on Agent 13.

In this symbiotic relationship, Wilkinson's spendthrift habits made Carondelet equally essential to him. His need for more money was underlined by the return of Nancy from Philadelphia in May 1793 after a ten-month absence.

The boys, including eight-year-old Joseph, the youngest, had been left behind in Philadelphia. None of his letters suggests that Wilkinson missed them, but his writing is full of references to what Nancy's absence meant to him. It was, he said, "Hell on earth" without her. He urged the Biddles to "hurry her back." Extravagantly, he declared to his commanding officer that he was "panting, sighing, dying for her embrace," and he demanded that Wayne either arrange for her to be sent down the Ohio or "give me plenty of Indian fighting." Although it was a convention, amounting to a military joke, that lovelorn warriors were supposed to drown their sorrows in blood, everything suggests that Wilkinson's words came as close to sincerity as was possible for him.

Extravagance was the most obvious sign of his affection. As an officer, he rode everywhere on horseback, but even on the frontier he always had a horse-drawn carriage for Nancy. In Kentucky the vehicle was remembered as a coach with four matched black horses; in Cincinnati it was drawn by no more than a pair, but it was "the only carriage in the place." He named a major street in Frankfort after her. At a time when Virginia law treated real estate as belonging to the husband alone, he bought land in her name as well as his. Her popularity with his fellow soldiers from privates through General Wayne—she was said to be the one person who could persuade him to show mercy to a soldier condemned to death by court-martial—and beyond him to Henry Knox, clearly caused Wilkinson pride rather than jealousy because he never ceased to involve her in the army's social events, and that despite the obvious fact that most people preferred her to him. The disparity appeared in anecdotes, and more lastingly in the compliments paid by Thomas Chapman, an English traveler, in his *Journal of a Journey through the United States*. Of Wilkinson, he could offer little more than a wooden tribute, not altogether believable, to his "unimpeached integrity, unexampled liberality & Hospitality," but what really moved the Englishman was "the good sence, Affable deportment & elegant manners of the General's amiable Wife, who surpasses any Lady I have met with in the course of my Travels through the United States."

They were too intimately attached, and she was too sensitive, for Nancy not to have had some idea of the Spanish connection, but it is doubtful that she understood its full complexity. To his dying day, he would publicly insist that every payment from New Orleans was a profit or insurance payment on his tobacco trade, and even to himself he never seemed to acknowledge what was involved. Yet Nancy's need for little luxuries such as sugar and coffee, and his desire to see her in an elegant carriage, and their joint pleasure in parties and liberal hospitality, were inseparable from his need for Carondelet's dollars.

NANCY'S ARRIVAL AT Fort Washington was followed barely a month later by the distinctly less welcome appearance of Wayne and a long convoy of boats carrying the Legion, now more than eleven hundred strong. The decision to ship his men down the Ohio was prompted by Wayne's conviction that they were being corrupted by their proximity to the taverns and brothels of Pittsburgh—"that Gomorrah," as he called it. A hint of the commander's state of mind emerged when he landed at Cincinnati and, to Wilkinson's relief, discovered it to be "filled with ardent poison & Caitiff wretches to dispose of it . . . a man possessed of the least tincture of morality must wish his stay here as short as possible." The army was moved to a site between the river and a swamp that Wayne named Hobson's Choice, implying that no alternative place could be found.

But Wayne faced more problems than creating an encampment in rough country. The most serious was the information from Philadelphia that a lack of recruits would limit the size of the Legion to three thousand men, and that to make up the numbers fifteen hundred Kentucky volunteers would have to be taken on. The least of his anxieties seemed to be the conduct of his second-in-command, which, Wayne assured Knox, "bespeaks the officer & merits my highest approbation." Knox, however, was more cautious and felt it necessary to issue a thinly veiled warning to Wilkinson in May 1793: "I am persuaded your good sense as well as inclination will lead you to unite cordially with General Wayne, and promote a spirit of harmony throughout the whole corps."

The general's arrival did indeed bring to the surface the jealousy and bitterness Wilkinson felt at being passed over for command. Through the summer, each of Wayne's many failings was passed on to the formidable array of political contacts that Wilkinson still maintained in Philadelphia. The most prominent was his brother-in-law, Clement Biddle, the president's lawyer, who had always received a heavy correspondence from Wilkinson detailing the difficulties he encountered with quarreling officers and inadequate equipment.

The Biddle influence was reinforced by Knox's liking for Nancy Wilkinson, who, until her return to the Ohio in May 1793, served as a two-way channel of communication between her husband and the War Department. "I have often expressed to her and to Colonel Biddle," Knox assured Wilkinson that spring, "the pleasure your conduct gave to the President of the United States." And to reinforce the coziness, the president himself was the recipient of gifts from Wilkinson, such as two kegs of fish taken from the Miami River on the uttermost limits of the United States and presented in the modest hope that "the novelty of the thing may render it acceptable." Washington accepted the fish, politely agreeing that they were "truly a Novelty here," but a second gift, sent in April 1793, pleased him more. This was a map drawn by Wilkinson of the country north of the Ohio where war with the Indians could be expected. It was, the president assured him, "the best description extant of the country to which it relates" and "affords me the greatest satisfaction."

By contrast Wayne's reputation in Philadelphia was corroded by reports of his "petulant" behavior toward his officers, and his authoritarian regime amounting to what one subordinate called "abject servitude." Some of the complaints stemmed from the commander's natural abrasiveness—"There is no calculating on anything but insult and oppression [from him]," one subordinate complained. But Wayne's behavior clearly became more extreme as the pressure of molding his new army mounted. In November 1793, the general lost all self-control when Major Thomas Cushing complained about an inefficient captain on Wayne's staff.

Instead of investigating the complaint, Wayne placed the major under arrest and charged a junior officer, Captain Isaac Guion, with unmilitary conduct for daring to offer evidence to substantiate Cushing's original complaint. When Colonel John Hamtramck, the solid, unexcitable commander of the First Sub-Legion, explained that Wayne's staff officer really had failed to carry out general orders, Wayne issued him an official reprimand for his "disrespectful" intervention. "There is no doubt about it," Hamtramck concluded, "the old man really is mad."

Like others slighted by Wayne, the three officers turned to the convivial Wilkinson for sympathy, and he supported them because he, too, felt disparaged by the autocratic Wayne. "My General treats me with great civility, and with much professed Friendship," he told Harry Innes in October, "yet I am an O, for he conceals his intentions from me, never asks my opinion, & when sense of Duty forces me to give it, he acts against it."

To retaliate, Wilkinson instigated a string of pinprick complaints about unsatisfactory supplies at Fort Washington of gunpowder, uniforms, food, and disciplinary power, all of which required Knox to send Wayne irritating reminders ordering him to inquire "into the nature and degree of the Confusion of Stores and Clothing complained of by Brigadier General Wilkinson," and to remedy instantly "complaints relative to the pay department in the district of Brigadier General Wilkinson." Even on the question of discipline, Wilkinson found cause for criticism. "Your remarks of the disproportionate punishments of death, or one hundred lashes, are just," Knox agreed, "and the suggestions of hard labour, seem to promise better success, and I shall communicate the same to Major-general Wayne."

With growing conviction, Wilkinson believed he could persuade Knox to replace Wayne as commander. When Wayne demanded more troops, Wilkinson sent Philadelphia his plan for a lightning strike into the heart of Indian territory with an army half the Legion's size. When Wayne declared that he required two hundred cavalry to protect each supply train to the forts, Wilkinson let the War Department know that he had needed only one hundred militia. When Wayne had to order the Kentucky cavalry to come under his direct command, Wilkinson was quick to remind Knox how those same horsemen volunteered to serve under him.

To Wayne himself, however, Wilkinson remained loyal and friendly. "Ever anxious for action & ready for duty," he wrote Wayne from Fort Jefferson, "you have only to order & the execution will follow, with promptitude & Energy." As Christmas 1793 approached, a festive invitation was sent to the Legion's commander: "Mrs. W. ventures to hope your Excellency may find it convenient & consistent to take dinner with Her on the 25th inst. with your suite, & any eight or ten gentlemen of your cantonment you may think proper should attend you; she begs leave to assure you the Dinner shall be a Christian one, in commemoration of the Day, and in Honor of Her Guest, and on my part I will promise a welcome from the

Heart, a warm fire, and a big-bellied Bottle of the veritable Lachrymae Christi. We pray you answer."

LACHRYMA CHRISTI, a sweet, succulent Mediterranean wine, did not come cheap in the land of raw, moonshine whiskey. That the near-bankrupt Wilkinson could afford it on a general's salary of $104 a month pointed to his successful role as Agent 13. He already had four thousand dollars from Carondelet, but the sudden collapse of the French threat to Louisiana promised still more.

Overconfident about the outcome of George Rogers Clark's raid, Genêt had been slow to send him the orders and money needed to recruit an armed force. The delay proved fatal. Genêt's flouting of diplomatic protocol led Washington to demand the ambassador's recall in December 1793. Deprived of funds, Clark found it difficult to acquire a credible quantity of boats and arms. In February 1794, when he advertised for "volunteers for the reduction of Spanish posts on the Mississippi," offering to pay them a thousand acres each or a dollar a day, fewer than a hundred men came forward. The expedition finally drifted to a halt fifty miles short of the nearest Spanish fort.

Wilkinson immediately wrote Carondelet in April 1794 claiming credit for Clark's failure. His lobbying had undermined popular support in Kentucky for the adventure, and he assured the governor that he had receipts showing he had spent no less than $8,640 "to retard, disjoint and defeat the mediated irruption of General Clark in L[ouisian]a." He was also responsible for the army's efforts to prevent sympathizers from shipping supplies for Clark's men down the Ohio River. Together with further payments on his pension now due, he expected to be paid $12,000.

The satisfactory nature of his activities as a Spanish agent contrasted sharply with the frustration of being an American general. By the time this letter was sent, his quarrel with Wayne had spilled into the open and threatened to split the Legion apart.

13

POISONED VICTORY

IN HIS FIERCELY DRIVEN WAY, General Anthony Wayne was not at first aware of what was happening. Only in January 1794 did he realize that his officers had split, as he told Knox, into "two distinct Parties." The hostility of the newest intake of junior officers alerted him to the situation. On the smallest excuse, he complained, they "offered their Resignations and prepared to depart without further Ceremony, saying they were *advised* to do so by *experienced* officers." Yet even then, he did not suspect his former friend of being at the root of the problem.

The invitation to share Christmas and a bottle of Lachryma Christi with the Wilkinsons had been refused only because, as Wayne tersely explained, he was busy moving his headquarters to Fort Greeneville, a new outpost constructed even farther into Indian territory. Early in the new year the Legion was moved to this gigantic stockade enclosing fifty acres, where the final stages of its training would take place. Supplying an army in such a remote post created incessant problems. Wayne constantly had to drive the victuallers Elliott and Williams to produce fatter cattle and fresher casks of beef, and the War Department to provide more blankets and blue and buff uniforms, and to deliver promptly the silver dollars needed to pay his men their four dollars a month. But he did not at first connect these difficulties with his second-in-command.

Always sensitive to the smallest insult to his vanity, Wilkinson had been infuriated by Wayne's refusal of the Christmas invitation. During the early months of 1794, Wilkinson periodically declared himself to be close to resignation. "I am unsettled in my purpose whether I shall join the army or not," he told Innes, and with still more of a flourish told Brown, "I owe so

much to my own feelings and to Professional reputation, that I cannot consent to sacrifice the one, or to hazard the other, under the administration of
a weak, corrupt minister or a despotic, Vainglorious, ignorant General." But
in truth, as he recognized himself, he could never quit the army "because
I know the profession of arms to be my Fort[e], and I verily believe that the
Hour may possibly come when my talents into that line might be of important account to our Country."

Instead, he devoted himself to encouraging the opposition to Wayne until camp gossip took to labeling the two camps using terms such as "such an
Officer is in favor of Wayne—and such a one is in favor of Wilkinson."
The depth of Wilkinson's hatred could be gauged from an article he sent to
a Cincinnati newspaper signed "Army Wretched" that damned Wayne for
drunkenness, incompetence, wastefulness, and favoritism toward "his pimps
and parasites." Unfortunately for this attempt to stampede public opinion,
General Charles Scott visited Wayne's command headquarters at Fort
Greeneville soon afterward and offered a different perspective on the general's conduct. "During my stay I found him attending with great Sobriety
& extream attention to the Duty of army," Scott reported to Knox, "he
paid the most Unwearied attention to the most minute thing possible *in
person*." When the government published Scott's testimony in rebuttal,
Wilkinson contemptuously dismissed Scott, once his friend and comrade-
in-arms, as "a fool, a poltroon and a scoundrel."

By the spring, Wayne's supporters had made him aware of Wilkinson's
hostility. Wayne's suspicions were directed particularly at the failure of the
victuallers Elliott and Williams to supply the army with enough food. In
Wayne's view, this was a deliberate attempt to sabotage his preparations for
war, and he accused Wilkinson to his face of being "the cause of the fault
of the Contractors." His second-in-command retaliated in his own fashion,
as Wayne discovered when a Philadelphia merchant reported that some
senators were proposing to impeach the Legion's commander "at the request of Wilkinson for Pedulation, Speculation, Fraud &c."

The longer the Legion remained inactive, the more poisonous the conflict
became. No army can remain ready for battle—"in the crouch," to use modern jargon—for long without the aggression beginning to spill over into
feuds and quarrels. But for the Legion, the lengthy delay was especially damaging. Even after training was completed, federal negotiators continued their
talks with Little Turtle and other Native American leaders in an attempt to
arrange a new boundary that would guarantee Indian land rights, but allow
settlers to move into the Ohio Valley. In the summer, as though the waiting

had undermined their physical health as much as their morale, an epidemic of illness ravaged the troops. "We labor under a universal influenza," Wilkinson told his friends, "and tertians [fevers], quotidians & intermittents rage beyond anything I have ever seen."

Yet while there remained a chance of signing a peace treaty with the Six Nations in the north and the western confederation in the northwest, Washington and Knox forbade Wayne to take any aggressive action. Chafing against the restraint, Wayne inched northward, constructing a fort that he named Recovery on the site of St. Clair's defeat.

Quite suddenly the talks broke down because Little Turtle, Blue Jacket, and their allies could not bring themselves to yield up the swath of land in the Northwest Territory demanded by U.S. negotiators. In a historic misjudgment, they insisted on maintaining the Ohio River as the border. On June 30, 1794, more than a thousand Shawnee and other warriors under Blue Jacket launched a surprise attack on Fort Recovery, the site where St. Clair's army had been annihilated. This time the attack failed, but it put an end to negotiations. Immediately Scott and the Kentucky horsemen were summoned to join the regulars, and on July 28 the Legion of the United States at last marched from Fort Greeneville.

As THE SECONDMOST SENIOR OFFICER, Brigadier General James Wilkinson had command of the right wing. It gave him a close-up position from which to criticize Wayne. He duly carped at the decision to leave the biggest cannons behind and, more insistently, at the slowness of the advance—twelve careful miles a day, always surrounded by a swarm of cavalry and riflemen, and halting well before nightfall so that entrenchments and fortifications could be put in place. Instead of following the St. Marys River westward, out into the open prairie where centers of Indian population were situated, Wayne struck due north, still keeping to rough territory so that the army had to force its way through "Thickets almost impervious," one of his men complained, "thru Marassies [morasses], Defiles & beds of Nettles more than waist high & miles in length." This unexpected maneuver, made possible by the absence of heavy artillery, wrong-footed the western confederation's army and put the Legion between Blue Jacket and supplies he expected from the British in Fort Miami, a newly constructed outpost, close to present Toledo, Ohio.

When the Legion at last emerged from the undergrowth, they found themselves on the banks of the Maumee River, which flows northward into Lake Erie. Even Wilkinson, who had spent the previous days offering

Wayne unsought advice on where they might be, was overwhelmed by the pristine beauty of the open countryside before them. "The River meandering in various directions thro a natural meadow in high cultivation & of great extent," he wrote John Brown, "this meadow bounded by noble eminences, crowned with lofty timber on either side, with Indian Villages, scattered along the Eastern [bank] & the British flag [flying] upon the Western Bank; after a dreary Journey of more than 200 miles from the Ohio, thro an uncultivated Wilderness, [the scene] fills the mind with the most Interesting Emotions, and affords the most pleasing recreation to the Eye."

Once more, Wayne ignored his second-in-command's advice to make a rapid move against Blue Jacket and instead spent days erecting yet another armed camp, Fort Deposit, where the army stored its tents and wagons. With his soldiers refreshed and unburdened, Wayne then marched northeast along the Maumee River towards the wooded hillside from which Fort Miami dominated the valley. On August 19, the Legion's scouts found the Indians' abandoned camp. Again Wilkinson and other senior officers urged immediate pursuit and attack, the kind of rapid maneuver that the Legion was designed for, but again Wayne chose the safer option of setting up camp.

The delay allowed Blue Jacket to assemble a force of about thirteen hundred men, strengthened by some sixty Canadian militia, and to take up position between the Legion and Fort Miami with their center in a clearing in the wood where a cyclone had torn up the trees. Here, late on the morning of August 20, 1794, cautiously advancing in two columns behind a double screen of sharpshooters and light infantry, the Legion met the enemy they had spent eighteen months training to fight.

The outlying skirmishers were halted by a volley of shots and, minutes later, were driven back by a charge from the Indian position. Immediately Wilkinson formed the right wing of the First and Third Sub-Legions numbering about one thousand men into line. Taking cover, the attackers began firing from a range of 160 yards at the nearest troops, Wilkinson's right wing. The two forces were packed into broken, boggy ground between the Maumee River on Wilkinson's right, forest in front, and low hills covered in heavy undergrowth on the American left. As the entire Legion extended in line, Wayne ordered forward the cavalry at the rear of his force, the regular dragoons under Captain Robert Mis Campbell behind Wilkinson on the right, and Scott's Kentucky volunteers on the left.

With drifts of musket smoke creating a heavy haze, and retreating riflemen hurrying back into the infantry lines while advancing cavalry came forward at speed, the Legion's training paid its dividend. Instead of confusion, the line on the right wing opened to let Campbell's horsemen gallop through, then reformed so that when Wilkinson gave the order to charge, the the broken defenders had no time to reform. Closest to the enemy, Wilkinson's men became the front line of attack following up the cavalry to send the Indians' left flank into headlong retreat.

From the clearing of torn-up trees that provided a defensive strongpoint, a counterattack under Little Turtle was launched against the Second and Fourth Sub-Legions on the left wing and in severe fighting threatened to turn them back. Here casualties were heaviest, and modern researchers have found the area most thickly strewn with spent buckshot and musket balls. But Little Turtle's men were first outflanked by Wilkinson's troops, then faced counterattack from the Legion's left wing. In a maneuver practiced endlessly beforehand, the Second and Fourth Sub-Legions delivered a close-range volley and at once stormed toward the position in a roaring bayonet charge. The survivors fled, melting into the woodland so that the Kentucky horsemen, slowed by heavy undergrowth, never caught up, although the regular cavalry operating in open country along the riverbank pursued the enemy for two miles.

The Native Americans never had any doubt about the significance of what happened at the battle that became known as Fallen Timbers. "We were driven by the sharp ends of the guns of the Long Knives, and we threw away our guns and fought with our knives and tomahawks," a Shawnee chief confessed. "But the Great Spirit was in the clouds, and weeping over the folly of his red children [because they] refused to smoke in the lodge of the great chief, Chenoten [Wayne]." Wayne, the victorious commander, made it equally clear in his report that "the enemy are . . . at length taught to dread—& our soldiery to believe—in the Bayonet." Reporting his own casualties of thirty-three killed and one hundred wounded, Wayne estimated the enemy losses at "more than double" his own. But to James Wilkinson and others who examined the result more closely, the issue seemed less clear-cut.

Describing the battle to his most important ally in Congress, John Brown, now a senator for Kentucky, Wilkinson doubted the enemy had more than nine hundred troops and jeered at Wayne's claims to have faced as many as two thousand. He criticized the Legion's inability to force the British out of Fort Miami, blaming Wayne's decision to leave the heavy artillery behind so that he only had a "little popgun Howitzer" to threaten its defenses. "We are Victorious & triumphant where ever we go," Wilkinson declared in his best sarcastic tone. "We have been all the way to the British Post, we have beat thousands of Indians in a pitched Battle, we have commanded the British officer to abandon his Post, we have pillaged his gardens, insulted his flag, which we left flying, & yesterday got back to this place [Fort Deposit]."

Some of these were valid criticisms—modern estimates of casualties, for example, suggest the United States lost forty-six killed and dead of wounds against fewer than forty Indian deaths—but they led to a profoundly damaging conclusion. Wilkinson convinced himself that the western confederation had not really been defeated, and that another campaign would be necessary "should the Savages determine to prosecute the War & at this moment I see nothing to contradict the Idea of the prosecution." All that had been achieved, in his view, was an immensely expensive punishment raid involving a few casualties, some destroyed villages, and many burned fields—"We have in truth done nothing which might not have been better done by 1500 mounted Volunteers in 30 days."

His failure to appreciate the strategic impact of the battle had a long-lasting influence. Throughout his subsequent career as the senior military authority in four successive administrations, Wilkinson remained convinced that large forces of regular soldiers were an unnecessary luxury on the frontier. Militia and volunteers, he assured his political masters, could be just as effective.

In reality, Wayne's victory at Fallen Timbers, demonstrating as it did the overwhelming armed might of the United States, combined with the construction of a chain of forts from the Ohio to the Great Lakes, changed the thinking of a generation of Native Americans. Leaders such as Little Turtle of the Miami, Cornplanter of the Seneca, Blue Jacket of the Shawnee, and even the volatile Oneida Red Jacket accepted the pragmatic consequence that their people had to find some accommodation to the inevitability of U.S. expansion.

So long as those Native Americans who remembered Fallen Timbers exerted influence, George Washington's successors could build on the inclusive Indian policy that he and Knox had established. But one vital ingredient was the existence of an army large enough to overawe the native occupants of the land and restrain the movement of settlers who wanted to expand into their territory. The failure of Washington's policy of assimilation was due not least to the activities of James Wilkinson.

THE BATTLE FOR COMMAND

Victory should have drained the poison from the Legion. In a generous report on the battle to Knox, General Wayne praised the entire force for the "spirit & promptitude" with which it obeyed orders. Having commended all his troops, he singled out a few "whose rank and situation placed their conduct in a very conspicuous point of view, and which I observe with pleasure, and the most lively gratitude. Among whom I beg leave to mention Brigadier General Wilkinson and Colonel Hamtramck, the commandants of the right and left wings of the Legion, whose brave example inspired the troops."

Nothing Wayne could say, however, would deflect Wilkinson from his campaign to displace his commanding officer. Writing to Brown, he contrived to take the equality of praise in Wayne's report as a calculated insult, insisting that the right wing had played a more important role and been led by a more dashing commander than the left. He also alleged, falsely, that it had suffered more casualties. Wayne, he declared, knew nothing of what had happened on the right, and his ignorance was typical of his "feeble & improvident" leadership through the entire campaign. "Yet the specious name of Victory & the gloss of misrepresentation, will doubtless gild the Character of our Chief. For my own I am content, conscious as I am, that I have in several instances partially saved my country, and . . . extorted applause from my most bitter enemy, and the most finished scoundrel on Earth."

This outburst was followed by more savage attacks in other letters to his Kentucky friends. Writing to Innes, he repeated the allegations of incompetence: "The whole operation presents us a tissue of improvidence, disarray, precipitancy, Error & Ignorance." Victory was due simply to the inferior numbers and "injudicious Conduct of the enemy." To underline the message, he wrote Innes again in December describing Wayne as "a liar, a drunkard, a Fool, the associate of the lowest order of Society, & the companion of their vices, of desperate Fortune, my rancorous enemy, a coward, a Hypocrite, and the contempt of every man of sense and virtue."

There was something mad about such a tirade—and jealousy at Wayne's growing reputation undoubtedly gave an edge to the fury. Henry Knox assumed Wilkinson's enmity arose from lack of self-confidence. Even before Fallen Timbers, Knox had received two letters from Wilkinson demanding a court of inquiry into Wayne's incompetence, but had chosen not to reply because the complaint "appears to me . . . to be more the effect of nice [sensitive] feelings than any palpable cause." When Knox finally responded in December, he first sent a private letter asking Wilkinson to give up the quarrel, and assuring him that Wayne had not criticized him, that Charles Scott would not be promoted to command over him, that he was not being investigated as the cause of dissension in the army, and ending, "You must rest assured that your military reputation stands as well as you could desire." In the formal letter that followed, Wilkinson was promised that if he made his complaint more precise and legal in tone, the president would consider it and decide "what steps he ought to take." Knox, in short, did not take seriously the cries of Wilkinson's wounded ego.

Yet, wise and tolerant though he was, the war secretary missed the almost chesslike shrewdness behind Wilkinson's paranoid outbursts. The unrelenting belittlement of the Legion and its commander, publicized both in the press and through friends such as Senator John Brown, had a political context.

In Congress, opponents of Washington's Federalist administration, led by James Madison in Philadelphia but orchestrated by Thomas Jefferson in Monticello, had focused on the expense of the Legion—an annual military budget of $155,500 in 1790 had risen to $1,130,000—and were demanding that its size be reduced by two thirds. By diminishing Wayne's achievement, Wilkinson strengthened the anti-Federalists in their belief that a large standing army was an unjustified extravagance. It also served his personal ambition. Military regulations would not allow a major general to command a force the size of a brigade. Consequently, a reduced army would force Wayne into retirement, leaving Brigadier General James Wilkinson in command.

With Congress due to debate the size of the army in February 1795, his timing could not have been better. Desperate to keep the quarrel private,

Washington's administration could neither reprimand him for insubordination nor refuse his request for an inquiry into Wayne's incompetence. Knox's demand that he present his charges in specific, legal form was an attempt to play for time. But, having acknowledged them formally, Knox also felt obliged to pass on a copy of Wilkinson's allegations to Wayne. Aided by the flukiest of chances, Knox thereby saved the Legion and came close to exposing Spain's chief agent in the United States.

UNTIL KNOX'S LETTER was delivered to Fort Greeneville in January 1795, Wayne had no inkling that his second-in-command was plotting against him. The realization that this "vile invidious man" had been creating divisions in the Legion while pretending to treat his commander with "attention, politeness & delicacy" outraged him. In an incandescent reply to Knox, Wayne angrily dismissed Wilkinson's charges: "They are as unexpected as they are groundless, and as false as they are base and insidious; and had I not known the real character and disposition of the man, I should have considered the whole as the idle Phantom of a disturbed immaginration [*sic*]." Recalling how "I always indulged the Brigadier, in all that he wished or requested," the general reached the same conclusion as dozens before and after him and damned Wilkinson for being "as devoid of principle as he is of honor or fortune."

Once alerted to his subordinate's true character, however, Wayne quickly came up with what seemed to him evidence of treachery. On October 12, 1794, a deserter named Robert Newman was discovered on a boat preparing to descend the Ohio River on his way to Fort Washington. Under questioning, Newman claimed to have been employed by Wilkinson and James Hawkins, a Kentucky land speculator, to deliver information about Wayne's campaign to the British. For good measure, he added that Wilkinson and Hawkins were planning to persuade Kentucky and the Northwest Territory to secede and join Canada in a northern version of the Spanish Conspiracy.

Newman's story caused disbelief and consternation. The lieutenant governor of Canada thought it must have been concocted for "a sinister purpose," perhaps to justify an attack on Fort Miami, while Wilkinson, guilty of selling out elsewhere, was furious at the imputation he would have done so to the British—"a base and vile calumny." Investigations by Philip Nolan suggested that Newman's information was invented and paid for by Wayne himself, and the general admitted that the supposed spy's "answers are rather mysterious, negative & equivocal." Nevertheless, Wayne felt justified in warning Knox, as he graphically put it, "There is 'something rotten in the State of Denmark' & which ought to be guarded against."

Perhaps typical of Wayne's impetuous nature, he got the direction of Wilkinson's treachery wrong by 180 degrees, but the precautions he took were unexpectedly effective and came within a hairbreadth of trapping his enemy. In addition to a general alert for foreign agents, he specifically ordered Captain John Pierce, commandant of Fort Washington, to arrest James Hawkins as a foreign agent should he set foot in Cincinnati and warned Major Thomas Doyle, in command of Fort Massac near the mouth of the Ohio, to investigate thoroughly any suspicious boats coming upriver. The timing could not have been worse for Wilkinson. In October, his activities as a secret agent were about to yield him a fortune.

Whereas Miró had understood Wilkinson's instinct for intrigue and accepted that it would always be used to further his own interests, Carondelet, who had never met him, betrayed a touching faith in his truthfulness. Wilkinson must sensed this in his letters because, having presented a demand for twelve thousand dollars in April 1794 for his success in foiling Clark's expedition, he wrote again in June with a project that would incur still greater expense for Carondelet. Resurrecting the bribery suggestion he had unsuccessfully presented to Miró, Wilkinson explained that the long-term safety of Louisiana depended on persuading Kentucky to secede, and this could be achieved by purchasing the loyalty of the state's "notables" for only two hundred thousand dollars. He promised to give his advice on how the money should be spent, and if funds could be provided, he would bring his friends Harry Innes and Benjamin Sebastian to confer with Carondelet. Finally, he had a list of sixteeen officers in the U.S. army whose commitment to Spain could also be bought.

"Do not believe me avaricious," he assured the governor earnestly, "as the sensation never found place in my bosom. Constant in my attachments, ardent in my affections, and an enthusiast in the cause I espoused, my character is the reverse."

The reply that Carondelet sent on August 6 could hardly have been more satisfactory. Indeed, the extravagant governor and avaricious general might have been made for each other. Only the suggestion of military bribes was turned down. The twelve thousand dollars Wilkinson had requested would be paid without delay. Once authorization of the two hundred thousand dollars had been received, Wilkinson would be expected to advise on its expenditure. Meanwhile, Innes and Sebastian would receive Spanish pensions, and a conference with them would be arranged in New Madrid. As

a sign of his personal gratitude, the governor had recommended to Madrid
that the general's pension be increased to four thousand dollars a year.

TWO DANGEROUS EVENTS PENETRATE a spy's cocoon of secrecy, the trans-
mission of information and the receipt of payment. For Wilkinson, the
problem of getting his hands on Carondelet's munificent reward without
arousing suspicion required particular care. In a letter to the governor written just before Fallen Timbers, he had recommended that the money
be entrusted to two messengers. Captain Joseph Collins, a reliable but
unimaginative officer from his staff, would travel to New Orleans posing as
a trader in flour, and he was to be accompanied by Henry Owens, a quick-
witted but unsuccessful Kentucky settler. Both understood the money to
be payment for Wilkinson's tobacco sales and, since it was in silver dollars,
it needed to be shipped in utmost secrecy. When they arrived in New Orleans, Carondelet divided the twelve thousand dollars between them and
sent each north by a different route.

On August 6, while the Legion was still struggling through the morasses
and stinging nettles, Owens left New Orleans heading up the Mississippi
with $6,000 in coins packed into three barrels of sugar in the hold of a Span-
ish galley. Two weeks later, on the very day that Fallen Timbers was fought,
Collins took passage in a ship sailing for Charleston, carrying $6,333, a sum
sufficient to pay all the expenses allegedly incurred by Wilkinson in check-
mating the expedition planned by George Rogers Clark. The knowledge
that this gigantic windfall was on its way and had somehow to be smuggled
past watchful eyes and wagging tongues that might alert Wayne no doubt
contributed to the stress that marked Wilkinson's increasingly strident attacks
on the commander.

By October, Owens had reached the Spanish fort of New Madrid. The
most difficult part of the transfer, taking the money up the Ohio and past
U.S. strongpoints such as Fort Massac, now began. New Madrid's commander, Tomás Portell, and François Langlois, a militia officer in charge of
galleys on the river, discussed with Owens the best way to escape detection.
Langlois proposed that Owens travel openly as a trader with a new crew recruited in the settlement, but was overruled by the other two, who preferred
secrecy. Accordingly in November, Langlois took a nervous Owens and his
three precious casks in a Spanish boat to the mouth of the Ohio, where they
transferred to a small canoe manned by six Spanish sailors. At the last moment, Langlois thought it too dangerous to allow so much money to be
transported in an open boat and took the barrels back, but Owens, who stood

to make about $600 from the delivery, insisted on taking the dollars in the canoe before winter came and ice blocked the river.

This very public quarrel destroyed any semblance of secrecy. Within days, Wilkinson's courier was dead, murdered by one of the paddlers in his canoe, a Spaniard named Vexerano, for the silver dollars inside the barrels. The crime was soon known on the Spanish side because one of the paddlers hurried back to New Madrid to alert Portell, but four others including Vexerano continued up the Ohio before splitting the cash and scattering into the Kentucky countryside. Unable to speak English, and in possession of large sums of money, they immediately aroused suspicions in the closely knit rural communities they traveled through.

For Wilkinson, waiting in Fort Washington for the money, Owens's murder was the worst possible outcome. Not only was he deprived of cash he needed to pay his debts, but somewhere at large were four criminals who could provide tangible evidence that he was being paid by Spain. In December, three of the boatmen were arrested in Kentucky and brought before the federal judge in Frankfort. Fortunately this happened to be Harry Innes, who was almost as deep in the conspiracy as his client. He immediately informed Wilkinson that the three men were under arrest and had them shipped in irons to Fort Washington in Cincinnati.

Yet with Captain Pierce, the fort's commander, on the lookout for foreign agents, Wilkinson could not afford to keep the three Spaniards there. On the grounds that Spain had jurisdiction over them, he ordered them to be taken down to the fort at New Madrid on December 29, escorted by Lieutenant Aaron Gregg and a Kentucky lawyer, Charles Smith. But the boat got no farther than Fort Massac, where Major Doyle, equally suspicious of strange movements on the river, had lookouts posted. The boat was spotted as it tried to slip past under cover of night, and at musket point it was ordered to shore, where those on board were brought in for questioning. Smith produced a written order from Wilkinson giving them free passage, but Doyle decided that because the three prisoners had committed their crime on U.S. soil, they could proceed no farther until he had questioned them himself.

Had anyone in Fort Massac spoken Spanish, Wilkinson's career would have been ended. Doyle was Wayne's man, and the murderers' evidence would have given the general incontrovertible information linking his enemy to Spain. But for the second time, luck went Wilkinson's way. The fort was manned by monoglot English speakers, and Doyle had to send to New Madrid for an interpreter.

In January 1795, Thomas Power, a bilingual Irishman who acted as Carondelet's confidential messenger, arrived from New Madrid to translate. Intimately aware of the sensitive information the prisoners possessed, Power carefully censored any reference to Owens's mission from the answers they gave to Doyle's questions. Although unaware of the prize he held, Doyle remained sufficiently suspicious to send them downriver to Louisville for trial. Still acting as interpreter, Power went with them and again doctored their replies to court officials there because, as he later admitted, "it was the wish of the Spanish officers to have the men delivered to them rather than tried in the territory of the United States, and such a wish arose from a fear of divulging the secret of Owens' mission." By this time the prisoners knew their lines, and all denied being concerned in the murder. Frustrated, the Louisville court at length remanded the prisoners to their starting point, Judge Innes in Frankfort.

An increasingly anxious Wilkinson let his old friend know that, to buy the prisoners' silence, he was ready "to pay the three two hundred dollars if they should not be compensated by the Spanish government." But Innes found a cheaper solution. In the weeks since he'd first questioned them no new evidence had come forward, and in March he discreetly concluded that the lack of witnesses made a trial impossible, and that the prisoners should be set free on condition they left Kentucky at once. In June 1795 the unfortunate Major Doyle was summoned upriver to Fort Washington, where he paid the price for his initiative by being put under arrest for disobeying Wilkinson's orders to let the men through. At about the same time, Vexerano was arrested in New Madrid, and his execution in New Orleans later that year removed the last threat to Wilkinson of exposure by Owens's murderers.

Nevertheless, suspicion still hung round him—the angry Doyle blamed "a base and ambitious faction" for his arrest—and Wilkinson's money had gone missing. Most damagingly as it turned out, the distraction had prevented him from feeding anti-Wayne propaganda either to the press or to Congress during the debates on the future size of the army. Although the House voted to reduce its numbers and, as a result, to abolish the post of major general, popular opinion was swinging in favor of the Legion and its commander as the effects of Fallen Timbers made themselves felt.

At the end of 1794, the Legion had marched into the Indiana prairie, the breadbasket of many of the nations that made up the western confederation, and not only destroyed most of their farmland, but erected the looming edifice of Fort Wayne. Before the winter was over, hunger drove the confederation's sachems and war leaders to begin negotiating a peace agreement. Whatever the ideological argument about the merits of a regular army and a militia, it was becoming obvious that, as Cornelius Sedam, a straight-talking New Jersey soldier, put it, "by many Genl. Wayne has been Sensured . . . [but] Saying here and Saying there has no Effect. He has Done the Business and that Settles the Dispute." On March 3 the Senate agreed, and its vote guaranteed the Legion's existence for another three years. Nailing Wilkinson's ambition into its coffin, the Senate also voted to make its commander a major general.

DEATH OF A RIVAL

C ONFIRMED IN HIS POST and convinced of Wilkinson's treachery, Major General Anthony Wayne made it his mission to deny his fellow general any part in the army's business. Wilkinson, he told Knox, was "a vile assassin," "the worst of all bad men," who intended to break up the United States with the help of the British in Canada and of secessionists in Kentucky. So far as the major general was concerned, his subordinate "had no command in the army, and if he had any modesty he would resign."

Thus, while negotiations with the western confederation continued at Wayne's headquarters in Fort Greeneville, Wilkinson was effectively sidelined in Fort Washington. He missed the steadily increasing pressure that was brought to bear by the Legion's powerful presence in the Indians' heartland. He had no part in the negotiations with Blue Jacket, Little Turtle, and other leaders of the western confederation. Finally, on August 3, 1795, he was absent when they assembled at the fort and accepted a new boundary that opened up the first prairies to settlement, including most of western Ohio and much of Indiana. In keeping with Knox's vision of co-existence, a binding guarantee was also given in the Treaty of Greeneville that "the United States will protect all the said Indian tribes in the quiet enjoyment of their lands against all citizens of the United States."

That same year, Wayne's decision not to attack Fort Miami was vindicated when diplomatic negotiations in London resulted in the Jay's Treaty and Britain's peaceful withdrawal from all forts on U.S. territory. Quite suddenly, the northern frontier was opened up. Wayne's triumph completed the humiliation of his subordinate.

Knox, who probably understood Wilkinson as well as any American, had resigned at the beginning of the year. The last two messages Wilkinson sent the former secretary of war concerned Wayne and perfectly reflected the split between his private feelings and public behavior. In reply to Knox's formal letter offering a court of inquiry, Wilkinson formally promised on January 1, 1795, to drop all public complaint against Wayne—"My Lips are now Sealed, my Pen is dismissed from depicting well founded grievances"— but on January 2 he sent an answer to the secretary's private letter in which he repeated all his denunciations.

Knox could accept such contradictions, but not his successor, the bald, Puritan disciplinarian Timothy Pickering. Caught between a military rock and a political hard place, Wilkinson found himself unable to plot openly against Wayne. Fearing that a head-on confrontation might bring the risk of his expulsion from the army, he abandoned his call for an inquiry.

IN FORT WASHINGTON, he and Nancy still kept up their lavish displays of hospitality, to the admiration of the *Kentucky Gazette*. They still ran their carriage through the muddy streets of rapidly growing Cincinnati, despite the presence of hogs scavenging among the refuse and despite the seasonal flooding of the lower part of town. They now had three children being educated in Philadelphia and had to find money for the necessary clothes, shoes, and tutors.

Economic stability had eluded Wilkinson all his life, but the prospect of Carondelet's dollars had briefly seemed to bring it within his grasp. In the fall of 1794, he had begun buying land again, this time from John Cleves Symmes, whose million acres lay on the northwest side of the Ohio River. Away from the stranglehold of lawsuits and chicanery that was killing Kentucky's land market, Ohio property was rising in value so fast that in 1795 the *Pittsburgh Gazette* reported, "Land that two or three years ago was sold for ten shillings [$1.50] per acre, will now bring upwards of three pounds [$9]."

It should have provided the sort of profitable investment in land that Wilkinson had sought ever since he first came west. But by the sort of bad luck that seemed to dog the general's real estate deals, a surveyor's error meant that the valuable acres he had bought from Symmes turned out to belong to the U.S. government and were not for sale. Since he had paid with borrowed money and Symmes had run out of funds, Wilkinson again found himself facing creditors, but this time without land he could sell.

In April 1795, a lifeline arrived in the shape of Captain Joseph Collins, who came downriver from Pittsburgh, thereby escaping Major Doyle's eagle eye. Yet here, too, it seemed that fortune was against Wilkinson. In a message to Gayoso, Wilkinson revealed that Collins had somehow contrived to lose $2,500 in a land speculation that went sour. Since Wilkinson continued to trust Collins as a messenger, he was probably lying slightly and this was actually money owed on the Symmes deal. Nevertheless, once travel expenses, incidental debts, and Collins's fee as a courier had been paid, Wilkinson was left with just $1,740 instead of the $6,333 he had expected. Altogether, less than one seventh of the money that he had been promised by Carondelet the year before had actually arrived in his hands.

"If my very damned and unparalleled crosses and misfortunes, did not uncash me, I would be with you in flour," he replied regretfully when an old friend, John Adair, invited him to join a trading expedition to New Orleans that summer. He still hoped to recoup some of the stolen money— "this sum is not lost, but is not within my control"—but even when it was eventually paid, other demands would be made upon it. He was still being sued for $3,000 by his former partner Peyton Short, and Harry Innes continued to demand money to pay off bonds he had underwritten. Small wonder that Wilkinson should have scrabbled so desperately to retain his dual role as general and spy.

HECTOR DE CARONDELET had many reasons for treating the general generously, and all were conneected to the fragile defense of Louisiana. Its protection depended heavily on alliances made with the Cherokee, Choctaw, and Creek nations, which lived along its borders. With a stiffening of Spanish regulars and militia operating from forts along the Mississippi, the threat of Indian war parties provided a deterrent to the sort of expeditions that bellicose settlers often talked of sending down the river to attack New Orleans. But the awesome power exhibited at Fallen Timbers by the Legion of the United States was on a different scale. Against such an army Carondelet had no defense.

The threat it posed became more real when Jay's Treaty was ratified in June 1795, signaling the imminent withdrawal of British troops from the forts they occupied south of the Great Lakes. Once the distraction on its northern border had been removed, the United States became free to enforce its interests in the south. At the same time, the risk of an attack from France had suddenly increased following the invasion of Spain by French armies in 1795. In such circumstances, Louisiana became a legitimate target. From the standpoint of those in New Orleans, her most useful resource appeared to be the secret information and hidden influence of a senior American general.

Wilkinson had already proved his usefulness in several specific ways. Although Carondelet mistakenly attached particular value to his role in undermining the George Rogers Clark expedition, the most valuable results came from the flow of intelligence he provided about U.S. military intentions and capability, and from the insights he offered about how they might be countered. The most obvious example was his recommendation to Miró to build a fort at New Madrid. Its construction immediately curbed U.S. expansion down the Mississippi and encouraged a surge of settlement into what would become Missouri, not just by Anglo-Americans but by more than a thousand Shawnees and Delawares, who were given land, as Gayoso explained, "with a view to their rendering us aid in case of war with the whites as well as with the Osages." And as Carondelet found, the fort became increasingly useful as a jumping-off point for agents and couriers who needed to enter the United States.

In June 1794, Wilkinson passed on General Wayne's plan to rebuild Fort Massac, near the junction of the Ohio and Mississippi rivers, and strongly advised Spain to counter with an outpost of its own. In response, Gayoso ordered the construction of a stockade almost opposite the mouth of the Ohio. Although it never became a major defense post, Wilkinson's insistence on the need for more Spanish fortifications on the Mississippi persuaded Carondelet to authorize the creation of a new fortress below New Madrid. In 1795, Gayoso negotiated the necessary transfer of land from the Chickasaws and in the fall traveled north to supervise the building of an ambitious new fort at Chickasaw Bluffs, the site of modern Memphis, Tennessee.

In Carondelet's eyes, however, the greatest prize remained the secession of Kentucky, which would in itself safeguard Louisiana. His interest had been aroused early in 1794 by a letter written by Harry Innes at Wilkinson's instigation that suggested Kentuckians had grown disenchanted with a federal government that had taxed their whiskey for three years and still not secured free navigation of the Mississippi. In April 1795 the general himself added confirmatory evidence by mailing Carondelet a copy of the *Kentucky Gazette* containing letters from Innes and the state governor, Isaac Shelby, about Kentucky's growing impatience to have the Mississippi opened to navigation. The possibility of detaching the state excited Carondelet's imagination in a way that blinded him to both the reality of the United States' growing power and the deceitfulness of Agent 13.

Yet clearly, Wilkinson's information and advice had earned him such respect in New Orleans, it was difficult to ignore his suggestion. His standing was referred to in a memorandum prepared some years later by an outsider, a patriotic Frenchman, Joseph de Pontalba, who lived in Louisiana but looked forward eagerly to the moment when France again ruled the province. In the paper that he presented to Napoléon in 1800, Pontalba emphasized the pervasive influence exerted on the Spanish authorities "by a powerful inhabitant of Kentucky, who possesses much influence with his countrymen, and enjoys great consideration for the services he has rendered to the cause of liberty, when occupying high grades in the army of the United States; [but] who . . . has never ceased to serve Spain in all her views."

Based on his own experience, he pinpointed two essential priorities to be followed by whichever country held New Orleans—and Pontalba was certain this should be France. It must aim to secure the economic loyalties of Kentucky's citizens by guaranteeing to buy their tobacco, and it should "renew the intelligences which the Government of Louisiana had with the individual of whom I have spoken." So long as these rules were followed, Louisiana would become a source of prosperity, power, and "the most brilliant destinies" for France.

But the most concrete tribute to Wilkinson's value was Carondelet's decision to make good the loss caused by Owens's murder. Replying to Wilkinson in July 1795, he promised to send the general another $9,640 on top of the original $12,333. To encourage the renewal of the Spanish Conspiracy, Wilkinson's friends were to have pensions as well—"You must not entertain the least doubt of the advantages they will derive," Carondelet declared—and there existed a still more glittering prize. Carondelet could only hint at it, but an independent Kentucky, united with Tennessee and the Northwest Territory, would make a new Mississippi nation requiring its own president. "And G.W. can aspire to the same dignity in the western states that P.W. has in the eastern," Carondelet suggested beguilingly. That the initials stood for General Wilkinson and President Washington respectively needed no elucidation. Over the next twenty years, the vision of a western United States was to occur in various forms to many people, not least to Thomas Jefferson and his vice president Aaron Burr, but it lodged most tenaciously in the mind of James Wilkinson.

SPEED WAS ESSENTIAL if the conspiracy to bring about Kentucky's secession was to succeed. Since Gayoso was already in New Madrid to supervise fort construction on the Mississippi, Carondelet promised that he would be available to confer with members of the Spanish Conspiracy. The latter were to come "authentically empowered by the State of Kentucky to treat with us secretly," while Gayoso would be authorized on behalf of the Spanish to offer "full execution concerning the navigation of the Misisipi [*sic*]." Meanwhile Wilkinson could guarantee pensions of two thousand dollars to Innes, Sebastian, the Federalist William Murray, and George Nicholas—reputedly the wealthiest man in Kentucky.

This proposal was delivered to Wilkinson, still isolated in Fort Washington, by Carondelet's personal messenger, the resourceful Thomas Power, who came upriver in October 1795. Unfortunately for Power's attempts at secrecy, his movements were reported to General Wayne. At a public dinner in Cincinnati, Wayne declared Power to be "a spy for the British, a spy for the Spanish, and a spy for somebody else." No one doubted that the "somebody else" was James Wilkinson.

It was not difficult to identify something alien in Power. Almost everyone knew him as a Spanish courier—Wilkinson himself referred to him as "the celebrated Power"—and none who met him more than once seems to have liked him. He apparently had no home life—"traveling was my ruling passion," he admitted—and his letters have a voluble, petulant tone. Furious at being outed by Wayne, he denounced the spying accusation as "ungenerous, illiberal, wanton, groundless, cruel, false, stupid, base and contemptible." Perhaps his sensitive, emotional nature made him a good spy—Carondelet certainly credited him with an exceptional "power of penetration," and the secrets he picked up in his restless journeying made him valuable to several different employers.

Despite the attention Wayne directed at him, Power smuggled a letter from Wilkinson to New Orleans in November 1795. Carondelet lost no time in passing its most important point on to Madrid. "I shall watch all the movements which the army of Gen'l Wayne may undertake," he told the royal council, "whereof W[ilkinson] will punctually inform me, as I have just had a letter from him on this subject in which he assures me that he will be informed of all that may be done."

Confident that Wilkinson intended to deliver both information and Kentucky itself, Carondelet authorized Power to return north with the promised $9,640 and to contact all those concerned with the Spanish Conspiracy.

WILKINSON'S PROMISE TO PROVIDE informaton on the army's movements signaled that he was no longer to be kept in isolation. Wayne had not changed his mind about Wilkinson's treachery, but after three years' service in the field, Wayne needed rest. Physically, he was suffering from recurring stomach pains that were described as "gout of the stomach," a diagnosis invalid in modern medicine, which identifies gout as the crystallization of uric acid in the joints. The association of sharp pain with high levels of stress suggests an ulcer. He was overdue for leave, and Congress wanted him to testify about his military and diplomatic achievements in the west.

With deep reluctance Wayne finally departed for Philadelphia in December 1795, having left Wilkinson as acting head of the army. His subordinate's power, however, was severely circumscribed. Wayne had summoned him to Fort Greeneville and coldly presented him with a list of instructions detailing exactly how he was to supervise the duties and movements of the Legion. On the advice of Pickering, secretary of war, Wilkinson was "enjoined not to make any the least alteration to them."

This attempt to limit his authority—the final insult in a year of humiliations—ratcheted Wilkinson's hatred of his superior to a new level of toxicity. To Harry Innes, he made it clear that he was ready to risk dismissal to bring Wayne down: "This accomplished, you will most probably have me for a neighbour [in Frankfort], as I am tired of the shackles of Military Life."

His first step, however, was to stretch the restrictions on his command. Within days of Wayne's departure for Philadelphia, Wilkinson issued a general order to the army announcing his "determination to inculcate, to enforce and to maintain a Uniform System of Subordination and Discipline through all Ranks, without Partiality, Prejudice, Favor or Affection." The implication, that Mad Anthony Wayne had allowed the army's command structure to be undermined by factionalism, was cleverly judged, since the quarrel between the two generals gave it a basis in reality. Even officers suspicious of Wilkinson supported a return to impartial discipline.

He followed up his announcement with a prolonged tour of inspection of the line of outposts that stretched to Fort Wayne, as though he needed space after his confinement in Fort Washington. Before he left, orders for rations and pay and clothing sprayed out from Fort Greeneville. Captain Shaumburgh was hurried north to negotiate the handover of Detroit from the British, Colonel Hamtramck was commanded to bring about a peaceful solution to a quarrel with the Chippewa in his area, and supplies and dollars were despatched to Fort Massac to feed and pay the garrison now commanded by Captain Zebulon Pike, father of the future explorer.

Wherever he went, Wilkinson deliberately spread his influence at the ex-

pense of Wayne's. But as always his chief weapon lay in Congress. The opportunity to strike was provided by a seismic shift in the relationship between Spain and the United States.

THE CHANGE WAS CAUSED by the war in Europe. In July 1795 a French
army came within striking distance of Madrid, forcing Carlos IV's government to make a hasty peace with France. By the logic of power politics, this
set Spain against Britain, forcing Spain to make a new alliance in North
America as protection against a possible British attack on Louisiana. The
price of friendship with the United States was high, an agreement to open
the Mississippi to the flatboats of Kentucky farmers. In October 1795, the
Treaty of San Lorenzo was signed between the two nations. It promised not
only that the river would be open to trade, but that a clearly defined frontier
would be run along the thirty-first parallel between the United States and
the Spanish colonies of East and West Florida.

No one was more directly affected by the treaty than the governor of
Louisiana, who had invested thousands of dollars in a conspiracy to detach
Kentucky from a country that was now Spain's ally. Defiantly Carondelet
continued with his plan, sending Thomas Power from New Orleans with
the promised $9,640 for Wilkinson.

The arrival of Carondelet's messenger in May 1796 should have caused
the acting head of the army some embarrassment. But in answer to Power's
formal request to travel to Fort Greeneville for their meeting, Wilkinson
answered grandly—and conveniently for someone acting as Carondelet's
eyes—that since the United States was at peace with everyone, "the officers
of the American army have no concealments to make, and therefore our
camps and our forts are free to the ingress and egress of all persons who de-
port themselves with propriety."

Catering to the general's taste for expensive living, Power had brought a
gift of "segars from Havana," but what cheered Wilkinson's spirits more was
the news that the money promised by Carondelet had finally arrived in the
north and was waiting for him at New Madrid. The cash, as Power confided
to Gayoso, was urgently needed because of "the [financial] embarrassments
of gen. Wilkinson . . . For a long time past he has been expecting this money,
the delay of which has been the cause of much trouble to him, involving him
in great difficulties." To escape detection and avoid the risk of another murder, he and Power agreed that the dollars should be packed in barrels of sugar
and coffee ostensibly being sent for sale in Louisville with no more than a
thousand coins in each barrel so that the extra weight would not be noticed.

Power was back in New Madrid within ten days of leaving Fort Greeneville, but without written authorization from Wilkinson to pick up the money on his behalf. This minor problem, caused by the general's reluctance to entrust compromising material to someone so liable to be searched, had large consequences. Since it would have taken months to obtain permission from New Orleans, Colonel Tomás Portell, commandant of the fort at New Madrid, agreed to make the handover anyway, but he and Power wrote formal explanations for Carondelet to show why they had ignored his instructions. Thus of all the payments Wilkinson received from Spain, none was better documented than this sum of $9,640, and none would figure more prominently in the accusations leveled against him.

Yet it was already clear to Wilkinson at least that the San Lorenzo treaty had snuffed out any lingering prospect of Kentucky's secession. Granted their long-held wish, the western settlers no longer had any motive for leaving the Union. That was the assumption made in Philadelphia, and accepted by Madrid. In New Orleans, Natchez, and New Madrid, however, the colonial administration thought otherwise. For Carondelet and Gayoso, the Spanish Conspiracy remained alive, and neither had any intention of abandoning the Mississippi forts built on Wilkinson's recommendation to limit American expansion. Having fortified and garrisoned the Chickasaw Bluffs post, Gayoso even went on to construct an armed stockade almost opposite the mouth of the Ohio itself. In the summer of 1796, Carondelet wrote explicitly to Benjamin Sebastian, and the other members of the conspiracy, "It may be confidently asserted, without incurring the reproach of presumption, that his Catholic Majesty *will not carry the above mentioned treaty into execution.*"

Sebastian, who personally worked on details of the conspiracy with both Gayoso and Carondelet during the first half of 1796, was rewarded with a pension and was authorized to offer $100,000 to the usual list of "notables" who could help bring about secession. As the linchpin of the entire conspiracy, Wilkinson was to be recompensed still more highly, not simply with fame and the governorship of the future Mississippi republic, but with the solid inducement of one hundred thousand acres in Illinois.

SECURE IN THE KNOWLEDGE that $9,640 was waiting for him in New Madrid, Wilkinson was more concerned with the opportunity that suddenly presented itself of destroying General Anthony Wayne. Taken with the two other treaties of 1795—the Jay agreement establishing good relations with

Britain and the Greeneville treaty with the western confederation—San Lorenzo left the United States without an obvious enemy, and, as Wilkinson's allies adamantly insisted, without the need for a large army commanded by a major general. With the support of Thomas Jefferson's Democratic-Republican Party, the House voted in April 1796 for an army of two thousand led by a brigadier general. The issue of personalities loomed so large that Chauncey Goodrich, a Federalist congressman from Connecticut, called it a plot "to get rid of General Wayne and place the army in the hands of a Jacobin and what is worse a western incendiary."

The president, however, still clung to his vision of an inclusive United States that depended on a large army. In a paper presented to Congress in February, Timothy Pickering, the secretary of war, declared the Legion to be essential "to preserve peace with the Indians, and to protect theirs and the public lands." The pendulum began to swing back, and helped by Wayne's presence in Philadelphia, the Federalist majority in the Senate voted in May to keep the major general and the Legion. Since money had to be saved, they would instead abolish Wilkinson's rank. Suddenly Wayne seemed about to win. As the heat of a Washington summer grew intolerable, however, a compromise deal was hammered out that reduced the army but retained both generals until the military budget was discussed again the following year.

Nevertheless, the contest between the two men remained in the balance, with Wilkinson acutely vulnerable to any revelation about his Spanish connections. That same summer, Wilkinson became aware of the widening circle of Kentuckians contacted by Power as part of the conspiracy. Fearful that someone would mention the name of the ringleader, Wilkinson pleaded with Gayoso, "For the love of God, my friend, enjoin greater secrecy and caution in all our concerns . . . Never suffer my name to be written or spoken. The suspicion of Washington is wide awake."

Not only was Spanish security lax, but the barrels of money in New Madrid that were due to come up the Ohio in July or August were lethal evidence of his treachery. The danger of discovery was underlined when one of Wilkinson's messengers was arrested as he returned from New Madrid by the commander of Fort Massac, Captain Zebulon Pike. With flattery, good humor, and the promise of promotion, Wilkinson cajoled Pike into releasing the messenger. The captain duly became a major, and the friendship forged in such unlikely conditions ensured that a few years later his son, Zebulon Pike the explorer, would become Wilkinson's right-hand man. But the incident showed that any boat coming up the river was liable to be stopped and searched.

In June, shortly before leaving Philadelphia, General Wayne was summoned to see the new secretary of war, James McHenry, who passed on the administration's own intelligence about Wilkinson's activities. Much was tainted, coming as it did from Federalist opponents, or personal enemies such as Humphrey Marshall. In the latest round of their contest, he had been debarred from his Senate seat in January 1796 while charges of "gross fraud" and "perjury" brought on evidence supplied by Wilkinson's friends were investigated. Nevertheless, Wayne saw enough to realize that Wilkinson was a Spanish rather than a British "pensioner," and the name of Thomas Power figured so prominently there could be no doubt that he was the general's link with New Orleans.

Hurrying back west, Wayne arrived in mid-July and immediately relieved Wilkinson of his command, putting him again in seclusion at Fort Washington. At the same time he sent Pike an urgent order to arrest Power whenever he appeared, with particular instructions to search for hidden documents. Days later, Wayne received specific warning from a Kentucky merchant, Elisha Winters, that Power would be coming upriver with "a royal chest" containing money and dispatches for Wilkinson. Mad Anthony had every reason to believe that the trap was about to close on his enemy.

On August 8, 1796, Lieutenant John Steele on river patrol halfway between Massac and Louisville stopped a large boat rowed by ten oarsmen. Boarding it, he discovered Thomas Power in the cabin with a cargo of barrels of sugar, coffee, and rum destined, according to Power's documents, for sale in Louisville. Power protested vigorously that he was a legitimate merchant flying the Spanish flag, and that a diplomatic incident would be created if Steele damaged his cargo. Later the steersman on the boat recollected, "Had Steel [*sic*] looked into a bucket on the top of the boat, containing old tobacco, he would have found papers enough to hang Wilkinson himself." However, the lieutenant was not the most enterprising officer in the army—after twenty years' service he still retained the same rank as when he enlisted. Although suspicious because Power was not a regular merchant, he merely examined the barrels without opening them, then waved the Irishman on.

In a breathless account of the incident to Carondelet, Power admitted that he had used up a fortnight's rum ration as a reward to keep the oarsmen rowing at full speed in case Steele changed his mind and came after them, "because, had I fallen into his hands for a second time, I was lost." In Louisville, Power lodged the barrels of cash with a friend, then bought a horse to gallop to Cincinnati, where he gave Wilkinson the news that he had again escaped disaster by the skin of his teeth. The dollars were eventually taken to Frankfort, where all but $640 that Power kept for himself was put into Nolan's safekeeping. In November, much of it seems to have been laundered through a bond for $4,000 drawn on Harry Innes. By then Wilkinson had taken the battle against Wayne to Philadelphia.

THE KNOWLEDGE THAT HE WAS once more in funds had an immediate effect on Wilkinson's outlook. In a long letter sent to Carondelet in September, he briskly outlined the ambitious program he intended to follow in the nation's capital: "My views at Philadelphia are to keep down the military establishment, to disgrace my commander, and to secure myself the commandant of the army; should you advise such action otherwise, I will throw up my commission and return to Kentucky: on this point write me particularly by Power." There was not the slightest chance that the baron would do anything but encourage his prize asset in his ruthless ambition to take command of the U.S. army.

In the same letter, Wilkinson also described the basic strategy he would adopt to account for the money received from Spain: "If I am questioned by Washington on my arrival at Philadelphia, I will avow a mercantile connection with New Orleans since [1788] and in which I still remain interested." In effect whatever cash Carondelet sent would appear as profits on tobacco sold, or as insurance payouts for goods that had been ruined. "I will deny receiving a dollar by Power and I will add that a balance is still due me. To circumstantiate this assertion I will cause the faithful Philip Nolan now with me to make an account in form with a letter of advice dated at New Orleans last autumn." Throughout the years ahead, Wilkinson would always follow this strategy to explain away the one incontrovertible proof of his relationship with Spain.

Rich once more and secure in his cover story, General James Wilkinson left Cincinnati in October with Nancy and their youngest son, James Biddle, and was rowed up the Ohio in the army's comfortable keelboat. At Pittsburgh, he met Andrew Ellicott, the commissioner appointed to survey the southern boundary of the United States under the terms of the San Lorenzo treaty, as he was traveling downstream with a large party of soldiers and scientists. Generously, Wilkinson handed over the boat for Ellicott's use.

An upright Quaker dedicated to astronomy, Ellicott was the antithesis of the volatile, spendthrift general. His reputation for painstaking, meticulous accuracy was unmatched. Computing his position by celestial observation, he had established the state borders of Pennsylvania, Virginia, New York, and the District of Columbia and laid out the future federal capital on the banks of the Potomac River. Yet this serious man was immediately seduced by Wilkinson's kindness and ease of manner. Ahead of Ellicott lay an epic journey around the borders of the United States that would last almost four years, but throughout that time, during which he stumbled upon the general's terrible secret, Ellicott never ceased to regard him as a friend.

At Pittsburgh, Nancy received the devastating news that fourteen-year-old John, their eldest son, had died of a fever. "I am proud of my little Sons," she had once written, "they are allowed to be very handsome & that I think the Smallest of there Perfections." But the eldest was her favorite, the one who most took after her, who "reads prettily" and "has an amazing turn to writing" and, like her, always wanted to be back in Philadelphia, away from the frontier. The loss could only have caused her utmost grief. It may well have contributed to Wilkinson's strangely downbeat message to Gayoso in November, ostensibly about the direction of Spanish policy but ending on an unmistakably low note: "Involved as I am in uncertainty, it is impossible to act with energy or even propriety."

If sadness had sapped his buoyant spirits, it did not alter his determination to bring down General Wayne. Demanding a court of inquiry, Wilkinson added one new charge to the old ones of negligence in the Fallen Timbers campaign. He now wanted Wayne to explain why he had hired Newman to smear him as a British spy. Although the accusations were petty, and Wayne was supported by both Washington and McHenry, Wilkinson's supporters in Congress, led by John Brown in the Senate and in the House by Jonathan Dayton, the Speaker, had enough political weight to force the War Department to cave in and authorize a court of inquiry into Wayne's behavior. In one of his last messages to McHenry, Wayne wrote bluntly, "The fact is my presence with the army is very inconvenient to the nefarious machinations of the Enemies of Government & may eventually prevent them from dissolving the Union."

He should have been beyond reach of his enemies. Aggressive, harsh, and insensitive he might be, but General Anthony Wayne had "done the Business." When he moved his headquarters to the recently evacuated British fort at Detroit on the Michigan peninsula in August, it marked the beginning of a new epoch in the expansion of the United States that emerged directly from the campaign he led in 1794. The northern frontier had been opened. The U.S. Public Lands Survey was moving through Ohio, transforming the territory into property that could be owned with clear title, unlike the chaos in Kentucky. Ahead lay the prairies.

The greatest test of George Washington's inclusive vision for his country would come when these mighty grasslands were occupied. Critically it depended upon the existence of General Wayne's victorious army. Neither settler nor Indian could have ignored that overwhelming force. Had it remained in existence, it might have made possible a coherent, organized westward expansion that did not sweep aside the rights of Native American owners. That at least was the president's dream.

Instead Wayne faced a double-edged onslaught, politically on the size of the Legion, and judicially on his generalship. The stress produced an exacerbated attack of the stabbing pains in his stomach that became so severe he was often unable to leave his army cot. As winter closed in, Wayne moved eastward, planning to take his headquarters back to Pittsburgh. In December he arrived at Presqu'isle, a harbor on Lake Erie, and there the stomach ulcer, if that is what it was, finally burst. His subordinates watched helplessly as he writhed in excruciating agony. "How long he can continue to suffer such torture is hard to say," wrote one on December 14, 1796, having seen his general convulsed all day by uncontrollable pain. But at two o'clock the following morning, death at last relieved Major General Anthony Wayne from all his torments.

For Washington and McHenry, the loss of Wayne was a blow in itself, but the timing made it worse. The army could not wait long for a new chief: orders had to be given, courts-martial appointed, detachments moved, officers transferred, the chain of command kept taut. To promote anyone other than the politically popular second-in-command during the last weeks before John Adams became president, when the existing administration was not so much a lame duck as a dead duck, would have been impossible. Whatever the executive's suspicions about Wilkinson's connections with Spain, he was the only possible candidate. Consequently, the highest post in the army devolved automatically onto James Wilkinson and was tacitly approved by President George Washington in February 1797.

In his last message to Congress as president, Washington made a final appeal on behalf of his Indian policy when he asked congressmen to exempt the cavalry from their bill to reduce the size of the army. "It is generally agreed that some cavalry, either militia or regular, are necessary," he pointed out, "and . . . the latter will be less expensive and more useful in maintaining the peace between the frontier settlers and the Indians." Three days later, on March 3, Congress ignored Washington's plea, cut the army by one third, and, by abolishing the rank of major general, confirmed that the brigadier general should be its "commander-in-chief."

In November 1796, General James Wilkinson had urged his Spanish handler, Baron Hector de Carondelet, to "point out with precision the object to be pursued, and, if attainable, you shall find my activity and exertions equal to your most sanguine expectations." Barely three months later, on March 4, 1797, he attended President John Adams's inauguration as a guest of honor, and commander in chief of the U.S. army.

The New Commander in Chief

Less than ten years had passed since James Wilkinson, land speculator and free trader, first traveled to New Orleans and declared that self-interest justified his transfer of loyalties to His Catholic Majesty. As a colonel, he found that the need for a spy's income reinforced his original decision. And so long as Anthony Wayne, the friend turned hated rival, was his superior, jealousy pointed him in the same direction. But as Brigadier General James Wilkinson, commander in chief of the U.S. army, it was less clear where his interests lay.

Wilkinson did not lie when he declared that his strength lay in military matters. His tactical sense was obvious in a brilliant analysis of the army's disposition that he drew up for Alexander Hamilton in 1798, and unlike Wayne, he had an insatiable hunger, matched only by Washington's, for the software of war—maps and intelligence about the territory in which he might need to fight. His theatrical temperament gave him an instinctive understanding of the mysterious effect that display and smartness have upon soldiers' morale. When applied to a peacetime army, starved of funds, lacking any obvious enemy, and usually split up into small, isolated garrisons, it was an invaluable insight. In place of anything more substantial, Wilkinson offered what he had in abundance, energy, personal warmth, and a sense of style, especially in his flamboyant, self-romanticizing portrayal of a general, to which most of his officers responded positively.

It was not a large stage on which he played—across the Atlantic, the French had thirteen armies totaling around eight hundred thousand men under arms, and Wilkinson's entire force was equivalent to about half a brigade in one of them. Knowing his ambition, his Spanish handlers could not believe that he would be satisfied with so small a part. Hector de Carondelet was genuinely bewildered when Wilkinson dispatched a formal notification to New Orleans in May 1797 that U.S. troops were being prepared to take over Spanish forts on the east bank of the Mississippi in accordance with the San Lorenzo treaty. Thomas Power was sent north to find out whether the general was still tempted by the wider horizons that Spain and the defection of Kentucky could provide.

"You will endeavour to discover, with your natural penetration, the General's dispositions," Carondelet wrote. "I doubt that a person of his character would prefer, through vanity, the advantage of commanding the army of the Atlantic states, to that of being the founder, the liberator in fine, the Washington of the Western states. His part is as brilliant as it is easy; all eyes are drawn toward him; he possesses the confidence of his fellow-citizens and of the Kentucky volunteers; at the slightest movement the people will name him the General of the new republic; his reputation will raise an army for him, and Spain, as well as France, will furnish him the means for paying for it." In a separate letter sent by Philip Nolan to Wilkinson himself, Carondelet reminded him of the land in Illinois that was to be his and promised that his pay would be doubled and he could "depend upon an annual bounty of four thousand dollars which shall be delivered to you at your order and to the person you may indicate."

Nevertheless, Wilkinson's state of mind might have been guessed from the manner in which Power was treated. There was no invitation to enjoy the freedom of "ingress and egress" to American forts. The general was inspecting the northerly fort of Mackinac when Power arrived in Detroit, but he immediately ordered the notorious Spanish courier confined to barracks until his return.

When they did meet in September, Power noted that "General Wilkinson received me very coolly." Undeterred, Power outlined an unlikely plot that began with Wilkinson seizing Fort Massac and calling for Kentucky's independence, at which point Spain and France would send him the artillery, weapons, and money needed to establish the new independent republic of the Mississippi. This was the ultimate goal of the Spanish Conspiracy, which had, as Power rightly stated, always been Wilkinson's idea. If he did not like the scenario, he might at least suggest some alternative. Instead, Power reported, the general summarily dismissed Carondelet's thinking as deluded—"chimerical" was his actual word—because the Treaty of San Lorenzo had given the western settlers all that they required.

In his account of their conversation, Power quoted him as saying, "The fermentation which had existed for four years was now subsided, &c.; that Spain had nothing else to do but to give complete effect to the treaty *which had overturned all his plans, and rendered useless the work of more than ten years.* And . . . he had, as he said, destroyed his cyphers and all his correspondence with our government, and that his duty and his honour did not permit him to continue it."

Quite clearly, as commander in chief Wilkinson had decided to give up his double life. He wanted no more communication with New Orleans, Power said, because he feared that "the secret of his connections with our government had been divulged through want of prudence on our part." Having brought his career as a spy to a close, the general ordered Power to be escorted off U.S. territory by Captain Shaumburgh and taken to the nearest Spanish fort.

The messenger resented not just this offhand treatment, but that he had been so totally misled. Before their meeting, he had assured Carondelet of Wilkinson's adherence to the conspiracy—"the ambitions and politics of this General are a certain guaranty to me that he will support our plans"—and having spoken to Sebastian, Power had been convinced that "the principal characters of the place are united to us by ambition and interest." Although Power attempted a feeble defense, suggesting that "the influence of General Wilkinson in Kentucky has become very limited," it was undeniable that without his support the conspiracy was over. "If [my mission] has not had a more happy issue," Power pleaded, "it ought not be attributed in any manner to indiscretion, or other deficiency, on my part, since it is evident that it sprung from a cause which no human penetration could foresee."

In fact the cause could easily have been predicted. Self-interest guided everything Wilkinson did. Once he had what he wanted, nothing would be allowed to jeopardize his enjoyment of it. Promotion had deprived Spain of its most useful spy.

Wilkinson's altered outlook was apparent in other, less obvious ways. In freezing winter temperatures, the new commander in chief had immediately undertaken a whirlwind tour of inspection, west to Fort Wayne and south to Fort Washington, then north along the line of forts that Wayne and he had built. The tide of settlement promoted by Wayne's Greeneville Treaty had already moved farther west, and Wilkinson recommended closing all these posts and sending their garrisons south to strengthen the force being assembled in Fort Washington to take over the Spanish forts. Its command he assigned to one of his favorite young officers, Captain Isaac Guion. In the early summer of 1797, when Power had hoped to meet him, the general hurried north again, to Detroit, then beyond to the farthermost post of all, Michilimackinac, usually contracted to Mackinac, on the northern shores of the Michigan peninsula. In this respect at least, James Wilkinson showed his desire to be a model commander in chief.

IN MARCH 1797, at the time of Wilkinson's appointment, the secretary of war, James McHenry, gave direction to Wilkinson's galvanizing energy. In a lengthy memorandum, akin to that prepared by Anthony Wayne a year earlier, McHenry laid down the priorities that the general was to observe— saving money, maintaining discipline, and keeping peace with the Indians. One typical passage on economizing required him to order garrison commanders to have damaged weapons repaired within the fort, but in doing so "it is not deemed expedient to incur any expense." But the officebound, regulation-minded McHenry had no conception of what it took to maintain order and morale among young soldiers marooned for months within their wooden stockades. Even Thomas Power had a better idea after ten days confined to the barracks in Fort Detroit.

"There is strict discipline observed in the army," he told Carondelet. "The soldiers are almost all youths from 16 to 26 years of age; they go through some military [drill] with sufficient precision. With respect to the officers, from the lowest to the highest (excepting very few) they are deficient of those qualities which adorn a good officer except fierceness, and are overwhelmed in ignorance and in the most base vice."

Spanish officers cultivated the manners of the higher classes because the military hierarchy faithfully reflected the gradations of an aristocratic society. No such pattern existed for U.S. officers—Colonel John Hamtramck was the son of a Quebec barber and wigmaker, for example, and the family of Colonel David Strong were Connecticut farmers. No military academy existed to give officers a grounding in their trade—training came from being attached to a company as a cadet; and there was little continuity of service to build a military tradition because fluctuations in the size of the army forced so many officers to leave the service—more than 60 percent of those commissioned in the 1780s had gone by 1795. Finally, American officers had to cope with the particular challenge of maintaining a command structure in an increasingly egalitarian society. This contradiction fascinated British observers.

"In fact the American peasant, though a brave and hardy man, and expert in the use of the rifle and musket, is naturally the worst soldier in the world as regards obedience and discipline," a British officer, Charles Murray, commented loftily in the 1790s. "He has been brought up to believe himself equal to the officers who command him, and never forgets that when his three years of enlistment are over, he will again be their equal."

An officer's right to command rested ultimately on the Articles of War, which required obedience to the orders of a superior, but in most situations the critical factor was an individual's leadership ability. The fierceness that Power noted, or at least a capacity to impose one's will, was a necessity. In battle, as Ebenezer Denny had dramatically described at St. Clair's rout, and Wayne's Legion proved at Fallen Timbers, ferocious officers could rely on their men to follow their lead. But in peacetime, when about two thousand men were scattered between forty-one military outposts—an average of roughly fifty men at each—other qualities were needed.

In a well-run garrison, much of what Denny himself called "the noise and bustle of military life" came from officers and noncommissioned officers enforcing an endless schedule of roll calls and fatigue duties at the tops of their voices backed by the beat of a drum. Desertion rates rising to 20 percent annually demonstrated how difficult it was to maintain discipline and a viable army. Nevertheless, more than half of those soldiers who completed their three-year enlistment signed on again, suggesting that their officers did get it mostly right.

For private soldiers, the rewards came to between four and five dollars a month with shelter, food, and two uniforms a year provided free. To young men unable to find more rewarding work, this was certainly an inducement. So, too, was the prospect of adventure, and the opportunity to be on the frontier, where a discharged soldier, or a deserter, could find cheap land, and a skillful marksman could live from hunting and selling furs. But many also enlisted while drunk and, as a later secretary of war admitted, "awoke from their stupor with abhorrence, anxious only to devise means how they are to escape from their dread condition."

To reduce the chances of desertion, the soldiers were subjected to four muster calls a day, the first at dawn and the last an hour after retreat or nightfall. In between, they were repeatedly drilled, sent on work parties to repair walls or dig entrenchments, and occasionally detached as escorts to guard surveyors or Indian agents operating in dangerous territory. Liquor dulled the monotony, starting with the distribution at daybreak of the daily four-ounce ration of rum or whiskey, and continuing with whatever could be bought from the garrison sutler, who had a store of tobacco, soap, and above all spirits for any soldier with enough credit to pay for them. And, despite repeated calls to garrison commanders to stamp out "drunkenness, desertion and licentiousness," camp prostitutes, recruited from the washer-women authorized to be in camp, or from Native Americans, provided the one other comfort that made a soldier's life tolerable.

IN DEALING WITH CHALLENGES to good discipline, drama was James Wilkinson's favored style. Arriving in Detroit in June 1797, he declared that the fort "presents a frightful picture to the scientific soldier; ignorance & licentiousness have been fostered, while intelligence and virtue have been persecuted & exiled." To punish William Mitchell and his girlfriend, Lydia Connor, for selling liquor illegally, he had them marched out of town with bottles hanging from their necks accompanied by the garrison band play-ing "The Rogues' March." A deserter, sentenced to hang on the Fourth of July, was pardoned at the last moment, but ordered to kneel before the flag grasping it with his right hand and, with his left uplifted, "to renew the oath of fidelity" before being ejected from the camp.

Back in his headquarters in Pittsburgh, Wilkinson discovered that a high proportion of men in one company had been arrested for "drunkenness and debauchery." As punishment, he ordered the entire company to be confined to barracks, with doubled sentries changed every hour and the guardhouse turned out every fifteen minutes day and night so that no one could sleep or rest, and then, to McHenry's dismay, publicized their shame by getting the *Pittsburgh Gazette* to run a story naming the guilty and their punishment.

Whether his methods had any effect on military morals is doubtful—as Rudyard Kipling put it, single men in barracks don't grow into plaster saints—but they reduced the toll of flogging and execution that Wayne had exacted. Private soldiers had additional reason to be grateful when he in-tervened on their behalf by prohibiting their superiors from using them "as hunters, fishermen, hostlers, Gardeners, fatigue men, scullions, etc. at the expense of the meritorious soldier and to the great injury and disgrace of the service." At a time when morale was suffering from Congress's savage cuts, Wilkinson's passion about good soldiering won him friends and per-sonal loyalty among a widening circle of officers.

ABANDONING ESPIONAGE CREATED its own dangers, above all the risk of ex-posure by former paymasters. Wilkinson's prime concern was Carondelet, who had invested so much in the general's participation in the conspiracy. In his meeting with Power, the general had referred to the possibility that their past connection might be made public and promised that Carondelet "ought not to be apprehensive of his abusing the confidence which [Carondelet] had placed in him."

The general was far more at risk than the governor, however, and in a somewhat incoherent sentence apparently taken from notes, Power recorded Wilkinson's explanation why Carondelet, too, should keep silent. When Spain eventually handed over the territory of Natchez, "[the United States] might perhaps name [Wilkinson] Governor of it, and then he would not want opportunities to take more effectual measures to comply with his political projects." In other words, as governor of Natchez Wilkinson might once more become an agent, so long as his past was kept a secret.

It was, however, a more immediate consideration that kept both Carondelet and Gayoso silent. At any moment, Wilkinson could have enforced the terms of the San Lorenzo treaty. Spain had undertaken to open the Mississippi to trade. In March 1797, James McHenry issued Wilkinson direct instructions to occupy the Spanish forts of Chickasaw Bluffs, Walnut Hills, and Natchez. Captain Isaac Guion was ready at the head of four hundred men. Captured documents showed that Spanish fort commanders were not expected to prevent the passage of American troops. Nevertheless, Guion did not enter Natchez until the last days of December.

There were reasons. At first, Gayoso, as governor of Natchez, insisted on detailed negotiations about how the evacuation should be arranged. Then in the summer he suspended the handover altogether, alleging the threat of a British invasion from Canada that would put Louisiana in peril. Since Wilkinson, like the other secessionists, had been told by Carondelet "that his Catholic Majesty *will not carry the above mentioned treaty into execution*," he might have guessed that these were delaying tactics. Instead, he ordered Guion not to approach any of the Spanish forts without permission. Guion duly halted at Chickasaw Bluffs and waited for permission. When McHenry demanded to know why Guion had not moved, the general deliberately invented evidence to support Gayoso's fears of a British invasion.

In June 1797, while Wilkinson was in Detroit, he suddenly discovered that a joint British and Indian attack on the fort was so imminent that he had to introduce martial law "for the safety of the troops against a coup." McHenry uselessly protested that "the danger from the savages or invasion is not very pressing and evident" as Wilkinson loudly annouced that the courts were suspended, and he had taken executive power until the emergency was over.

Secretary of State Timothy Pickering, who knew Wilkinson from the campaign against Wayne, was convinced that no threat existed. In August

1797 he warned Winthrop Sargent, secretary of the Northwest Territory, "that there is too much ground to think that we have *internal* enemies disposed to favor the view of the French and Spanish—perhaps to detach the whole western country from the United States." In case Sargent could not guess whom this pointed to, Pickering added, "Such a conspiracy must have conspicuous men for leaders, and such demands the closest observation."

The presence of Andrew Ellicott in Natchez all this time made Wilkinson's failure to move still more inexplicable. Given responsibility for running the southern boundary of the United States, Ellicott had simply ignored all attempts to stop him on the river. To Gayoso's irritation, he had landed at Natchez in February 1797, marched his bodyguard up the bluff above the river, and planted his tent with the Union flag within sight of the fort. An angry demand that he haul down the Stars and Stripes "met with a positive refusal," Ellicott later recalled, "and the flag wore out upon its staff."

Amid the swirling confusion of loyalties and motives, Ellicott's resolution was as solid as his science. Using his expertise as an astronomer, he made celestial observations that established beyond doubt that Natchez lay half a degree north of the thirty-first parallel marking the frontier agreed to by the San Lorenzo treaty. The town was American and the Spanish had no legal right to remain there, or in any of the other forts farther north.

Long before the fabric of his flag had unraveled, Ellicott discovered just how weak Gayoso's position really was. To defend all of Louisiania and the entire length of the Mississippi, Spain had two regiments of regular soldiers, and between Illinois and Mobile there were no more than 5,440 militia, insignificant beside the 80,000 citizen-soldiers ready "to march at a moment's notice" that the U.S. president was authorized to raise under the 1794 Militia Act. Behind the vast panoply of Spanish imperial power lurked a reality as puny as the Wizard of Oz.

Much of this information came from the magnetic, twenty-six-year-old Philip Nolan, who joined Ellicott on his way down the Mississippi. Characteristic of the dazzling effect Nolan had on all who met him was that Ellicott should have believed he was "strongly attached to the interest and welfare of our country," while the young man was in fact the bearer of a letter from Wilkinson to Gayoso that read, "Nolan . . . is a child of my own raising, true to his profession, and firm in his attachments to Spain. I consider him a powerful instrument in *our* hand should occasion offer. I will answer for his conduct."

Despite the melodrama in Detroit, the pressure to move troops south continued to grow during the summer and fall of 1797. Knowing the frailty of the Spanish defenses and their intention to ignore the treaty, Ellicott begged both Wilkinson and Guion to send forces downriver to secure control of Natchez. In their absence, the town and surrounding district threatened to break up in disorder as competing factions struggled to take over. Despite his lack of official status, Ellicott steered the volatile inhabitants away from violence and, in July, underlined Spain's weakness by persuading the most influential planters to set up a de facto government on behalf of the United States that took over administration of the district.

In September, Wilkinson blandly told Ellicott, "You have a warm place in my affections . . . and I regret the obstacles you have experienced to the execution of your commission." But, far from promising support, Wilkinson warned that in the opinion of influential senators Ellicott had "been too stern and peremptory" with the Spanish. The official army position, as Guion informed Ellicott from Chickasaw Bluffs, was that no troops would be moved farther south without direct orders from the general or permission from Gayoso. The general's attitude was made abundantly clear that summer when he withdrew three companies from a regiment in Tennessee under the command of a fire-eating martinet, Colonel Thomas Butler, who was aggressively protecting farmers against the threat of Indian and Spanish attack.

In exasperation, McHenry tried to counter the effect of the general's tactics. He wrote directly to Butler, suggesting that he should keep all his men in Tennessee, then to Guion insisting that he move on to Natchez, and finally to Wilkinson demanding that he tell Guion not to let himself be distracted by "any frivolous pretences which may be presented to him on his passage." McHenry's attempt to bypass a general's orders provoked a blistering response. Wilkinson accused McHenry of unwarranted interference by issuing orders "to my subordinates immediately under my eye," by breaking "the chain of dependence that exists from the ranks to the chief in immediate command," and by taking action that "could be construed into a want of confidence in my command." Wrong-footed, McHenry offered an apology, but Wilkinson refused to be mollified. The bullying tone of his letters showed who held the upper hand.

WILKINSON NEVER DOUBTED his hold over the army. What he feared was the sort of political ambush he had mounted against Wayne. Several members of Adams's Federalist administration, including Secretary of State Timothy Pickering, regarded him with suspicion, not only for his Spanish connection, but as "a Jacobin" and a Republican. In Congress, Humphrey Marshall had finally proved his right to be admitted as Kentucky's junior senator and was thirsting for vengeance. These enemies knew where the general was most vulnerable, and Wilkinson had good cause to fear the leakiness of Spanish security, especially the confidence placed by Carondelet and Gayoso in the thin-skinned Thomas Power.

Infuriated by the way the general had treated him, Power had in fact approached Daniel Clark Jr., a well-known New Orleans merchant, in October 1797 with damaging information. The Clark family and Wilkinson went back a long way. Clark's Irish-born uncle, also Daniel, acted as Wilkinson's New Orleans agent in his first trading scheme in 1787, and both uncle and nephew had represented him in the city until Nolan came south in 1791. In the New Orleans commercial community, the Clarks were recognized as among the city's most secretive and successful merchants, and in 1795 when the uncle retired to live in Natchez, Daniel Clark Jr. took over the business—and its secrets.

Although a Spanish citizen, Clark had already decided to switch loyalties from Spain to the United States when Power contacted him and was lobbying Ellicott to be made American consul in New Orleans. After consulting his uncle, Clark decided to demonstrate his newfound loyalty to the United States by bringing Power with him to tell Ellicott about the general's behavior.

In a dispatch sent to Pickering on November 14, 1797, Ellicott described how Power had traveled upriver to confer with members of the conspiracy and with "Gen. Wilkinson at Cincinnati . . . The first object of these plotters is to detach the States of Kentucky and Tenesee [sic] from the union and place them under the protection of Spain." Ellicott told Pickering about the payments to the conspirators and the use of the pocket dictionary as a key to their cipher. His dispatch also carried the outline of another, larger plan, presumably taken from the general's own speculations, about the expedition he would lead into Mexico once the Mississippi republic was established, and the "new empire" he intended to carve out there.

This information should have destroyed Wilkinson's career. That it had the opposite effect of strengthening his position was due to the general's brilliant countermove. With the cool calculation that contrasted so surprisingly with his histrionic behavior, Wilkinson forged a personal link with the unlikeliest of allies, President John Adams.

His means was Little Turtle. Discovering a sudden enthusiasm for Native American ways, Wilkinson sent the Miami chief in late December to meet the president so that he could plead for what was essentially Washington's old inclusive policy toward the Indians. "Could I be made instrumental in any way to ameliorate the condition of these people," the general wrote in an accompanying letter, "and to lay the foundation of their permanent prosperity, it would be more acceptable to me than the most distinguished triumph of arms."

Adams was delighted both by the chief and by the general's desire to see what was still Federalist policy carried out in the Northwest Territory. "He is certainly a remarkable man," the president told Wilkinson. "We shall endeavor to make him happy here and contented after his return. I thank you for introducing him to me and for the infomation you have given me concerning him."

Wilkinson's real purpose, however, appeared in the letter that he gave the chief to present to Adams. In it, the commander in chief personally informed the president about the rumors that he was being paid by Spain. "I most sincerely wish an inquiry into my conduct military and political. I know, sir, that a sinister connection with Spain is slanderously imputed to me . . . but conscious of my innocence I court inquiry to obtain an opportunity of vindication, which I have amply in my power."

Adopting the excuse originally prepared for Washington, he explained away the money from New Orleans as payment for tobacco sales or insurance losses. He reminded the president of a conversation at his inauguration when, as a patriot, Wilkinson had sworn he would employ any means in defense of the United States against British attack. He ended with the superb declaration "It is the invisibility of my enemies only which I fear; for while I dare the open assault, I dread the secret stab."

Adams habitually relied more on his solitary judgment than the advice of his colleagues—a permanent cause of dissension in his administration— and on this occasion, too, he dismissed the doubts of leading members of his cabinet. In his reply he told the general that he had heard many such allegations, especially that Wilkinson was an officer in the Spanish army— "scarcely any man arrives from [the Mississippi] who does not bring the report along with him," Adams asserted—but that he believed them to be motivated by malice and jealousy. "I esteem your talents, I respect your services and feel an attachment to your person," he wrote in February 1798. "What measures you may think fit to take to silence the villainous rumours and clamours of your connections with Spain and France I know not; but no violent or military ones will do any good. I shall give no countenance to any imputations unless accusations should come & then you will have room to justify yourself. But I assure you I do not expect that any charge will be seriously made."

It was an extraordinary endorsement. Effectively it nullified both Elli-cott's warning and any other that might be made to the Adams administra-tion. Yet in reality the president had little room for maneuver. The federal government was still too new to be sure of its power. The previous sum-mer, Senator William Blount of Tennessee had been discovered plotting with the British to seize New Orleans and the Mississippi Valley, but despite the near unanimous vote of his fellow senators that he was guilty of "a high misdemeanour inconsistent with public trust and duty," he had simply re-turned to Tennessee and the U.S. government proved powerless to bring him to trial. Any attempt to remove the efficient, popular Wilkinson might also fail and thereby risk causing a mutiny. Speculating some years later on how the head of the army could be removed in such a situation, Adams posed the question that must have occurred to him in 1797: "How is the subordination of the military to the civil power to be supported?"

WITH ADAMS'S LETTER IN HIS FILES, Wilkinson became virtually impreg-nable to a Federalist ambush. He reveled in his new security. In October 1797, he had moved the army's headquarters to Pittsburgh, conveniently located between the western states and the federal government. Although Pittsburgh was no Philadelphia, what had been a frontier settlement when Wilkinson first descended the Ohio was now "a thriving town containing about 200 houses, fifty of which are brick and Fram'd, & the remainder Log." On the army's budget, he transformed a large frame house on the east side of town into an imposing dwelling fit for a commander in chief. "The surrounding grounds were handsomely laid out, planted, and ornamented by General Wilkinson," an English traveler noted in 1807, "and considering the smallness of the field he had to work on, [they] show much taste and are an ornament to the eastern and principal approach to the town."

The setting was comfortable enough to satisfy the demanding Nancy, and Wilkinson's credit had so improved that in July he could tell the army pay-master "that provisions will always be made at Headquarters under whatever events to honor Mrs Wilkinson's drafts at sight." A draft was in effect a check: one payable at sight, rather than a month or year later, as good as cash, and an unmistakable sign of wealth. "I prefer this plan," he assured Samuel Hodgdon, now in charge of military finances, with the confidence of a man whose chaotic accounts were temporarily in order, "because it enables her to appropriate [money] to her expenditure with precision."

To reach this satisfactory position, it seems clear that Wilkinson had be-gun to replace his pay as a spy by taking rake-offs from contractors who wanted to open trading stores in Indian territory or close to military bar-racks. One of the first was the Canadian company of Leith, Shepherd & Duff, which paid a fee in 1797 for the privilege of operating among the Chippewa near Detroit, but the practice soon became so habitual that the general thought nothing of writing to a food company hoping to land an army contract "to apprise you of my ready disposition *to enter into your Ser-vice & of my determination to do it well for you.*"

Cushioned by these extracurricular payments and by the use of army resources, such as the military wagons that carried their furniture and wine from the East Coast, the entire family could live together in comfort for the first time since James Wilkinson left to make a fortune in Kentucky. "Your dear Sister and our Sons are near me in good health," he wrote his brother-in-law Owen Biddle in December 1797. "My Ann unusually hearty. We are comfortably fixed and I suppose shall spend the winter here."

Yet security was impossible for a double agent as deeply involved as Wilkinson. Almost as he wrote, Gayoso received word from Madrid that Captain Isaac Guion's force could at last be allowed into Natchez. An as-tounded Ellicott described to Pickering how, immediately after Guion's ar-rival, the captain burst into a meeting of the American planters' committee that administered Natchez, demanding to know "by what authority they met, that it was improper, and by G-d he would dissolve them the next day—he knew better than to be made a cypher of and by G-d he would rule the district with a rod of iron . . . after a debate of some length, he took his leave very politely saying 'you may all kiss my a★se.'"

Ellicott may have been right to blame Guion's behavior on drink, but the captain was acting on orders. Behind his rudeness to Americans lay the general's fear of giving offense to Spaniards. Once Gayoso was ready to evacuate the forts along the Mississippi, the commander in chief of the U.S. army lost his insurance policy against betrayal. Even if Gayoso kept silent, Wilkinson could be sure that the citizens of Natchez would not.

In the spring of 1798, he sent an urgent coded message to Gayoso, newly promoted to be govenor of Louisiana in place of the openhanded Caron-delet: "Observed everywhere, I dare not communicate with you, nor should you try to do so with me; Marshall has attacked my honor and fi-delity. You should not trust the western people, because some are traitors. Fortify your frontiers well. While I remain as at present all is safe. Have buried my cipher, but I will recover it. You have many spies in your coun-try. Do not mention me nor write my name, I implore you in the name of God and our friendship."

The key phrase was "I will recover it." The hint that he might return to spying was thrown in to give Gayoso a renewed interest in keeping his secret. Everything that Wilkinson did over the next three years was conditioned by the need to persuade the Spanish authorities that as an agent he was a sleeper rather than retired.

ELLICOTT'S DISCOVERY

IN AUGUST 1798, Brigadier General Wilkinson himself took four hundred men in a convoy of thirty boats down the muddy current of the Mississippi. They floated past Natchez, to the last curve in the river before it cut through the thirty-first parallel. At a point where the ground rose to a small hill above the east bank, known locally as Loftus Heights, the general ordered several acres of canebrake and prickly thorn to be cleared for the construction of a fort. In honor of his unexpected benefactor, he named it Fort Adams. A year earlier, Fort Massac, five hundred miles to the north, had marked the extent of U.S. power. Now New Orleans lay tantalizingly close.

That dramatic change owed nothing to the efforts of the U.S. army under its commander in chief, but much to Andrew Ellicott's success in guiding American loyalties toward independence in the face of Gayoso's refusal to implement the treaty. When he saw the Spanish troops begin to evacuate the Natchez fort in February 1798, Ellicott wrote in understandable triumph to his wife, Sally, "My Love,—I have at length worried the Spaniards out." By the time Wilkinson made his late arrival, Winthrop Sargent, former secretary of the Northwest Territory, had been installed as governor of Natchez, and Ellicott was deep in the wilderness east of the Mississippi cutting a trail through the matted undergrowth along the line of the thirty-first parallel with a team of American and Spanish astronomers, surveyors, and axmen.

In October, the general visited the two boundary commissioners, Ellicott and Spain's Esteban Minor, in their camp. His motives caused deep suspicion on both sides. Ostensibly the purpose was to join Sargent and Ellicott in a conference to choose who should be involved in the government of the future Mississippi Territory. The discussions were dominated by Wilkinson, partly because Sargent was ill, but mostly because Ellicott felt himself to be under an obligation to the general.

In steamy heat and attacked by clouds of gnats and mosquitoes, the scientist's unyielding determination to make exact astronomical measurements had driven the leading surveyor, Thomas Freeman, and the head of the military detachment, Lieutenant John McLary, to outright mutiny. As the U.S. boundary commissioner, Ellicott had the authority to suspend Freeman, but to deal with McLary, a military appointee, he needed Wilkinson's intervention. Before the meeting at the camp, Ellicott asked the general for help and received a heartwarming reply: "My friend, you are warranted in drawing upon my confidence and my friendship at your discretion . . . Your refractory subaltern shall be relieved and his successor shall be taught how to respect a national Minister."

As he later admitted, Ellicott had already begun to discount the importance of the information he had sent Pickering, and it was certainly outweighed by the value of such prompt assistance. At the meeting, he supported Wilkinson in the appointment of judges and other federal officials. He also gladly promised to comply with the general's private request for sketch maps of the terrain that would show "the interesting Roads, and practicable points of approach from below with such remarks on the face of the country as may assist a military man in his conceptions and intelligence of the theatre before him." Then, freed of his two troublemakers, Ellicott returned to his scientific odyssey through the unmapped wilderness.

At the very end of October, Wilkinson spent several days in discussions at Loftus Heights with Daniel Clark Jr., who had traveled up from New Orleans to see him. On Ellicott's recommendation, Clark had been appointed U.S. consul in New Orleans. When the evacuation of Natchez took place, Clark formally applied to become a citizen of the United States. Less formally, he developed a plan with his uncle for his future country to seize New Orleans by force without further delay. They feared that the power of the gigantic French armies terrorizing Europe would be used to force its frail ally to hand over New Orleans and all Louisiana. Clark's journey to see Wilkinson was undertaken to persuade him join in a preemptive strike before the formidable French took control.

Wilkinson pretended to be enthusiastic about the plan for seizing New Orleans but claimed that the government's policy of avoiding war with Spain prevented him from taking any action. "I would to heaven I could procure an order for the operation you wish," he assured Clark senior in a letter from Fort Adams. "I would hazard my fame and fortune without much hesitation to precipitate an event which is to happen." In reality, he could not afford to risk Gayoso's enmity, and there was never the slightest chance that he would undertake any action against Spanish forces.

Suspicious about Wilkinson's real motives, Clark may have asked whether the general was still being paid by Gayoso, because it is equally clear that Wilkinson informed Clark, truthfully, that since the western settlers had achieved their goal with the opening of the Mississippi, the Spanish Conspiracy was at an end. From Fort Adams, Clark wrote his uncle that he believed this "assurance that the disgraceful connexion should be broken off." On November 4, the young man left the fort having failed to achieve his object. The meeting might have been utterly inconsequential, except that out of it grew a campaign to expose Wilkinson that proved so damaging, his past as a paid agent of Spain came in the end to haunt him like Banquo's ghost.

THE FIRST STEP WAS TAKEN, inadvertently, by the guileless Andrew Ellicott. On November 8, Ellicott reached Darling's Creek, a tributary of the Pearl River, and was preparing a map of the area that Wilkinson had requested. Then, as he put it in his journal, "by a very extraordinary accident, a letter from the Governor General [Gayoso] on its way to a confidential officer in the Spanish service [Power] fell into my hands for a few hours." In fact what he had was Power's copy of the letter. Ellicott's refusal to explain how it came into his hands suggests it was stolen and had to be returned before the loss was discovered. Only Clark could have engineered the theft of the letter, and its swift conveyance to Ellicott. His motives can be deduced from its contents.

Gayoso's letter was written in response to the news of Wilkinson's visit to the commissioners' camp. This, the governor suggested, had to be seen in relation to the Spanish Conspiracy, and the fears of those involved that their participation might be exposed by publication of their letters. "I wonder you could not see the design of General Wilkinson's visit to Mr Ellicott's and Mr Minor's camp," Gayoso explained to Power. "It was to fall upon some measures to obtain his papers. They are all safe and never will be made use of against him if he conducts himself with propriety. In fact the originals are at the court [in Madrid], the copies only are here."

To Clark, the most important item was the evidence of blackmail—it explained Wilkinson's refusal to participate in his projected attack on New

Orleans—but the implications were different for Ellicott. He saw in the letter "unequivocal proof" of the conspiracy, and as he later explained, this document more than any other evidence convinced him that Wilkinson must have been involved in a plot "calculated to injure the United States." He promptly sent Pickering another long and deeply ciphered dispatch with this fresh indication of the general's treachery. Yet even then, he felt compelled to discover whether there might not be some other, more innocent explanation.

With the folly of the truly innocent, he wrote Wilkinson on December 16, 1798, "I have seen a letter of Mr. Power's, in his own hand writing, dated the 23d ultimo, in which your name is mentioned in a manner, that astonished me; I dare not commit any part of it to paper, but if I should ever have the pleasure of another interview with you, I will communicate the substance of it under the injunction of secrecy. If the design of it, has been to injure you in my opinion, it has failed in its effect, for in the most material point I am confident it is false."

However friendly the tone of the Quaker's letter, the general could not afford to let someone with Ellicott's moral authority possess such damning knowledge. Since denial was impossible, Wilkinson set about destroying Ellicott's reputation. From friends in Natchez, the astronomer learned that Wilkinson and Thomas Freeman had become companions and were intent on smearing his name. The least harmful allegation they circulated was that he had been in the pay of Spain, but what almost broke Ellicott's heart was the story that he and his son, Andy, a surveyor on the boundary-marking team, had, as Freeman put it, "a beastly, criminal, and disgraceful intercourse" with their washerwoman, Betsy. "It was said, and generally believed," Freeman declared, "that that extraordinary trio, father, son, and washerwoman, slept in the same bed, at the same time—I did not see, but I believed it. I was even pressed myself by the old sinner, Ellicott, to take part of his bed with his washerwoman and himself, for the night."

A more wounding charge could hardly have been made against someone with Ellicott's grave, Quaker background, undeviating scientific integrity, and utter devotion to his wife, Sally, who bore him thirteen children and all her life moved him to such endearments as "My darling," "My love," and "Dearest of all earthly beings."

The episode showed how dangerous it was to be a threat, however inadvertent, to Wilkinson. It also demonstrated how armored against exposure the general had become. In his next message, Pickering sharply reprimanded Ellicott for passing on malicious allegations and refused to hear any more. Consequently the boundary commissioner said nothing about his encounter some months later with Captain Tomás Portell, the former commandant of New Madrid. Having supervised the packing of $9,640 into sugar and coffee barrels for Wilkinson, Portell was able to give the shaken commissioner firsthand testimony that the money was earned by spying, and not, as the general insisted, by trade.

Another year passed before Andrew Ellicott returned from the wilderness. By the time he reached his home in Philadelphia, he was a changed man, physically run-down, as he admitted, and psychologically scarred. But he was no less determined to see General Wilkinson uncovered as a Spanish spy.

THE FEDERALIST FAVORITE

B Y THE END OF 1798, it seemed that no one, whether Federalist or Republican, American or Spaniard, wanted to hear anything bad against Wilkinson. Even the French were prepared to think well of him as they began to exert pressure on Spain to hand over Louisiana. In Paris, Joseph de Pontalba, former citizen of New Orleans and self-appointed expert on the Spanish colony, recommended the general's immediate recruitment. "Four times from 1786 to 1792, preparations were made in Kentucky and Cumberland to attack Louisiana," Pontalba recklessly declared in his memorandum to Napoléon, "and every time this same individual caused them to fail through his influence over his countrymen. I make these facts known to show that France must not neglect to enlist this individual in her service."

Had Napoléon's plans to land an army of forty thousand troops in Louisiana been realized, Wilkinson might have received such an approach. But the threat of French hostilities produced for him an offer that flattered his vanity beyond anything that Napoléon might have offered.

In April 1798, the growing arrogance of France's military government provoked a crisis in its dealings with the United States. The flashpoint was the diplomatic insult, known as the XYZ affair, when three representatives of Foreign Secretary Talleyrand demanded a bribe of fifty thousand pounds sterling, approximately $150,000, before the U.S. ambassadors could present their credentials. The news provoked an outraged Congress to authorize a dramatic increase in the army. In a first installment, twelve regiments, each of one thousand men, were to be raised to create what was called the New Army, and this was followed by further increases until Congress had approved a force of more than forty thousand men. In overall command was George Washington, newly promoted to lieutenant general, with two major generals, Alexander Hamilton and Charles Cotesworth Pinckney, as operational commanders, all superseding Wilkinson in seniority. Yet astonishingly he did not appear to resent his demotion.

That George Washington had been placed in supreme command of the New Army made the loss easier to bear, but it was Alexander Hamilton, Washington's deputy, who found the key to Wilkinson's volatile loyalties.

As early as February 1799, when the recruits began to come in, Hamilton had promised Wilkinson that he wanted their relationship to result in "great mutual satisfaction." When Wilkinson replied offering his full support, Hamilton suggested to Washington, "It strikes me forcibly that it be right and expedient to advance this gentlemen to the grade of major general." Hamilton had only sporadically met Wilkinson since the Conway cabal, but he clearly understood Wilkinson's temperament. "I am aware that some doubts have been entertained of him," Hamilton acknowledged, "and that his character, on certain sides, gives room for doubt. Yet he is at present in the service; is a man of more than ordinary talent, of courage and enterprise . . . and will naturally find his interest as an ambitious man in deserving the favour of the government; while he will be apt to become disgusted if neglected, and through disgust may be rendered really what he is now only suspected to be." On June 25, George Washington agreed to recommend to the president "promoting Brigadier Wilkinson to the Rank of Maj[o]r General." Conspicuously he said nothing about the brigadier's abilities, only that "it would feed his ambition, soothe his vanity, and by arresting discontent, produce the good effect you contemplate."

Their reading of his character showed insight, and Wilkinson responded to the encouragement as they had hoped. But what Washington and Hamilton could not imagine was how deeply ingrained his double life had become. In a curious way, it freed him from any sense of social obligation. His ambition might be fed and his vanity soothed, but the only real constraints that affected him were a desire to be popular and a fear of being found out. With one notable exception, he never seems to have felt that he was betraying anyone, merely that he was seizing an opportunity.

THE EXCEPTION WAS HIS WIFE. Sensitive, gentle, and, in middle age, possibly depressive, Nancy had a neediness that Wilkinson had to meet. Whether from love, or an egocentric desire not to let her down, he always struggled to fulfill her wants. Hamilton's request that he come to Philadelphia in early 1799 to advise on the disposition of the New Army consequently threw Wilkinson into a dilemma. It was a necessary step toward promotion, but Nancy became distraught at the prospect of being left alone in Natchez. "The anxiety of my wife at the idea of our separation, gives us both agony, and so sensibly affects her whole frame, that I shall not be able to tear myself from her as soon as I expected," Wilkinson confided to Gayoso in May.

She had arrived from Pittsburgh just a few months earlier, and her reluctance to return to a frontier society could be guessed from a line in one of Wilkinson's letters to Sargent begging him to write her with some words "commendatory of the climate and society [of Natchez]." Coached by her popular, outgoing husband, she had brought with her suitable gifts to offer southern society, including "a few cranberries, a northern berry valuable for its rarity in this quarter and its fine aromatic flavor when properly prepared," for Gayoso's American wife, Margaret.

During those months an unmistakable intimacy grew up between the two families, despite the barbed relations between the husbands. The Wilkinsons rented Gayoso's exquisite estate of Concordia, perched high above the Mississippi, and they planned for their children to exchange visits. Gayoso might exert some discreet blackmail on Wilkinson, and Wilkinson might complain of his landlord, "The Mingo asks too much for his dirty acres," but when Nancy pleaded to be allowed to accompany her husband back to Pennsylvania, Wilkinson had no hesitation in enlisting Gayoso's help: "Would you take the trouble to point out the dangers and the incommodations of the voyage? It would have great weight with my Ann, and will oblige me, but the thing must appear like a suggestion of your own—you perceive I treat you with the intimacy and unreserve of a Brother."

Aside from the habitual distaste for honesty, his tendency to enlist others in dealing with his wife does suggest a tenderness toward her that no one else evoked. It even softened his feelings toward Ellicott. As he was about to sail from New Orleans, he wrote the boundary commissioner, "I left Mrs. Wilkinson with our friend Walker at Concord House, in tolerable health but deep affliction. My own solicitude exceeds anything I have before experienced on Her account and my absence will be shortened by every means in my power. I shall find pleasure in reporting your progress to the President, and rendering you any service in my power."

———————————

James Wilkinson in 1797, by Charles Willson Peale.

Benedict Arnold and Horatio Gates, Continental Army generals
on whose staff Wilkinson served during the American Revolution.

General Anthony Wayne, whom Wilkinson replaced as
commander in chief of the U.S. Army.

Ann Biddle Wilkinson, beloved wife. (Courtesy of
the Historical Society of Frederick County, Maryland)

The four presidents Wilkinson served as commander in chief of the army: George Washington, John Adams, Thomas Jefferson, James Madison.

Secretaries of war Henry Knox and Henry Dearborn.

Aaron Burr.

William Claiborne, first governor of Louisiana.

Andrew Ellicott, master surveyor. (Courtesy of the
Pennsylvania Historical and Museum Commission)

James Wilkinson later in life, after a painting by Gilbert Stuart.
(Courtesy of the Historical Society of Frederick County, Maryland)

THE SUMMER IN PHILADELPHIA sealed an unlikely friendship with Hamilton, based personally on a shared excess of physical energy, and professionally on a desire to reform the army. Since neither wanted to see French ideas of liberty and equality undermining its discipline, Wilkinson was drawn into the Federalist strategy of weeding out any officer who was a Republican sympathizer and, in the words of a critic, "has had the audacity to mount the French cockade." This threatened to make the New Army an overtly political animal—"We were very attentive to the importance of appointing friends of the Govern[ment] to military stations," Hamilton assured McHenry.

It was exactly what Republicans had warned would happen once a standing army was permitted—professional soldiers would be loyal to the government and could be used to intimidate its opponents. Their fears had been reinforced by the restrictions on public criticism of the government brought in under the 1798 Alien and Sedition Acts. When the Kentucky and Virginia legislatures, under the covert prompting of Thomas Jefferson and James Madison, resolved that the acts were unconstitutional, it drew from Hamilton, the army's operational commander, a reaction that was the stuff of Republican nightmares. The resolves, he told Theodore Sedgwick of Massachusetts on February 12, 1799, were evidence of "a regular conspiracy to overturn the government," and armed force was the proper response: "when a clever force has been collected let them be drawn towards Virginia, for which there is an obvious pretext—and then let measures be taken to act upon the laws, and put Virginia to the test of resistance."

Even John Adams declared, "This man is stark mad," when he learned of Hamilton's proposal. But significantly, he responded to the riots led by Captain John Fries that broke out in western Pennsylvania over taxes in March 1799 by sending in the army. Although barely remembered compared to the more notorious Whiskey Rebellion by the same people, Fries's revolt had much greater consequences for the military.

Hamilton insisted that overwhelming force had to be employed because "whenever the Government appears in arms it ought to appear like a *Hercules* and inspire respect by a display of strength." Accordingly five companies of professionals accompanied by artillery were ordered to join the militia. But the reports of armed soldiers searching Pennsylvania homes and tearing women and screaming children from their beds quickly triggered a wave of anger against the government. Scores of petitions flooded into Congress against standing armies and the alien and sedition laws. In his newspaper, *Aurora*, the influential editor William Duane warned ominously that "[people] may see from this what they have to expect from a military force under the orders of the administration."

Detained in the south by his concerns over Nancy, Wilkinson missed the popular fury, but once in Philadelphia he associated himself closely with Hamilton's increasingly beleaguered command. That August, in response to the major general's request, he produced within ten days a long, detailed report for the future disposition of the army. Stressing the importance of defending the nation at its borders, he also recommended closing down forts in the interior and transferring their garrisons to ports and defensive positions on the frontier, especially in the south, where they could repel any attack from the French. Hamilton was delighted. He passed the report to Washington, praising it as "intelligent and interesting," and wrote to Adams with a new plea for Wilkinson's promotion on the grounds that he was "brave, enterprising, active and diligent, warmly animated by the spirit of his profession and devoted to it."

Washington, however, gave the report a cool reception. Voicing his military opinion in September for virtually the last time before his death, he returned to the strategy that had served him so well—not committing troops too early, keeping the main force in reserve, being ready to counterattack at speed. It followed that the bulk of the army should be located in the north, "from where it could descend the [Mississippi] like lightening, with all its munitions and equipments; which could be accumulated with ease, and without noise, at the upper Posts, and make the surprise more complete." Distilled into those vivid words was the military wisdom learned in the war that won independence, the fighting on the back foot against superior numbers, the dazzling ripostes at Trenton and Princeton, and the final victory over an enemy that had never been allowed to land a decisive blow. Nevertheless, he said, he offered his wisdom "more for consideration than decision."

The strategic argument was never resolved. Three months later Washington was dead, war with France was averted by Adams's diplomacy, and Wilkinson was back in Fort Adams. He left Hamilton a farewell message just before he sailed from Baltimore in November: "I cannot more safely consign my own Interest than to the delicacies and the sensibilities of your own bosom . . . 20 years a Brigadier, a patient one too. I pant for promotion." But Hamilton could no longer help. Incensed by the Federalists' use of troops, the Democratic-Republicans in Congress had made, as Jefferson declared in December, "the disbanding of the army" a priority. Adams, too, wanted to clip Hamilton's wings. In the spring of 1800, Congress voted to abolish the New Army and the provisional and volunteer forces that had been so enthusiastically endorsed a year earlier. The reduction made major generals redundant and left a brigadier general in command of the old army once more.

JEFFERSON'S GENERAL

THE INSTINCT OF "THE COMMANDING GENERAL" as Congress now referred to Wilkinson, was as always to strengthen his political base. He had the endorsements of Washington and Hamilton to add to that of the president, but his connections to Jefferson's party suffered from his association with Hamilton's military policies. Already antimilitarist Republicans such as Elbridge Gerry and the freshman congressman Edmund Randolph were calling for the elimination of his rank as well.

Barely two months after arriving back in the south, he sailed again from New Orleans to return north, this time with Nancy—"Blooming still as Hebe," he reported, "and fully qualified quickly to repay for the pain and pangs of absence"—and their two sons. By July, he was in Georgetown, neighboring the new federal capital, where the next president would officially reside. There he went to work.

The intimacy with Hamilton was kept warm with a gift sent to New York of pecan nuts and orange shrubs for his family, and a male-bonding letter commenting on the luscious "women of figure" Wilkinson had met at a ball in Havana. "I defy the most prized mortal to behold them steadily for a second," he confided nudgingly, "without strong emotions of admiration and desire." Science was what excited Thomas Jefferson, and so rare Indian pottery and weaving brought from Louisiana and Texas, courtesy of Nolan, were dispatched, with a superb map of the territory, to Monticello. For Aaron Burr, the Federalist candidate for the presidency, and a friend of Nancy's cousin Charles Biddle, there were meetings and coded letters whose import would not become clear until five years later, and the kind of godfatherly exchanges that led to Burr's securing a place at Princeton College for Wilkinson's youngest son, Joseph. Even faithless John Adams, who had failed to push for Wilkinson's promotion to major general, received a sociable invitation to a party in the muddy wasteland of the District of Columbia. Mrs. Thornton, wife of William, the Capitol's architect, wrote in her diary of seeing the president's secretary stumbling "across the fields to Mrs General Wilkinson's party . . . [whence came] the enlivening strains of a military band with which his company was entertained." All that could be done politically was done.

The need to bolster his position was underlined by the unwelcome arrival of a letter from Andrew Ellicott in August. Despite its friendly tone and congratulations on being made "head of the army again," the reminder that the scientist had returned from the wilderness was a cause for concern. It was fortunate therefore that shortly before the general left Washington, one further event helped his cause, although no one could tell who was responsible.

In May, John Adams had dismissed James McHenry, a Hamilton ally, in a fine outburst of fury: "Through all parts of the Country, Sir, Your conduct in the Department is complained of. Every member of Congress I have spoken with tells me that you want capacity to discharge its duties . . . You cannot, Sir, remain longer in Office." Until the fall, when Samuel Dexter took over, the War Department had no leader, and overwhelmed officials besought the commanding general to help them deal with its business. For several months, Wilkinson had unrestricted access to the records containing the many accusations against him that had accumulated since he rejoined the army. In November, while Dexter was away, a fire broke out in a building that had been "locked for two weeks," as the *Federal Gazette* pointed out, destroying all the records. Suspicions tended to rest on Treasury Secretary Oliver Wolcott Jr., who was first at the scene, although he had nothing to gain from the blaze. A few days later, Brigadier General James Wilkinson and his wife left town for military headquarters in Pittsburgh.

Whatever or whoever caused the fire, he must have felt he was free. In July 1799, his blackmailing friend and dear enemy Manuel Gayoso de Lemos, who knew all Wilkinson's secrets from the Spanish side, had contracted yellow fever and died. Now most of the official papers on the American side had gone up in smoke. However the election turned out, one of his friends, Jefferson or Burr, would become president, and his future could unfold without his being haunted by the old suspicions.

DURING THAT WINTER WHILE FORT FAYETTE, the army's headquarters, was being refurbished, the Wilkinsons resumed their dominance of Pittsburgh's small but growing society. This was congenial to both. Nancy was among friends, and the brigadier general was in unchallenged command. He was by nature hospitable and generous, and as a garrison town, Pittsburgh could be relied on to provide the appreciative audience he needed. A portrait painted by Charles Willson Peale a little earlier shows him plump and authoritative, his bright, dark eyes gleaming from a jowly pink face, and the bristly gray hair no longer curling but brushed straight back from his high forehead. Not even Peale's flattering technique can disguise the double chin or the hard expression, but there is also the alertness and appetite for sensation that made him attractive.

His talk was wide-ranging and engaging. In 1800 no one had seen more of the United States, both geographically and socially, than Wilkinson. His extensive travels had made him familiar with life in New Orleans and Michigan and much in between. He had known well the first two presidents—and would surely be a friend of the third—as well as Miami chiefs, clothing contractors, and sutlers. He attended lectures at the American Philosophical Society as equably as he faced Little Turtle's bullets at Fallen Timbers. He was a passionate gardener and adored music—any fifer or trumpeter who showed talent could expect a transfer from his frontier fort to a soft life at headquarters. He preferred his cigars to come from Havana, and his Madeira to be served chilled. He still showed off—a habit that sounded increasingly pompous—but he encouraged his friends to do the same.

Young men with a taste for adventure were exhilarated by his theatrical style, and it showed not only in their devotion to him but in the operatic phrasing they learned from him. Thus a quarrel with the genial Gayoso prompted Philip Nolan to term him "a vile man and my implacable enemy," while Zebulon Pike compared the clouds around the summit of Pikes Peak to "the ocean in a storm, wave piled on wave and foaming."

On formal parades, Wilkinson chose to wear the peacock uniform that he dressed in for Peale's portrait. The shoulders were decorated with epaulets the size of platters overflowing with gold braid, each studded with a single enormous silver star denoting the rank of a brigadier; the facings on the topcoat were yellow, as was the waistcoat, the buttons gold, and white ruffles exploded from beneath an elaborately knotted black silk stock. The display was excessive, but served a purpose. Both personally and professionally, he was the army's figurehead. In a society deeply suspicious of a large, standing force of regular soldiers, it was no bad thing for military morale to see the senior general so obviously proud of his position.

Presumably he would have worn his full dress uniform at the formal party the Wilkinsons planned to celebrate the inauguration of the new president. On February 17, 1801, however, the long drama of the hung election between Burr and Jefferson was at last resolved. With each receiving seventy-three electoral-college votes, the decision had gone to the House of Representatives, where thirty-five ballots had failed to break the agonizing tie. On the thirty-sixth, the stalemate broke, and the moment it was known that Jefferson would become the next president, Wilkinson's faithful subordinate Major Thomas Cushing sent an urgent warning to Richmond: "It is understood on all sides that an entire new administration is to be formed and that many other alterations are to take place." For the army, change could only be bad. Abruptly Wilkinson departed for Washington, leaving Nancy to stand in for him, welcoming the officers "in front of her apartments where a large collection of ladies were previously assembled," before leading the entire company to listen to the handpicked band and watch a fireworks display.

POLITICALLY, CUSHING EXPECTED THE ARMY "to go to the right about," meaning it would turn to face in the opposite direction from in the Adams administration. Thomas Jefferson put it more diplomatically, explaining, "The Army is undergoing a chaste reformation." But Cushing's version was more accurate. When the commanding general arrived in Washington, he found the beginnings of a bloodbath, ostensibly designed to save five hundred thousand dollars a year.

The army's authorized strength was 5,438 men. Even before he was appointed, the new secretary of war, Henry Dearborn, intended to cut this by one third. The Military Peace Establishment Bill, which he began preparing the day after Jefferson's election, set the new level at 3,300 men distributed among three regiments—two of infantry and one of artillery. It required at least one in three of the 269 serving officers to be dismissed, and the immediate question was, who should be weeded out? On February 23, Jefferson asked Wilkinson to transfer Captain Meriwether Lewis, paymaster of the First Infantry Regiment, to the presidential staff because he needed someone "possessing a knoledge [*sic*] of the Western country, of the army & it's [*sic*] situation [who] might sometimes aid us with informations of interest, which we may not otherwise possess."

Today, it is Lewis's knowledge of the "Western country" that receives most attention, but his familiarity with "the army and its situation," and specifically its officers, was Jefferson's first priority. By July 1801, Lewis had listed every officer and rated each according to his professional abilities and his political affiliation. The military category was divided into

"1st Class," "Respectable," and "Unfit," while the political had labels that ranged from "Republican" through "Apathy" and "no known affiliation" to "Opposed to the Administration" and "Most violently opposed to the administration and still active in its vilification."

Within twelve months, Lewis's list had been used to purge the largely Federalist officer corps. More than half left the army, some forced into resignation, but most simply dismissed. Angry Federalists accused the administration of politicizing the military, and Dearborn himself virtually admitted it was retaliation for Hamilton's attempt to pack the army in 1799. "We have been much more liberal towards [the Federalists] than they would be towards us," he told the congressman Joseph Vamum, "and in future I think we ought to give them measure for measure." Military efficiency was not ignored—of forty-four officers deemed unfit, thirty-eight were dismissed, Republicans and Federalists alike—but in the end the army had a more distinctly Republican tinge than the raw numbers suggest, because the ax fell most heavily on the senior, strongly Federalist officers, especially those on the general staff. Many of Wilkinson's favorites were culled, among them Captain Bartholomew Shaumburgh, deemed to be "opposed to the administration," and Major Isaac Guion, "violently opposed." According to Federalist congressman James Bayard, the commanding general should have been among them because the slimmer army no longer required even a brigadier general in command.

Had Jefferson and Dearborn really wanted to save money, they might have been tempted. It was soon apparent that the cuts would reduce military spending by less than expected—in the end by forty thousand dollars rather than half a million dollars—and Wilkinson's salary was now more than twenty-five hundred dollars a year, with almost half as much again in expenses. Many Republicans also believed him to be too closely associated with Hamilton and the Federalists. Against the commanding general's name, however, no mark appeared. Possibly Lewis felt it would have been presumptuous, but more plausibly he had been told that none was needed. The president had a specific role for the general to play in the new Republican army. Wilkinson's survival depended on his acquiescence.

ONE OF THE FIRST to become aware of the general's closeness to the new administration was Andrew Ellicott. Since his return to Philadelphia in the dying days of John Adams's government, he had been pleading to be paid eight thousand dollars in unclaimed salary for his years in the wilderness. Despairing of the Federalists, he wrote as a friend and fellow member of the American Philosophical Society to Thomas Jefferson, asking for his help. Instead of a reply from the president, he received one in March 1801 from Wilkinson, oozing friendliness, and offering him one of the best-paid jobs in the federal government: "What do you think of the surveyor-general's office in the N.Western Territory—you could fill it and I am sure it is not filled now."

The surveyor general was responsible for organizing the Public Lands Survey, the great government enterprise that would eventually measure out one million square miles of land between the Appalachians and the Pacific Ocean, transforming wilderness into property and capital. It paid two thousand dollars a year with another five hundred dollars for his clerk, a suitable post for Ellicott's son Andy. Desperate for the financial security it represented, but appalled by the implicit condition of silence that came with it, the astronomer replied in a tortured letter to his crooked would-be benefactor, begging for time to make up his mind and wailing at the unfairness that forced him to sell his scientific books and instruments so that he could feed his family. "I now find that I am inevitably ruined and know not for what," he exclaimed. "I never betrayed the interests of my country, I never used a farthing of money that was not my own, I never lost a single observation by absence of inattention, and never when out on public business was caught in bed by the sun."

After five weeks' wrestling with temptation, Ellicott finally turned the offer down and, in June 1801, wrote Jefferson a complete account of what he knew of the general's Spanish connections. It began with a specific warning about Wilkinson's activities that Ellicott had received from President Washington; it included testimony from Thomas Power and Daniel Clark; and it ended with the final detail of Captain Tomás Portell's recollection that the $9,640 "was not on account of any mercantile transactions, but of the pension allowed the General by the Spanish government." The letter ended, as Ellicott recalled, with the blunt warning that "General W. was not a man to be trusted; and if continued in employ, would one day or other disgrace and involve the government in his schemes."

Neither then nor in the future did President Jefferson ever acknowledge receipt of this letter. On a later occasion before Congress, he even denied its existence. Yet he clearly not only received Ellicott's warning, but almost certainly passed it on to the man most directly concerned, Secretary of War Henry Dearborn. The following year, when a disgruntled Wilkinson toyed with the idea of leaving the army and taking the job of surveyor general himself, Dearborn deemed him unsuitable, scrawling across his letter of application, "Such a situation would enable him to associate with Spanish agents without suspicion."

It is impossible not to find Jefferson's prolonged dealings with Brigadier General James Wilkinson equivocal and troubling. Knowing his past as a spy, the president still trusted him as commander in chief. More than that, he added civil and diplomatic posts to the general's military command until at a crucial moment Wilkinson single-handedly possessed enough power to decide the fate of the nation. The general once described Jefferson as "a fool" to his Spanish handler, and the risk taken by the president was an undeniable folly that could have destroyed the still-unformed nation. Yet, it was also a cold calculation. In exchange for trusting Wilkinson, the president expected to gain what he considered to be the priceless return of a compliant army.

ON APRIL 30, 1801, the commanding general demonstrated in a small but unmistakable way his intention to comply with the wishes of the Republican president. He issued a general order requiring every man under his command to cut off the queue or pigtail of long hair worn by all eighteenth-century soldiers. As a fashion, it had come in during the early eighteenth century when shoulder-length wigs were discarded, but in civilian life it was rapidly disappearing, partly on hygienic grounds, and, after the French Revolution spread a taste for simplicity, partly because it seemed old-fashioned. For a conservative institution like the army, that was its value. The queue served as a reminder of its past.

Washington wore it to his dying day, as did all the officers in the heroic days of the Revolution. Indeed, the difficulty in making it look smart helped to distinguish a good soldier. To achieve the best result, it was essential to add tallow grease as the hair was braided and to powder the finished queue liberally with flour. The result might be what the general order called "a filthy and insalubrious ornament," but it served as the outward and visible sign of the army's difference from the civilian population. Wilkinson's order consequently caused deep anguish, especially to tradition-minded, predominantly Federalist officers.

"I was determined not to [cut my hair], provided a less sacrifice to my feelings would have sufficed," Captain Russell Bissell of Connecticut confessed to his father. "I wrote my Resignation, & showed it, but . . . the Col[onel]. was not impowered to accept . . . I was obliged to submit to the act that I despised, and if ever you see me you will find that I have been closely cropped." Others did resign over the issue, but the adamant refusal of Lieutenant Colonel Thomas Butler, a cantankerous, dyed-in-the-wool

traditionalist, to deprive himself of what he regarded as "the greatest ornament of a soldier" demonstrated how deep resistance ran.

It was useless for Wilkinson to explain that pigtails were as out-of-date as
knee breeches, and that short hair was "recommended by the ablest generals
of the day," meaning the crop-haired Napoléon Bonaparte. Despite being
twice court-martialed, Butler refused to accept that the general had the authority to order a haircut. Gradually Butler's queue became the rallying
point for conservatives opposed to Jefferson's reforms. Bystanders such as
Andrew Jackson condemned Wilkinson's order as "despotic," others called
him a "detestable persecutor," and, most woundingly, "a time-serving, su-
perannuated coxcomb, the fawning flatterer of Adams and Jefferson, a perfect Vicar of Bray"—a reference to the eighteenth-century satire on an
English clergyman whose political sympathies changed from Whig to Tory
and back according to the views of each new monarch on the throne.

The fury that the mere cutting of a pigtail aroused explains why Thomas
Jefferson needed Wilkinson. Had the general thrown his weight against the
Republican reforms of the army, the Federalist backlash, inside its ranks and
among former officers, would have had a leader, and as Adams had recognized earlier, a disaffected army could create a constitutional crisis with unpredictable consequences. Wilkinson's switch of allegiance was therefore
crucial, as the barrage of attacks on him made clear. According to the Federalist senator and former soldier William North, the general was the only senior officer "friendly to the politics of the now reigning party." Without him,
the ten-year-old federal government, so easily defied by lawbreakers such as
William Blount, might not be able to impose its will on a determined army.

The lesson of France was fresh in the mind of every Republican: on
November 9, 1799, the French military, led by General Napoléon Bonaparte, had overthrown the legitimate government, the Directory, despite
the country's constitution having been approved by more than a million
voters. Even with Wilkinson's support, Elbridge Gerry still felt bound to
warn the president in May 1801 that forts and arsenals should be "placed
under the protection of faithful officers and corps," meaning Republicans,
to prevent "their seizure or destruction . . . by a desperate faction."

While Wilkinson was expected to hold the existing army in check, Jefferson and Dearborn instituted the decisive reform that was to shape its future
by creating a military academy at West Point. Although set up specifically to
train artillery and engineer officers, it, too, was expected to tilt the army
away from its old Federalist roots. One of its first cadets, Joseph Swift, later a
commandant of the academy himself, remembered being interviewed by

Jefferson, who asked, " 'To which of the political creeds do you adhere?' My reply was that as yet I had done no political act, but that my family were Federalists. Mr Jefferson rejoined, 'There are many men of high talent and integrity in that party, but it is not the rising party.' " The hint, repeated by Dearborn, convinced Swift to keep his opinions to himself. In the long term, however, West Point performed its function, not by fostering Republicanism but by encouraging a professional ethic that displaced political loyalties.

By making Jefferson's "chaste reformation" possible, Wilkinson lost popularity, but preserved an important constitutional principle. He had acquiesced in the axing of some of his closest military friends—only Major Thomas Cushing, marked down as "violently opposed to the administration," survived—and thereby incurred the hatred of Federalists. But on a larger canvas, what mattered was that he had defended the fundamental basis of any democracy's relationship with the army, that the military must always be at the service of the civil power. Jefferson's appreciation of that important service provides the best explanation for his subsequent dealings with the general.

WITHIN THE WAR DEPARTMENT, however, Wilkinson continued to be regarded with suspicion. During the Saratoga campaign, Henry Dearborn was one of those who regarded Wilkinson as a turncoat for betraying Benedict Arnold and, more openly than any other secretary of war, set out to restrict Wilkinson's capacity for doing mischief. Administratively, functions concerning pay and equipment once performed by military officers, who might be beholden to the commanding general, were transferred to civilian staff answerable to the war secretary. The general's direct command over operational duties now had to be mediated through three colonels appointed to command the three regiments that constituted the fighting forces of the army. West Point was put under the direct control of the war secretary. Above all, the whole thrust of Jefferson's famous program of "frugal government" hobbled any scope for maneuver by leaving troops perpetually short of uniforms, ammunition, and transport. As though to underline the weakness of the commander in chief, Dearborn's directives ensured that from the summer of 1801 Wilkinson spent most of the next eighteen months away from headquarters in Pittsburgh where his family lived. Instead, he was required to supervise the construction of a road linking Lakes Erie and Ontario on the northern frontier, then to negotiate a series of land treaties with Choctaw and Cherokee Indians so that settlers could move into western Tennessee and the Mississippi Territory.

Depressed by his lack of prospects, Wilkinson attempted unsuccessfully to secure the governorship of the Mississippi Territory following Winthrop Sargent's dismissal. When Jefferson refused on the grounds that a general could not be a chief executive—"no military man should be so placed as to have no civil superior"—he then applied to be made surveyor general, only to be frozen out by Dearborn's bleak mistrust.

After six months in the wilderness "under extreme ill health, during an inclement season," Wilkinson passed his first night under a solid roof in Fort Adams on January 27, 1803. There he found the United States facing an international crisis over the long-settled question of navigation rights on the Mississippi. The emergency was precipitated by Juan Morales, acting intendant of Louisiana, who in October 1802 aribitrarily closed the depot at New Orleans to American goods. This precipitate move, interrupting trade worth almost two million dollars a year, was widely thought to be an aberration attributable to his interfering character.

In reality Morales's orders came directly from King Carlos IV. Their purpose was to create an opening for French traders and represented the first public evidence of the secret treaty by which Spain had ceded Louisiana to France. When the treaty was signed in 1800, Talleyrand promised that French power would transform Louisiana into a "wall of brass" preventing further American expansion, and Napoléon gave an explicit assurance that the former French colony would never be transferred. A French army under General Charles Leclerc presently engaged in restoring order in Saint Domingue, present-day Haiti, was expected to land at the end of the year to take possession of the colony. His arrival would create an immediate French empire stretching from Guadeloupe in the West Indies to the Canadian border, with the French-dominated province of Quebec just beyond.

To Wilkinson's frustration, even in this extreme situation he was given no orders to prepare the army for action. Lacking any direct information on the government's intentions, he wrote Dearborn urging the need for the United States to move first to "get possession of New Orleans by treaty or by arms" before Leclerc arrived. In either event, he pleaded to be involved: "In the first case . . . my intimacy with the inhabitants, their prejudices, habits and interests, would enable me to conciliate and attach all parties to our government; in the last case, my knowledge of every approach and every defense, and the firm adherents which I have within the place, might be of important avail in the attempt [to capture it]."

In fact, the general was already in contact with people in the city, including two old friends-turned-enemies, Daniel Clark and Thomas Power. The prospect of being ruled by France put them in the same camp as the general once more, and both had begun to supply him with information about French intentions and the city's defenses. Despite lack of instructions from the War Department, Wilkinson concentrated close to five hundred men at Fort Adams ready for an assault on New Orleans.

The transfer of New Orleans from Spain's fragile possession to France's immense power was not an outcome that the United States could accept. "There is on the globe one single port, the possessor of which is our natural and habitual enemy," Jefferson instructed his minister to France, Robert Livingston. "It is New Orleans, through which the produce of three-eighths of our territory must pass to market, and from its fertility it will ere long yield more than half of our whole produce, and contain more than half of our inhabitants." In February 1803 James Monroe was sent to join Livingston with the goal of purchasing the city from France.

Still kept out of the loop, General Wilkinson could reply only in the vaguest terms to officers who pestered him for information. "If Mr Monroe succeeds all will be well," he told one young favorite, Captain Jacob Kingsbury, "but if he should fail, we shall have noise, bustle & Bloodshed. Keep your sword with a good Edge & be quiet."

As Livingston and Monroe's negotations with François Barbé-Marbois, Napoléon's minister of finance, dragged on through the spring, Dearborn sent the army's senior general to negotiate more Indian treaties, this time with Creek communities, to release land for the benefit of Georgia settlers. In 1802 and 1803, Wilkinson reckoned he covered more than sixteen thousand miles by land and sea in pursuit of unmartial duties. He took the opportunity to explore "every critical pass, every direct route & every devious way between the Mexican Gulph & the Tennessee river" so that American forces would have the opportunity to seize not just New Orleans but the Floridas as well. But his knowledge was never called upon.

In July 1803 a near-desperate Wilkinson was back in Fort Adams. In an anguished letter to Dearborn, he complained that although he had enough troops to seize the city at any time, he could make no detailed plans because he was still being kept in the dark about the government's intentions. "If anything professional is to be done which may imply trust & hazard—I hope you may confide the execution to me," he declared, "or give an order to someone to knock me on the head."

Writing to Alexander Hamilton, Wilkinson revealed his growing impatience: "I have extended my capacities for utility but not my sphere of action & in the present moment my destination is extremely precarious. To divorce my sword is to rend a strong ligament of my affections & to wear it without active service is becoming disreputable." His use of this allusive, overelaborate language, enabling him to hint at possibilities rather than reveal intentions, was a sure sign that he was looking for more rewarding opportunities than those allowed by Dearborn.

Given Ellicott's warning, Dearborn's desire to restrain his general's room for maneuver was understandable, but it seriously underestimated his capacity for usefulness as well as resentment and intrigue. Hamilton, who understood him well, advised that where Wilkinson was concerned "to act towards him so as to convince him that he is not trusted . . . is the most effectual way that can be adopted to make him unfaithful." In his memoirs, the general not only quoted that advice, but capitalized the words to give them extra emphasis.

Not until July 1803 did the news finally arrive in Washington of Livingston and Monroe's agreement to purchase not just New Orleans but the entire vulnerable province of Louisiana that Miró, Carondelet, and Gayoso had struggled so hard to keep out of American hands. What precipitated the deal was the decimation of Leclerc's army in Saint Domingue by disease and warfare. Once the dream of an American empire had gone, Napoléon abruptly cut his losses and, to finance his planned invasion of Britain, accepted Monroe and Livingston's offer of fifteen million dollars for the 885,000 square miles of territory.

At once, Jefferson's administration set about finding a suitable commissioner to take charge of the massive new province it had acquired. Unfortunately the ideal candidate, General Thomas Sumter of South Carolina, refused to leave the Senate, then the Marquis de Lafayette declined, as did James Monroe. Rumors that Spain was protesting the validity of the sale, and that France was having second thoughts, made any long delay dangerous.

In October, with time running out for the handover in December, Jefferson reluctantly selected as civil commissioner twenty-nine-year-old William C. Claiborne, governor of Mississippi Territory, and, as his military counterpart, forty-six-year-old Brigadier General James Wilkinson. Dearborn's opinion was not recorded, but Wilkinson's length of service was strictly limited. The moment the last fort in Louisiana was handed over, his power as commissioner would end.

NOTHING IN THE GENERAL'S BEHAVIOR could have aroused any doubt about his loyalty. Within weeks of receiving his orders and a copy of the Paris agreement, he had embarked a force of 450 regulars and 100 militia with all their equipment on a fleet of seventeen flatboats and two baggage barges at Fort Adams. To ensure a smooth handover, he privately visited New Orleans to make the necessary arrangements beforehand with Pierre de Laussat, the designated French governor of Louisiana. On December 10, after Claiborne had joined him from Natchez, Wilkinson sailed down to New Orleans and a week later pitched camp on the outskirts of the city.

There Wilkinson issued a grandiloquent but necessary reminder to the soldiers of the delicate nature of their mission, and the need for toleration of foreign customs: "We behold a polished people (strangers to our manners, our laws and our language) cast into our arms. Be it our pride and our glory to receive them into the great family of our happy country with cordial embraces." On December 20, the two commissioners marched at the head of the U.S. troops along the levees on the riverfront, and into the huge central square, the Place d'Armes, in front of the City Hall of New Orleans.

In a bittersweet mood Laussat, who had received the keys of New Orleans from the Spanish only three weeks before, noted in his journal, "The day was beautiful and the temperature as balmy as a day in May. Lovely ladies and city dandies graced all the balconies on the Place d'Armes. The Spanish officers could be distinguished in the crowd by their plumage . . . The American troops appeared and, with drums beating, marched by platoons, and placed themselves on the river side of the square. Facing them, on the other side were the [French] militia."

To his chagrin, Laussat now had to repeat the earlier ceremony in which he had formally received Louisiana from Spain's two commissioners, the ancient Manuel de Salcedo—"an impotent old man in his dotage," the forty-two-year-old Laussat noted—and the aristocratic Marqués de Casa Calvo, "a violent man who hated the French." But this time Laussat had to give away a third of a continent. In the conference chamber, he greeted the two commissioners. Claiborne, Laussat wrote, was "tall and erect with an American complexion," while Wilkinson was "short, also erect, of handsome though pompous mien." Having proclaimed that he was "transferring the country to the United States," Laussat presented the general with the keys to the city, tied with a tricolor ribbon; then all three signed the documents that officially conveyed ownership of Louisiana to the United States. Finally they went out on the balcony, where "the French colors were lowered and the American flag was raised," and a salvo of cannon fire signaled that the United States had almost doubled in size.

Exactly six weeks later, Brigadier General James Wilkinson, commanding general of the U.S. army, and his country's military commissioner for the province of Louisiana, had a private interview in New Orleans with the visiting Spanish governor of West Florida, Don Vizente Folch. He suggested that he should be paid twenty thousand dollars, the arrears on his pension as a Spanish agent. In return he promised to pass on information vital to Spain, including Jefferson's plans regarding Spanish America. "I know," he boasted, "what is concealed in the President's heart."

AGENT 13 REBORN

NEW ORLEANS WAS WHERE JAMES WILKINSON had first transferred his loyalties to Spain. Two years later, it was where he had returned to negotiate his transition from trader to Spanish agent. But despite the precedents, it could hardly have been imagined that he would behave there in the same way three times in a row. So much had changed since the 1780s. Even before the purchase of Louisiana, the balance of power in North America had clearly shifted from Spain to the United States. The Spanish Conspiracy was a distant memory. Most important, Wilkinson himself was in command of the U.S. army, the great prize for which he had cut off his original connection with Spain.

Nor did his public behavior suggest any secret agenda. Seen through the jaundiced eyes of Pierre de Laussat, he appeared as a loud buffoon. In a report to Paris, the French commissioner compared the performance of both Wilkinson and Claiborne unfavorably to his own suave efficiency and rated them below even the disorganized but self-possessed Spaniards:

"It was hardly possible that the Government of the United States should have a worse beginning, and that it should have sent two men more deficient in the proper requisites to conciliate the hearts of the Louisianians. The first, with estimable qualities as a private man, has little intellect, a good deal of awkwardness, and is extremely [inadequate to] the position in which he has been placed. The second, who has been long known here in the most unfavorable manner, is a rattle-headed fellow, full of odd fantasies. He is frequently drunk, and has committed a hundred inconsistent and impertinent acts. Neither the one nor the other understands one word of French, or Spanish. They have, on all occasions, and without the slightest circumspection, shocked the habits, the prejudices and the natural dispositions of the inhabitants of this country."

The sort of incident Laussat had in mind occurred at a public ball on January 22, 1804, attended by American and French officers as well as New Orleans high society. Wilkinson noticed among the dancers in a quadrille a French official who had just returned from Saint Domingue and so should have been in quarantine for yellow fever. He plunged into the dancers and marched him off the floor. The French officers began to protest. Wilkinson jumped up on a bench and, with Claiborne standing loyally beside him, delivered a bombastic lecture on social responsibility in bad French and his own elaborate English. The French began to jeer, and their response provoked the general to launch into "Hail, Columbia," the national anthem of the time, accompanied by Claiborne and members of their staffs. When this failed to silence the protests, Wilkinson inexplicably, unless to annoy the French, who had spent ten years at war with the British, decided to sing "God Save the King," to which the French responded stridently with "La Marseillaise" amid a mounting storm of shouts and whistling. At that point, with scuffles breaking out and pandemonium descending, Wilkinson and Claiborne prudently abandoned the war of songs and withdrew.

None of this suggested the anonymity and self-control expected of a secret agent, but Wilkinson's bluster was always a good disguise to his shrewdness. Despite the explosive mixture of nationalities in the city, the confusion arising from three different governments holding power in as many weeks, and the presence of armed soldiers from three separate armies, New Orleans avoided disorder. "The Prefect of France and the Spanish troops are still in town, and the magazines and storehouses still in their possession," Wilkinson complained to Dearborn almost three months after the transfer of power, "while we are obliged to pay rent for our own accommodation." Despite provocations from Spanish militia "which a state of war alone would justify," as one of Wilkinson's officers put it, the army's presence kept the peace until April, when both Spanish and French forces sailed for home.

In his arrogance, Laussat failed to see that at least part of the credit for this orderly transition was due to Wilkinson's shrewd disposition of his troops across the city, and his very public tours of inspection to ensure their good behavior. The punishments inflicted after he discovered the guard in Fort St. Louis dead drunk on the very first night ensured that the offense was never repeated, or at least not found out, while he was there. "I apprehend no Danger," the general wrote dramatically to Secretary of War Henry Dearborn after a night on patrol with his men in the streets, "but the horrors of a sinister attempt make it my duty to prevent one." French residents complained of heavy-handed policing, but not of laxness.

Wilkinson's very public commitment makes the decision to betray his country again still more mysterious. Had it been his intention to sabotage the American takeover, an incident could easily have been allowed to blow up. French resentment remained especially fierce, and as Claiborne reported, they "seem determined to sour the Inhabitants as much as possible with the American government." Yet the general clearly did everything he could to prevent such an explosion from taking place.

One immediate motive in approaching the Spanish again was, as always, financial. His salary as general was now $225 a month, and on top of that he received generous expenses, and a special allowance of $8 a day while negotiating Indian treaties. Wilkinson estimated that altogether he received something close to $4,000 a year from the army. But tighter regulations and constant travel clearly reduced the scope for payoffs from contractors, and he had received nothing from the Spaniards since the notorious $9,640 had arrived covered in sugar and coffee. Meanwhile, he had one son at Princeton—Ensign James Biddle Wilkinson having followed his father into the army—and a wife whose nervousness grew more pronounced the longer he was away from home, and whose demands he could not deny.

Psychology must also have played its part. For two years Wilkinson had been sidelined by Henry Dearborn, behavior guaranteed to wound his vanity and trigger a vicious urge to retaliate. Furthermore, he was in his late forties, a midlife point when unsatisfied men are prone to dreams of sudden transformation from routine to excitement. Finally there was Mexico. Ever since Philip Nolan's first report of the road to Santa Fe, it had occupied his mind, and the key to his serpentine activities lay in the extraordinary, meteoric career of the young Irishman.

BORN IN BELFAST, NORTHERN IRELAND, in 1771 and destined to be buried in Texas before his thirty-first birthday, Nolan had at the age of twenty exchanged the imaginative bookkeeping practiced in Wilkinson's Lexington store and in his shipping agency in New Orleans for the more daring life of a horse trader, rounding up wild mustangs in Texas and Chihuahua for sale in Louisiana and Natchez. Such activities required a passport from the governor of each region. Wilkinson, Nolan's mentor, persuaded Miró to grant him his first permit to import horses for the Louisiana militia, but Nolan's happy relish for adventure made it easy for him to procure these valuable documents—"He is," said Carondelet, "a charming young man whom I regard very highly," and the governors of Texas and New Mexico agreed. Nor was his appeal limited to European Americans.

After his goods and money were stolen on his first expedition in Texas, Nolan lived for two years with the notoriously aggressive Comanche and "acquired a perfect knowledge" of the sign language they used to communicate with other tribes in the Southwest. Even Daniel Clark Jr., notoriously cold and calculating in his judgments, was seduced by Nolan's careless courage and joyful spirits, assuring Thomas Jefferson that he was someone "whom Nature seems to have formed for Enterprizes of which the rest of Mankind are incapable." Only Gayoso, after an initial friendship, suddenly realized that his repeated trips into Spanish territory might serve another purpose and issued an urgent warning to his fellow governors that Nolan was "popular and enterprising" but at the same time "a dangerous man and a sacrilegious hypocrite."

Yet the Irishman never deviated from his loyalty to the general, whom he called "the friend and protector of my youth." Just before leaving on his first horse-trading expedition to Texas, he promised Wilkinson, "*I am wholly yours until I do the business of the season,*" and just before his last trip he told a friend, "Whatever discoveries I can make shall be carefully preserved for General Wilkinson." By 1797, his information about the trail to Santa Fe and Mexico had begun to excite his mentor's volatile imagination.

This was the background to Nolan's calculated friendship with the trusting Ellicott. The horse trader shared his intelligence about Spanish intentions and troop numbers and received in return private instruction in the art of navigation from the United States' foremost mapmaker. "I have instruments to enable me to make a more correct map than the one you saw," Nolan told Wilkinson before his next trip to Texas. "Ellicott assisted me in acquiring a more perfect knowledge of astronomy and [telescopes]; and Gayoso himself has made me a present of a portable sextant."

That promise of a more accurate map of the trail to Santa Fe suggests the direction of Wilkinson's thoughts. As a soldier, he valued nothing so much as reliable information about ground that might become strategically important. In 1801 Nolan was killed by a Spanish patrol in Texas to prevent him from exploring further, but his maps had planted the seeds of another ambition. The general's dream of a Mississippi republic might be over, but the idea of another, richer empire farther west was taking root.

THERE WAS NOTHING IMPULSIVE about his decision to approach Vizente Folch, governor of West Florida. Wilkinson already knew him as Miró's nephew, and another encounter in 1803 while working on the Indian frontier had convinced him that he could trust Folch. Their meeting in New Orleans in February 1804 was carefully minuted in Folch's report to his immediate senior, the captain general in Havana, Marqués Salvador de Someruelos. Having extracted a pledge that their conversation should be kept utterly secret, Wilkinson had made "various reflections" on the strategy Spain should pursue following the Louisiana Purchase. Folch was wary, suspecting that this might be an attempt to extract information on Spanish intentions, and so asked Wilkinson to write out his ideas.

The suggestion was accepted, but then Wilkinson raised a matter that caused him "considerable embarrassment"—his salary of two thousand dollars a year as a Spanish agent had not been paid for ten years. He would soon travel north to report to Thomas Jefferson. While in Washington, he would discover not only the administration's plans for Louisiana but, as Jefferson's friend, the president's innermost thoughts. Before he left New Orleans, Wilkinson suggested, Spain should pay him the twenty thousand dollars he was owed, "for the services which I shall render and more particularly to indemnify me for the eventual loss of the office which I hold and which probably it will seem necessary for me to abandon in case of hostilities." In return he would commit his reflections to paper and report back after his meetings in Washington.

That Folch should have taken seriously the request for such a gigantic sum says much for the value of the general's past services. Nevertheless, the governor explained, he could not personally pay so much—at this, Wilkinson apparently lowered his price to just ten thousand dollars—but Casa Calvo, the aristocrat who hated the French, was still in town, and he had one hundred thousand dollars from Mexico. On learning this, Wilkinson suddenly became extremely difficult, forbidding Folch to approach Casa Calvo because the aristocrat's secretary, Andrés Arnesto, represented a security risk. "I am a lost man," he declared with operatic intensity, "if the secretary should learn what I propose."

Even through the measured language of Folch's report, it is clear that Wilkinson wanted a personal interview with the man holding the money. His maneuvering succeeded, and the following Sunday Wilkinson met

Casa Calvo face-to-face and succeeded in wringing from him the promise of an immediate payment of twelve thousand dollars. During the interview, the general not only found it convenient to use Arnesto as an interpreter but praised him lavishly for his "wisdom and probity."

"Reflections," the paper Wilkinson wrote for Folch and Casa Calvo, was the third strategy document he had prepared for Spain's colonial authorities and, like its predecessors, demonstrated why he deserved the confidence they placed in him. With great clarity, he delineated the consequences of the Louisiana Purchase, that the irresistible drive of settlement would now sweep westward across the Mississippi, unless Spain could stop it. In the long term, the most effective way was to divert the torrent southward by granting the United States the economically important Floridas in exchange for Louisiana. To sweeten the deal, Spain should offer to repay the fifteen-million-dollar price of the purchase and any other expenses the United States might have incurred, otherwise Mexico stood in danger of being overrun by "an army of adventurers similar to the ancient Goths and Vandals."

In the short term, he suggested two tactical moves, one of which directly betrayed one of the president's most vital secrets, the proposed exploration of a route to the Pacific by an expedition under Captains Meriwether Lewis and William Clark, which was due to depart from St. Louis later that year. Since any weakness would encourage the westward expansion of the United States, Wilkinson urged the Spanish authorities to "detach a sufficient body of chasseurs to intercept Captain Lewis and his party . . . and force them to retire or take them prisoners." Second, and perhaps more surprisingly since it affected his own burgeoning plans, he recommended that Spain should "drive back every illegal usurpation toward the region of Texas" and prevent any exploration of the Red and Arkansas rivers; otherwise "they will very quickly explore the right path which will lead them to the capital of Santa Fe." Finally, the governors of Texas and Florida should fortify their frontiers to prevent American incursions.

As a general survey, Wilkinson's "Reflections" offered a realistic assessment of the unpromising situation facing Spain. The territorial exchange was not an impossible scenario: the Floridas were what Jefferson had originally instructed his negotiators to acquire. They contained good harbors and the mouths of the Mobile, Tombigbee, and Apalachicola rivers, all important routes for western producers aiming to transport flour and tobacco to the outside world. Many influential figures believed that in economic terms the Floridas made a more immediately useful addition to the United

States than the empty desert of Louisiana, whose open spaces would only encourage settlers to scatter across an area too large to govern.

His advice on frontiers certainly convinced the Council of the Indies to recommend later that year the establishment of an inviolable boundary between Texas and Louisiana stretching north from the Gulf Coast along the Arroyo Hondo River, today the Calcasieu River. Folch himself rigidly turned down every American request to descend the three great rivers flowing through the Floridas.

But the greatest immediate value of Wilkinson's paper lay in the intelligence about Lewis and Clark, which by any standard represented high-grade information. Publicly Jefferson had characterized Lewis and Clark's expedition as no more than the kind of "literary pursuit which [Spain] is in the habit of permitting within its own dominions." Nevertheless, their proposed route following the upper reaches of the Missouri would take them through territory still claimed by Spain. Furthermore, in a secret message to Congress in January 1803, Jefferson had revealed that the expedition's real purpose was to "explore the whole line, even to the Western ocean," thus establishing a claim to the entire region.

Recognizing the importance of Wilkinson's information, Casa Calvo immediately instructed Antonio Cordero y Bustamante, the energetic acting governor of Texas, to take steps to counter this "daring undertaking" and to make every effort to "divert and even to destroy such expeditions." As a result, at least three attempts by an armed patrol of two hundred men sent out under Captain Pedro Vial were made to kill or capture Lewis and Clark's party. Had they succeeded, the history of western exploration would have been delayed for a generation, with far-reaching consequences including the unopposed expansion of British settlement throughout Oregon.

With the added prospect of Wilkinson's report on the president's thinking, Casa Calvo and Folch agreed it was worth paying him twelve thousand dollars. As a bonus, they also gave Wilkinson a permit to export sixteen hundred barrels of flour annually to Havana, a source of profit with the potential to make good some of the shortfall on his original demand.

For the first time, Wilkinson received the full amount of his reward for treachery without having to pay intermediaries or risk the murder of messengers. And unlike in previous betrayals, on this occasion he intended to replicate his success by betraying Spain's secrets to the United States.

IN THE UNITED STATES nothing was known of his return to active work as a Spanish agent, but doubts about his loyalty were never far from the surface.

Apart from his initial report on the peaceful state of the city, Wilkinson had gone silent in New Orleans, ignoring Dearborn's increasingly frantic demands for information. "You have taken no notice of any of my letters," the secretary of war wrote in February, "[at a time] when information had been highly important relative to any Military operations." When Wilkinson did reply, it was to cast doubts on Claiborne's capacity, declaring that the province would be better run by "a Military executive Magistrate." Alerted by Daniel Clark to rising anti-American feeling in the city, and apparently fearing some sort of military coup, Jefferson asked Dearborn in February to intervene: "It is so important that Wilkenson's [sic] maneuvers should be understood. He is turning on us the batteries of our friends in aid of his own . . . he should be brought away as soon as possible, or I should not wonder if some disturbance be produced to keep him there."

On March 4, all of Louisiana was officially handed over to the United States, and in those outlying forts and towns that had not yet registered the original transfer from Spain to France, the flags of all three nations were flown within a single day. On that day the general's term of office as military commissioner officially ended, and Dearborn wasted no time in ordering his return to Washington. By then rumors were beginning to spread through New Orleans about Wilkinson's sudden purchases of sugar. Suspecting another Spanish payment, Clark persuaded an equally dubious Morales to let him examine the Louisiana books, but, as he reported back to Claiborne, found nothing—the twelve thousand dollars appeared only in the Mexico accounts. Wilkinson's assertion that an old tobacco deal had at last paid off strained credulity, but there seemed no other explanation.

When the general sailed for Washington in April 1804, he took with him the mirror image of "Reflections," a twenty-two-page strategy document prepared for American eyes, accompanied by eighteen hand-drawn maps of the country between the Mississippi and the Rio Grande—the very territory he suggested that Spain should fortify against U.S. expansion. He also transported a large cargo of sugar purchased with part of the payment for "Reflections," and the assurance that once more his Spanish handlers would not refer to him by name, only by his old *nom d'espionnage*, Agent 13.

WITHIN WEEKS OF HIS RETURN to Washington, Wilkinson had developed a relationship with Jefferson close enough to suggest he did have an inkling of what the president concealed in his heart. If so, part of the secret concerned Jefferson's continuing apprehension of the dangers of a standing army, and his wish for greater control over it.

To meet Jefferson's needs, Wilkinson drew up a new set of Articles of War on his return from New Orleans that dramatically increased the president's power in matters of military discipline. The most contentious change concerned the individual soldier's allegiance. Under the old Articles of War, composed in 1776, a soldier swore "to be true to the United States of America" and was forbidden to utter "traitorous and disrespectful words against the authority of the United States in Congress assembled." The Constitution had designated the president as commander in chief, but so far as the army was concerned, the chain of command stopped at the senior general. The president had to exert control through him over the military, the most potent instrument of executive authority.

Wilkinson proposed to alter the Articles so that each officer and soldier swore to "observe and obey the orders of the President of the United States, and the orders of the officers appointed over me," and it would become an offense to utter "traitorous and disrespectful words against the President" or other government officers. The suggested change made the military structure constitutional, but it also shifted the primary loyalty of a soldier from his country to his government.

The change seemed to give dangerous power to the executive, and opposition to the new Articles immediately became entangled in the continuing saga of Colonel Thomas Butler's uncropped pigtail, which had, by 1804, become the focal point of resentment against Wilkinson among forcibly retired officers of the once Federalist army. The issue created an unholy alliance between the Federalist stronghold of New England and the frontiersmen of Tennessee, where the colonel was stationed with the Second Regiment. Acting together, they mustered enough support in the Senate to approve a petition against the order for short hair and to throw out the new Articles of War. Until the twin issues of the pigtail and the Articles were resolved, Jefferson could not ignore the importance of the general's support for the Constitution and the Republican administration.

Beyond his political usefulness, Wilkinson had another more immediate claim on the president's attention. The general's unparalleled knowledge of the west met one of the abiding passions in Jefferson's life. From his childhood, when his father, Peter Jefferson, founded the Loyal Land Company to buy territory beyond the Appalachians, through the purchase of Louisiana and the creation of the Lewis and Clark expedition, the western lands occupied a strikingly important place in Jefferson's imagination. In the winter of 1783–84, as a Virginia delegate to the Continental Congress, he had specified how they should be purchased from the Native Americans, how they should be surveyed and sold to eastern settlers, and how their structure of government should be created. The west was the canvas on which Jefferson envisioned a new republican society being drawn. His desire for information about the region was insatiable.

When James Wilkinson arrived in Washington with his sketch maps and direct information of the area, the president had already sent two ambassadors, James Monroe and John Armstrong, to Madrid to negotiate the exact dividing line between the Louisiana Purchase and Mexico. Since Louisiana had originally been discovered and settled by the French, this resolved itself into a question of how much land their colonists had explored in the eighteenth century. Jefferson believed that French exploration had taken them several hundred miles west of the Mississippi, justifying a border along the Sabine River. Encouraged by Wilkinson's "Reflections," however, Spain insisted that the boundary ran almost eighty miles east of the Sabine River. Their own detailed maps showed the line following the Arroyo Hondo, then extending northward until it crossed the Red River close to Natchitoches. Lack of knowledge about the geography of the area handicapped the American response. Wilkinson's advice was consequently as welcome in Washington as it had been in New Orleans.

His maps no longer exist, but his information about the Red River can be deduced from the report he sent Dearborn in July. A mixture of fact and fiction, some of which came from Philip Nolan, and some from French maps procured in New Orleans, it revealed for the first time to non–Native Americans that this mighty feeder of the lower Mississippi had "its source in the East side of a height, the top of which presents an open plain, so extensive as to require the Indians four days in crossing it." This was the high, flat tableland that straddles the New Mexico/Texas border called the Llano Estacado.

The next section, however, led Jefferson astray. "West of this high plain," Wilkinson went on, "my informants report certain waters (which run to the Southward) probably those of the Rio Bravo, and beyond these they report a ridge of high mountains extending North and South." What made this misleading was that it compressed the actual geography, narrowing the distances involved. The Pecos River was confused with the Rio Bravo (alternatively named the Rio Grande), and the Sangre de Cristo mountains merged with the Rockies farther to the west.

By an extraordinary coincidence, the arrival of the distinguished German explorer Alexander von Humboldt in Washington that summer made it possible to compare Wilkinson's information and sketches with the first authoritative map of the region. While in Mexico City, Humboldt had been given the rare privilege of examining the government's closely guarded charts and atlases and, from them, had produced his magisterial *Chart of the Kingdom of New Spain*, covering Texas and New Mexico.

When he appeared in Washington in June 1804, Jefferson questioned Humboldt closely, then invited Wilkinson to dinner so that he and the German could compare information. Unfortunately, a fever required Wilkinson to be bled so heavily the day before that he was unable to leave his bed. By way of apology, the next day he sent Jefferson two souvenirs of the Southwest, a buffalo hide with an Osage drawing of a horned toad, and the leaves and fruit of a cotton tree.

His absence hardly mattered because at the president's urging Humboldt later met Wilkinson in person and let him borrow his precious chart. For Jefferson, the information it contained was intoxicating. What it showed was indeed that the Red River rose in the high plateau, as Wilkinson had described; that the narrow ridge of the Rockies lay a little farther west; and that on the other side of the ridge the land sloped down to California and the Pacific Ocean. In other words, it appeared that the Red River would take an explorer almost to the watershed between the Mississippi basin and the Pacific, with a clear run down to the ocean on the other side.

That Humboldt's chart should have confirmed the information from Nolan so closely makes it probable they had both studied the same Spanish maps, the Irishman presumably having had access to copies in the offices of the governors who found him so delightful. Alternatively, Humboldt may have incorporated data from Wilkinson's inaccurate sketches into the map shown to the president. Whatever the explanation, the coincidence confirmed Wilkinson in Jefferson's estimation as an utterly reliable source of information about the west.

The discovery that the Red River offered a clear route toward the Pacific prompted the president to immediate action. He commissioned the Scottish scientists William Dunbar and George Hunter to make a preliminary study of its lowest reaches and, in the fall of 1804, began to organize a much larger expedition led by Thomas Freeman, Wilkinson's old ally against Ellicott, to explore the river to its source. This was to be the southern counterpart to Lewis and Clark's northern exploration of the upper Missouri, and Congress was asked to set aside five thousand dollars to fund it. The Red River expedition was born out of Jefferson's passion, but was made possible by Wilkinson's information. Shortly afterward the president gave tangible proof of the value he attached to the general's unsurpassed knowledge of the west.

In November, Jefferson announced to Congress that the Louisiana Purchase was to be split into two, the southern portion being known as the Orleans Territory, and the rest to be called the Louisiana Territory. Before the end of 1804, William Claiborne, already governor of New Orleans, had his power extended to cover all the southern part of the Purchase. At the same time, the president appointed as governor of the Louisiana Territory, General James Wilkinson.

BURR'S AMBITION

W HAT PREOCCUPIED THE THOUGHTS of every westward-looking American were signs of the imminent collapse of the Spanish empire. As Spain was squeezed harder between Napoléon's army and Britain's navy, the fantastic three-hundred-year-old machinery of its colonial administration began to seize up. The fleets carrying silver from Peru and Mexico still sailed twice a year to Cádiz, but soldiers went unpaid for longer, local officials were left unsupervised, and Madrid's slackening grip was sharply evident in Casa Calvo's unilateral decision to divert twelve thousand dollars of Mexico's revenue to Wilkinson without Spain's direct permission. In similar circumstances in 1787 Miró had not felt able to do more than make the American a loan, while Carondelet's payments were possible only because they were in line with the existing policy of the royal council. The empire's shuddering edifice positively invited outsiders to think of what might replace it.

According to Alexander von Humboldt's recollection of his conversations in 1804, Jefferson speculated that after the Spanish empire disappeared the republic of the United States would become the model for a still larger project, "a future division of the American continent into three great republics which were to include Mexico and the South American states." But while Jefferson dreamed of the spread of republican virtue, other Americans, inspired by Francisco de Miranda, the Venezuelan-born liberationist and veteran of the Revolution, imagined a general Creole uprising leading to an independent South American empire. The remainder, including Wilkinson and perhaps most adventurers, found it hard to think beyond the mother lodes of silver ore that surfaced repeatedly in the western range of Mexico's Sierra Madre.

Although Wilkinson shared his information about the different roads to Mexico with President Jefferson, he had already discussed it with another would-be adventurer, the vice president, Colonel Aaron Burr. "To save time of which I need much and have little," Wilkinson wrote urgently in May 1804 immediately after landing in Charleston, "I propose to take a Bed with you this night, if it may be done without observation or intrusion—Answer me and if in the affirmative I will be with [you] at 30 after the 8th Hour."

A clandestine meeting, set up without preliminaries, indicated that Burr and Wilkinson already knew each other's mind, but that their thoughts needed to be kept secret. Since Burr's house in Richmond Hill lay on the road from Charleston to Washington, it was easy for Wilkinson to break his journey unobserved. The nature of their discussions was never divulged, but they must have concerned the opportunities that Burr might find in the west. In particular, Wilkinson wanted the youthful Claiborne replaced as governor of Louisiana, and his eagerness to meet Burr suggested that the vice president was his preferred candidate as successor.

The timing of their encounter was significant. Burr had another ten months before his term of office ended, but no obvious political future. He had just been defeated in the race for governor of his home state, New York, a result he blamed on the scurrilous allegations about his financial probity made by his bitter political rival Alexander Hamilton. Burr was in a dangerous mood when he met Wilkinson. As Charles Biddle reported, the vice president was ready "to call out the first man of any respectability concerned in the infamous publications concerning him."

The provocation came just six weeks after his meeting with Wilkinson. Hamilton's comment that Burr was "a dangerous man unfit to be entrusted with the reins of power" was enough for the challenge to be issued, answered, and shots exchanged on the hillside of Weehawken, New Jersey, overlooking the Hudson River. What destroyed Burr's political career, in the north at least, was the report that Hamilton had intentionally fired wide before the colonel deliberately shot his opponent in the gut.

With a warrant issued for his arrest in New York, Burr took refuge with Charles Biddle in Pennsylvania. Lacking any obvious outlet for his energies, he returned to the topic that Wilkinson had raised. During the rest of the year, they exchanged ciphered messages and held occasional meetings.

From these emerged the outline of what became known as the Burr conspiracy.

THE CONSPIRATORS MADE AN INCONGRUOUS PAIR. The general growing stouter, increasingly rosy and swollen in the face, and addicted to ever more Ruritanian uniforms; the colonel, tall, elegantly dressed, an eighteenth-century aristocrat, who took it as a truth that "a gentleman is free to do whatever he pleases so long as he does it with style." John Adams wrote that he had "never known, in any country, the prejudice in favor of birth, parentage, and descent more conspicuous than in the instance of Colonel Burr." Marriage had made Wilkinson part of the Biddles' influential circle, but Burr, grandson of the great Calvinist theologian Jonathan Edwards, "was connected by blood," as Adams put it, "to many leading families in New England." Wilkinson had never been to college, and most of his life had been spent on the frontier or in the coarse world of licentious soldiery, while Burr, the successful New York attorney and brilliant politician who came within a single vote of being the third president, had been educated at Princeton and had never strayed far from the Atlantic coast, rarely even beyond its law courts and drawing rooms.

Yet they shared some notable characteristics. Both grew up fatherless and indulged by wealthy relatives. Each displayed a mesmerizing ability to win influential friends, outstanding initiative and courage during the Revolutionary War, and in peacetime a taste for extravagance that drove them to stretch morality to the point of illegality in the pursuit of money. In Burr's case, he sold political favors and made a flagrant attempt to turn the credit-issuing powers of the Manhattan water company into a full banking service. And by the time they began discussing operations in Mexico, both were facing a bleak future, according to one astute observer, the French ambassador, General Louis-Marie Turreau.

"Mr. Burr's career is generally looked upon as finished; but he is far from sharing that opinion, and I believe he would rather sacrifice the interests of his country than renounce celebrity and fortune," Turreau told Talleyrand in March 1805. Wilkinson, he wrote, "complains rather indiscreetly, and especially after dinner, of the form of his government, which leaves officers few chances of fortune, advancement, and glory, and which does not pay its military chiefs enough to support a proper style."

Nevertheless, those who had dealings with Burr and Wilkinson made a sharp distinction between the two. Both Alexander Hamilton and Thomas Jefferson, natural opposites in other matters, shared a visceral antagonism to

Burr and his ambitions. Jefferson expressed his dislike circumspectly, noting that from their first encounter in the 1790s "his conduct very soon inspired me with distrust" because Burr had no principles and "was always at market" for political gain. Hamilton, on the other hand, did not mince his words, writing, "[Burr] loves nothing but himself. He is sanguine enough to hope every thing—daring enough to attempt every thing—wicked enough to scruple [at] nothing." By contrast, despite their doubts about Wilkinson's financial dealings with the Spaniards, both were ready to entrust him with power, Hamilton by recommending his promotion to major general in 1799, and Jefferson by confirming him as army commander in 1801. If either of the conspirators at Richmond Hill were to betray the other, everything suggested it would be Burr.

WILKINSON'S MAPS AND NOTES SHOWED two obvious ways of entering Mexico from the United States. The first was championed by the French general Victor Collot, who explored the Mississippi Valley in 1796. In his book, *Voyage dans l'Amérique Septentrionale*, Collot selected Santa Fe as the most desirable point of access. Troops could either descend from the Missouri River in the north, following a line that would become the Santa Fe Trail, or ascend the Arkansas River from the Mississippi. Because the final approach "presents neither mountains nor rivers which might be serious obstacles," Collot concluded, "one may easily appreciate how important it is for Spain that these two passages be closed."

Much of Collot's geography was wrong, but his military instinct was right. So long as a commander chose the right rivers to follow through the dry land that lay beyond the Mississippi, Santa Fe could be reached without overwhelming difficulty. And from Santa Fe, the royal road, El Camino Real, led due south to Chihuahua and Mexico City. The route left New Orleans more than one thousand miles to the east. The city could be ignored in any advance through Santa Fe.

The alternative was to sail directly to Veracruz on the coast of Mexico and march less than two hundred miles inland to Mexico City. In every way it was simpler than the Santa Fe route, except that the commander would have to decide what to do about New Orleans, the port where his army had to be assembled for embarkation to Mexico. If it could not be cajoled into giving its support willingly, New Orleans would have to be captured.

After his first discussions with Wilkinson, Burr contacted the British ambassador, Anthony Merry, to enlist Britain's aid. The plan, Merry tersely informed London, was "to effect a separation of the Western Part of the United States from that which lies between the Atlantick and the Mountains, in its whole Extent." What Burr wanted, as he soon made clear, was a squadron of British warships from the West Indies to prevent the United States navy from reaching the mouth of the Mississippi. This would stop New Orleans from being reinforced from the sea and allow a force bound for Veracruz free passage to the coast of Mexico.

From an early stage, therefore, the colonel favored a plan for, directly or indirectly, the secession of the western states, and an invasion of Mexico through Veracruz. The general's interests, by contrast, were always drawn toward Santa Fe. Nor was his name mentioned in Merry's report, even though the secessionist plan outlined there was essentially the Spanish Conspiracy in British colors. Long experience had inoculated Wilkinson against any scheme that involved detaching the western states from the Union.

IN JANUARY 1805, the president nominated James Wilkinson to the Senate to be governor of the new Louisiana Territory. The choice drew immediate criticism in Congress that "it was anti-republican to unite civil and military office in one person," and in defending it Jefferson had to contradict his own principle that "no military man should be so placed as to have no civil superior." Louisiana Territory, the president claimed, was a military outpost—an officer administered each of its five districts—thus requiring a general to be in command. But the casuistry did not alter the reality. From his headquarters in St. Louis, Brigadier General James Wilkinson would not only have command of an army whose troops were increasingly concentrated in the south and the west, but would also exercise civilian control over an area that reached from Canada to the Arkansas River, and from the Mississippi westward to the indeterminate border with the Spanish empire.

Criticism was not confined to Congress. From Kentucky, Judge Joseph Daveiss wrote in alarm to the president, "You have appointed General Wilkinson a governor of St. Louis, who I am convinced has been for years, and now is, a pensioner of Spain." Almost apologetically, the judge referred to the earlier warning given to Jefferson: "I am told that Mr. Ellicott, in his journal, communicated to the office of state the names of the Americans concerned [in the Spanish Conspiracy]. If this is true you are long since guarded; but I suspect either that it is not, or has escaped you; or you have considered the affair dead." Jefferson immediately acknowledged the importance of his allegation and requested "a full communication of everything known by you." Daveiss's reply revealed, however, that he was relying on Humphrey Marshall's suspicions dating back to the 1780s and had nothing more substantial to offer than gossip about the barrels of money Wilkinson had received. In Washington, where the general's role was becoming more important, it was easy to dismiss this as politically motivated abuse.

Within the administration, Wilkinson's warmest supporter was Gideon Granger, the postmaster general, who described the general that spring as "one of the most agreeable, best informed, most genteel, moderate & sensible Republicans in the Nation." What most of Jefferson's cabinet felt was best expressed by Treasury Secretary Albert Gallatin, when he said, "Of the General I have no very exalted opinion; he is extravagant and needy and would not, I think, feel much delicacy in speculating on public money or public lands. In both these respects he must be closely watched . . . But tho' perhaps not very scrupulous in that respect and although I fear he may sacrifice to a certain degree the interests of the United States to his desire of being popular in his government, he is honorable in his private dealings and of betraying it to a foreign country I believe him altogether incapable."

This profound misjudgment by Jefferson's sharpest political adviser points to the difficulty that everyone would shortly face in deciding where the general's loyalties really lay. Unmistakably he was capable of betraying his country: since his payment of twelve thousand dollars, he had twice briefed the Spanish ambassador, the Marqués de Casa-Yrujo, on U.S. strategy, and when spring came, Captain Pedro Vial's column was roaming the headwaters of the Missouri in search of Lewis and Clark. As tensions about the border grew angrier in the early months of 1805, leading to talk of war, the advantage of having Agent 13 in command of the U.S. army and governor of a border province must have seemed unmistakable to his Spanish handlers. Yet even they could hardly have known which way he would jump if hostilities did break out.

The governor's post carried with it a salary of two thousand dollars a year, as well as the power of patronage, the chance of bribery, and a preferential position for land speculation in the wide-open prairies beyond the Mississippi River. Nevertheless, when Charles Biddle, Nancy's cousin and Burr's friend, wrote to congratulate Wilkinson on the appointment, his reply alluded to an entirely different advantage. It would take a year to show how rewarding the post would be, Wilkinson said, but "in the meantime I can only say the country is a healthy one and I shall be on the high road to Mexico."

His florid style always made the import of such remarks equivocal—was this rhetoric or reality? For a plain-talking frontiersman such as John Adair, his old comrade-in-arms and expert in horseflesh, it had to be real. In December 1804 he had written Wilkinson lamenting the failure of the United States to declare war on Spain and thereby provide an excuse for invading Mexico. "The Kentuckians are full of enterprise," he assured the general, "and, although not poor, as greedy after plunder as ever the old Romans were. Mexico glitters in our Eyes—the word is all we wait for." In June 1805, Adair received a teasing reply. It was an apology for Wilkinson's failure to introduce him to Aaron Burr, who "understands your merits, and *reckons* on you." The general promised to make up for it when they next met. "I will tell you *all*. We must have a *peep* at the unknown world beyond me." The world beyond Louisiana was Mexico.

For every adventurer, not just those in Kentucky, the dream of seizing Mexico's silver and gold mines did indeed dazzle the imagination.

On March 4, 1805, Jefferson's new vice president, George Clinton, was sworn in and Colonel Aaron Burr ceased to have a job. A few days earlier, at Wilkinson's recommendation Congressman Matthew Lyon from Kentucky had gone to Burr with a plan for reviving his political career. His suggestion was that the colonel should immediately relocate to Tennessee, where his national reputation would almost guarantee his immediate election to the next Congress. Lyon was forced to wait for almost an hour to see Burr at his lodgings in Washington because the former vice president was locked in conference with Wilkinson and Jonathan Dayton, an old political ally of both men's.

When Burr at last emerged, he made his lack of enthusiasm for the Tennessee project apparent by informing Lyon that his first priority was to go to Philadelphia—"He talked as if the business was indispensable," the congressman commented. The reason for this visit, kept secret from Lyon, was to make another approach to the British minister, Merry. According to the report that was later sent to London, Burr asked for "two or three frigates and the same number of smaller vessels to be stationed at the mouth of the Mississippi to prevent its being blockaded by such force as the United States could send." He also wanted a loan of about $350,000. Neither money nor ships were forthcoming, but Aaron Burr's preference for invading Mexico by the Veracruz route was unmistakable.

In April, having had his appointment as governor reluctantly confirmed by the Senate, General James Wilkinson set out for St. Louis with Nancy and his son James Biddle, now a lieutenant, and an entourage of officials and their families, including his secretary, Joseph Browne, Burr's brother-in-law. During the winter, Burr and Wilkinson had communicated with each other using a cipher devised by Wilkinson and based on his Spanish model. Since Burr was about to undertake an exploratory journey to New Orleans, they would now follow the same route as far as the Mississippi River. Fresh from his meeting with Merry, Burr wrote Wilkinson to say he would wait for him in Pittsburgh until May 1 but no longer because he had a pressing schedule and "there is so much uncertainty and contingency in your march with a family."

By the time the general arrived in Pittsburgh, the former vice president had left, and Wilkinson with his followers floated down the Ohio in a small convoy of boats without encountering anyone of importance. Waiting for him at Cincinnati, however, was Jonathan Dayton. Since almost everything that Dayton did was tainted by corruption, few people believed Wilkinson's explanation that they were discussing the construction of a canal to bypass the Falls of the Ohio. It was noted, too, that when Burr had passed through earlier, he had spent much of a day in conversation with Dayton. Burr had then made a detour into Tennessee to consult with Andrew Jackson, and during the five days he spent with the Tennessean, Wilkinson drifted ahead of him. Early in June, the general came to the grassy hillside where Fort Massac overlooked the river, and the convoy docked there.

The fort was built in an old-fashioned, star-shaped style to allow defenders to give covering fire wherever possible. Dearborn had just introduced a design for a cheaper, square blockhouse that would become the classic fort of the western prairies. With the Indian threat pushed back beyond the Mississippi, Fort Massac was about to become redundant, but it played a curiously fraught role in Wilkinson's life. There he had come closest to exposure as a Spanish agent, first with the arrest of Owens's murderers, and again when Thomas Power was stopped with Wilkinson's barrels of silver dollars. There, too, he now became entrapped in the events that would see him branded forever as a traitor.

On June 8, 1805, Aaron Burr's boat was rowed briskly into shore. He was in a hurry and drove his boatmen hard. During the next thirty-six hours, he and Wilkinson spent much time in private conversation. According to Wilkinson, they discussed Burr's political ambitions, and in particular the discovery that his chances of being elected in Tennessee had gone because he'd arrived there too late. Instead, Wilkinson had suggested "he might be returned [as a delegate] from New Orleans." For Daniel Clark, the man who became Wilkinson's most damaging accuser, this was simply implausible.

"Here," he wrote in his *Proofs of the Corruption of General James Wilkinson*, "is the first period at which I have positive proof of the general's participation in Burr's plans." After Fort Massac, every move made by the two men would come to be studied in detail by contemporaries and by historians in order to understand the roles they played in the Burr Conspiracy.

THE ONE SALIENT FEATURE of the conspiracy was the position of power occupied by the general. To Burr and Dayton, it was obvious that whatever they might plan depended on Wilkinson's cooperation. Everything hung on that. Not only had he been given the supreme military and political authority in the territory bordering Mexico, but within the army he possessed a dominating, personal influence. Its extent was made apparent when the long chronicle of Colonel Thomas Butler's pigtail reached its final chapter.

Summoned to a second court-martial in New Orleans in July 1805, Butler was found guilty of "disobedience of orders" and "mutinous conduct" and was sentenced to suspension from his command of the Second Regiment for one year without pay. The city itself, however, had a more terminal punishment for his insubordination. On September 7, the colonel died of the yellow fever that repeatedly plagued New Orleans. His death triggered a final outburst of fury against Wilkinson, but also left vacant the command of the Second Regiment. The appointment of Butler's successor started a turf war between the commanding general and the secretary of war that determined where power lay within the army.

By right of seniority, Butler's successor should have been Lieutenant Colonel Thomas Cushing, adjutant general and Wilkinson's close friend. But before the appointment could be made, Dearborn warned the general, "No measures should be taken in the consequence of the death of Colonel Butler in regard to promotions until you receive further information from this department." The department's preferred candidate for command of the Second Regiment was Colonel Samuel Hammond, a militia officer well-known to Dearborn as Wilkinson's sworn enemy. The choice was deliberate. In Dearborn's jaundiced view, the bloodbath of Federalist officers had produced a paradoxical result. Their places had been taken not by Republicans but by Wilkinson supporters.

The commander of the First Regiment, Colonel Thomas Hunt, was Wilkinson's friend, as was Major Andrew Nicoli, next in line to become adjutant general. The superintendent of West Point military academy,

Colonel Jonathan Williams, was a convivial companion whose enthusiasm for good living and military music once led the general to send him a mock-serious warning: "For your own amusment puff every Cheek at your will—let the Hills resound & the vallies sing—but give no occasion for those who listen with invidious pleasure, to fasten upon us the *foul* imputation of Ariostocratic Pomp & parade at the public expence." With Cushing in command of the Second Regiment, Wilkinson's allies would be everywhere.

Among senior officers below the rank of colonel, a high proportion put their names to a remarkable memorial just eighteen months later attesting to the qualities of Wilkinson's character: "Generous, benevolent, and humane—his heart, his hand, and his purse, are ever open, and ready to succour distress, and relieve misfortune—hardy, enterprising, daring and brave, he encounters obstacles with alacrity, and is most exalted when pressed by difficulties . . . With him for a leader, we shall neither fear dangers, nor foresee difficulties—but shall march to battle, with the assurance of victory."

Alarmed by the extent of Wilkinson's following within the army, Dearborn needed to put Hammond in a position of power where he could create a rival source of patronage within the army. But as each of Dearborn's predecessors, going back to Henry Knox, had discovered, it was difficult to defeat the general in a head-on confrontation. Because Hammond was not a regular officer, giving him command of the Second Regiment threatened to block a long chain of potential promotions that allowed each rank down to mere lieutenants to count on moving up to the vacancy immediately above them. Such a move, protested Lieutenant Zebulon Pike, was "striking at the very root of ambition & stifling in the bud every noble sentiment." Similar denunciations of Dearborn's flouting of military convention streamed in from other outraged officers. When Wilkinson's allies in the Senate, led by Samuel Smith, discovered that Hammond had once actively supported the subversive French minister Genêt, the excuse was enough to have his appointment overturned. Cushing duly took command of the Second Regiment, and a shuffling of promotions restored harmony to the army.

The result left Dearborn's attempt to limit Wilkinson's power in ruins. All three colonels—Hunt and Cushing in command of the infantry regiments, and Henry Burbeck, commander of the artillery—opposed Dearborn's political interference and gave the Senate "great credit" for overturning Hammond's appointment. The result was unmistakable. With the Burr Conspiracy beginning to take shape, Wilkinson's sympathizers held every key post in the army. He had a clear-cut plan for seizing Texas, New Mexico, and possibly silver-rich Chihuahua. The one necessary condition for action was the outbreak of war, and the worsening dispute over the borders of Louisiana seemed certain to provide what he wanted.

BETRAYER BETRAYED

O N JULY 3, 1805, some hours after breakfast, General James Wilkinson's convoy arrived at the St. Louis levee. He should have been there two days earlier, but had to make a detour to St. Genevieve so that a judge could administer the oath of office that the governor had forgotten to take in Washington; in the only public apology of his life, Wilkinson confessed to Jefferson that the omission "excites the sharpest self-reproach and exposes me to severe reprehension." From the levee, a troop of cavalry escorted him as he rode on horseback up the slope to the central square, where he was greeted by a ragged volley of shots fired by 100 armed Indians, then by a sharper salute from the 240 soldiers drawn up for his inspection. This was followed by speeches of welcome in French, the language of the long-established Creole inhabitants, and in English, the language of the newcomers.

The next day, on the Fourth of July, he and his officers sat down to dinner at a three-hundred-foot-long table decorated with eighteen gilded pyramids, seventeen representing the number of states, each inscribed, "Prudence, Morality, Wisdom, Law," and the eighteenth decorated in gold letters reading, "United States—Glory & Power—*Sic Semper Omnia* [So everything should be forever]," on one face and on the other, "James Wilkinson—Protection." Inspired by music from the military band and the "courteous and affable manners and fascinating charms" of the ladies of St. Louis, the festivity continued through the night and "did not cease," the *National Intelligencer* confided in its inimitable style, "till the gentle Aurora with lighted taper in her rosy fingers conducted each angelic form to her downy pillow." Almost from the moment the revelers awoke, relations between governor and citizens went downhill.

The reception reflected St. Louis's pride in its sophistication. The city was more than forty years old and boasted around two hundred houses, the majority built of stone, and a population that included prosperous citizens such as Auguste Chouteau, aspiring new arrivals such as Timothy Kibby, and almost one thousand other inhabitants, largely French Canadian, Native American, and mixed race, with a scattering of British and Spanish. The economy depended on the fur trade and mining—iron, lead, and salt—but as in all frontier communities the central concern was land, the fundamental source of wealth in a preindustrial economy. At the heart of that concern were two questions: Who owned it? How could they prove it?

The answers affected everyone living within the Louisiana Purchase, both around St. Louis and in the Orleans Territory. They fostered popular resentment against the United States, soured the reputations of the two governors, Claiborne and Wilkinson, and powerfully influenced the development of the Burr Conspiracy.

The problem began with the confusion caused by the rapid transfer of sovereignty between Spain, France, and the United States. The difficulty of harmonizing three different kinds of property law was compounded by systematic tampering with the land registry files. "There has been Leaves cut out of the Books and others pasted in with Large Plats of Surveys on them," Silas Bent, the American-appointed surveyor general of the Louisiana Territory, reported in 1806. "The dates have been evidently altered in a large proportion of the certificates. Plats have been altered from smaller to Larger. Names erased and others incerted and striking difference in collour of the ink etc."

To clear up the confusion, Congress appointed a board of land commissioners to examine the legal title of all property owners within the Louisiana Purchase. Their investigation sparked fury among the Creole inhabitants. The standard demanded was that of United States law, meaning there had to be documentary evidence of the original grant, a surveyor's plat of the property, and registration of it in a land office. Any disputes would be decided in court by the American adversarial system rather than the French and Spanish legal process that depended on a consensual pursuit of facts. According to Amos Stoddard, the temporary governor who first had to confront the problem, nineteen out of twenty existing French and Spanish owners were likely to lose their property under this process.

From the safety of Washington, Wilkinson had repeatedly urged Stoddard "to conciliate the people," by which he meant the Creoles, but all five of the military officers who administered Louisiana Territory supported the newcomers who wanted the land. Most claims were still working their way through the courts, but already properties were being transferred from French to American owners. Now the explosive issue was Wilkinson's responsibility.

From his first day in office, when he chose to avoid a settlers' welcoming banquet in favor of lunch with Auguste Chouteau, Wilkinson showed a consistent bias in favor of the Creoles. Although justified in terms of democratic justice—when Louisiana became the Missouri Territory in 1812, the legislature would quickly vote to restore much of the Creoles' land—this was a dangerous policy. It not only made enemies among Anglo-American settlers, but turned the military administrators against him. Two in particular, Major James Bruff, whose banquet Wilkinson spurned, and Colonel Samuel Hammond, were landowners as well, and each was to become a dangerous enemy. Both were retired professional soldiers, now in the militia, and as their military and civilian superior General Wilkinson loftily dismissed their opposition. Hammond he termed "a hackneyed scoundrel," and Bruff nothing more than "a damned cunning fellow."

For someone so subtle in playing off one individual against another, Wilkinson's confrontation with the Anglo-American settlers seemed almost willful. Edward Hempstead, a leading St. Louis citizen, expressed a widely shared feeling when he wrote of the governor, "From a rank Federalist to a suspected Republican, he became a bigot and is now a petty tyrant." Yet there was method in his quarreling. Many of the actions that aroused antagonism among the newcomers—his hostility to the judges, and his refusal to pardon Hammond's nephew for murdering a Kickapoo man, for example—conciliated Creole and Native American feelings. Since these people constituted a majority in the territory, his policy was more democratic than tyrannical. Unpopular though he was with the Anglo-Americans, Wilkinson's stance helped reconcile a diffuse, frontier population to U.S. government.

In New Orleans by contrast, Governor Claiborne imposed the land laws and legal system of the United States without regard to the feelings of the majority Creole population and was faced with near rebellion. As Jefferson himself acknowledged, they were driven to this extreme by "the call on them by the land commissioners for their deeds" and by "the administration of justice in our forms, principles & language." Whatever private reservations he might have about the roughshod tactics of the governor of

Louisiana Territory, in public Jefferson unequivocally approved of his policy. "Not a single fact has appeared," he told Senator Samuel Smith of Maryland in May 1806, "which occasions me doubt that I could have made a fitter appointment than Genl. Wilkenson [*sic*]."

IT WAS PRECISELY THE HOSTILITY of the French inhabitants toward their new rulers that Colonel Aaron Burr hoped to exploit when he was rowed into New Orleans in June 1805. He arrived, as he told his daughter, Theodosia, on "an elegant barge, [with] sails, colors, ten oars, [and] a sergeant and ten able, faithful hands." Burr boasted that it had been supplied by the army's commanding general, although it actually belonged to Captain Daniel Bissell and was carrying officers to Colonel Butler's court-martial. More impressive than the boat, however, was the letter that Burr carried with him from James Wilkinson to his former agent Daniel Clark Jr. Written at Fort Massac and couched in typically misty terms, it recommended the former vice president as someone "whose worth you know well how to estimate. If the persecutions of a great and honourable man can give title to generous attentions, he has claims to all your civilities and your services. You cannot oblige me more than by such conduct, and I pledge my life to you it will not be misapplied. To him I refer you for many things improper to a letter, and which he will not say to any other."

The "improper" phrase would come back to haunt Wilkinson when it was assumed to refer to his complicity in Burr's plans. But in a letter liable to fall into the wrong hands, the general might have wanted to keep other sensitive topics secret—his wish to see Burr replace Claiborne as governor of Orleans Territory, and, as it turned out, Burr's intention of involving Daniel Clark himself in his schemes. Clark always dismissed this last option. He vigorously denied any ties to Burr and made much of the fact that he saw the colonel only once during his twelve days in New Orleans. Clark's actions, however, belied his protestations.

As he had anticipated, Burr found his hints of secession rapturously welcomed by the alienated French community in New Orleans. Their anger at Claiborne's governorship had boiled over the previous fall, and two spokesmen, sent to Washington to protest against the destruction of their democratic rights, predicted widespread revolt unless his policies softened. Burr's Veracruz venture also drew support from an informal network of traders calling themselves the Mexico Association, who hoped to back a coup d'état there, and from a group of Ursuline nuns hoping for the restoration of Catholic rule. Nevertheless, the high point of Burr's short visit to New

Orleans was a magnificent dinner given in his honor by the French merchants who dominated the city.

When he started to return north in late June, heading initially for a second consultation with Andrew Jackson, the support of New Orleans and its wealthy inhabitants must have become a factor in his plans. The exact nature of those plans were still a mystery, but in September 1805 a curious letter sent by Clark to Wilkinson shed some light on them.

Ostensibly Clark's message was a warning about the "many absurd and evil reports circulated here . . . respecting our ex-Vice-President . . . The tale is a horrid one, if well told. Kentucky, Tennessee, the state of Ohio, with part of Georgia and part of Carolina, are to be bribed with plunder of the Spanish countries west of us to separate from the Union; this is but a part of the business." The writer's tone was amused and disbelieving. One wild rumor struck him as particularly incredible: "You are spoken of as his right hand man." Like every public figure of his time, however, Clark appreciated the likelihood of his mail being opened, and his message carried an inner private meaning.

In the winter of 1805, after sending this letter, Clark made the first of two trading voyages to Veracruz, during which he made extensive notes of the military forces in the area, and, according to John Graham, secretary at the time of the Orleans Territory, who saw his report, "particularly of the garrison-towns between Vera Cruz and Mexico [City]." At a time when war with Spain seemed imminent, Graham was intrigued and later testified that he made "several inquiries of Mr. Clark concerning Mexico; he was of opinion it might be invaded with every prospect of success. I asked him, whether, if the United States should undertake the invasion he would bear a part; he evidenced an unwillingness to have any thing to do with an expedition carried on by the government; but expressed himself willing to join in such an enterprize undertaken and carried on by individuals."

Clark's motives for aligning himself with Burr's schemes were both personal and political. He had just been frustrated by Governor Claiborne in his attempt to be appointed the Orleans Territory representative to Congress, but he was also infuriated by the treatment of the Creoles. "I have encouraged, and will continue to encourage, the outcry and opposition to [U.S.] measures," he promised Wilkinson in 1804, and the strength of his feelings was widely known. "He has often said that the Union could not last," Claiborne reported, "and that, had he children, he would impress early on their minds the expediency of a separation between the Atlantic and Western States."

These evident sympathies for the goals that Burr had in mind give a different meaning to the letter Clark sent Wilkinson. Rather than a general warning, his real intention was to share in coded form Burr's latest thinking. The plan that Clark described looked very like the old Spanish Conspiracy that was so familiar to them both. Thus the critical sentence about Wilkinson being "spoken of as his right hand man" had a double significance.

On September 11, about the time when this letter was sent, Aaron Burr himself came in person to St. Louis for another meeting with the man who appeared more and more clearly to be the linchpin of all his plans. The priorities of James Wilkinson were not what he expected.

ON HIS JOURNEY NORTH, Burr had held extensive consultations with two militia generals, Andrew Jackson in Tennessee and John Adair in Kentucky. Although the details of their conversations remained private, their shape was clear. Both generals publicly stated that once war was declared with Spain, they would lead the militia and thousands of volunteers to seize the Floridas and "Mexico," an ambiguous label that referred sometimes just to Texas, but sometimes included the Floridas, and occasionally all the Spanish border provinces including the silver state of Chihuahua. It was a prospect they both eagerly looked forward to.

In contrast to their ebullient spirits, Burr found Wilkinson depressed, exhausted by his battles with the settlers, but affected more deeply than anything else by his wife's deteriorating health. Nancy Wilkinson had developed tuberculosis and, during the steamy heat of the St. Louis summer, suffered difficulty in breathing. Her illness added a bitter note to Wilkinson's patronizing onslaughts against his enemies. One particular target, Judge John Lucas, who combined speculation with his official position as a land commissioner, was accused not only of venality, but of attacking Wilkinson "because I do not acknowledge his superiority, because I sometimes wear a cocked hat and a sword, and am fond of a clean shirt, which are Eyesores to him, [and] because my infirm wife rides daily for her Health in a carriage, which he considers aristocratic." In the months ahead, Wilkinson's erratic behavior would bewilder friend and foe, but one explanation for it lay in the anxiety he felt for his wife's condition.

His gloomy outlook cast a shadow over his first meeting with Burr. A major difference arose over Burr's belief that the western settlers could be induced to secede from the United States. According to his own account, Wilkinson exclaimed, "My friend, no person was ever more mistaken! The western people disaffected to the government! They are bigoted to Jefferson and democracy."

Having lived in the west for more than twenty years and spent ten of them unsuccessfully promoting the Spanish Conspiracy, it was understandable that he should have been exasperated by the easterner's assumption that sentiments in the west were as volatile as in the 1780s. In the argument that ensued, Burr apparently questioned the depth of Wilkinson's commitment to the plan to invade Mexico, demanding angrily, in the governor's recollection, " 'whether I could be content to vegitate or moulder in that d—d government?' meaning the government of Louisiana." Wilkinson replied in subdued terms that "I was making arrangements to retire to private life; that I was tired of the erratic life I had long led; and that the delicate situation of my wife, to whom I owed more than I could render, made it necessary."

Quite implausibly, the governor claimed that this was when Burr first broached his Mexican plan: "But suppose some grand enterprize should present, which would lead direct to fame and fortune?" This lie apart, there clearly was a disagreement between them, because a second, hurried meeting was held as Burr was leaving. By way of compromise, they apparently decided to put aside the matter of secession and concentrate on what was essential for Burr, Wilkinson's proposals to march on Santa Fe. War would bring out Jackson and Adair, and so long as the army was engaged in the west, New Orleans would be defenseless, and its French inhabitants would willingly turn it over to Burr. Beyond that, any conflict around Santa Fe would draw Spanish troops away to the north of Mexico, leaving little opposition to an invasion of Veracruz in the south.

Their discussions took place at a time of high alert, when the mounting tensions over the border between Louisiana and Texas seemed to make war with Spain inevitable. In the summer, the U.S. representatives in Spain, James Monroe and John Armstrong, broke off negotiations and secretly advised the president simply to seize Texas. Days before Burr's arrival, Wilkinson had actually sent the war secretary a lucid and obviously well-considered proposal for invading Mexico by way of Santa Fe, approaching the city either by the Santa Fe trail or the Arkansas River, and employing "a Corps of 100 Artillerists, 400 Cavalry, 400 Rifle men and 1100 Musquetry." An otherwise bizarre proposal to bring along "a band of Irish Priests who have been educated in Spain, (of whom I have a dozen)" indicated that the general planned not merely to seize "the Northern Provinces" but to take permanent possession. Clearly Wilkinson envisioned the silver-bearing Sierra Madre as a prize.

That fall, Dearborn wrote to advise Wilkinson that the army should be kept on alert. In a rare show of harmony, he commented approvingly on the general's plan to invade Mexico with guns and priests: "I am not sure that a project of that kind may not become necessary." In November, after Burr's departure, Wilkinson promised Dearborn, "If I do not reduce New Mexico, at least, in one campaign, I will forfeit my command."

It was Aaron Burr's habit, according to the modern editor of his papers, "to hear what he wanted to hear." What he evidently heard was that Wilkinson intended to move against Santa Fe shortly. People he tried to recruit testified later that Burr talked as though the Veracruz attack was part of the official strategy to invade Mexico. What he did not hear was the caveat that the general added when he told Dearborn of his invasion plan, that it would only take place "should we be involved in a War, (which Heaven avert)."

They parted with sufficient goodwill for Wilkinson to give Burr an introduction to Governor William Harrison of Indiana Territory, and a warm letter asking him to consider appointing Burr as the territory's delegate to Congress. Soon after the colonel's departure, however, the governor received another warning, this time from Dearborn: "There is a strong rumor that you, Burr, etc are too intimate. You ought to keep every suspicious person at arms length, and be as wise as a serpent and as harmless as a dove." Wilkinson's reaction was carefully designed to distance himself from Burr but without giving him away.

In a friendly message to Robert Smith, secretary of the navy, and brother of Samuel, Wilkinson dropped in a significant phrase: "Burr is about something, but whether internal or external, I cannot discover. I think you should keep an eye on him." So vague was the wording that Smith did not notice its import and did nothing to act on it. The tone was not so much a warning from someone anxious about possible insurrection as insurance by someone concerned to protect his own back. Should war come, and Burr encourage secession in Kentucky and Tennesee, General Wilkinson could at least claim to have alerted the government.

Yet the general remained troubled. In December 1805, he contacted his old friend John Adair, fishing for information about Burr's secessionist plans. Adair sent a teasing reply. "You observe to me," he wrote in January 1806, "that I 'have seen Colonel Burr, and ask me what was his Business in the west?' Answer. Only to avoid a prosecution in New York. Now, Sir, you will oblige me by answering a question in turn for I know you can, Pray how far is it, and what kind of way from St. Louis to Santa Fé, and from thence to Mexico?" The answer he received sounded boastful on first reading, but more cautious on the second. "Do you know that I have reserved these places for my own triumphal entry," Wilkinson declared, "that I not only know the way but all the difficulties and how to surmount them? I wish we could get leave, Mexico could soon be ours."

Since Jefferson's policy was to avoid the expense of fighting, no leave was given for attack. In the absence of war, Wilkinson would not move. As a result, Aaron Burr and his chief of staff, Jonathan Dayton, were forced to resort to blackmail.

DESPITE FAILING TO GET any encouragement for his plans from Governor Harrison, Burr immediately set about fund-raising on his return to Philadelphia. During the winter he was promised more than fifty thousand dollars, ostensibly to buy land west of the Mississippi on the Ouachita River. Burr's son-in-law, Joseph Alston, governor of South Carolina, provided substantial financial guarantees, but the most generous supporter was Jonathan Dayton, who personally lent twenty thousand dollars. He did so on the specific understanding that the commanding general would be an active participant. Dayton had known Wilkinson since 1794 and was well-informed about his connection to the Spanish Conspiracy. But he had not been in contact with the general since their meeting at Cincinnati in June 1805.

Apart from a note sent shortly after Burr left St. Louis, Wilkinson had in fact ceased to communicate with the leaders of the conspiracy. "Nothing has been heard from the Brigadier since October," Burr wrote in exasperation in April 1806. By contrast Burr had written several times to Wilkinson to keep him in touch with the conspiracy's development. "On the subject of a certain speculation, it is not deemed material to write till the whole can be communicated," Burr told him guardedly in December. And in April 1806 when it appeared that not enough funds were available, he announced, "The execution of our project is postponed till December: want of water in Ohio [i.e., money] rendered movement impracticable: other reasons rendered delay expedient. The association is enlarged, and comprises all that Wilkinson could wish."

The general's silence clearly alarmed Burr and Dayton. They needed war with Spain, and when it failed to materialize, they realized that he would have to be forced to cooperate. As early as December 1805, Burr wrote suggesting that had war broken out earlier in the year, "[General] Lee would have been commander in chief: truth I assure you." A month later in another letter, he retailed the gossip of Washington insiders that a road that Wilkinson claimed to have built through Tennessee had never really existed—"One, professing to be your friend, whispered to me soon afterwards that this conversation was calculated to do you injury"—but, Burr added innocently, Jefferson knew all about the allegation, "and I could not perceive that any inference unfriendly to you was drawn from the fact."

The direction of the hints was always the same—Wilkinson could no longer depend on Jefferson's support. When the letters drew no response, Dayton took more drastic action. In the summer of 1806, he financed a Kentucky newspaper, *Western World*, and supplied it with a series of stories exposing Wilkinson as "a Spanish pensioner." In great detail, and with much imagination, it described how he had been commissioned into the Spanish army, how his money arrived in leather bags, and how he repeatedly tried to get Kentucky to secede from the Union. The motive was clear, to make him unemployable by the federal government and thus force him to fall in with Burr's plans.

Not entirely by coincidence, the governor's enemies in St. Louis began to step up their attacks. During the winter of 1805–6, Bruff and Hammond had sent repeated complaints about his behavior to Congress and petitioned for his removal. Once the allegations of the *Western World* began to be published, they openly predicted that he would be replaced before the end of the year. In the summer of 1806, one critic, Seth Hunt, even specified the month, September, and the identity of his successor, Samuel Hammond.

WILKINSON WAS NOWHERE MORE VULNERABLE than in his concern about Jefferson's commitment to him. The most consistent feature of his time as governor of Louisiana was neither his friendship with the Creoles nor his vendetta with the settlers, but his unstinted efforts to cement his personal relationship with the man who'd appointed him. His behavior suggested something akin to the emotional seduction that he once displayed toward his generals.

Early in September 1805, just before Burr's arrival, Wilkinson sent east a stunning array of gifts designed to appeal to the president. Packed into a wooden trunk were twenty-seven mineral samples—iron ore from the Platte and Osage rivers, lead and galena from the upper Missouri, pumice stone from the Yellowstone, crystallized gypsum and salt rock from the Arkansas— evidence of enough wealth beneath the earth, he explained, "to employ Thousands of Hands, and to produce Millions of Dollars." With the help of a Ricara or Pawnee chief, named Ankedoucharo, who spoke seven languages including the lingua franca of the Plains Indians, sign language, the governor also assembled for the president a rough census of the eight thousand Plains Indians living southwest of the Missouri. Finally and most enticingly of all, he sent Jefferson a Native American map drawn on buffalo hide showing the courses of the Platte and Yellowstone rivers and what might have been a geyser in the area of what is now the Yellowstone National Park, thirteen hundred miles to the west.

Nothing was better calculated to earn Jefferson's gratitude than a gift of Indian lore. But Wilkinson's sumptuous offering also had an official justification. In addition to making him governor of Louisiana Territory, the president had appointed Wilkinson to be commissioner for Indian affairs, and therefore responsible for putting into practice Jefferson's policy of relocating Native Americans away from land wanted by settlers. In a report sent with the specimens, Wilkinson suggested that northern Louisiana could be made a repository for Native Americans living in the more desirable south, although this would be "opposed by busy and short-sighted politicians" in the Louisiana Territory. Because it was important to keep white settlers out of land intended for Indians, he urged the president to prevent "Aliens and Suspicious Characters mingling with the Natives, and to suspend all Commerce with them at your discretion."

On the document Jefferson's firm tick of approval can be seen beside the paragraph with Wilkinson's proposals, indicating that president and commissioner were at one on the future of the Louisiana Territory. Recognizing that the policy would not be popular, Wilkinson promised to carry out his president's instructions "without regard to personal consequences."

Although it was impossible to read Jefferson's sphinxlike mind, he clearly valued what Wilkinson could offer. The general had kept the army loyal, shown a passion for western exploration, defied unpopularity to carry out the president's Indian policies, justified the Red River expedition, and written the new Articles of War, which were about to receive congressional approval. The reward had been the decision to entrust him with almost unlimited power in the west. But Wilkinson's anxiety to earn Jefferson's good opinion only increased.

To satisfy the president's desire for knowledge about the west, he sent off a series of expeditions to explore the unknown country beyond him. Led by Lieutenant Zebulon Pike, the first departed northward a few weeks after the governor's arrival in St. Louis with a mission to explore the headwaters of the Mississippi and clear any British fur traders from the area. Pike fought his way through the swamps and pine forests of northern Minnesota and spent a hard winter near Cass Lake, which he identified as the source of the river— Lake Itasca, the real source, is about thirty miles away—before returning in April 1806. While he was away, Wilkinson dispatched two other lieutenants to explore the country to the west: George Peter was sent up the Osage

River, accompanied by the fur trader Pierre Chouteau; and Wilkinson's son, James Biddle, was directed to the upper Missouri, an enterprise cut short after a soldier was killed in a skirmish with Kickapoo warriors.

Like the maps that had first caught the president's attention, all this activity was for Jefferson's benefit. "My last breath, my last drop of blood shall be for Him," Wilkinson assured Samuel Smith in March 1806, "would that I had more to give." Yet, whatever he did, the evidence of his treachery was all around.

While the Red River expedition was being planned on the basis of Wilkinson's maps, Casa Calvo was advising the acting governor of Texas, in accordance with Wilkinson's "Reflections," that Spain should "drive back every illegal usurpation toward the region of Texas." Consequently, when Wilkinson's old associate Thomas Freeman led the expedition up the river in the spring of 1806, with Wilkinson's latest protégé, Captain Richard Sparks, in command of the military detachment, Wilkinson's advice also ensured that a troop of two hundred Mexican cavalry were being dispatched from Nacogdoches under Captain Francisco Viana to intercept them.

The general's anxieties were understandable. His adherence to Jefferson had begun as political calculation. But no one had entrusted him with more power, and Wilkinson had responded as he always did to those who flattered his vanity—with wholehearted devotion. That Jefferson might withdraw his trust created an almost intolerable anxiety.

IN THE TWO YEARS since Wilkinson had written "Reflections," General Salcedo, the commandant of the Internal Provinces, had moved more than seven hundred troops forward to beef up defenses on the Texas border, and Antonio Cordero, the energetic governor of Chihuahua, had been transferred to take over the forward province of Texas. This aggressive policy had been recommended by Agent 13 as a way of preventing the United States from expanding farther west. Rising tension reached a new pitch in October 1805 when Spanish forces occupied two fortified positions east of the Sabine River, the border with Texas as designated by the United States.

On June 11, 1806, Wilkinson received a letter from Henry Dearborn concerning the military situation in the south. Negotiations had failed to persuade the Spanish to withdraw. The presence of their forces on U.S. territory was effectively an invasion. "You will therefore with as little delay as possible repair to the Territory of New Orleans," the war secretary ordered, "and take upon yourself command of the Troops in that quarter, together with such Militia or Volunteers as you may need for the defence of the country."

He was being given the chance of war, with overall command. It would enhance his position as commanding general and bring him "fame and honor," as he acknowledged. At worst, the mere threat of attack might procure a Spanish bribe to keep the peace. At best, it would allow Burr to make his attack on Veracruz and might lead to the seizure of the Mexican silver mines. It should have been the culmination of all Wilkinson's preparations.

Instead, Dearborn's letter threw Wilkinson into rage and despair. All he could see was that his enemies had won. This was what Burr had hinted at, and Hunt had predicted. Until that moment Wilkinson had dismissed their reports as groundless. That very month, his confidence had been reinforced by a letter from Samuel Smith passing on Jefferson's opinion that he could not have made "a fitter appointment" as governor. Now, as Wilkinson told Dearborn, "your letter [has] corrected my delusions."

The order to leave St. Louis might be dressed up as a military deployment, but to Wilkinson's eyes, the harsh reality was to force him out of Louisiana. "Bruff, Lucas &c say it is done to get me out of the way to make room for Hammond," he told Smith. What made it "more afflicting" was the consequent need to move his now seriously ill wife. To Dearborn, he complained that Bruff's attempt to stir up trouble between "a General in Chief and a Minister of War" and to "draw down unmerited suspicions upon men of purest honor" was tantamount to treason. But to Smith he raged about the worst betrayal of all: how could Jefferson have praised him one day and condoned his dismissal the next?

The letters to Dearborn and Smith were sent on June 17. Then there was silence. Throughout the summer and fall of 1806, it was as though the commanding general of the U.S. army and Burr's right-hand man had simply disappeared. In the absence of any communication, neither the federal government nor the conspirators knew what had happened to him. On the Ohio, Aaron Burr and Jonathan Dayton gathered funds, men, and equipment for their next move and wondered why they had not heard from their collaborator. In Washington, Thomas Jefferson and Henry Dearborn debated with increasing anxiety why the army commander was no longer replying to letters or complying with orders. No one knew which way James Wilkinson would jump.

The General at Bay

O N October 22, 1806, the president summoned a cabinet meeting in the White House to be attended by his senior heads of department, Secretary of State James Madison, Albert Gallatin from Treasury, Henry Dearborn from War, and Gideon Granger, the postmaster general. Three critically important items were on the agenda—the Spanish threat east of the Sabine River, the nature of Aaron Burr's movements, and the loyalty of General James Wilkinson. The first two matters were quickly dealt with— they agreed that troops should be moved to the most southwesterly city in the United States, Natchitoches, to mount a credible deterrent to Spain, and Burr needed to be "strictly watched" to ensure that he did not put into action any plan that might injure the United States. The third question really tested the best political minds in the nation: "General Wilkinson being expressly declared by Burr to be engaged with him in this design as his Lieutenant or first in command, and suspicion of infidelity in Wilkinson being now become very general, a question is proposed what is proper to be done as to him?"

Gideon Granger, once Wilkinson's outspoken supporter, was responsible for raising the question. Three days earlier he had taken a sworn statement from William Eaton, formerly the U.S. consul in Tripoli, who had won a famous victory at Derna in 1805 leading a force that included the Marine Corps against the Barbary pirates in North Africa. Eaton claimed that after his return to the United States, Aaron Burr had approached him and "laid open his project of revolutionizing the western country, separating it from the Union, establishing a monarchy there, of which he was to be the sovereign, New Orleans to be his capital; organizing a force on the Mississippi, and extending conquest to Mexico." Burr offered to appoint Eaton second-in-command of the army that was to be led by General James Wilkinson.

The extravagance of the plot invited skepticism, and Eaton, who was seeking compensation from the government for debts he had incurred in North Africa, was not entirely reliable. When he originally brought his story to the attention of the president earlier in the year, Jefferson had dismissed it, saying he had "too much confidence in the integrity and the attachment to the Union of the citizens of [the western] country to admit an apprehension." The ease with which the cabinet disposed of the Burr question suggests that even at this late date his plans were not their chief concern. The real problem lay with the most powerful man in the Mississippi Valley, and its urgency was contained in the phrase "suspicion of infidelity in Wilkinson being now become very general."

The one person in the cabinet who had up to that point consistently refused to entertain any such suspicion was the president himself, and the consequences were starkly obvious. In New Orleans, the Creole population was close to rebellion against Claiborne's government, and the Spanish ambassador, Carlos Martinez de Casa-Yrujo, had let it be known that both Burr and Dayton had approached him with plans to exploit the unrest and use it to split off the western states from the Union. Everyone in the room must have been aware that the fate of the country now depended on what Wilkinson decided to do.

If he acted as a loyal commander against Spain, its invasion was easily countered. If he acted as a Spanish agent, the consequences were incalculable. Protected by the army, New Orleans was safe. Left vulnerable, it could fall to assault from the Mississippi or to an internal revolt. Unsupported by Wilkinson, Burr could be contained. Supported by Wilkinson, and the military following he could count on, Burr's conspiracy became a genuine insurrection. The cabinet agonized over these questions, and Dearborn, at least, could have been forgiven for wanting to say to the president, "You were warned."

Yet however they approached it, there was no easy answer to the question "What is proper to be done as to him?" because no one had been able to contact Wilkinson. He was out of reach and out of control. Dearborn had alerted the president to the problem early in September. "Genrl Wilkinson had not left St Louis on 28th July and I cannot account for his delay," Dearborn reported. "In his letters to me after the rcpt. of his orders, he ingaged at all events to be in Fort Adams by the twenty-fifth of July. I have received no letters from him for several weeks."

It took three or four weeks for a letter to come from St. Louis to Washington, and as much as two months from Fort Adams, depending on the level of the Ohio. But clearly Wilkinson had not moved from St. Louis six weeks after Dearborn's instructions to go to the Sabine "with as little delay as possible." Not until the end of August, ten weeks after the original order reached him, did the general finally take a boat south to Natchez, news that only reached Dearborn a month later. Meanwhile Claiborne and Mississippi's acting governor, Cowles Mead, had been ordered to call out the militia, but Colonel Cushing's refusal to allow any troops to move forward to Natchitoches without direct orders from Wilkinson prevented them from being deployed. From Washington it was difficult to make sense of what was happening. They could only be sure that, as Claiborne put it, "all was not right."

The desperation in the White House made itself apparent in an extraordinary order to Navy Secretary Robert Smith to call in two senior captains, Stephen Decatur and Edward Preble, for a secret briefing before leaving for New Orleans. Smith was instructed to give the officers command of all defensive operations in the city, meaning that the army would have to follow their orders. It was vivid evidence of the cabinet's distrust of the army's loyalty. Almost at once, however, the explosive consequences began to sink in of requiring Colonel Cushing and his fellow officers to ignore their general and instead take orders from a navy captain whose only force at New Orleans was a fleet of seven small gunships manned by militia sailors. The risk of setting military and naval commands at each other's throat was deemed too great, and Preble and Decatur's instructions were canceled at the last minute, thereby confirming the administration's impotence. The next day and the day after that, Jefferson's cabinet returned to the Wilkinson question. To deal with Burr, they decided to send John Graham, the Orleans Territory secretary, who happened to be in Washington, to spy on the colonel's followers. But even after hours of fruitless discussion, no decision was taken about Wilkinson. The president's policy had left the federal government powerless to prevent the general from exercising his magisterial power in whatever way he chose.

AARON BURR'S CAMP WAS ALSO CONCERNED about Wilkinson's intentions. Through the winter of 1806 Burr had exercised his magnetic personality on almost everyone on the east coast who might be able to aid his fortunes. The fund-raising campaign surprisingly included approaches by Burr and Jonathan Dayton, acting as his chief of staff, to the Spanish ambassador, the

Marquis de Casa-Yrujo. The scenario that Burr and Dayton presented to him—a separatist movement in the Mississippi Valley backed by a British fleet—had attractions for any Spanish diplomat. Although their plot had elements of fantasy as well, including an armed putsch in Washington with Burr forcibly replacing Jefferson, the power of the Creoles' independence movement in New Orleans convinced Yrujo of its feasibility. He contributed a much needed three thousand dollars and, in his dispatches to the Spanish foreign minister, Pedro Cevallos, confirmed that Wilkinson was involved and that Burr's goal was secession rather than an attack on Mexico.

In late May 1806, Burr finally received a letter from Wilkinson, but one so anodyne that Burr could not later recall its contents. The absence of any expression of support told its own story. With twenty thousand dollars at stake, Dayton finally lost patience. "It is now well ascertained that you are to be displaced in the next session," he wrote Wilkinson bluntly. "Jefferson will affect to yield reluctantly to the public sentiment, but yield he will; prepare yourself therefore for it; you know the rest. You are not a man to despair, or even despond, especially when such prospects offer in another quarter. Are you ready? Are your numerous associates ready? Wealth and Glory. Louisiana and Mexico."

In July 1806, Burr approached Albert Gallatin, the recognized fixer in Jefferson's administration, and inquired whether "Wilkinson had resigned or been removed from the office of governor of Louisiana." The nature of the questions indicated that Burr hoped the answer would be yes, but Gallatin replied with a double negative. In truth, however, Wilkinson's long silence meant that neither side knew where the general's shifting loyalties might turn. On the eve of the Burr Conspiracy, the participation of the one person who could make or break it remained a mystery.

WHETHER EVEN THE GENERAL HIMSELF knew what he would do is questionable. By coincidence, Dearborn's command to move south arrived just after Wilkinson had drafted orders for Cushing to advance up the Red River to Natchitoches with three companies of infantry to confront the Spanish threat. Immediately he added an urgent postscript giving Cushing sweeping power over all troops west of the Mississippi, and warning him to be ready for war, but to do nothing to provoke it, "as war is not only opposite to the genius and disposition of our country, but also to its substantial interests and happiness."

While this suggested the loyal commander, Wilkinson was at the same time urgently making arrangements for the departure of Lieutenant Pike's second expedition. Ostensibly its purpose was to explore the Red River, but covertly its orders seemed designed to take it to Santa Fe. The character of Pike himself might have been made for such a desperate mission.

Born into the army, Pike had followed his military father from post to post until he could enlist himself as a fifteen-year-old cadet, just in time to fight at Fallen Timbers. He never received more than a smattering of an education, and he had failed in all the tasks set for his 1805 expedition—discovery of the source of the Mississippi, removal of British traders, and suppression of their illegal fur business. But he had demonstrated a priceless ability to persuade others to accept his leadership whatever the cost. Hauling their boats through snowstorms and freezing, ice-thickened rivers, his twenty men worked until they vomited blood and collapsed with frostbite, so that Pike himself admitted, "[Even] if I had no regard for my own health and constitution, I should have some for these poor fellows, who were killing themselves to obey my orders."

The overt purpose of Pike's new expedition was to return a party of Osage hostages to their village high on the Missouri River, then reach the source of the Arkansas River, before pushing south to the Red River and descending from its source to the Mississippi. Geography suggested another goal. Hundreds of mountainous miles separate the source of the Arkansas from the Red River, but amid the web of waterways that rise from the southern Rockies in Colorado, barely eighty miles lie between the head of the Arkansas and the Rio Bravo or Grande, which flows past Santa Fe and south toward Mexico.

Private messages exchanged with Wilkinson indicated that Pike expected his party to be made "prisoners of war," and that Wilkinson would "send to look for him" with a force of three thousand or four thousand men "if Christmas Eve should pass without his return." Since his instructions to Pike were dated June 24, weeks after Wilkinson was ordered south, the general may well have conceived the expedition as a response to Dearborn's command. In other words, it seems probable that in the summer of 1806 Burr's strategy was working, and that as Wilkinson felt himself being pushed out of favor with Jefferson, he was creating an excuse to invade Mexico by way of Santa Fe and the Camino Real.

In early October, at a point high up on the Arkansas River, Pike detached James Biddle Wilkinson with five boatmen to paddle down the river with a report to his father. It read, "Any number of men who may reasonably be calculated on would find no difficulty in marching by the route we came, with baggage wagons, field artillery, and all the usual appendages of a small army; and if all the route to Santa Fe should be of the same description, in case of war I would pledge my life and what is infinitely dearer, my honor, for the successful march of a reasonable body of troops into the province of New Mexico."

WILKINSON FINALLY SAILED from St. Louis on August 22. To his confidant in the Senate, Samuel Smith, he attributed the delay to "the extreme ill health of Mrs W." The symptoms of her tuberculosis—a hard cough accompanied by bright specks of blood sprayed out from the congested lungs—were made worse by the fetid summer. Accordingly he waited until the worst of the heat was over before gently taking her down the river. Despite the emergency, he then spent a week in Natchez settling Nancy into the familiar surroundings of the Concordia mansion, once Gayoso's but now the property of Esteban Minor.

As always with Wilkinson, any change that removed a weight of obligations, even those to his beloved wife, and allowed him to give orders to others transformed his mood. During his slow progress south, a platoon of Spanish troops had occupied a small outpost on U.S. soil called Bayou Pierre. This had become the potential flashpoint that could lead to war. Once Nancy was settled, the general immediately ordered up all the regular troops in the vicinity that could be spared, together with seven hundred militia from Mississippi and Orleans territories, and, as he confidently assured Dearborn on September 27, "With this Force I have no doubts of success in the outset, and think I shall be able to drive our opponents before me and take Nacodoches" several miles to the west of the Sabine River.

While in Natchez, his optimism tempted him into a dangerous joke about the allegations in the *Western World* when he encountered the surveyor general of the Mississippi Territory, Isaac Briggs, a sobersided, upright Quaker. "It must appear strange to you, friend Briggs," he declared during a chance meeting in the mansion of Cowles Mead, acting governor of the territory, "that I, a Spanish officer, am now on my way, to fight the Spaniards, should they not retire." It was said, Briggs recalled, "with great vivacity" and "a very cheerful air." But Briggs was not the sort of person to laugh at such matters, even when they had appeared in a rag such as the *Western World*. Suddenly turning on Wilkinson, he demanded, " 'But, General, what about the Spanish money? I have heard that thou receivedst, previous to thy departure from New Orleans, in the spring of 1804, from Spanish officers, about 10,000 dollars, of a late Mexican coinage, in Campeachy bags.' He answered, still with the same gay and easy air, 'It is a fact, Sir, I did receive about that sum of a late

Mexican coinage, in Campeachy bags, and from Spanish officers, and what then? It was due to me on account of former mercantile contracts.' "

Leaving Natchez and the astonished Briggs behind, the general took a boat up the Red River to Cushing's headquarters in Natchitoches, where he arrived on September 22. For several electric days, it seemed that the long-awaited conflict was about to begin. The general sent a message to the new governor of Texas, Antonio Cordero, in Nacogdoches, telling him to withdraw his forces from Bayou Pierre and all the territory east of the Sabine because it lay "fully within the limits . . . of the United States," and Wilkinson was authorized to "sustain the jurisdiction of the United States against any force." Wilkinson had about twelve hundred men at Natchitoches, and apart from a shortage of mules and tents he had sufficient supplies and intelligence for a successful campaign. Writing to John Adair, his old companion, he promised, "The time looked for by many and wished for by more has now arrived for subverting the Spanish government in Mexico. Be you ready to join me; we will want little more than light-armed troops . . . 5000 men will give us the Rio Bravo, 10,000 Monterey . . . 30,000 men to conquer the whole province of Mexico. We cannot fail of success." On the other side, however, Cordero, with more than a thousand soldiers in Nacogdoches under the command of Lieutenant Colonel Simon de Herrera, was in no mood to back down. Yet so adroitly had Wilkinson maneuvered that either peace or war would suit him.

Some 750 miles to the north east, Aaron Burr was staying with Andrew Jackson in Nashville, Tennessee. The final arrangements for his descent of the Mississippi were put in place, including the provision of four thousand dollars to Jackson to buy boats and supplies. Such largesse was made possible by the financial backing of the hugely wealthy Harman Blennerhassett, whose elegant mansion on an island in the Ohio River served as Burr's headquarters. Just a month earlier, Blennerhassett had helped Burr pay for the construction of fifteen boats big enough to ferry five hundred men downriver, and for sufficient pork, cornmeal, and whiskey to supply them for a month. About fifty recruits had already come forward, but once hostilities broke out, Jackson, Adair, and Senator John Smith of Ohio had made it clear they were ready to call out thousands of militia-trained volunteers from Tennessee, Kentucky, and Ohio eager for the Mexican adventure. Everyone was poised for the first shots to be fired.

Then unexpectedly, General Nemecio Salcedo, in overall command of defense on the frontier, intervened. At the end of September, he ordered troops to be withdrawn from east of the Sabine. Immediately tension in the area eased. The new situation apparently caught Wilkinson by surprise. Although he made arrangements to send the militia home and assured Cordero of his wish for a peaceful solution, he also informed Dearborn of his intention to occupy the land up to the Sabine. That this was deliberate provocation was made clear in a letter to Samuel Smith warning that war might still break out, and that the army was unprepared for it. With magnificent disregard for the ten weeks he had wasted in St. Louis, he blamed the lack of readiness for hostilities on Henry Dearborn's failure to supply enough mules and tents. "You should immediately put a competent character at the Head of the War Department," he informed the senator, "and prepare to reinforce me with from three to five thousand more [troops]." The president was to be informed, Wilkinson went on, that owing to the shortage of men and equipment "it is my opinion that we are approaching a crisis."

It should have been a safe prediction—either the Spanish would react or Zebulon Pike would be captured. What the commander in chief did not expect was the arrival on the evening of October 8 of a twenty-three-year-old New Yorker named Samuel Swartwout.

Wilkinson and Cushing were seated together when the young man was shown in. He claimed to have come as a volunteer, ready to serve against the Spaniards, and he had with him a letter of recommendation from Jonathan Dayton to the general. But when Cushing stepped out of the room for a moment, Swartwout drew from his coat pocket a package that he slipped furtively into Wilkinson's hand. It contained, he said, a message from Aaron Burr. Immediately Wilkinson asked where Burr was. Swartwout replied that he was still in Philadelphia, or had been when he left. But Wilkinson's lack of contact with Burr had forced the young man to spend more than two months searching for him, first turning upriver toward St. Louis before learning that the general was in the south. The news was out-of-date. Burr might be anywhere. The general waited until Swartwout had left the room before taking the package to his "private chamber" and opening it in secret.

The letter was written partly in plain English and partly in the symbol-substitution cipher that Burr and Wilkinson often used when the writer was uncertain whether the recipient had access to Entick's spelling dictionary. According to Wilkinson's later testimony, he did not succeed in deciphering the entire message that evening, but he could read enough to know that he faced a devastating threat to his career.

The letter was dated July 29 and began with news of what Burr had achieved up to that date: "Yours postmarked 13th May is received. I have obtained funds, and have actually commenced the enterprise. Detachments from different points under different pretences will rendezvous on the Ohio, 1st November—everything internal and external favors views—protection of England is secured. T- [Commodore Thomas Truxton] is gone to Jamaica to arrange with the admiral on that station, and will meet at the Mississippi—England—Navy of the United States are ready to join, and final orders are given to my friends and followers—it will be a host of choice spirits."

So far there was no direct mention of the general's involvement. The next sentence must have chilled his blood, however. "Wilkinson shall be second to Burr only—Wilkinson shall dictate the rank and promotion of his officers." Then came organizational details pointing to their close collaboration: "Burr will proceed westward 1st August, never to return: with him go his daughter . . . Send forthwith an intelligent and confidential friend with whom Burr may confer . . . Send a list of all persons known to Wilkinson west of the mountains, who could be useful, with a note delineating their characters . . . send me four or five of the commissions of your officers [blank forms to be filled in] . . . orders to the contractor [have been] given to forward six months' provisions to points Wilkinson may name . . . the project is brought to the point so long desired: Burr guarantees the result with his life and honor—the lives, the honor and fortunes of hundreds, the best blood of our country."

Finally and worst of all were the plans for the conspiracy's immediate implementation: "Burr's plan of operations is to move rapidly from the falls [of the Ohio] on the 15th of November, with the first five hundred or one thousand men, in light boats now constructing for that purpose—to be at Natchez between the 5th and 15th of December—then to meet Wilkinson—then to determine whether it will be expedient in the first instance to seize on or pass by Baton Rouge. On receipt of this, send Burr an answer—draw on Burr for all expenses, &c. The people of the country to which we are going are prepared to receive us—their agents now with Burr say that if we will protect their religion, and will not subject them to a foreign power, that in three weeks all will be settled. The gods invite to glory and fortune—it remains to be seen whether we deserve the boon."

24

HIS COUNTRY'S SAVIOR

T HE TIMING MADE THE LETTER TOXIC. Had war with Spain broken out
 in September, Burr's project would have been welcome and legitimate.
Equally, had Burr held off until Pike was captured, national outrage against
Spain would have seen his attack on Veracruz as patriotic assistance to
Wilkinson's efforts to liberate the prisoners. But, as it was, the United States
and Spain were at peace, and the general had diverted nearly all American
troops in the south, regular and militia, hundreds of miles from New Orleans,
leaving the city virtually defenseless, with a population hostile to the United
States, at the very moment when Burr was apparently shipping a thousand
armed men down the Mississippi.

Whatever thoughts possessed the general's mind, one impulse must have
been to destroy the letter with its evidence of his complicity. But in the
dark hours of the night he would have realized that other copies were in
circulation, and that the truthful Swartwout, described by Burr as "a man
of inviolable honor and perfect discretion . . . capable of relating facts with
fidelity," was able to tie him closer to Burr than any letter.

In the package was a second letter from Dayton. This was the one written in July crudely threatening that he would be dismissed in the next
Congress—"Jefferson will affect to yield reluctantly to the public sentiment,
but yield he will." To Wilkinson, so deeply wounded by the president's
compliance with the order to leave St. Louis, this scenario must have seemed
all too plausible.

By early next morning, he had still not decided what course to follow. He
found Cushing striding up and down on the gallery before his office and

called him aside for consultation. To his second-in-command, the general revealed only that the letter referred to some "illicit design" that Burr had in mind. The loyal Cushing never doubted that Wilkinson's connection with Burr was innocent, and that their plans were concerted only in the context of war breaking out. Together they decided to pump Swartwout for more information, keeping him in camp so that he could not take information back to Burr.

According to Wilkinson, he affected a friendly air with Swartwout, expressing admiration when he heard of plans to recruit no fewer than seven thousand men for the Mexican expedition, and to finance it with silver taken from the New Orleans banks. The general explained that "although I could not join the expedition, [the border dispute] might prevent my opposing it." Swartwout said that he was due to meet Burr on November 20 and invited Wilkinson to write the colonel with his response.

Most of what the young man had to say would have been familiar to the general from his discussions with Burr. The numbers involved would have surprised him, however, as would the highly significant information—mistaken, as it turned out—that Commodore Truxton, Burr's adviser on naval matters, had enlisted the help of the British navy. Every plot aimed at New Orleans had always assumed that its fall would be guaranteed by the arrival of two or three frigates at the mouth of the Mississippi. Yet even knowing this apparently crucial fact, Wilkinson still hesitated. For ten days, he remained in Natchitoches considering how the military should react.

Even in his *Memoirs*, written to show his unswerving patriotism, he could not help revealing the attractions of accepting that the conspiracy was too far advanced to be stopped and simply launching an attack across the Sabine River: "If I had faultered [*sic*] in duty at that critical moment; if I had been inclined to close with the splendid offers of Colonel Burr, I should have struck the Spaniards, which my orders would have fully justified, and Burr would then have reached New Orleans, without opposition; and I could have deliberated on the part I should take, with entire safety." It was a possibility he considered in detail, working out that he could wait to see whether Burr succeeded in taking New Orleans, "and without hazarding blame on either side, I should have been left at liberty to take advantage of events and choose my part."

As late as October 17, Wilkinson wrote to Dearborn suggesting that a hundred picked men could seize the Spanish headquarters at Nacogdoches. Although he stressed that the purpose would only be to negotiate its return in exchange for a truce in the area, any kind of conflict with Spain, whatever the excuse, would obviously have given a vital impetus to Burr's conspiracy and have blurred his own association with it.

During those days, Wilkinson held the fate of the United States in his hands. Had fighting with Spain broken out on the Sabine River, Andrew Jackson made it clear he would have led the Tennessee militia to seize the Floridas, and John Adair was undeniably prepared to take Kentuckians into Mexico. In the confusion, New Orleans would have given itself up to Burr. What the final outcome might have been is impossible to say, but the radical Republican John Randolph was clearly correct when he later declared to Congress, "The agency of the Army was the whole pivot on which that plot turned."

While he still wrestled with the problem, Wilkinson did write Burr, as Swartwout had asked, and sent the letter to Natchez to await the colonel's arrival. What he said was never known. He might have explained that the border situation made it impossible to help or mentioned the possibility of a surprise assault across the Sabine or merely asked for more information. Certainly he did not declare the conspiracy to be an act of treason; otherwise, when asked about the letter later, Wilkinson would have said so. All he offered by way of explanation was that when he returned to Natchez, "I recovered [the letter] and destroyed it."

For most of the time, it is clear that the general and his second-in-command leaned toward war. But two obstacles stood in the way. The more obvious was the risk. Command of three thousand trained soldiers, however meanly paid, gave Wilkinson control of the largest single source of power within the republic, and he was desperate not to lose the prize. But psychology may have counted for more. In court, William Eaton declared on oath that when Burr told him Wilkinson was to be his lieutenant, "I replied, 'Wilkinson will be a lieutenant to no man in existence.'" That was an unchanging truth. In the end, Wilkinson always destroyed any friendship that threatened his self-esteem.

Given his emotional volatility, the anger and anxiety produced by Burr's letter may have contributed to Wilkinson's indecision. Briggs, who saw him three weeks later, remarked that he seemed a changed man from the sunny figure he had encountered in September.

In the end, Wilkinson decided to play for time. On October 18, Swartwout was sent away from camp so that he could not observe what was happening. Then Wilkinson composed two documents for the president that contained the first authentic news of the Burr Conspiracy. In a personal letter, dated October 21, he wrote of his discovery that "a numerous and powerful association, extending from New York through the Western states to the territories bordering on the Mississippi, has been formed with the design to levy and rendezvous eight or ten thousand men in New Orleans . . . I have no doubt the revolt of this Territory will be made an auxiliary step to the main design of attacking Mexico, to give it a New Master in place of the promised liberty." To frustrate this plot, the general proposed to make "the best compromise with Salcedo in my power, and throw myself with my little Band into New Orleans to be ready to defend that Capital against usurpation and violence."

Yet, as he himself admitted, "I have never, in my whole life, found myself under such circumstances of perplexity and embarrassment as at present." To give himself room for maneuver, he pretended to believe that Jefferson might still give approval to Burr's scheme in the event of war. "It is my desire," he wrote, "to avert a great public calamity, and not to mar a salutary design." On the back of the letter, he scribbled an alternative scenario: "Should Spain be disposed to war seriously with us, might not some plan be adopted to correct the destination of the associates, and by a suitable appeal to their patriotism, engage them in the service of their country?" Then he made out a copy of the ciphered letter together with a hasty translation, omitting or doctoring the more compromising details.

On October 22, these papers, together with a note to Dearborn telling him that he would advance to the Sabine River immediately to negotiate the withdrawal of both armies from the disputed border, were given to Lieutenant Thomas Smith with strict instructions that they were to be seen by no one but the president. Resourcefully the lieutenant sewed them into the souls of his slippers and set off for Washington.

On October 23, Wilkinson sent a cryptic message to the senior officer in New Orleans, Lieutenant Colonel Thomas Freeman, telling him of a "threat too highly confidential to be whispered," but which required the city's ineffective defenses to be put in order immediately. On the same day, the general and Cushing set out on a forced march with a company of soldiers to the Sabine River, sixty miles away. Once there, Wilkinson dispatched a trusted officer, Captain Walter Burling, to contact Governor Cordero in Nacogdoches, proposing that each army withdrew from the disputed area, "without yielding a Pretension, ceding a right, or interferring with the discussion which belongs to our superiors." In practice, this would entail the Spanish remaining behind the Sabine River, while the Americans retreated east of the Arroyo Hondo, the deep stream that Spain claimed as its frontier. The result would create a buffer territory, about fifty miles wide east to west, and stretching north from the Gulf of Mexico to the thirty-first parallel, the line specified by the Treaty of San Lorenzo as the border between the two nations.

Cordero, sensing the weakness behind the proposal, wanted to reject it, but Colonel Herrera had his orders from Salcedo and quickly accepted. On November 6, an agreement was signed by both sides, creating the Neutral Ground, which would for almost twenty years serve as a buffer dividing the two powers in the west. Devoid of government, it gradually became peopled by citizens of every country—the very embodiment of the border society—and its eventual collapse into lawlessness exemplified the built-in weakness of such communities.

With the border problem temporarily solved, the general immediately rode hard back to Natchitoches, covering the sixty miles in a day, and leaving Cushing to bring back the troops. At Natchitoches, he found a copy of the original Burr letter, delivered in his absence by another courier, Erick Bollman. Also waiting for him was a mysterious message sent by James Lowry Donaldson, one of Louisiana's land commissioners, "that a plan to revolutionise the western country has been formed, matured, and is ready to explode—that Kentucky, Ohio, Tennessee, Orleans, and Indiana, are combined, to declare themselves independent on the 15th November."

The mystery lay less in the message than in its alleged effect on Wilkinson. It was "decisive on my conduct," he declared in his *Memoirs*, as though even then he had half hoped not to have to commit himself. "I had not formed a decided opinion, of the nature and objects of Burr's enterprise before the receipt of Mr Donaldson's letter. I then first perceived [the enterprise] was wholly unauthorised by the government—highly criminal in the design,—most alarming in its extent; and I had no longer any difficulty as to the course of conduct, my duty and the interests of the nation required me to pursue."

Donaldson's letter, however, said nothing of the kind. It stressed Donaldson's belief that the story was so like "a second Spanish Conspiracy" it could only be a trick—"a stratagem set on foot by the patrons of the *Western World*." But it carried a different meaning for Wilkinson. The letter demonstrated the changed emphasis of Burr's conspiracy—New Orleans was to be seized, not as a jumping-off point for Mexico, but to bring about the secession of the western states. It was indeed a second Spanish Conspiracy, and as the creator of the first one, Wilkinson would be inescapably tied into it. No matter what he and the army did on the frontier, he would be seen as participating in an attempt to separate the western states from the Union.

Even to Thomas Jefferson, desperate though he was to believe the best of his general, the diversion of troops looked deliberate. Writing to warn Claiborne in December of Burr's coming attack, he explained, "Genrl. Wilkenson [*sic*] is believed to be kept at bay on the west side of the Misisipi [*sic*] by a Spanish force under advice from Yrujo who has been duped by Burr to believe he means only the capture of N Orleans and the separation of the western country." The president was ready to see Wilkinson as a victim, but others might not be so kind. As Chief Justice John Marshall would repeatedly explain in his court, the law treated an attempt to wage war on a country at peace with the United States as a misdemeanor, but war against a province governed by the United States was treason.

This was why Wilkinson could no longer afford to stand back. He had to oppose Burr outright. And the equivocal letter sent to the colonel to await his arrival in Natchez had to be destroyed instantly.

The choice had been forced on him, but the decision to portray himself as the savior of the nation, and the histrionic manner in which he played the role, was Wilkinson's entirely. "The plot thickens," he wrote in a message to Cushing, urging him to bring all available troops to New Orleans, "yet all but those concerned sleep profoundly! My God! what a situation has our Country reached. Let us save it if we can . . . hurry, hurry after me and if necessary let us be buried together in the place we shall defend." Apart from a single company, the entire garrison of Natchitoches, under the command of Major Moses Porter, was ordered to New Orleans, with fresh orders to Freeman to repair the city's defenses urgently, but "manifest no hurry or emotion for you are surrounded by secret agents, yet use every exertion in your power."

With men sweating at the oars, the general's boat then swept down the Red River, covering more than one hundred and fifty miles in three days. But when they reached the Mississippi, the general demonstrated how little he believed in the melodrama he was creating. Instead of hastening downriver to protect beleaguered New Orleans, he turned upriver to Natchez, where his letter was awaiting Burr, and where the genuine tragedy of Ann Wilkinson's approaching death was unfolding.

NANCY'S FAMILY WAS ALL HER LIFE. She needed to have tenderness around her. Until she met James Wilkinson, the affection that nourished her had come from her father and brothers and sisters. While her husband was away, she found it in her children, and to a lesser extent in the military circles surrounding her. What she could not bear was loneliness. But in the last febrile stages of her illness, her elder son, James Biddle, was still lost in the mountains, the younger was living far off in Philadelphia, and her husband was distracted by a military emergency. His brief return must have come as a gift. But an undeniably operatic atmosphere existed in the elegant mansion as Ann lay dying of tuberculosis and her husband sat nearby scribbling messages of increasing wildness to save himself from disgrace.

A second letter was written to the president on November 12 warning of "a deep, dark and wide-spread conspiracy, embracing the young and the old, the democrat and the federalist, the native and the foreigner, the patriot at '76 and the exotic of yesterday, the opulent and the needy, the ins and the outs." Superbly, the general promised to use "indefatigable industry, incessant vigilance and hardy courage" to defend New Orleans, admitting only to a slight trepidation at the thought of the "desperate enthusiasts who would seek my life, and although I may be able to smile at danger in open conflict, I will confess I dread the stroke of the assassin, because it cannot confer an honourable death." But wrapped in the hyperbole lay the shape of the plan he had conceived. "To give effect to my military arrangements, it is absolutely indispensable New Orleans and its environs should be placed under martial law." Ten years earlier, he had used the same stratagem in Detroit in response to a supposed threat of British invasion. The experience had shown that martial law had the double merit of creating a state of panic and giving him total control.

Two more letters went to Freeman with further orders for improving the defense of the city, and the assurance that "I have made up my mind to perish in the storm, in defence of the government and integrity of the union, and every officer I have the honour to command will do the same." On the same day he wrote William Claiborne with instructions to act urgently in repairing New Orleans's defenses, but to "demonstrate no hurry" because "you are surrounded by disaffection where you least suspect it." That letter was no sooner sealed than he began another to Samuel Smith, insisting that Claiborne be dismissed for failing to prepare adequate defenses; then, having asserted that the "Integrity of the Union is menaced by the impious ambition of a desperate Band," he demanded that his salary should be increased— "Shall I be suffered to starve or to exhaust the last Cent of my private purse, or abandon every thing like respectability in office?"

Finally, the ever reliable Walter Burling was sent all the way to Mexico City with a message for José de Iturrigaray, viceroy of Mexico, explaining the heroic efforts Wilkinson had already made to protect Spain's possessions against Burr, his immediate intention to "spring like Leonidas into the breach defending it, or perish in the attempt," and his pressing need to be repaid for the expenses he had incurred—eighty-five thousand pesos spent "in shattering the plans and destroying the union and harmony among the bandits being enrolled along the Ohio, and thirty-six thousand in the dispatch of supplies and counter-revolutionists—which sums I trust will be reimbursed to the bearer."

Aside from the calculated need to squeeze a profit from the emergency, this was not the language of a cold-blooded plotter, as his enemies later alleged. With his wife dying in an upstairs bedroom, James Wilkinson was performing his different roles as patriot, as spy, as military hero, with the desperate intensity of a man on the edge of breakdown. Failure to convince his audience would kill off his characters as surely as tuberculosis was killing his wife and condemn him to cope with intolerable reality.

Invited to the Concordia mansion on about November 15, Isaac Briggs was struck by the change in the general's demeanor since September. "I confess I approached him with caution," Briggs recounted. "His wife lay at this time, in the same house, apparently at the point of death. The General met me in a mood the reverse of that described in the former conversation: then, all was gaiety; now, every thing in his manner was throughout, solemn, impressive and pregnant with alarm. He took me aside, and immediately put the question: 'Can you go to the seat of government of the United States?' "

The recruitment of Briggs to act as messenger to Jefferson, not only carrying his dispatches, but testifying to his patriotism with a Quaker's unshakable integrity, was essential to Wilkinson's plans. Briggs's initial skepticism, even after being told of the conspiracy, only added to his usefulness. "How dost thou know these things?" he demanded. "May all this not be a deception?" To satisfy his doubts, Wilkinson had to produce Burr's and Dayton's letters, to point to the connection between the *Western World* stories and Dayton's blackmailing suggestion that he was about to be dismissed, and to pave the way for the conclusion that Briggs reached after a night's sleep. "I could not resist the inference," the Quaker wrote, "that did Colonel Burr aim to secure the co-operation of General Wilkinson, the use of such means perfectly accorded with the opinion I had acquired of [Burr's] character—to impose on [Wilkinson] the conviction on the one hand that his reputation with his country was destroyed beyond his power to redeem it; and on the other to hold up to his view such allurements as were well calculated to fascinate his ambition."

Convinced that Jefferson had to be informed of what was really happening, Briggs set off for Washington on November 18 with the general's dispatches and copies of Burr's and Dayton's letters. Any hope of rescuing Wilkinson's reputation rested with him. Elsewhere in the south, Burr and Dayton had already shredded it beyond repair. Cowles Mead, acting governor of Mississippi, was so convinced of Wilkinson's complicity that he refused the general's request to call out the militia for fear they would be used in the plot and instead told William Claiborne in New Orleans, "It is here believed that General Wilkinson is the soul of the conspiracy." Andrew Jackson, himself uncomfortably close to Burr, followed up with a second warning to Claiborne sent on November 12: "Be upon the alert; keep a watchful eye upon our General and beware of an attack, as well from our own country as Spain. I fear there is something rotten in the State of Denmark." Theater was already blurring with reality when the general arrived in New Orleans on November 25 ready to take the stage in the greatest role of his life, not as Hamlet, but something closer to Julius Caesar.

THE GENERAL REDEEMED

O N THE VERY DAY that James Wilkinson entered New Orleans, a weary Lieutenant Thomas Smith stepped into President Jefferson's study in the White House and removed his slippers. When he had unpicked the soles, he handed over the general's two letters for the president, and his message to the secretary of war. Smith left no account of his record journey—almost fourteen hundred miles covered in thirty-three days—or of the president's response to this first indication of Wilkinson's loyalty. But Smith's fatigue must have been as extreme as the president's relief.

During the weeks without news, and the continuing doubts about how the general might use the troops under his command, the administration had remained paralyzed. Dearborn had guessed that Wilkinson would try to make war on Spain. Urgent messages had been sent south instructing him to keep the peace, and ordering Captain Thomas Swaine, commander of the eastern defenses on the Mobile River, not to leave his post to attack the Spanish, whatever Wilkinson might command. But until the creased pages were removed from their wrapping, and Jefferson began to read Wilkinson's looped handwriting, no one knew what had actually happened.

However alarming the references to the "deep and dark conspiracy" and the "eight or ten thousand men" who were to rendezvous in New Orleans, the discovery that the army's commander in chief was loyal and planned to defend the city outweighed every other consideration. The difference it made to Jefferson's administration was immediately evident when the cabinet met the following day. For the first time, decisive action could be taken to frustrate Burr's plans. As the president explained to Congress, "Two days after the receipt of General Wilkinson's information . . . orders were despatched to every intersecting point on the Ohio and Mississippi, from Pittsburgh to New Orleans, for the employment of such force either of the regulars or of the militia, and of such proceedings also of the civil authorities, as might enable them to seize on all the boats and stores provided for the enterprise, to arrest the persons concerned, and to suppress effectually the further progress of the enterprise."

The first action against Burr was taken by Governor Edward Tiffin of Ohio, based on information that the cabinet's confidential agent, John Graham, had gained from men recruited by Blennerhassett. Shortly before the president's proclamation arrived, Ohio militia raided Blennerhassett's island home. They were just too late to capture its owner, who had left hours earlier with his friend Colonel Comfort Tyler. In their absence, the soldiers seized about a dozen boats and two hundred barrels of provisions, as well as destroying Blennerhassett's library and beautiful furniture. In late December, Blennerhassett, Tyler, and a force numbering no more than eighty men joined up with Burr, who had acquired two more large boats from Andrew Jackson. By the end of the year, their small convoy was sailing down the Mississippi just ahead of the news of Jefferson's proclamation that was spreading southward like a tide.

AHEAD OF THEM IN NEW ORLEANS, James Wilkinson was working feverishly to repair the city's defenses. A force of fewer than eight hundred troops had been set to rebuilding the ruined walls of Fort St. Louis, and constructing new barriers across strategic roads and canals into the city. Governor William Claiborne ordered the tiny fleet of four gunboats and two bomb ketches to be put under Wilkinson's command, and an urgent meeting was convened with leading merchants to ask them for money and men to equip the vessels for action. The first indication that Wilkinson had something more extreme in mind came on December 6, just before this meeting, when he wrote Claiborne, "Under circumstances so imperious, extraordinary measures must be resorted to, and the ordinary forms of our civil institutions must, for a short period, yield to the strong arm of military law . . . I most earnestly entreat you to proclaim martial law over this city, its ports and precincts."

During the long months of uncertainty about Wilkinson's loyalty, Claiborne had received no communication from Washington. Both Jackson and Mead, had, however, counseled him not to trust the general. In a message announcing his intention to defend Natchez at all costs, Mead told the governor, "Burr may come—and he is no doubt desperate . . . Should he pass us, your fate will depend on the General, not on the Colonel. If I stop Burr, this may hold the General in his allegiance to the United States. But if Burr passes this Territory with two thousand men, I have no doubt but the General will be your worst enemy." Forced to choose between losing the city to Burr or to Wilkinson, Claiborne temporized. On December 7, he refused Wilkinson's demand for martial law, but only on the technical grounds that it suspended the citizen's right of habeas corpus, a power that resided solely with the legislature, which was not in session.

Two days later, New Orleans's merchants met and volunteered to supply crews and money for the navy. With their agreement, Claiborne simultaneously put an embargo on ships leaving the port during the emergency. This measure halted all trade, and if sustained long would drive the merchants and the city into bankruptcy, but for a few weeks it was acceptable because everyone shared the burden. To the merchants' consternation, Wilkinson dismissed their offer as inadequate. In the expectation of a naval attack from the Gulf of Mexico backed by British frigates, he demanded the use of New Orleans's sailors for a minimum of six months. When this was refused, he told Claiborne that he would round up the seamen forcibly, pressing them into service as the British navy did.

By now the governor was deeply alarmed. "I submit it to your cool reflection," he replied, "whether *at this time* I could be justifiable in compelling men by force to enter the service. Many good-disposed citizens do not appear to think the danger considerable, and there are others who (perhaps from wicked intentions) endeavor to turn our preparations into ridicule."

Wilkinson, however, was unrelenting. The argument he used for attacking civil liberties has become familiar. "We have reached an extremity in our public affairs," he brusquely informed Claiborne, "which will not only justify, but which imperiously demands, the partial and momentary dispensation of the ordinary course of our civil institutions, to preserve the sanctuary of public liberty from total dilapidation."

The general estimated Burr's forces at between seven and twelve thousand men, but it was not just this outside threat he had to confront. In New Orleans, Burr sympathizers could be found in the resentful Creole population, and among the shadowy but influential membership of the Mexico Association. Privately, Wilkinson assured Samuel Smith that three quarters of the population were unreliable. Consequently the sweeping powers of martial law and impressment were essential because "unless I am authorized to repress the seditious and arrest the disaffected, and to call the resources of the place into active operation, the defects of my force may expose me to be overwhelmed by numbers; and the cause and the place will be lost." With increasing feebleness, Claiborne still held out, insisting that the judiciary alone had the power to enforce the law, "nor can any acts of mine arrest or suspend their powers."

By mid-December, however, his protests had become irrelevant. Sensing the governor's weakness, Wilkinson simply bypassed the constitutional safeguards and carried out what amounted to a military coup in the city. On December 14 a series of arbitrary arrests began. First, the courier Erick Bollman was seized on suspicion of treason by Wilkinson's soldiers, then Swartwout and his traveling companion, Peter Ogden. Bollman was hustled onto a gunboat and shipped out of the city, while Swartwout, as he later told a friend, "was taken from prison in the night under a guard of soldiers and hurried through swamps and marshes to an unfrequented place in the woods . . . and threatened by the officer if [I] attempted to escape, death would be the consequence." According to Swartwout, they did shoot when he tried to get away, but their muskets misfired. Later he and Ogden were both chained up on a bomb ketch moored in the river.

The arrests, coming on top of the rumors of Burr's approaching army, created panic in the city. A judge, James Workman, issued writs of habeas corpus for the release of all three men, but Wilkinson immediately re-arrested them, declaring that he took full responsibility for "the two traitors who were the subjects of the writs." He promised to continue to arrest "all those against whom I have positive proof of being accomplices in the machinations against the state." Angrily Workman told Claiborne that by law his next step should be to call on the sheriff to have the general arrested, but in such dangerous circumstances he was prepared to let the governor intervene. When Claiborne refused to act, Workman resigned. As an early historian of Louisiana put it, "This was acknowledging the fact that Wilkinson was supreme dictator, and that henceforth his will was to be the law."

Most of this was motivated by his need to act the superpatriot. But another factor was at work. Nancy Wilkinson lay dying.

Carried downriver from Natchez in December, she was lodged in the house of the Creole millionaire Bernard de Marigny. Shortly before she died on February 23, her son James returned from his epic journey down the Arkansas River so that she was not alone at her death. "Oh god how heavy have been my afflictions," Wilkinson confided to Jonathan Williams, and it would be strange if the awful waiting for her end, and the eventual grief, did not contribute to his savagery. Always a convivial drinker, the general seems now to have begun drinking to dull his senses, to the tragedy in his private life and, perhaps, to the monstrous edifice he was creating in public. In an unsigned letter to the *Aurora* newspaper, edited by the sympathetic William Duane, he portrayed himself isolated in the midst of "acknowledged traitors and masked confederates." This was, he wrote, a different Wilkinson, "unmoved and indefatigable . . . no more jocose, volatile or convivial. He seemed wrought in thought and silence! and was to be found only with the troops, at the works, or in his office."

Early in January, John Adair, his friend for more than fifteen years, arrived in the city. Whatever his expectations of Wilkinson—it was said that Adair still hoped to arrange the handover of the city to Burr—Adair was too ill to do anything but send word that he wanted to see the general. The same afternoon, a detachment of 120 troops under the command of Wilkinson's trusted aide Lieutenant Colonel Jacob Kingsbury surrounded his hotel. Adair was dragged from his room and taken to military headquarters, where he was held until he could be put on a ship bound for Washington alongside Swartwout, Bollman, and Ogden. Adair's arrest was followed by that of Workman, on the grounds that the judge was "strongly suspected for being connected with Burr," and that of the editor of the *Orleans Gazette*, James Bradford, and a financier, Lewis Kerr, who was accused of plotting "to plunder the bank."

All mail addressed to Burr and his associates was intercepted and opened, and travel outside the city was restricted to those with military permits. The streets were patrolled by detachments of armed soldiers with the power to apprehend anyone the general wanted to detain. Such was his authority, he had only to issue a warrant. The list of his suspects lengthened rapidly until by February it extended to printers, legislators, traders, lawyers, and "the Bar in general."

ON JANUARY 10, 1807, Burr with his small band of followers landed at Vicksburg and, for the first time, learned that the president had ordered his arrest. Wilkinson, who might have enabled the conspiracy to succeed, had made its failure inevitable. In despair, Burr surrendered to Cowles Mead, Mississippi's acting governor.

The disparity between the eighty men who came ashore with him and the "eight to twelve thousand" that Wilkinson talked of later caused the general to be ridiculed. There were, however, signs of the support that Burr commanded in the south, even after Jefferson's proclamation was known. Only thirty or forty of the Natchez militia responded to the muster call to defend the city, and when Burr was indicted before a grand jury in Washington, Mississippi, its members not only denounced Burr's arrest as a triumph for "the enemies of our glorious Constitution" but immediately found him "not guilty of any crime or misdemeanor against the United States." Jefferson and Dearborn believed that a grand jury in New Orleans would have brought in similar verdicts had his supporters been arraigned there.

Once set free, Burr bade an emotional farewell to his men on February 13 and disappeared into the wilderness. The failure to capture him in Mississippi despite Wilkinson's offer of a five-hundred-dollar reward, and the deployment of a snatch squad of officers in civilian clothes, meant that the potential threat continued. So, too, did Wilkinson's hard-line policy despite the release of some of his prisoners, including Bradford. Reconvened in January, the legislature protested angrily against the general's destruction of civil liberties, forcing Claiborne to offer a partial apology on his behalf. "I believe the General is actuated by a sincere disposition to serve the best interest of his country," he declared, "but his zeal, I fear, has carried him too far." By then, however, it was apparent that the general's methods were endorsed by President Jefferson and his administration.

Two DAYS AFTER DEARBORN learned of Wilkinson's loyalty from Lieutenant Smith, he gave the general blanket powers to "dispose of the troops in such manner, as will most effectually intercept and prevent any unlawful enterprize." In addition Dearborn ordered, "Any person or persons who may be found in or about your camp or post, with evident intention of sounding either officer or soldier, with a view to an unlawful expedition, should be arrested."

Any lingering doubts about his past associations—Dearborn commented, "Your name has been very frequently mentioned with Burr, Dayton and others"—evaporated with the arrival of the upright Isaac Briggs. As the Quaker recounted, "After a most arduous journey, in the midst of a severe winter, of more than 1200 miles, 600 of it through wilderness, on the first day of the year, 1807, I arrived in Washington city, and waited on the President with my despatches. Immediately on his opening them, he exclaimed with earnestness, 'Is Wilkinson sound in this business?' I replied very promptly, 'There is not the slightest doubt of it.'"

From that moment, Jefferson showed himself ready to support whatever Wilkinson did, regardless of the cost to the principles of individual liberty and the rule of law. In reply to the letters that Briggs delivered, including copies of those from Burr and Dayton, Jefferson urged the general on January

3, 1807, to "act on the possibility that the resources of our enemies may be greater and deeper than we are yet informed." A month later, answering a flood of letters from Wilkinson detailing his measures to protect New Orleans, Jefferson wrote approvingly, "We were pleased to see that without waiting for [the orders sent in November] you adopted nearly the same plan yourself and acted on it with promptitude."

By then Bollman and Swartwout, the first of the prisoners to be arbitrarily arrested and deported, had arrived in the capital, yet the president still insisted that the threat of attack by an "overwheming force" from the Mississippi justified Wilkinson in what he did. He offered a single note of caution. Referring to popular opinion "in a nation tender as to anything infringing liberty, especially from the military," Jefferson expressed the hope that "you will not extend this deportation where there is only suspicion . . . in that case public sentiment will desert you, because seeing no danger here, violations of the law are felt with strength." Even then, the president made a specific exception for the ringleaders, Burr and Blennerhassett, who should be deported immediately and without trial to Washington, "should they fall into your hands." Of Wilkinson's military rule, he said nothing directly, but alluding to rumors that the administration was distancing itself from the general, the president ended, "Be assured you will be cordially supported in the line of your duties."

Until then no one had been more tender about the military infringing liberty than Jefferson—even years later, in correspondence with John Adams, he did not hesitate to describe the comparatively mild restrictions on free speech contained in the alien and sedition laws as "terrorism." The explanation that Jefferson himself offered for his endorsement of Wilkinson's behavior was sent to John Colvin, editor of two Republican newspapers and of Jefferson's own memoirs: "A strict observance of the written laws is doubtless one of the high duties of a good citizen, but it is not the highest. The laws of necessity, of self-preservation, of saving our country when in danger, are of higher obligation. To lose our country by a scrupulous adherence to written law, would be to lose the law itself, with life, liberty, property and all those who are enjoying them with us; thus absurdly sacrificing the end to the means." Wilkinson's need to defeat the threat posed by Burr "constituted a law of necessity and self-preservation, and rendered the *salus populi* [safety of the people] supreme over the written law."

This was—and is—a specious argument, one based on circular logic, since the agency that restricts liberty invariably maintains that it is the only competent judge of the danger. As Adams tartly pointed out, he could claim that the alien and sedition laws were made necessary by the threat of "terrorism" from Jefferson's own Republican clubs with their close links to the Jacobins in France, who were, after all, the originators of terror as a political tactic.

Recognizing the inherent weakness of his reasoning, Jefferson did suggest an extra safeguard to Colvin, that of retrospective judgment. "The officer who is called to act on this supreme ground, does indeed risk himself on the justice of the controlling powers of the constitution, and his station makes it his duty to incur that risk." Thus Wilkinson might later find himself held criminally responsible for his actions. In his defense, however, he had only to claim honest intention, because as Jefferson insisted, "In all these cases, the purity and the patriotism of the motives should shield the agent from blame."

Guided by the hints in Jefferson's letters, Wilkinson adopted this as his own defense. "I have never attempted to justify the infractions of the law which were forced on me in New Orleans by an impending great calamity," he told Daniel Clark in May 1807. "Yet I can never repent what I have done, and would repeat it a thousand times, for if a destructive evil to a national community can be arrested by the ruin of an individual, should he pause? I think not, and under this impression I have acted."

On March 3 Burr was arrested on the Mobile River by a member of Wilkinson's snatch squad, Lieutenant Edmund Gaines. When the news arrived in New Orleans at the end of the month, the mood in the city changed abruptly. The general relaxed his grip, armed patrols ceased, the seamen were released, and normal commercial life began to return.

On April 20, Wilkinson left New Orleans to return to Washington. He had reason to believe that his performance as the patriotic hero had been a triumph. Not only had he defeated Burr's conspiracy, but he had done so in a way that commanded the warm approval of the government and, most important, of Thomas Jefferson himself.

TWO TRAITORS ON TRIAL

THE ONE AREA WHERE JAMES WILKINSON remained vulnerable was his past. It was certain that Jonathan Dayton and Aaron Burr would in their defense revive the *Western World*'s allegations of his "holding a commission and drawing a pension from the government of Spain." His first, surprising step, taken while still in New Orleans, was to approach the governor of West Florida, Vizente Folch, to help clear his name. Relying, as he put it, "upon those sympathies which connect military men throughout the civilized world," he asked Folch to give an assurance that Wilkinson had never been paid by Spain or held a Spanish commission. Since Folch had been living with Miró in 1787 when Wilkinson first appeared in New Orleans and "possessed his confidences in a greater degree" than anyone else, this was tantamount to asking him to lie.

Folch was well prepared, however, because, as he informed Captain General Someruelos, "during the Burr disturbances, the general has by means of a person in his confidence [Thomas Power] constantly maintained a correspondence with me, in which he has laid before me not only the information which he has acquired, but also his intentions for the various exigencies in which he might feel himself." To give Wilkinson the clearance he wanted, Folch first declared that had the general been guilty, Spanish archives would certainly contain some record of his commission and pension. Then, he announced grandly, "Under my sacred word of honour, no such document, nor any other paper tending to substantiate such assertions, exists in the records in my possession."

As one critic pointed out, Folch's declaration was narrow and qualified since he made it in Pensacola while the relevant papers were held in Havana.

But at least his Spanish handlers were now prevented from making any embarrassing revelations. In similar fashion, the general persuaded Thomas Power to provide a certificate—to be shown only to the president, Power specified—declaring that Wilkinson had never acted as a Spanish agent. Finally Wilkinson set about insulating himself against the damaging information held by Daniel Clark.

During the summer of 1806, Clark's loyalties had made another dizzying turn when he at last secured the nomination to be the Orleans Territory's representative to Congress. In the fall, when rumors of Burr's movements first reached the city, Claiborne immediately assumed that "the delegate to Congress from this Territory, Daniel Clark, is one of the leaders [of the conspiracy]." But, forced to choose which way to jump, Clark turned against Burr. In mid-October, he advised members of the legislature, including Joseph Bellechasse, commander of the city's militia, "to forget any personal animosity towards the Governor, and to rally round the government, and die, if necessary, in its defence." Then he hastily left the city to take up his duties in Washington.

As early as December, Wilkinson had sent Clark a reminder that each of them knew too much about the other's links to Burr. "Suspicion is afloat! and numbers are implicated," he wrote, and added with dramatic underlining, *"Thank God, your advice to Bellechasse, if your character was not a sufficient guarantee, would vindicate you against any imputation."*

In January 1807, at the height of his dictatorial rule, the general recalled in another letter Clark's pro-Creole comment about not wanting his children to be part of the United States. "It is a fact," Wilkinson wrote, "that our fool [Claiborne] has written to his contemptible fabricator [the president] that you had declared if you had children you would teach them to curse the United States as soon as they were able to lisp." The theme appeared for a third time in March 1807: "Mr. Burr and his accredited agents have made, or endeavour to make, much use of Mr. Clark's name." Wilkinson assured him, "General W. has never mentioned it."

This letter crossed with one sent by Clark from Washington warning Wilkinson, "You are calumniated from all quarters," with rumors "of your having received 10,000 dollars, at Orleans, of the Spaniards when you went to take possession. I have pointed out the utter impossibility of such a thing." To this, Wilkinson replied in May, smoothly assuring Clark, "A friendship, founded on almost twenty years acquaintance makes it my peculiar duty, pending the highly important developments which are at issue, to watch over and defend your fame, should it be implicated in the discussion."

It was a dangerous strategy. As preparations were made for Aaron Burr's trial, and public excitement mounted about who else had been involved, one or another might conclude more was to be gained from blowing the whistle than keeping such dangerous information secret.

Unnoticed amid the storm of interest stirred up by Burr's appearance in court was the return to the United States on July 1 of Captain Zebulon Pike and most of his party. An epic of courage and hardiness had taken them close to Santa Fe, where they were, as expected, captured by the Spanish, but not until February 1807. As prisoners, they were then taken down the Camino Real deep into Mexico, ending up, ironically, in Chihuahua, Wilkinson's ultimate goal. There Salcedo ordered Pike and his men to be released, and they were escorted back through Texas to the border. The expected rescue had never come, the expected war with Spain was not fought, and what was perhaps the real conspiracy with Burr remained hidden.

BY THE TIME JAMES WILKINSON reached Washington, his enemies were waiting for him in force. Chief among them was Aaron Burr. At the time of his arrest, he exclaimed bitterly to Mississippi's attorney general, "As to any projects or plans which may have been formed between General Wilkinson and myself heretofore, they are now completely frustrated by the perfidious conduct of Wilkinson, and the world must pronounce him a perfidious villain." With the help of his daughter, Theodosia, and the wealthy Blennerhassett, a powerful legal team under the leadership of Edmund Randolph, George Washington's attorney general, was assembled to defend Burr, their overt aim being to prove both Burr's innocence and the general's guilt.

"Our ground of defence is that Mr. Burr's expedition was in concurrence with General Wilkinson, against the dominions of the king of Spain, in case of a war," George Wickham, the most damaging of Burr's counsel, stated bluntly. "If we prove that, at the time Wilkinson was pretending to favor Burr's expedition . . . he was receiving a Spanish pension, this will explain his conduct. He defeated the enterprize of Burr by hatching a charge of treason against the United States, on purpose to serve the king whose money he was receiving!"

Others were ready to provide corroborating detail. Even before his arrest, John Adair had pinned the blame for failure on Wilkinson. "Why, something would have been done if Wilkinson had not turned out a damned coward," he declared on hearing the news from the Sabine River, "for if he had attacked the Spaniards, and the blood of one man had been spilt, the government could not have stopped the western people." Arrested and shipped north as a prisoner by his former friend, Adair had immediately been released on a writ of habeas corpus and gladly supplied the defense with copies of Wilkinson's numerous letters encouraging him to "come on" to Mexico.

Luther Martin, the grandstanding, alcoholic, self-appointed guardian of democracy, and best known of Burr's team, tracked down Major James Bruff and encouraged him to testify. As Bruff excitedly told everyone in the stagecoach carrying him to Richmond, Martin had promised "he would lash General Wilkinson into tortures" with his cross-examination. The major brought not only his own, far from credible, testimony concerning alleged confessions of conspiracy that Wilkinson had chosen to reveal privately to him behind locked doors and convenient bushes, but affidavits to the same effect from Wilkinson's other enemies in St. Louis, inlcuding Samuel Hammond, "with whom General Wilkinson had a conversation nearly similar to the one held with me." Bruff was joined by Swartwout, and a reluctant Thomas Power, who had been subpoenaed in New Orleans. All contributed to the impression that, as Luther Martin put it, "General Wilkinson is the alpha and the omega of the present prosecution."

Quite apart from his personal hostility to Burr, Jefferson's tactics left them little option but to pursue the general. When the president first told Congress about the conspiracy on January 22, 1807, he dated the moment at which the administration realized what was being planned not to William Eaton's information in October, but to Wilkinson's letter on November 25. This conveniently obscured the nightmare period when the cabinet lost control of events, but it portrayed the general as solely responsible for detecting the conspiracy, and deserving most of the credit for defeating it. By destroying Wilkinson, Burr's team undermined the very existence of a plot. And behind him was a larger target.

In his address to Congress, Jefferson had declared that Burr "contemplated two distinct objects, which might be carried on either jointly or separately . . . One of these was the severance of the Union of these States by the Alleghany mountains; the other, an attack on Mexico." His public statements hammered at the theme of Burr's undoubted guilt in seeking to destroy the Union. In private he went further, referring to "treason stalking through the land," and accusing the Federalists of "making Burr's cause their own, mortified only that he did not separate the Union or overturn the government."

Burr's defense team responded by issuing subpoenas for the presidential papers, and especially for his letters to the general. "The president has undertaken to prejudge my client by declaring 'of his guilt there can be no doubt,'" Martin thundered in court. "He has let slip the dogs of war, the hellhounds of prosecution, to hunt down my friend. And would this president of the United States, who has raised all this absurd clamor, pretend to keep back the papers which are wanted for this trial, where life itself is at stake?" It was, on both sides, a political as well as a legal contest.

To Jefferson's intense frustration, at every hearing, from the first application in February 1807 before the Supreme Court for a writ of habeas corpus for Swartwout and Bollman, the leading judge was the chief justice, John Marshall, an overt Federalist appointed to his position by John Adams in 1801. In releasing Burr's two messengers, Marshall had laid out what was to be his unchanging opinion, that the constitution specified that "treason against the United States shall consist only in levying war against them," and that "conspiracy is not treason . . . To conspire, and actually to levy war are distinct offences." As a result, when Burr appeared before Marshall at a preliminary hearing on March 31 in Richmond, the capital of Burr's home state, Marshall would indict him only on the grounds of levying war against a foreign power, a charge that amounted to a misdemeanor. It was left to the grand jury, whose hearings began on May 22, to decide whether to reinstate the charge of treason. Again in charge of the case, this time as judge of the circuit court in Virginia, Marshall did not challenge the president's refusal to let his papers be subpoenaed, although he continued to make plain his opinion that the treason charge was unsound.

The appearance in court of General James Wilkinson on June 15 was consequently one of high drama, bringing onto the stage the prosecution's chief witness and the defense's primary target. For political connoisseurs, he would serve as a surrogate for the president; for conspiracy theorists, he was the one person who might be able to throw light on Burr's real intentions; but for enthusiasts of crude emotional confrontation, nothing matched the electric moment when Wilkinson approached Burr in the handsome, white-paneled hall of Virginia's House of Delegates.

"Wilkinson strutted into court and took his stand in a parallel line with Burr on his right hand," wrote Washington Irving. "Here he stood for a moment, swelling like a turkey cock and bracing himself for the encounter of Burr's eye. The latter did not take any notice of him until the judge directed the clerk to swear General Wilkinson; at the mention of the name Burr turned his head, looked him full in the face with one of his piercing regards, swept his eye over his whole person from head to foot, as if to scan its dimensions, and then cooly resumed his former position, and went on versing with his counsel as tranquilly as ever. The whole look was over in an instant, but it was an admirable one. There was no appearance of study or constraint in it; no affectation of disdain or defiance; a slight expression of contempt played over his countenance."

Irving wrote from the point of view of a New York Federalist and someone who confessed to feeling "no sensation but compassion for [Burr]." From Wilkinson's perspective, the scene played differently. "I was introduced to a position within the bar very near my adversary," he wrote Jefferson two days later. "I saluted the bench and inspite of myself my eyes darted a flash of indignation at the little traitor, on whom they continued fixed until I was called to the Book; here, sir, I found my expectations verified— this lion-hearted, eagle-eyed Hero, jerking under the weight of conscious guilt, with haggard eyes in an effort to meet the indignant salutation of outraged honor; but it was in vain, his audacity failed him. He averted his face, grew pale, and affected passion to conceal his perturbation."

For the next four days Wilkinson gave evidence before the grand jury. Seeing himself as the nation's savior confronting its betrayer must have left him ill-prepared for the hostility he faced, not just from Burr's lawyers, but from the foreman of the jury, John Randolph. A disease in adolescence had left him with a childlike voice and no facial hair, condemning him to be an outsider in Virginia's testosterone-fueled society. Politically, he exploited his position on the sidelines to become a coruscating, merciless critic of any frailty or compromise that he detected among the main players. "He is a very slight man but of the common stature," his fellow congressman William Plumer noted. "At a little distance, he does not appear older than you are; but, upon a nearer approach, you perceive his wrinkles and grey hairs . . . [His opponents] ridicule and affect to despise him; but a despised foe often proves a dangerous enemy."

Although nominally a Republican, he made a particular target of Jefferson's extensive use of federal power, basing his criticism, to the president's intense irritation, on the doctrine of state sovereignty put forward in 1798 by Jefferson himself. This stance ensured that Randolph was also adamantly opposed to a standing army—in 1800 he dismissed it in Congress as "a handful of Ragamuffins." In Wilkinson himself, Randolph discerned a wickedness that had tempted Jefferson into compromising his former values, and he roundly declared that the general was "the only man I ever saw who was a villain from the bark to the core." It became Randolph's mission to persuade his fellow jurors to indict the general as a traitor, more vicious than Burr.

The hearings were secret, but both protagonists agreed, for their own purposes, that the general had become the main focus of the grand jury hearings. Wilkinson portrayed himself as victim, while Randolph declared, "There was scarcely a variance of opinion amongst us [in the grand jury] as to his guilt." In fact, most jurors opposed Randolph's move to arraign Wilkinson, but did vote to indict Burr on a charge of treason on the basis of the general's testimony and the ciphered letter he produced. And at a later hearing, when Burr's lawyers called three grand jurors to give evidence intended to demonstrate the general's untrustworthiness, their accounts strengthened rather than undermined Wilkinson's standing as a witness.

With Burr bailed out on ten thousand dollars and directed to appear for trial on August 3 on charges of treason, referring to the threat to New Orleans, and high misdemeanor, relating to the attack on Mexico, Wilkinson was released from his ordeal. "Your enemies have filled the public ear with slanders, & your mind with trouble on that account," the president wrote consolingly from Washington. "The establishment of their guilt will let the world see what they ought to think of their clamors; it will dissipate the doubts of those who doubted for want of knolege [*sic*], and will place you on higher ground in the public estimate and public confidence. No one is more sensible than myself of the injustice which has been aimed at you."

THE PROSECUTION BEGAN with William Eaton's recollected conversations in the winter of 1805–6 with the accused: "Colonel Burr now laid open his project of revolutionizing the territory west of the Allegheny, establishing an independent empire there; New Orleans to be the capital, and he himself to be the chief; organizing a military force on the waters of the Mississippi, and carrying conquest to Mexico." Eaton was partially supported by Commodore Truxton, who said nothing of secession, but remembered Burr declaring at that time that he "intended to attack Veracruz and Mexico, give liberty to an enslaved world, and establish an independent government in Mexico."

Secession returned in an affidavit from Colonel George Morgan, founder of New Madrid, and a pioneer settler in the west from the 1780s, who told of Burr's conversation when he came to stay in the summer of 1806. "After dinner I spoke of our fine country," the old man testified. "I observed that when I first went there, there was not a single family between the Allegheny mountains and the Ohio; and that by and by we should have congress sitting in this neighborhood or at Pittsburg [*sic*]. We were allowed to sport these things over a glass of wine: 'No, never' said Colonel Burr, 'for in less than five years you will be totally divided from the Atlantic states.' The colonel entered into some arguments to prove why it would and must be so." Before the argument was over, Burr had shocked Morgan further by insisting that "with two hundred men he could drive congress, with the president at its head, into the river Potomac."

Marshall's narrow interpretation of what constituted treason, however, pushed the focus of the trial to the events that took place on Blennerhassett's island in the Ohio River, since it was there that men, arms, and transport were most obviously brought together to "levy war." Blennerhassett's gardener, Peter Taylor, offered a vivid account of a conversation with his normally fastidious employer: "He made a sudden pause and said, 'I will tell you what, Peter, we are going to take Mexico, one of the finest and richest places in the whole world.' He said that Colonel Burr would be the king of Mexico, and Mrs. Alston, daughter of Colonel Burr, was to be the queen of Mexico whenever Colonel Burr died. He said that Colonel Burr had made fortunes for many in his time, but none for himself; but now he was going to make something for himself."

The evidence of other young men invited by Blennerhassett to join an undefined adventure in the west—the defense insisted it was merely to settle Burr's 300,000-acre holding on the Ouachita River—was inconclusive, and in any event while they were on the island, Burr was demonstrably a hundred miles away with Andrew Jackson. On August 20, Burr moved to have the trial ended because the evidence "utterly failed to prove any overt act of war had been committed." Marshall accepted that the Blennerhassett gathering was not treasonous and refused to hear any evidence relating to events subsequent to it. The prosecution case quickly lapsed, with many witnesses, including Wilkinson, unheard, and when the jurors were called upon to give their verdict, they did so with heavy qualification: "We of the jury say that Aaron Burr is not proved to be guilty under this indictment by any evidence submitted to us. We therefore find him not guilty."

The wording implied that a fuller hearing might have produced a different verdict, and on the street there was little doubt about Burr's guilt. Half of those called for jury service in the next trial admitted to entrenched opinions against him, and no one thought him innocent. Jefferson's fury was unrestrained. Marshall's handling of the trial, he told Wilkinson, amounted to "a proclamation of impunity to every traitorous combination which may be formed to destroy the Union."

Unhampered by the judge's narrow interpretation, Burr's second trial, beginning in September, for the misdemeanor of planning to attack Mexico, came closer to revealing the true nature of the conspiracy. From its opening debate about the failure of the president to respond to a subpoena duces tecum that required him to produce two letters from the general sent on October 21 and November 12, the defense had Wilkinson in their sights. "We shall prove that he turned traitor to Colonel Burr," Luther Martin rasped in his brandy-roughened voice, "and violated his engagement with him, by endeavoring to sacrifice him to the government."

The documents that Wilkinson sent the president on October 21 following Swartwout's surprise appearance provided the defense with their opening. In his copy and translation of Burr's ciphered letter, the general was shown to have omitted the opening sentence, "Yours postmarked 13th May is received," and to have doctored other passages to make them less compromising. In the accompanying letter to Jefferson, Wilkinson had stated, "I am not only uninformed of the prime mover and ultimate objects of the daring enterprize, I am ignorant of the foundation on which it rests, of the means by which it is to be supported," although Swartwout had told him that it was led by Burr and Mexico was its target. Finally, a postscript on the back of the letter suggested that "some plan be adopted to correct the destination of the associates." Read together, the inference was clear— that the general was closely associated with the traitor and at least half inclined to collaborate with him, and, as Luther Martin caustically observed, "that he has placed himself in such a situation, he must hang Mr. Burr or be himself eternally detested."

But in their eagerness to bring down the general, the defense went too far. Martin put Bruff on the stand to give evidence that Wilkinson had privately confessed his involvement in a conspiracy, only to see his story rendered unbelievable when the general produced a letter from Governor Harrison of Indiana warning him, before he even arrived in St. Louis, that Bruff was so unreliable no one in the city trusted him: "The bare idea of his being in your confidence would frighten some of them [the inhabitants] out of their senses." Nor did Wickham do any better with Thomas Power, who had been brought unwillingly from New Orleans to testify to delivering dollars from Carondelet to Wilkinson. In near hysteria, Power flatly refused as a Spanish citizen to say anything derogatory about the general.

Nevertheless, watching Wilkinson being assailed by his attorney's unrelenting cross-examination, Harman Blennerhassett noted with satisfaction, "He exhibited the manner of a sergeant under courtmartial rather than the demeanor of an accusing officer confronted with his culprit. His perplexity and derangement, even upon his direct examination, has placed beyond all doubt 'his honor as a soldier and his fidelity as a citizen.'"

The general's case was not helped by the decision of the government's lead attorney, George Hay, to throw him to the wolves. "My confidence in him is shaken, if not destroyed," Hay admitted to Jefferson. "I am sorry for it on his own account, on the public account, and because you have expressed opinions in his favor." As a result, the prosecution rarely challenged the defense's use of unsupported allegations, leading questions, and hearsay evidence to indict Wilkinson.

In his summing-up, Marshall accepted the central thrust of Burr's defense that the two men were inseparable: "It is obvious that Col. Burr, whether with or without reason, calculated on his co-operation with the army which [Wilkinson] commanded, and that on this co-operation, the execution of his plan greatly, if not absolutely depended." When the jury found Burr not guilty, they also implicitly cleared Wilkinson. But in popular opinion, both were judged to be treacherous to the core.

THE PRESIDENT'S EXTRAORDINARY efforts to see Burr convicted, and his endorsement of Wilkinson's unconstitutional regime in New Orleans, suggest how gravely he viewed the threat presented by the conspiracy. It was the ultimate test of the republican democracy he had tried to foster in the Mississippi Valley, where central government was denuded of power in favor of the states and the citizen. Addressing Congress on January 31, 1807, he declared that the conspiracy had been defeated by "the patriotic exertions of the militia wherever called into action, by the fidelity of the army, and energy of the commander-in-chief." In reality, however, these were not the vital ingredients.

Apart from the small detachment of Ohio militia that descended on Blennerhassett's island, and the thirty men of the Mississippi militia who arrested Burr at Natchez, the citizens' army was conspicuous by its absence. The fidelity of the regular army was unquestionable, but the soldiers would have marched to war with Spain as readily as they patrolled the streets of New Orleans. Equally the commanding general would have given the same bravura display in an attack across the Sabine as in his role as savior of the nation. What makes the Burr Conspiracy a pivotal event in American history lay in the evidence given by every witness who was invited to aid Burr in his enterprise. Sooner or later, each one made it plain that he was prepared to join the expedition only if it was part of the United States' war with Spain.

That was the transformation in the western settlers that Burr, the east-erner, never appreciated. Trying to recruit Colonel George Morgan's family, Burr had told the old man "that our taxes [in the west] were very heavy, and demanded why we should pay them to the Atlantic parts of the country?" as though he were talking to the whiskey rebels of the eighteenth century. But in the Mississippi Valley the border mentality that had allowed Rogers Clark, Blount, Sevier, and especially the younger Wilkinson to switch loyalties to serve their own advantage had gone. The certainty of the national frontier drawn by Andrew Ellicott in 1798, the pride in the sudden doubling of the U.S. landmass through the Louisiana Purchase, and the guarantee of property rights under U.S. law that each settler depended upon had created something new, a clear attachment to the nation.

The change was unmistakable in the response of the Morgans because Burr specifically told them of his efforts to recruit men "who had been engaged in the western insurraction," meaning the 1794 Whiskey Rebellion. Not only did the son, John, advise his father "to apprize the President of the United States that something was going forward," but the old colonel, who in 1788 had been ready to become a Spanish subject, went out of his way to express to Burr his pride in "our fine country." He was not alone. Time after time, those that Burr and Blennerhassett tried to recruit made it clear that they regarded the exploitation of their country as unpatriotic.

Andrew Jackson expressed the emotion in histrionic fashion: "I would delight to see Mexico reduced, but I will die in the last ditch before I would yield a foot to the Dons, or see the union disunited." More soberly, Lieutenant Jacob Jackson, in command of the garrison at Chickasaw Bluffs, said that he had agreed to join Burr "provided I found him patronized by the United States." Even Maurice Belknap, one of Blennerhassett's messengers, who had nothing to lose by enlisting, refused to do so because, as he testified, "I stated to him that I believed that the expedition was an unlawful one."

That was the dilemma that faced James Wilkinson from the moment Swartwout entered his camp. Would he side with the past or the future? At that point, the fate of the United States had hinged on his choice. John Adair was surely correct in assuming that an attack across the Sabine would have triggered the cascade of volunteers that Burr counted on. No one, perhaps not even Burr himself, knew what he would then have done with thousands of men at his back, money needed, New Orleans at his mercy, and Veracruz beyond. However disreputable Wilkinson's motives, his decision to oppose Burr was crucial in determining whether the American states remained united or not, whether they moved into the future or not. It was, in consequence, the depth of irony that after twenty highly successful and rewarding years of treachery, one single act of loyalty and patriotism should have plunged the rest of his life into ignominy.

The War with Randolph

I CAN DISTINCTLY TRACE the source of my persecutions to the celebrated John Randolph of Roanoke," James Wilkinson wrote in his *Memoirs*, "who is entitled to all the credit, to be derived from the cunning, zeal, perseverance, and perfidy displayed in his complottings against the character of a man, whom he feared and hated." Wilkinson overlooked, however, his own considerable contribution to his downfall.

In his attempt to indict Wilkinson for treachery, Randolph had termed him "a rogue," an insult that festered until, on Christmas Eve 1807, the general challenged Randolph to a duel for a comment "injurious to my reputation." His challenge was swept aside contemptuously. "In you, sir," Randolph replied, "I recognize no right to hold me accountable for my public or private opinion of your character . . . I cannot descend to your level." Frustrated, Wilkinson responded by plastering Washington with posters that boldy proclaimed, "In Justice to my Character, I denounce John Randolph, Member of Congress, to the world, as a prevaricating, base, calumniating scoundrel."

This imaginative retaliation tarnished Randolph's standing in the eyes of the Virginians who had elected him. But it also secured his inveterate hatred. Members of the Tenth Congress had more pressing issues to consider. They had reconvened early at the president's urgent request to consider how best to respond to the unprovoked attack in June by the British warship *Leopard* on the USS *Chesapeake* after the latter refused to allow a British search party on board to look for possible deserters. Without waiting for Congress, Jefferson had authorized additional spending to strengthen defenses, which, he admitted later, "were illy provided with some necessary articles," but his decision created a host of questions about defense, the Constitution, and the budget. Yet all this took second place after the posters appeared.

What made Wilkinson's accusation truly dangerous was that, for entirely different reasons, he had also made enemies of Thomas Power and Daniel Clark. To clear his name after the trial, he had published Power's declaration that Wilkinson had not spied for Spain, and the Irishman, who had thought his certificate was only for Jefferson's eyes, was mortified to be publicly revealed as a fool. Still more serious was Wilkinson's indiscreet remark in November at an Annapolis party that Clark was so short of money one of his bills of exchange had been offered for payment at a third of its face value. Unfortunately this was overheard by wealthy Richard Caton of Baltimore, whose sixteen-year-old daughter, Louisa, was being wooed by Clark. The girl was promptly banned from seeing Clark again and sent abroad to Britain, where she eventually married Francis George Godolphin D'Arcy D'Arcy-Osborne, the seventh duke of Leeds. Socially it was an improvement on a New Orleans merchant who was short of money and already married, but Clark's heart was broken. "The affair is *forever* ended," he wrote sadly, and as Wilkinson acknowledged, a man who "had always been my professed friend and obsequious servant, as his correspondence will testify, was suddenly converted into a remorseless enemy."

The result of his enmity became clear on the last day of 1807, when Randolph told his astonished colleagues in Congress that he intended to call for an inquiry to discover whether General Wilkinson "while in the service of the United States had corruptly received money from the government of Spain." To substantiate his demand, he produced three documents given him by Clark—a note from Baron Carondelet in January 1796 referring to the payment to Wilkinson of $9,640; Wilkinson's to Gayoso in September 1796 with its "let my name be never mentioned" demand for greater secrecy; and Thomas Power's characterically effusive but damning explanation of why he had lied (or as he preferred to put it, descended to "tergiversation, captious logic and sophistical evasion") on behalf of the general. The false certificate clearing Wilkinson was necessary, Power explained, because "I [was] a secret agent of the Spanish government and General Wilkinson was a pensioner of the said government," and it was the agent's duty to provide the general with cover.

Under pressure to explain his own involvement, Clark produced a hurried document that traced his long commercial connection with the general, and the firsthand knowledge he possessed of the general's treachery. In growing excitement, Congress suspended discussion in January 1808 of the

Embargo Act banning the export of United States goods to Europe and argued instead about the propriety of investigating General James Wilkinson. "Is it because this man assisted in the capture of General Burgoyne, the first step in securing the existence of our nation," James Sloan of New Jersey angrily demanded, "and has now arrested an infernal band—a host of traitors—is it for these things that he is now charged?"

It was soon clear the general was not the only target. Kentucky's John Rowan said that if the inquiry recommended Wilkinson's removal and the president did not comply, Congresss "should try, not General Wilkinson, but the President of the United States." From the Senate, Republican John Pope of Kentucky judged that "the object of [Randolph's attack] is to injure the administration." But the weight of Clark's evidence overwhelmed personal and party considerations. On January 13, 1808, a large majority voted to set up an inquiry into reports that General Wilkinson had "corruptly received money from the Government of Spain." They had, however, been preempted.

In response to Randolph's opening assault, Wilkinson had demanded a court of inquiry, as he had twice before, in Washington's and Adams's administrations. This time it was granted. Like Pope, Jefferson understood the attack on Wilkinson to be an assault on his increasingly unpopular administration. He did not intend to abandon his general.

On January 2, the president announced that a three-man military board would investigate the general's conduct. Since its membership consisted of three colonels whose careers could be made or broken by the general, and two of whom, Cushing and Jonathan Williams, the superintendent of West Point, were his close friends, it was widely criticized as inadequate. It sat for five months, with Wilkinson attending most of its hearings so that he could cross-examine witnesses and present testimony that vindicated his behavior. Many of the two thousand pages in his *Memoirs* were taken directly from his voluminous defense.

Daniel Clark refused to appear before the board, but in April, shortly before it was due to report, he presented Congress with more material from Power's archives, this time relating to the agent's two visits to Wilkinson, just before and after General Wayne's death. Among the documents were Power's letters to Carondelet and Gayoso telling in breathless prose of his narrow escape when Lieutenant Steele boarded his boat with the general's dollars hidden in coffee barrels. To these allegations, Wilkinson offered the familiar defense that the money was payment for commercial transactions, and that far from favoring Spain, he had sent troops south to push them out of Natchez.

The effervescent Power, a self-confessed liar, could be swatted aside by the sheer weight of the general's declaration, but the weighty testimony of Andrew Ellicott, the precise Quaker astronomer, presented a more formidable challenge. On January 20, Jefferson had bowed to Congress's demand that he provide all the documents relevant to their inquiry. Determined to release as little as possible, the president warned Congress that fire had destroyed everything in the War Office prior to 1800, that other papers might have been lost or misfiled, and that one letter sent by Ellicott to the War Department in November 1798 had at his request to be kept secret, although its author might reveal its contents. Apart from that, Jefferson declared, with astonishing lack of candor, Clark's evidence "is the first direct testimony ever made known to me charging General Wilkinson with the corrupt receipt of money."

When one of Clark's investigators approached Ellicott a few days later, he heard a different story. "To my knowledge," Ellicott declared, "the present administration has been minutely informed of the conduct of General Wilkinson; and why he has been supported, and patronized, after this information, is to me an inexplicable paradox." He duly provided Clark with an affidavit to be given to the board of inquiry that repeated the substance of the letter he had sent Jefferson in the first months of his administration. It detailed all the evidence he had received, from President Washington's warning against Wilkinson in 1796 to the information from Tomás Portell, obtained in November 1799, that the $9,640 was the general's "pension" from Spain. "I questioned [Portell] frequently whether this money was not on account of some mercantile transaction," Ellicott testified, "he declared it was not."

Had this testimony been given in person, it might well have swayed the board. But, unwilling to risk exposing Jefferson's cover-up, Ellicott refused to apear in person, and without his presence and transparent honesty to support its allegations, his affidavit lost much of its force.

Nevertheless, Wilkinson went to extraordinary lengths to counter Ellicott's evidence, beginning with the jocular aside that when he wrote his affidavit, "the celebrated astronomer must have been under the influence of the moon." With growing indignation, he declared Ellicott to be a self-appointed spy, then whipping himself to a fury claimed, "This witness in his fondness for the marvellous, his propensity for defamation, and his sympathy for Mr Clark, has perjured himself, over and over again." Finally in an uppercase frenzy of alliteration, he denounced "the pretended SPY, THE PERJURED, PROFLIGATE ELLICOTT [for] labouring to assassinate my humble, hard-earned reputation."

It is almost possible to sense the general's lobster-eyed delight in this demolition of Ellicott, the one witness who had no secrets to hide and no animosity to conceal. The others, including Clark, were easily exposed as hostile liars whose evidence counted for nothing beside the numerous testimonials to the general's loyalty and patriotism bestowed on him by three presidents, two secretaries of war, and others both great and good. Wilkinson's vigorous counterattack was unexpectedly helped by the rapid erosion of Clark's popularity in New Orleans, where, Claiborne reported, "His deposition against General Wilkinson has given rise to much severe animadversion on Mr Clark's general character."

It was hardly surprising that on June 28 the board of inquiry should have reported, "There is no evidence of Brigadier-general James Wilkinson, having, at any time, received a pension from the Spanish government, or of his having received money from the government of Spain, or any of its officers or agents, for corrupt purposes; and the court has no hesitation in saying, that, as far as his conduct has been developed by this enquiry, he appears to have discharged the duties of his station with honor to himself and fidelity to his country."

ALTHOUGH NOT A RINGING ENDORSEMENT, the verdict left the commanding general once more in full control of the army. And for the first time in Jefferson's administration, its numbers were increasing. The dominance of Britain's navy at sea and its aggressive inspection of neutral vessels suspected of trading strategic goods with Napoléon's empire exposed the flaws in Jefferson's minimalist defense policy. Responding to the perceived threat of British attack from Canada or the Gulf of Mexico, the president reversed the policy of the previous seven years. In February, he asked Congress for funding to pay for the recruitment of six thousand more regulars, and twenty-four thousand volunteers.

This represented a historic shift by the great advocate of militia as the nation's primary defense. The type of troops to be raised, artillery, riflemen, and light dragoons as well as infantry, explained why the change had to be made. To train a large number of citizen-soldiers in these skills was prohibitively expensive compared with the cost of producing a small corps of full-time specialists. In April, Congress dispensed with the volunteers and committed nearly all the resources to the recruitment of eight new regiments of regulars. Slapping down the last few holdouts who still echoed Samuel Adams's warnings against standing armies, South Carolina's John Taylor declared, "If I could believe that there was the least danger to the liberties of 800,000 or one million of freemen by the forces now to be raised, I should think very little of my country."

Nevertheless, no one could deny that the first use of the new force was directed at Americans. In an attempt to force Britain into negotiations, the Embargo Act banned all trade with her. Faced by bankruptcy, many merchants from New Orleans to Boston chose to find a way round the embargo by smuggling flour, cotton, and tobacco through Canada or Spanish Florida. Customs officials who tried to interfere were beaten up or otherwise intimidated, while local militia often preferred to ignore smugglers, who were liable to be their own neighbors.

As always in military matters, the president relied on his newly vindicated general to implement his political goals. In August 1808, Jefferson ordered Wilkinson to send newly trained recruits north to reinforce federal officials on the Canadian border. "The armed resistance to the embargo laws on the Canada line," the president explained, "[convinced] us at an early period that the new 'regular' recruits of the northern States should be rendezvoused there." The use of militia troops would have been, he acknowledged, "expensive, troublesome and less efficacious." Wilkinson promptly deployed three companies along the New York section of the border and ordered existing garrisons in smuggling ports to take extreme measures against smugglers. From Boston, artillery captain Joseph Swift eagerly reported back, "There would be no difficulty in planting a battery that would ensure an obedience to the law."

DESPITE HIS BEST EFFORTS, Jefferson could not prevent the United States from becoming embroiled in the cataclysm of Napoléon's attempt to dominate Europe. At sea, American ships were attacked by French privateers and boarded and often confiscated by the British navy. On land, the government was shaken by the nationalist earthquake that altered Latin American history—the uprising of the Spanish people on May 2 against France's military occupation. Once content to rule Spain through a puppet government under its king, Ferdinand VII, Napoléon now instituted direct rule, placing his own brother, Joseph, on the Spanish throne. From Chile to Florida, the legitimacy of this new Madrid government was immediately questioned. The dormant liberationist movement begun in 1806 by Francisco de Miranda in Venezuela revived and would, in the years ahead, spread across the continent.

The first American response to the new situation came from Wilkinson. On October 6 he wrote an alchoholic, rambling, but typically guileful memorandum on future policy in Latin America from his temporary head-quarters in Carlisle, Pennsylvania. Although addressed to Dearborn, its audience was clearly the president.

Wilkinson appealed first to Jefferson's well-known prejudices against the corrupting influence of European sophistication—"it multiplies our wants, depresses our tastes, infects our manners and corrupts our principles." He looked forward to "the Liberation of the American Continent from the Shackles of European Government, and the Nations of the West forming a distinct community united by common protection, defence and happiness." This community he called "United America." The only threat to its independence, he argued, came from the intervention of British power in the area, and he singled out the captain general of Cuba, Someruelos—"extremely feminine in his exterior and feeble in his intellect"—as particularly susceptible to British influence.

As always, Wilkinson's compelling description of a problem was followed by a solution that could be provided only by someone with his particular talents: "I know more of Spanish America, am better known by name and military character—impressive to despotic governments—than any other American." Bringing Someruelos into the U.S. camp was a task that would enable him to regain public confidence "by a display of zeal, integrity, devotion, perseverance and successful exertion. I would give my life for such an opportunity."

Reluctant to become involved, Jefferson preferred a policy of strict neutrality. "The patriots of Spain have no warmer friends than the Administration of the United States," he declared, "but it is our duty to say nothing for or against either [side]." Nevertheless, in a final, very public manifestation of confidence in his commanding general, he gave Wilkinson permission to approach Someruelos.

After eight years of compromising collaboration, the president and the general remained as mutually dependent as ever. Despite the dire effect on its fighting ability, Wilkinson turned a blind eye to the Republicans' relentless political screening of new officers in the enlarged army. The Federalist *Boston Gazette* complained that "beardless boys who belch beer and democracy" were promoted above non-Republican officers with experience, and fifty years later General Winfield Scott remembered, "Many of the appointments were positively bad, and a majority of the remainder indifferent. Party spirit of that day knew no bounds, and of course was blind to policy. Federalists were almost entirely excluded from selection, though great numbers were eager for the field."

For his part, Jefferson responded to Wilkinson's desperate appeal for help with his legal costs—"for half or even a third of the sum, my necessities being extreme"—by allowing the money to be paid in the form of recompense for extra rations the general must have bought during his time in New Orleans. The president also overlooked the fifty barrels of flour that the general took for sale in Cuba in breach of the Embargo Act. Nevertheless in February 1809, when Wilkinson was still on the high seas to Havana, the president also approved the appointment of two new brigadiers, Wade Hampton and Peter Gansevoort, both staunch Republicans. In the very last days of his administration, Jefferson was making sure that the general would never again have a monopoly of influence within the army.

WHEN WILKINSON SAILED FROM ANNAPOLIS on January 24, 1809, he was ostensibly making for New Orleans. Seven weeks earlier, responding to reports of British military preparations for an attack on the city, Dearborn had ordered him to assemble "as large a proportion of our regular troops at New Orleans and its vicinity as circumstances will permit." Although intended for the defense of the city, the presence of two thousand troops concentrated so close to Baton Rouge and West Florida, also constituted a diplomatic move and was, in Spanish eyes, seen as encouragement to potential rebels in the colonies. Consequently Wilkinson's mission to Havana caused a flurry of concerned messages along the borderland that was the commander in chief's natural home.

From Pensacola, Vizente Folch sent Someruelos a message that although Wilkinson had been "sincerely attached" to the Spanish cause and remained a personal friend, he was not to be trusted. The captain general replied in similar tone, observing that "His Majesty had some relations [with] No. 13" in the past, but Folch was to be wary of him now. These anxieties about Wilkinson's intentions were only increased by news from Norfolk, the first port at which he called, that at the end of a magnificent banquet given in his honor, he had proposed a toast to "the New World governed by itself and independent of the Old."

Unfortunately for Wilkinson's ambition to regain public confidence, Someruelos remained loyal to the Spanish royal family and, angered by the "New World" speech, refused to see him. Next, the general tried to visit Folch in Pensacola, but was again frustrated, this time by the governor's pressing need to be in Baton Rouge. When Wilkinson eventually arrived in New Orleans in April, his public diplomatic mission appeared to have failed. Nevertheless, his public support for the revolutionaries whose aims, he confessed to Dearborn, "excite in my Breast the Strangest Solicitude to participate in the glorious Atchievement" did have some effect.

Encouraged by the general's remarks and the nearby presence of U.S. troops, a force of American rebels seized Baton Rouge and proclaimed "the free and independent" republic of West Florida. Although swiftly annexed by the United States, this fragment of West Florida was the first district within the Spanish empire to achieve its independence—six months before Venezuela's more famous declaration—and could claim to be the precursor of the liberationist avalanche that would sweep Spanish rule away.

THE GENERAL WAS RECEIVED with surprising warmth on his return to New Orleans. Many turned out to cheer, and the merchant community who had come to hate Daniel Clark gave a dinner in his honor. But the popularity of a satirical pamphlet depicting him as "the Grand Pensioner" showed that the past was not entirely forgotten.

"Sweet was the song sung on Monday evening," the pamphlet, *The Pensioner's Mirror*, declared, "when it was announced by a herald from headquarters, that his Serene Highness, the Grand Pensioner de Godoy, was approaching the city and that he was to make his triumphal entry yesterday . . . When his serene highness entered the city, the bells they rung, *The pensioner is come, um, um, um,* and the drums re-echoed the joyful tidings. How grand the spectacle! What terror did it carry to the hearts of traitors!"

The barbs of a pamphlet might be ignored. Wilkinson's immediate concern was the situation of the two thousand troops sent to New Orleans in December. Taken from garrisons primarily on the Atlantic coast, and containing a high proportion of hastily trained recruits, both officers and soldiers, they had arrived in a city already overflowing with French refugees fleeing the anti-Napoleonic backlash in Cuba. Some had been billeted in the city, the remainder had been housed in tents and temporary wooden barracks across the river. For young men, the pleasures of New Orleans were ruinous, as Wilkinson put it, to "health, morals and discipline," and their largely untried, politically correct officers could not cope. By March 24, barely a month after their arrival, almost a quarter of the total force were on the sick list, others were not fit to bear arms, and desertion rates were soaring. When the general at last appeared on April 19, close to a third of his command were unfit for duty.

Within three days, he announced his intention to move the troops away from the city as soon as arrangements could be made, and that meanwhile mosquito nets were to be provided for all the tents. On May 12, three weeks after his arrival, he sent a long, angry letter to William Eustis, secretary of war in James Madison's new administration: "You will observe, Sir, we have an army without a general staff; and an hospital without surgeon, purveyor, matron, or nurse . . . The troops are without bunks or births to repose on, or musquitoe nets to protect them against that pestiferous insect with which this country abounds."

This crossed with a message from Eustis sent on April 29 in response to the sickness figures, urging Wilkinson to get the men out of New Orleans. "It will be desirable," he declared, "that [they] should be transported either to the high ground in the rear of Fort Adams or in the rear of Natchez." Since the first troops left the city only in early June, six weeks after Wilkinson discovered the situation, it is probable, although he denied it, that Wilkinson received this message before the men moved and deliberately ignored it.

The ostensible reason was that New Orleans wisdom insisted that in summer the heat and "effluvia" from the water made river journeys dangerously unhealthy, and a voyage upriver to Natchez would take at least a month. But it was also clear that Wilkinson wanted to teach Eustis, the sixth secretary of war he had dealt with, who was master in their relationship. As he informed his court-martial, "peremptory, unqualified orders, at a thousand miles distance, evince an excess of temerity, which no military man will justify."

The general was also distracted by the sort of intoxication that overtakes a fifty-two-year-old man when he falls in love with a twenty-two-year-old girl. Since Celestine Laveau Trudeau was the daughter of Louisiana's surveyor general, and one of the city's leading citizens, the courtship could not be rushed.

The place he chose for a new camp was Terre aux Boeufs, seven miles downriver from New Orleans where a defense could be mounted against a naval force coming up the Mississippi. Although three feet below the level of the river on the other side of the levee, Wilkinson assured Eustis that "it was perfectly dry" and in a later description made it sound idyllic with cattle grazing in lush clover fields and "a charming shade along the front . . . furnished by a grove of majestic live oak trees."

Once the ground had been cleared by a work party under the indefatigable Major Zebulon Pike, a tented encampment was set up for a force that had by then reached about 2,300 men. As the troops arrived, the sickness rate fell rapidly from its May peak of 600 with 53 further losses from death and desertion, to 442 at the end of June and only 13 other losses.

Unfortunately for General Wilkinson's calculated defiance, and tragically for the well-being of his men, the rain that had held off for most of June began to fall again. The river that had shrunk until it was half a mile from the camp began to rise until it lapped the levee only fifty-five yards away. Above and below Terre aux Boeufs, it broke through the embankments until the lower ground became lakes and swamps. Trodden down by hundreds of men, the clover fields turned to mud. Within the tents the men lay in pools of water until in mid-July the boats were broken up to make wooden floors. The latrines, long, makeshift ditches known as sinks, which had been dug at the back of the camp, overflowed, and raw sewage spread over the ground, contaminating water supplies, spreading disease, and attracting clouds of flies. The coffins of those that died could not be buried more than a few inches below the surface, and the corpses soon putrefied in the heat.

On July 16, Captain John Bentley of the military police inspected the camp and gave Wilkinson a devastating report on what he found: "The whole camp abounds with filth and nastiness of almost every kind . . . The kitchens are generally in a very bad state; in some instances holes have been dug to form them, which have become the receptacle of all manner of filth, and on the left of the dragoons, it is not uncommon to see men in the day time, easing themselves within a few yards of the kitchens! I beg leave to suggest the propriety of procuring necessary tubs for the use of the sick, who are not able to go to the sinks. The sewers have become the receptacle of stinking meat, refuse of vegetables, old clothes, and every species of filth. It is necessary that a number of new sinks should be dug, in place of those covered, and those that ought to be covered. You will be assailed with a very unpleasant smell, in walking down the levee, from the front to the flank guard . . . The burying ground requires immediate attention; the lids of many of the coffins are but very little, if any, below the surface, and covered with but a few inches of earth; the stench arising from the burying ground is sensibly observed on the left of the dragoons."

Missing from Bentley's report was anything about the food being prepared in the filthy kitchens, and that caused more complaints from soldiers than the filth. No one disputed that the flour was "generally mouldy, lumpy and sour" and infested with mealie bugs and worms, and that the bread was no better. The salted meat, usually pork, turned out to be a rusty brown color when it was ladled out of the barrel and often covered in mold, while the fresh meat, taken from cattle slaughtered close to the camp, was stringy and, on two occasions, proved so inedible that the provisioning officers took the salt meat instead.

Selfish and greedy though he was, Wilkinson responded quickly to Bentley's findings. He transferred his headquarters from New Orleans to be on-site and ordered new drains to be dug, and shading to be constructed for the guard posts and on the paths between the tents. He also overrode the existing food contract, ordering a hundred barrels of fresh flour, and regular supplies of fresh chickens for the sick.

These measures, however, brought a compromising response from the food supplier, James Morrison: "You know whether the contract is profitable depends on the commander-in-chief . . . Be as serviceable to me as you can, where you are, keeping the public in view, and it may be in my power to be in some way serviceable to you . . . Should a part [of the flour] become unfit for use, I have directed [my agents] to purchase and mix with sweet flour so as to make it palatable. Don't I pray you order an examination unless in the last resort."

On top of this witches' brew of cheeseparing, military mismanagement, and bad weather came the intervention of William Eustis. In an apoplectic response to Wilkinson's move downriver, the secretary of war issued a direct order "immediately to embark all the troops . . . and proceed to the high ground in the rear of Fort Adams and Natchez." The months at Terre aux Boeufs saw 145 losses from death and desertion. In an operation that eventually saw the force lose more than 1,100 men, approximately 750 of them died or deserted after the move ordered by Eustis. At his court-martial, Wilkinson insisted, probably correctly, that had the men been left where they were, with the river level falling, the ground drying, and the food improving, it would have cost fewer lives. But he had gambled on the weather before, and lost.

The navy, manned by militia sailors, had been ordered to provide all twenty-four of its gunboats to carry the army, but only supplied four. The military boats in Natchez that were supposed to supplement them turned out to be rotten and unseaworthy. Accordingly the troops were crammed onto the few boats that could be hired in New Orleans and, with agonizing slowness, were rowed upstream in the sultry summer heat. One regiment as well as the sickest on board were left behind in New Orleans, and another hundred invalids were put ashore at the army post at Pointe Coupee. Not until mid-October did the first boats reach Fort Washington behind Fort Adams, and the remainder were landed at Natchez near the end of the month. More than two hundred men had succumbed on the boats, but weakened by disease and recurrent fevers, including malaria, another five hundred died after they reached dry land.

Inevitably, the officer in charge of such a catastrophe would face a public inquiry. On December 19, 1809, before any conclusion was reached, President Madison suspended General James Wilkinson from command of the U.S. army pending the outcome of a congressional investigation.

28

MADISON'S ACCUSATIONS

I CONFESS, THE STRENGTH of my mind was shaken," James Wilkinson admitted when he learned of President James Madison's decision. For the first time in his career, the general had no allies in government. He faced an unfriendly Congress, and an administration that was downright hostile. Yet he soon recovered his mental alertness, thanks to a sense of "conscious rectitude, an implicit reliance on my Creator, an invincible flow of animal spirits, and a firmness of resolution which had supported me under almost every vicissitude of human life." Of these, the flow of animal spirits, meaning his remorseless, bounding energy, counted for most. That was apparent in early 1810, once command had formally been handed over to Brigadier Wade Hampton in Natchez. Instead of heading straight for Washington, Wilkinson first turned south for New Orleans and the embrace of Celestine Trudeau.

They were married on March 5. The ceremony took place in the chapel of the fashionable Ursuline nuns who, the groom must have been uneasily aware, had been enthusiastic supporters of Aaron Burr's. The honeymoon was brief, but indubitably passionate since Celestine bore him a daughter nine months later. Yet not even a young bride could keep him away from the battle to save his career. Less than a week after they were married, he sailed for Washington, and he and his wife would not see each other again for more than two years.

The long delay in bringing him to face a court was largely deliberate, a device adopted by Madison and Eustis to force him out of the army, but the process was also slowed by the long list of offenses that required investigation. During the disastrous summer of 1809, Daniel Clark's *Proofs of the*

Corruption of General Wilkinson and His Connexion with Aaron Burr had been published, containing every document that Clark and Power could unearth in New Orleans that pointed to the general's guilt. Although the Spanish records escaped them, the impact was more powerful than their piecemeal presentation the previous year. Accordingly Congress appointed two committees to investigate the separate issues of the general's role as a Spanish agent, and his responsibility for the army's loss of life.

Both eventually reported in February 1811. Within military circles, the more potentially damaging was the inquiry into the debacle at Terre aux Boeufs. To his frustration, the general was not allowed to appear personally, and witnesses who testified to filthy conditions and poor food were not cross-examined. The imputation that Wilkinson alone was to blame was thus left unchallenged except by one balky member of the committee, William Crawford of Pennsylvania. Convinced that other factors must be involved since almost three quarters of the deaths had occurred after leaving the camp, Crawford voted against recommending action against the general. Presented with a confused report, Congress decided simply to ignore it. The second committee under Ezekiel Bacon made no recommendation but passed directly to the executive the voluminous and familiar evidence that Daniel Clark had assembled about the general's connections to Spain.

Unlike their predecessors, neither President Madison nor Secretary of War Eustis had any intention of rescuing the general. For ten weeks, he was left in limbo, apart from an informal suggestion that he should return to New Orleans to be with Celestine "and wait there the farther pleasure of the House of Representatives, without the resumption of my command." The general indignantly refused, declaring that "sooner than consent to such a degradation, I would bare my bosom to the fire of a platoon." Eventually, eighteen months after his suspension, public pressure from both his friends and enemies to have him brought to trial at last forced the secretary of war to agree to a meeting on May 14, 1811.

"Mr. Eustis received me with great cordiality," Wilkinson recorded, "and pressed my hand, until it almost ached." With the same apparent friendliness, Eustis explained smoothly that "the President felt for my situation very sensibly, and felt every disposition to do me justice; that on the score of the Burr business, I stood perfectly acquitted, and in relation to the Spanish business, he was also satisfied." Nevertheless, Eustis continued, the awkward problem created by Ellicott's information about his spying still remained. Eustis hoped that the general might agree it needed to be cleared up, "but that this was a mere suggestion, which he offered to my consideration."

Turning to Terre aux Boeufs, Eustis acknowledged the president's wish for a third inquiry, this time under military auspices, in order "to satisfy the public mind, vindicate your character, and justify your conduct." It should take place, the secretary recommended, in New Orleans, far away from Washington.

As a master of military maneuvering, Wilkinson had no difficulty in perceiving the opportunities and pitfalls in this proposal. Without hesitation, he accepted the suggested inquiry and insisted that its scope should be as wide as possible. Although Celestine's absence caused "the keenest pangs which crossed my bosom," he also stipulated that it should take place on the Atlantic coast close to the center of power rather than in her home city. Madison agreed to these conditions, and on June 1, 1811, Wilkinson was ordered to stand trial at a court-martial, accused of aiding the Burr conspiracy, accepting a pension from the Spanish government, and being responsible for the disaster at Terre aux Boeufs.

By the time he entered the courthouse in Fredericktown, Maryland, the general faced an astonishing list of eight different charges, subdivided into twenty-five specific offenses. Chronologically they covered events from 1787 through 1809, and in seriousness from the waste of public money to disobedience to orders, which was punishable by death. In defiance of natural justice, they ignored the statute of limitations, ignored the double-jeopardy prohibition against being tried twice for the same alleged offense, and admitted hearsay evidence. Wilkinson made no objection and even encouraged the government to spread its net wide. This should have made Madison and Eustis pause for thought.

In May 1811, Wilkinson completed his first memoirs, entitled *Burr's Conspiracy exposed and General Wilkinson vindicated against the slanders of his enemies.* The book was in many ways a rehearsal of the case he would make at his court-martial. In it he painted a picture of himself as a former friend of Burr's, taken by surprise when the conspiracy became clear, but motivated at all times by upright, unshakable patriotism, and unjustly criticized by malignant enemies. From the opening paragraphs where he described himself as "persecuted to the verge of destruction, without a dawn of relief, his humble fortune ruined and his domestic happiness blasted, for his fidelity to his country," he adopted a tone of wounded innocence that was too contrived to be wholly believable. But as always, the posturing deflected attention from his cleverness.

Contained within the turgid pages was a formidable defense of his conduct based on a vast range of obsessively hoarded documents, an astonishing network of contacts, and an exhaustive ability to research information. Its strength was demonstrated by the impact on two brilliant lawyers, Roger B. Taney, a future Supreme Court chief justice, and John H. Thomas. Each had thought the general complicit in the conspiracy, but became so convinced of his innocence that they volunteered to defend him without fee. Thus when his court-martial began on September 4, 1811, before eleven army officers selected by a hostile administration and under the direction of a Republican loyalist, Brigadier Peter Gansevoort, the defendant had already secured one important victory.

GENERAL JAMES WILKINSON ARRIVED in the courtroom dressed in the gaudy gold-braided uniform he had devised for himself, with his sword strapped to his waist. When Gansevoort reminded him that as a prisoner he must surrender his weapon, the general unbuckled the sword and handed it over with the tragic observation that it was the first time he had been deprived of "the untarnished companion of my thigh for forty years."

The first days of the hearings were concerned with the charges related to the Spanish pension and the Burr Conspiracy. Under Taney's direction, the defense had little difficulty in disposing of the familiar evidence of the general's dealings with Spanish officials in New Orleans. The charge sheet began with the earliest connection with Spain in 1787, but because Wilkinson was still a civilian at that date, it had to be dropped. The allegation, based on Daniel Clark's *Proofs*, that "two mule loads of silver" had been sent to him in 1789 by the Spanish government, was shot down when Joseph Ballinger, who actually brought the money, testified that he delivered it to tobacco farmers in Lincoln County, Kentucky, who "were there to receive their money for tobacco which Wilkinson had purchased of them."

Clark himself did not appear and was in his absence discredited as a vindictive liar. Power's winsome character was said to be of "shocking depravity," the sober Ellicott was again presented as a lunatic perjurer, while Isaac Briggs was persuaded to admit that when Wilkinson had described himself as "a Spanish officer," the general had spoken "with a very cheerful air." The one new item was a balance sheet dated January 1796, supposedly drawn up by Philip Nolan, that showed conclusively that every cent of money Wilkinson received from Esteban Miró was a payment owed from two sources—the belated sale in 1791 of 235 hogsheads of tobacco that had been wrongly condemned the previous year, and insurance on the loss of the *Speedwell*'s cargo. That this precious document was a forgery by

Nolan did not detract from its value, since Nolan was long dead, like Miró and any others who might have questioned its authenticity.

More persuasive even than the fake balance sheet was the long array of documents attesting to the confidence that the nation's founding fathers had placed in the general's abilities and loyalties. Since Washington, Adams, Jefferson, and those in their administrations knew of the allegations against Wilkinson, the jury had to choose between two possible explanations: either the giants who had helped bring the United States into existence deemed the allegations to be frivolous, or they had deliberately shut their eyes to what he was doing. The first option was undoubtedly preferable.

The final fifteen specific charges concerned Terre aux Boeufs. Displaying a masterful command of the detail of military organization, Wilkinson concentrated on the culture of penny-pinching, begun by Dearborn and continued by Eustis, that left the army underequipped in such necessities as hospitals and mosquito nets. For the entire year of 1809, Eustis had allocated just $250,000 to pay for the wages, accommodation, transportation, medical care, and equipment of two thousand men sent to defend New Orleans. Unless directly authorized by Washington, no expenditure above fifty dollars was allowed, and the "military agent," a civilian appointed by the War Department to buy supplies, was forbidden to pay for anything "except for articles actually received or for services performed." This meant, Wilkinson carefully explained to the colonels and majors who made up the jury, that a civilian clerk could countermand any order given by a colonel or a major involving extra expense regardless of its military importance. The structure, designed for peacetime routine, made it impossible for a commander to respond to an emergency.

On the most serious charge of refusing to obey Eustis's order to move upriver to Fort Adams, Wilkinson simply showed that the move downriver was in obedience to Dearborn's earlier order to defend New Orleans. By the time he had presented weighty testimonials to his wisdom in choosing the site, to his efforts in caring for the sick, to the exceptional severity of the weather, and to the relatively small number of deaths while at Terre aux Boeufs, the prosecution's case was in tatters. Then the general demanded the right to make a personal statement that occupied six more days. Disheartened, the judge advocate general started to stay away from court until ordered to return by the president.

On Christmas Day, the jury returned its verdict. It could not be publicly announced until scrutinized by the president, but onlookers were able to guess its import from the way the jurors "very politely waited upon General Wilkinson" when the court was adjourned. About seven hundred pages of transcripts and conclusions were sent to President Madison, who spent almost six weeks plowing through what must have been uncomfortable reading. The government was savagely criticized, for failing to realize Wilkinson was a civilian when he first went to New Orleans, and for presenting evidence "much of which is unessential as to matter, and incorrect as to form, and inadmissible in judicial proceedings." On every count, the general was found not guilty, and the court concluded, "From a comparison of all the testimony, General Wilkinson appears to have performed his various and complicated duties with zeal and fidelity, and merits the approbation of his country."

The court-martial's judgment was not perverse. Wilkinson had transformed the case against him into a trial of the fundamental relationship between the army and the federal government since independence. In the range of testimonies that he brought to bear upon his conduct, from junior officers to heroes of the past such as George Washington, Henry Knox, and Anthony Wayne, the general provided a detailed picture of the political pressures that shaped the army during that period. In finding him not guilty, the jury implicitly placed the blame for the toleration of his ambivalent loyalties, and for the tragedy of Terre aux Boeufs, squarely upon the shoulders of his civilian masters.

For the president and his secretary of war, the verdict represented the utter failure of their two-year campaign to rid themselves of the general. On February 14, 1812, Madison commented grudgingly that although "there are instances in the Court, as well as in the conduct of the Officer on trial, which are evidently and justly objectionable, his acquittal of the several charges exhibited agst. him is approved, and his sword is accordingly ordered to be restored."

AT ONE MOMENT DURING THE TRIAL, Thomas Power was challenged about the vindictive tone of his evidence and exclaimed emotionally that in the duplicitous world where Wilkinson operated, there was no choice, it was "stab or be stabbed." Although Wilkinson pretended to be shocked by "the malice of his heart," Power's outburst was a fair assessment of the feral conditions in which the general operated. For more than five years, ever since Burr's conspiracy had put a blade to Wilkinson's throat by requiring him to collaborate or be revealed as a traitor, he had been knifing friends and enemies alike to keep his career alive. Now he alone remained standing surrounded by the corpses of his adversaries. Even James Madison and William Eustis, pursuing him with the full force of executive power and more enmity than Jefferson had brought to his vendetta against Burr, had been laid low. Having survived, the general might have felt a sense of triumph.

His military career, however, remained in the hands of the president and the secretary of war. Consequently Wilkinson's first reaction was not to gloat but to send Madison a cringing letter to explain that his diatribes in court against "Corruption & Power" were not directed at the executive, as everyone thought, but at Burr, Clark, and the House of Representatives. Going further, he proposed to amend any books that he had written, and the court-martial record if necessary, "to vary or expunge any rank Epithet or acrimonious expression which in an Agony of Mind may have escaped my Pen." And he hoped that this would be acceptable because "the impending Crisis of our public Affairs requires harmony, concord & cooperation among the public Servants."

For the first time in his career, his self-abasement was not an act. The long, bruising encounter with Madison and Eustis had brought the general close to bankruptcy, and something like depression replaced his customary ebullience. In a lengthy, rambling letter sent to Jefferson before his court-martial, he confessed to an unprecedented lack of confidence brought on by "the pressure of my persecution, the desolation of my fortunes, the abandonment of those who owed me support." To his dying day, he hated Madison for bringing him so low. But "the impending crisis" offered an opportunity that no professional soldier could ignore. By February 1812, it was certain that, for reasons that were not entirely clear, the country was sliding toward war with Britain.

THE ORIGINAL CAUSE AROSE from the British policy of stopping and searching neutral vessels on the high seas to ensure that they were not carrying strategic goods to France, or any other country under Napoléon's control. From the start of the Napoleonic wars, the United States had gradually taken the lion's share of world trade as Britain and France imposed ever stricter blockades on each other's shipping. Worth $43 million in 1792, the value of American cargoes rose inexorably to $138 million in 1807. American vessels not only carried American wheat, tobacco, and cotton to Europe, but West Indies sugar as well. As neutrals in the conflict, they also shipped British manufactured pottery, textiles, and brass lamps to Napoléon-dominated Europe, and French brandy to Britain. Consequently, the British blockade, and to a lesser extent the French blockade operated by privateers, fell most heavily on ships flying the stars and stripes.

Yet there was an anomaly. Outrages that most hurt the merchant communities in New York and New England triggered the most violent anger in the south and west. John C. Calhoun of South Carolina, Henry Clay of Kentucky, Felix Grundy of Tennessee, the young leaders of the Republican War Hawks, suffered no direct economic harm from the capture of a Boston ship, but took it as an incitement to war. By contrast, the Massachusetts legislature, representing shippers, merchants, insurers, and bankers who had lost fortunes to the British, petitioned Congress to negotiate a peaceful solution.

In November 1811, the House Committee on Foreign Relations reported on all the complaints against Britain, including the help given to Native Americans resisting American expansion in the west. Two months later, Congress, under the dominance of the War Hawks, voted to increase the army first to ten thousand, then twenty-five thousand regulars, and to create a volunteer force of fifty thousand from the militia of each state. A New England Federalist such as Rufus King might object, "I regard this war as a war of party not of country," and New York congressman Morris Miller might declare, "We will give you millions for defense but not a cent for the conquest of Canada," but Congress went ahead anyway to authorize a budget of eleven million dollars for the first year of the conflict. As a nineteenth-century historian succinctly observed, "The war may be said to have been a measure of the South and West to take care of the interests of the North, much against the will of the latter."

Behind the anomaly lay a shift in attitudes about the nature of the United States that James Wilkinson would have understood better than most. It had first made itself felt during the Burr Conspiracy. The western settlers, whose loyalties once swung with the touch of a feather, now felt themselves to be the center of the nation. Colonel Morgan had boasted to Burr that the capital would one day move from Washington to Pittsburgh, while others predicted it could end as far west as Cincinnati or even St. Louis. In Congress, John Randolph, who represented the voters and values of Virginia, mocked their ambitions, saying "he could almost fancy that he saw the Capitol in motion towards the falls of Ohio—after a short sojourn taking its flight to the Mississippi." But his mockery demonstrated an inability to appreciate the west's new, expansionist patriotism.

Beyond the Appalachians, the borderless mind-set of the original pioneers had disappeared. In 1787, when Tennessee was still a territory, John Sevier had been ready to pledge the loyalties of its settlers to His Catholic Majesty, and in 1797 Tennessee's first senator, William Blunt, was prepared to ally himself with Britain to further his plans. But in 1811, when Tennessee congressman Felix Grundy welcomed the prospect of war, he did so because it would benefit the United States. "I therefore feel anxious," he said, "not only to add the Floridas to the South, but the Canadas to the North of this empire." This was the new voice of the Mississippi Valley. In place of coexistence, it nourished the dream that one nation would overfill the continent.

In New England, the old Atlantic loyalty to an idea of American liberty, rather than an American nation, remained strong enough to allow opponents of the war to talk of secession, much as the settlers used to do in the Mississippi Valley. In 1809, their opinions encouraged Canada's governor general, Sir James Craig, to send the agent John Henry "to discover how far they would look to England for assistance, or be disposed to enter into a connection with us." The answer was not far, and a discouraged Henry soon gave up, before selling his secret to Madison for fifty thousand dollars. His efforts hardly amounted to a British conspiracy, but then Henry lacked the energy and inventiveness of James Wilkinson.

NEWLY CLEARED, THE GENERAL WAS DESPERATE to take advantage of the opportunities available in the larger army that Congress voted for in January 1812. Two old adversaries, Henry Dearborn and Wade Hampton, had already been promoted above him to major general, and he could not afford to be left without an active command. Yet Madison needed him at least as urgently. Three presidents had learned to handle the difficult, treacherous, but pliable general so that he carried out the contradictory duties they assigned him. In March 1812, politics forced Madison to follow their example.

On March 2, Republican Party chiefs informed Madison that he risked losing the party's nomination for president at the next election unless he showed a clear commitment to war. A week later, the president published Henry's papers to demonstrate British aggression and, on April 1, proposed a sixty-day embargo on ships leaving port, a recognized preparation for war. On April 10, James Wilkinson was ordered to take command of the defenses of New Orleans.

Appointed to the same position three years earlier, he had brusquely defied Eustis. This time in half a dozen letters, he meekly asked Eustis to specify exactly the powers he could exercise, and the precise goals the executive wished him to achieve. When a hostile paymaster's office blocked his claim for almost seven thousand dollars in expenses, he presented his case directly to the secretary of war rather than trying to fiddle the money through secret service funding. A chastened Wilkinson arrived in New Orleans in July to discover that his country had declared war on Britain on June 18.

He found the three regiments of infantry under his command woefully unprepared for hostilities. Senior officers had been detailed for service on the Canadian frontier, leaving gaps in command; so many soldiers were absent that most units were understrength; artillery had been neglected until it was incapable of firing; and long years of penury had caused "a frightful destitution of means in every branch of the service except the hospital." Overall, he concluded, "Imbecility and disorder prevailed throughout." In the past Wilkinson would have blamed his predecessor, in this case Wade Hampton, for such dismal conditions. Hampton's incompetence was never in doubt—William Duane, later Andrew Jackson's treasury secretary, once exclaimed, "I would not trust a corporal's guard nor the defense of a hen-roost to him"—but Hampton was Eustis's man. Now Wilkinson only referred to his own efforts to restore order.

The same downbeat, almost diffident tone persisted throughout his correspondence with the secretary. A rumor of Eustis's displeasure brought an instant, anxious response. "It has been hinted to me that I may be recalled from this quarter," he wrote in December. "I do not credit the report, yet I think it proper to express the hope that it may not be the case, because it would expose me to great expense and would separate me from my family, and because my constitution would not bear a northern clime."

In truth, Eustis was more at risk. Before the first shot was fired, he had promised a quick and overwhelming victory. "We can take the Canadas without soldiers," he declared with blind optimism, "we have only to send officers into the province and the people . . . will rally round our standard."

When the three-pronged invasion that was to conquer Canada took place, the reality of twelve years of pinched funding and political neutering became painfully apparent. In August 1812, General William Hull humiliatingly surrendered Detroit without a fight; in October, General Stephen van Rensselaer was defeated at Queenston Heights above Niagara; and from his base in Albany, General Henry Dearborn, handicapped by ill health, found it impossible even to reach the frontier. On January 13, 1813, faced by a rising storm of criticism, Eustis chose to resign.

In the discussions to choose his successor, Wilkinson's name was suggested, offering a hint of the glittering prospects that might have come his way in other circumstances. John Adams thought that on merit he should have been chosen, but, recognizing how deeply Wilkinson was distrusted, added, "His vanity and the collision of Factions have rendered his appointment improper and impossible." Instead, the president appointed John Armstrong, who had been a junior officer on General Gates's staff at Saratoga.

In his training regime and his efforts to restore morale, however, Wilkinson's showing as a general already compared favorably to anything in the north. And he was about to execute a textbook military operation to enlarge the territory of the United States.

IN JANUARY 1813, on the shaky grounds that the Spanish-held remnant of West Florida was part of the Louisiana Purchase, Congress authorized its seizure. In effect, this meant capturing Mobile, the capital. With maps drawn years earlier by Andrew Ellicott, and notes and sketches from his personal observations, Wilkinson had the intelligence to plan his attack with care. Supplies were concentrated upstream at Fort Stoddert on the Mobile River, a squadron of gunboats was readied for an attack from the sea, and in late March the general divided the twelve hundred men he had available into an overland detachment under Colonel John Bowyer and a seaborne force under his personal command.

His preparation was interrupted by the unexpected arrival of Andrew Jackson at the head of three thousand Tennessee volunteers, ready to undertake the invasion of the Floridas he must have discussed with Aaron Burr. On this occasion, John Armstrong frustrated the plan by ordering Jackson to disband the volunteers. Rather than obey this command, Jackson earned himself a devoted following and his imperishable nickname of Old Hickory by marching them back to Nashville intact. Their absence left Wilkinson free to achieve his goal with his original force.

Although on a miniature scale, his pincer movement with four hundred land troops under Colonel Bowyer coming down the Mobile River and a seaborne force of eight hundred coming ashore from gunboats was almost perfectly executed. Its only flaw occurred when the oarsmen rowing Wilkinson across Lake Pontchartrain equalized the boat, leaving the fifty-six-year-old general, his staff, and boatmen clinging to the upturned hull for several hours until rescued by passing fishermen. Before dawn on April 12, Bowyer's troops deployed opposite Fort Charlotte, and at daylight troops from the second and third regiments landed from gunboats in the bay. As Wilkinson's report boasted, the sleepy garrison realized they were surrounded only when they were awoken by the sound of bugles blowing outside.

Later that morning Wilkinson sent the Spanish commander, Cayetano Perez, a diplomatic message saying that they came "not as the enemies of

Spain, but on the order of the President to relieve the garrison which you command from the occupancy of a post within the legitimate limits of [the United] States." On April 15, Perez and his garrison surrendered and were shipped along the coast by American gunboats to Pensacola, where Wilkinson's old friend Vizente Folch was waiting to receive them. The very ease of it detracted from Wilkinson's achievement. But what might have happened had things gone wrong was illustrated eighteen months later when a garrison of barely a hundred soldiers in the wooden fort that Bowyer had constructed was able to hold off a seaborne assault by a squadron of four British warships with more than a thousand men on board and drive one of their frigates ashore. As it was, Wilkinson's bloodless operation secured the entire coastal region as far east as the Perdido River, the present border between Alabama and Florida, and represented the only territorial gains that the United States made in the entire war.

On May 19, Wilkinson returned to New Orleans a hero, and waiting for him was a reward—his promotion, after twenty-one years as a brigadier, to major general. The secretary of war had in fact already recommended the higher rank before news of Mobile's capture reached Washington. But Armstrong had in mind a still greater prize, as he was replacing General Henry Dearborn in command of the Ninth War District, comprising the Canadian border from Lake Erie to the Atlantic—the area of operations where the war could be won or lost. Accordingly the new major general was ordered to report immediately to the capital, and accompanying the official message, John Armstrong sent a flattering personal letter reminding Wilkinson of their participation in the great victory of 1777. "Why should you remain in your land of *cypress*," the secretary wrote, "when patriotism and ambition equally invite you to one where grows the *laurel*? . . . Come to the north and come quickly. If our cards be well played we may renew the scenes of Saratoga."

THE LAST BATTLE

I N THE DECADES THAT HAD PASSED since the victory at Saratoga, Armstrong had grown bald, Wilkinson gray-haired. Neither had the vigor of their youth, but Armstrong, who had never exercised independent command, still ached to do so. On the other hand, the effervescent Wilky, who had inspired Gates and kept a chaotic headquarters in order, seemed to have grown tired at last. Psychologically he had been whipped by Madison and Eustis, and physically a fever he had contracted at Terre aux Boeufs had left its mark. The three doctors who examined him at the time all agreed that the illness was serious, one reporting that he had suffered "violent paroxysms." To reduce the fever, Wilkinson had been bled five times. He also had to use laudanum heavily.

Composed of drops of morphine mixed with sweet wine, laudanum was widely prescribed not only to provide relief from pain but as an antidote to fevers, insomnia, and loose bowels. But Wilkinson first took it after Saratoga specifically to relieve stress. Although the general liked to refer to his "iron constitution," at times of tension he was almost invariably afflicted by diarrhea, and even today laudanum is prescribed as its antidote. He used the drug periodically throughout his career, but after Terre aux Boeufs, when all his doctors commented on his extreme anxiety, his consumption became habitual. With this change came an increasingly clear pattern of lassitude and depression alternating with high energy and application.

Replying to Armstrong, Wilkinson attempted his familiar, upbeat style: "I receive the order with pleasure and shall obey it with alacrity because it may furnish a more favorable opportunity than I can find elsewhere to testify to the world my readiness to offer my best faculties and to lay down my life if necessary for the honor and independence of our country." But physically he conveyed a different message.

Celestine, "my divine little Creole," as he complacently described her to his middle-aged friends, was pregnant, making his reluctance to move north understandable. When he did so on June 10, he took with him both Celestine and her sister, traveling first to Mobile, where his son James Biddle was stationed, then across country to Milledgeville, Georgia. The large party, slowed by Celestine's condition and the general's desire for comfort, took a month to bounce along the federal road.

In Georgia's capital, he learned of the first American success in the north when General William Harrison and Commander Oliver Perry seized control of Detroit and Lake Erie in the west, and Dearborn captured the British strongpoint Fort George in the center between Lakes Erie and Ontario. But for Wilkinson the triumph was shrouded by news of the heroic death of his protégé and ideal son, General Zebulon Pike, killed while leading his troops in a seaborne assault on York, subsequently renamed Toronto, the capital of Upper Canada. Sorrowfully Wilkinson wrote to his contemporary Morgan Lewis, once New York's governor, now a major general, lamenting Pike's courageous impetuosity. It was contrary to the lesson taught by Napoléon, that "a general officer does not expose his person but in the last resort," Wilkinson told Lewis. "Subordinates execute, while chiefs command; to mingle in the conflict is to abandon the power of direction."

On August 3, almost six weeks after Armstrong told him to come north, Major General James Wilkinson met the secretary of war and learned that he was to be given the supreme command on the Canadian frontier. It offered the opportunity to win undying glory by leading his nation's army to victory and driving the British out of North America. This was the ultimate reward any soldier could hope for, an accolade for years of service to his country. And for Wilkinson in particular, it offered the chance of redemption for a life soiled with accusations of iniquity.

Almost immediately, however, Wilkinson sensed a coolness in the secretary's manner. Its origin lay in the letter Wilkinson had sent to Lewis through the War Department. Armstrong had read its contents and decided that its commonsense advice about generals remaining above the fray was that of a coward. As he expostulated to the astonished Wilkinson, it "struck at the very foundation of military character and service and . . . was calculated to bring shame and dishonour upon the American arms." The suspicion of Wilkinson's cowardice, once formed, proved almost impossible to shift.

Whatever the supreme commander suggested thereafter appeared to Armstrong to arise from his reluctance to expose himself to danger.

On July 23 the secretary of war had formulated a new strategy for the invasion of Canada. In place of the original, failed idea of invading at three widely separated points, he proposed to concentrate forces at Sackets Harbor, a natural haven at the east end of Lake Ontario, close to the entrance to the St. Lawrence River, and opposite the major British supply base at Kingston in Canada. He would then leave it up to Wilkinson to choose whether to capture Kingston or to sail straight down the St. Lawrence and seize Montreal. Armstrong's proposal made no reference to the practicalities of command structure, supply lines, equipment, weather, or enemy strength. It assumed that the naval squadron under Commodore Isaac Chauncey had established control of Lake Ontario. It concluded that circumstances offered a unique opportunity that had to be grasped at once to end the war before Christmas.

Realistically, Wilkinson asked for more details about his own command, in particular about his relationship to Hampton, senior as a major general but junior for the proposed invasion. He also questioned the assumption that Chauncey had control of the lake. Aware that disheartened troops needed to be built up in morale, training, and experience after the first disastrous year of war, Wilkinson suggested that the campaign should begin with a series of small operations to exploit General Harrison's success at the west end of Lake Ontario, where British defenses were weakest. Still unconscious of Armstrong's doubts about his courage, he concluded, "These suggestions spring from my desire to hazard as little as possible in the outset, and to secure infallibly whatever may be attempted, with the intention to increase our own confidence, to diminish that of the enemy, and to *popularise* the war."

Convinced that the general lacked nerve, Armstrong brushed away this cautious strategy and the rationale of rebuilding skills and morale. The choice, he explained, was simply between taking Kingston or going straight down the St. Lawrence. Either plan would leave the U.S. army in control of the river and force the enemy "to fight his way to Quebec, to perish in the attempt, or to lay down his arms." At that moment, Wilkinson may have guessed that he was being handed a poisoned chalice. The problem did not lie in Armstrong's strategy of cutting the St. Lawrence, the vital artery linking Lower Canada in the east to Upper Canada in the west, but in his failure to appreciate the means needed to achieve that end.

From Eustis, Armstrong had inherited a crippling range of organizational failings created by the lack of staff officers, inefficient supply arrangements, and a chaotic system of recruitment that was further handicapped by the refusal of Massachusetts and Connecticut to muster their militia for the war. As a result, barely thirteen thousand soldiers of the twenty-five thousand on the muster list were available for service. Of those the great majority were new recruits with barely a year's training, and the acerbic Winfield Scott judged their officers to be "imbeciles and ignoramuses." Promotion through seniority resulted in Wilkinson's being surrounded by a generation of brigadiers and colonels as gray-haired as himself who lacked the vigor and abrasive drive to make an inefficient organization produce wagons, weapons, and reinforcements.

Armstrong's attention to these systemic weaknesses was spasmodic and ineffective. Of most immediate concern to Wilkinson, Armstrong not only failed to clear up the confusion of Hampton's role, but allowed General Lewis, Wilkinson's second-in-command, to go on leave for a month just before the operation began and appointed as his quartermaster general Robert Swartwout, brother of Burr's lieutenant, who would only take the post part-time. The project that aroused the secretary of war's real enthusiasm was planning the assault on Kingston.

In August, General Wilkinson traveled up the Hudson River and across country to Sackets Harbor, and on the twenty-fifth he held a council of war to decide which of Armstrong's two plans of attack should be adopted. The council was attended by Morgan Lewis, Swartwout, and the most dynamic officer in Wilkinson's army, Jacob Brown, whose religion and aggressive leadership won him the nickname the Fighting Quaker. The fifth member of the council, Commodore Isaac Chauncey, was, next to Wilkinson himself, the most important.

Since the attack on Kingston would require the army to be shipped across the open waters of Lake Ontario, Chauncey's squadron of eight vessels had to establish complete dominance over the British. They had shown their superiority each time the two fleets had met, but the British vessels were still at large. However, the decision was unexpectedly simplified when Swartwout announced that only twenty-five boats were available to carry Wilkinson's soldiers to Kingston instead of the three hundred that were needed. Unanimously, the council decided the army should march down the banks of the St. Lawrence to attack Montreal, leaving Chauncey's fleet with the task of guarding its entrance against British warships. Once the target was chosen, Wilkinson sent orders to Hampton on Lake Champlain to be ready to move against Montreal from the south.

For the first time since his appointment, the general's spirits soared. "All things go well here," he assured Armstrong the following day. Within a short time, he expected Chauncey to defeat the British, his men to become healthy, and Hampton to communicate with him: "I hope he does not mean to take the stud [start sulking]. But if so, we can do without him, and he should be sent home."

Nothing was quite as simple as Wilkinson in his burst of optimism imagined. Almost half his forces, thirty-five hundred men, were located at Fort George, near Niagara at the west end of the lake. Despite all efforts, Chauncey proved unable to trap the British squadron. One in three of the troops at Sackets Harbor remained sick. Transportation was crippled by a lack of boats and horses. The summer was coming to an end. And Hampton had unmistakably taken the stud, not only refusing to reply to Wilkinson's messages, but complaining to Armstrong that his "command instead of being a separate one has sunk within that of a district." To mollify him, Armstrong secretly promised that he intended to take personal command of the operation, then assured Wilkinson that Hampton and his four thousand troops would cooperate "cordially and vigorously."

None of these concerns affected Wilkinson's mood. He hired a spy to report on British positions in Kingston. He ordered the construction of a dozen large keelboats capable of carrying sixty men each. He was in command with people around him to execute his orders, and as always the sensation restored his confidence. In that rejuvenated state of mind, he decided to go in person to Fort George to hurry the transportation of the troops there back to Sackets Harbor. It entailed a journey of about 130 miles in an open boat, but the incompetence of the Fort George commander, Brigadier General John Boyd, described by Winfield Scott as "vacillating and imbecile beyond all endurance," made Wilkinson's presence necessary.

As the fall approached, time had become vital. Without the supreme commander's personal intervention, Boyd would certainly fail to bring his soldiers east before the weather broke. Armstrong's intention to visit Sackets Harbor at the end of the month might also have made escape attractive. "Two heads on the same shoulder," Wilkinson commented, "make a monster."

The voyage turned out to be a disaster. For six days he was exposed to sun, rain, and wind. By the time he arrived at Fort George, he was shivering

with fever. For the next ten days he was confined to his bed, forced to dictate orders while suffering "much depression of head and stomach." On
September 16 he told Armstrong, "I have escaped my pallet and with a
giddy head and trembling hand will scrawl you a few lines," and most of
what followed was devoted to listing the complex problem of transporting
several thousand soldiers from one end of the lake to the other. The next
day, his health was better, and he returned to his original idea of beginning
the campaign with small-scale operations in the west. The British he noted
had barely sixteen hundred combatant soldiers opposite him, and, he told
Armstrong, he was tempted to have "a sweep at them." Peremptorily Armstrong replied, "Let not the great objects of the campaign be hazarded," and
ordered him to return to Sackets Harbor as quickly as possible.

In the little ice age of the early nineteenth century, the onset of fall and
winter came early. By late September, the weather was rapidly deteriorating, and for days contrary winds delayed the fleet of transports that Wilkinson had finally assembled. Not until early October was he able to sail back
into the secluded waters of Sackets Harbor. There he found that he had
been comprehensively second-guessed by Armstrong. Sweeping aside the
council of war's plans to move directly down the St. Lawrence against
Montreal, the secretary of war had substituted his own project for attacking
Kingston. The terse entry in Armstrong's journal for October 4 told its
own story: "General Wilkinson arrived this day in Sackett's Harbor from
Fort George. He immediately visited the Secretary of War in the company
of Generals Lewis and Brown, and in the presence of these officers remon-
strated freely and warmly against making an attack on Kingston."

Wilkinson's fury at having the council of war's choice overturned had
no more effect than his detailed argument that the lack of transport, the
certainty of casualties, and the worsening weather made it impossible to assault both Kingston and Montreal. Armstrong was immovable. He had personally developed a detailed plan for capturing Kingston and insisted on its
being carried out. A healthy Wilkinson would have fought back. Before
Eustis broke his confidence, he had run rings round secretaries of war.
Now, weakened by his illness in Fort George, he collapsed, physically and
emotionally, and took to his bed.

While he lay there, the first autumn storms arrived, ten days of unremitting wind. Fearful that winter snows would soon follow, leaving too little
time to reach Montreal, Wilkinson agreed on October 19 that his army
should attack Kingston. Forty-eight hours later, with maddening perversity,
Armstrong decided that Kingston should be canceled because the weather

was too severe and the risks too high, and its failure "would extinguish every hope of grasping the other, the safer, the greater object."

Wilkinson learned of this latest twist as he was organizing the embarkation of troops for Kingston and, as he admitted, "in my feeble condition," could hardly do justice to his emotions. In the end, he felt capable only of demanding from the secretary of war a final, clear order "to direct the operations of my army particularly against Montreal." He must have known that the operation, harassed by British troops, overlooked by British fortifications, lacking supplies, plans, and intelligence, and at the mercy of the approaching winter, had only a slim chance of success.

Gales out of the northwest made it perilous even to round the cape guarding Sackets Harbor to reach the mouth of the St. Lawrence. Boats were wrecked, soldiers drowned, ammunition lost, and rations ruined. November had come before the fleet of about three hundred vessels at last assembled in the river. By then disease and the diversion of men to other projects had reduced a projected army of more than twelve thousand by a third. Any hope of surprise had been blown away by the long delays caused by the storm. Chauncey proved unable to prevent British gunboats from following them into the St. Lawrence, and British troops allocated to the defense of Kingston were hurried along the riverbank to reinforce the strongpoint at Prescott, halfway to their target, and to harass Wilkinson's army as it moved toward Montreal.

Yet with a strong column of about twenty-five hundred men including cavalry under Brown's vigorous command on the north bank, artillery and almost four thousand soldiers on the boats, and another smaller force led by Swartwout on the south bank, Wilkinson's force was greater than anything the British could put up in opposition. Once Hampton's regulars and a promised fifteen hundred New York militia were added, their dominance would become overwhelming. The capture of Montreal was not impossible.

The one essential ingredient was forceful leadership. The general's first test, passing by the fortified town of Prescott that overlooked the river, was successfully negotiated on November 5. Wilkinson had the powder and ammunition transferred from the boats into wagons, then, leaving only skeleton crews aboard, he ordered the fleet to drift down on the current at dead of night and led them himself in an open gig. The moon appearing through a gap in the clouds revealed some vessels to the sentries, but despite a rattle of fire the boats came through with only one casualty. Ahead lay an eight-mile rapid known as the Longue Saut, and beyond that thirty miles of open river to their target.

But the general's once galvanizing energy was only feebly apparent. For much of the time he veered between two extremes, prostrated in his bunk with a fever that might have been flu or malaria, alternating with periods when, according to the testimony of his fellow general, Morgan Lewis, he "seemed to be in high spirits, which I considered to be assumed to inspire confidence." To many, however, and in particular to Colonel William King, a messenger from General Hampton, his unpredictable behavior suggested that he was drunk.

King based his suspicions on an encounter with Wilkinson on November 6, the day after passing Prescott, on board the general's boat. He brought bad news from Hampton and approached Lewis first to ask "whether the old gentleman would be found in a good humour." General Lewis, who was himself frequently laid low with stomach pains and dysentery, restricted himself to the cold reply that "he might perhaps find the general a little petulant from his indisposition."

But Wilkinson's reaction went beyond petulance. When King revealed that three weeks earlier Hampton at the head of twenty-six hundred infantry, cavalry, and artillery regulars had let himself be driven back from the river Chateaugay by a numerically inferior force of sixteen hundred Canadian militia and volunteers, Wilkinson exploded, "Damn such an army! A man might as well be in hell as command it." Angrily he gave King an order for Hampton to rendezvous with him outside Montreal without fail, and to carry enough supplies for both their armies.

There were other reports of erratic behavior. Colonel Joseph G. Swift, a talented engineer, acknowledged that "under the influence of laudanaum the general became very merry and sang and repeated stories," but insisted "the only evil of which was that it was not of the dignified deportment to be expected from the commander in chief." Nevertheless, added to the shouting match with Armstrong at Sackets Harbor, the rumors of intoxication undermined confidence. In retrospect, however, the frustration of seeing the last faint chances of success being relentlessly chipped away must have done more damage to his temper than any drug. Armstrong had also fallen sick at the end of October and formally handed over command of the Montreal operation to Wilkinson. If the expedition failed, there could be no doubt where the blame would fall.

UNTIL NOVEMBER 10, Wilkinson kept a flickering hope of success alive. On land and water British forces maintained a harassing pursuit of the army. Despite his sickness, Wilkinson continued to be sufficiently energetic to keep them at bay. On two occasions, enemy schooners and galleys that had slipped past Chauncey's uncertain defenses were rapidly turned back by fire from a battery of heavy guns Wilkinson ordered to be unshipped and placed on the bank. On the north side of the river, Brown could always be relied on to outflank and drive off any would-be ambushers. As they approached the rapids of the Longue Saut, however, the boats threatened to race ahead of the marching soldiers, and to slow them down Wilkinson ordered them to anchor early. Overcome by a return of his fever, he took to his bed and gave command to Lewis. Meanwhile Jacob Brown went ahead to explore the land alongside the rapids, leaving John Boyd in command on the north side of the river. The delay also allowed a British pursuing force of about fifteen hundred regulars and militia under Lieutenant Colonel Joseph Morrison to catch up.

Late in the afternoon of that gray, overcast day, Boyd launched a series of ill-organized and uncoordinated attacks against Morrison's strongly held defensive position on the perimeter of some open ground known as Crysler's Field. By nightfall, 321 of Boyd's 3,000-strong force had been killed or wounded, and the survivors were forced to retreat to the river.

Subdued and sullen, Wilkinson's men boarded the boats, and the next day the long line of vessels hurtled down the rapids. Waiting at the foot of the Longue Saut was another messenger from Wade Hampton. He had one final blow to deliver. Instead of marching toward Montreal as ordered, Hampton had turned back to Lake Champlain, where he intended to go into winter quarters. On November 16 Wilkinson submitted this news to a council of senior officers. Unanimously they agreed that "the attack on Montreal should be suspended for the present season."

THERE COULD BE NO COMING BACK. He had been given the chance of winning the war and had failed. From Albany, Secretary of War John Armstrong wrote that he found it "quite incredible" that Wilkinson should have been defeated by an inferior force, adding, shamelessly, that if only Wilkinson had taken Kingston, "the upper province [of Canada] was won." Desperately the general replied by laying the blame on Hampton's refusal to obey orders and demanded he be arrested for his "outrage of every principle of subordination and discipline." But it was a useless appeal. Hampton had already resigned, and Wilkinson's tainted reputation was against him. A man already charged with responsibility for Terre aux Boeufs, participation in the Burr Conspiracy, and being a Spanish pensioner could hardly expect the public to believe he had nothing to do with the failure of the Montreal expedition.

Through the winter, his army shivered and sickened in makeshift huts constructed in the forest by French Mills, now Fort Covington, just south of the St. Lawrence. Inexplicably Hampton had furloughed all his officers before resigning himself. The confusion that ensued cut off supplies of food and medicine coming from Albany. Pneumonia, dysentery, and typhus spread until, as Wilkinson himself admitted, "The mortality spread so deep a gloom over our camps, that funeral dirges were countermanded." On his own responsibility, the general rented buildings to accommodate 450 patients in the settlement of Malone, ten miles to the south where he had his headquarters. But a steady stream of deserters testified to the demoralization of his army. On January 27, 1814, an official tally of the force at French Mills showed that of the 8,143 men who had left Sackets Harbor, only 4,777 remained ready for duty.

Nevertheless, in a final bid to escape the impending wreck of his career, the general searched for a last-ditch victory. Unable to ride because of his illness, he had himself towed in a sled "on which a box is placed to receive my bed" to Plattsburgh to discuss a winter offensive with General George Izard, who had been drafted to replace Hampton. From there Wilkinson went on to Albany to suggest to New York governor Daniel Tompkins an attack on Prescott, using the combined forces at French Mills and Plattsburgh, bulked up with New York militia. Tompkins, who had been warned by John Armstrong to expect a sick old man on the edge of resignation, was surprised by the veteran's unabated forcefulness. "He threatens to make a dash soon," he told Armstrong after the meeting. "I have great confidence in your penetration upon most subjects, but I fear you have not formed a correct judgment of the General's talents and qualifications. He is wonderfully tenacious of his authority and is very indifferent about his old carcass, and vapours too much."

Determined to prevent the general from exercising command again, Armstrong immediately ordered General Jacob Brown to take two thousand men from French Mills back to Sackets Harbor and withdrew the rest to Plattsburgh. Wilkinson protested that this order "blasted all my hopes, subjected the public to millions of expense, [and] sacrificed thrice the number of men Prescott would have cost." As he had done throughout his career, he responded by demanding a public inquiry, then, without waiting for Armstrong's reply, fixed on another, less ambitious target. This was a strongpoint called La Colle Mill, situated thirty miles farther down the Champlain Valley, whose capture would open the road to Montreal.

On March 29, a force of 3,999 men accompanied by eleven guns marched north from Plattsburgh. For the last time in his career, the general issued a stirring order—"Every officer and every man [must] return victorious or not at all, for with double the force of the enemy, this army must not give ground"—but for the first time in his career, he neglected intelligence. Without maps, his inexperienced scouts became lost, and the heaviest of his artillery, the eighteen-pounders, sank axle-deep in slushy mud.

Not until late on March 30 did the first men reach the target, an imposing, stone-built mill with stone walls on either side offering protection to the six hundred defenders. From about 150 yards, the attackers fired their muskets, and when they proved ineffective, the lighter guns, twelve-pounders, were brought up. Once it became clear that their shot could do no more than chip the stone walls, the conflict descended into stalemate until at dusk Wilkinson ordered his men to withdraw. Two days later, the last of his force dragged the guns back into camp. Even before the expedition had left Plattsburgh, orders had been sent from Washington relieving him of his command pending a court-martial. Thus the military career of Major General James Wilkinson ended with a whimper on April Fools' Day.

30

THE CHANGING OF THE GUARD

THE COURT-MARTIAL ORDERED for the general's failure on the Canadian frontier was the third military tribunal he had faced. On top of that, he had already been subjected to four congressional investigations into allegations of misdeeds, and two more unofficial trawls through his past by Luther Martin and Daniel Clark. Despite the wealth of allegations against him, he had not yet been found guilty, and it was said of him with increasing frequency that he had never won a battle but never lost an inquiry. The sheer number of probes testified to his public reputation among contemporaries, and from the perspective of two hundred years it is tempting to regard them as rough justice, a way of getting even for the undoubted lies he told to conceal his actions as a Spanish agent.

Yet with the hindsight of history, what seems overwhelmingly obvious is that the wrong accusations were leveled against him. Even the one charge of which he was certainly guilty, covert treachery to the United States, was less damaging than his overt and repeated betrayal of the army. Yet no court could try him for acquiescence in its political neutering and financial strangulation because the instigators were Presidents John Adams, Thomas Jefferson, and James Madison.

Thus when John Armstrong drew up the list of charges for Wilkinson's third court-martial, they ranged from his failure to ensure the army's swift departure from Fort George and Sackets Harbor through the fiasco at La Colle Mill, and for good measure included drunkenness, conduct unbecoming an officer and a gentleman, publicly disparaging the army, and cowardice. Those, however, were not the crimes with which he should have been

charged. The war itself, the ultimate prosecutor and judge of military mis-
doings, revealed where he was truly culpable. The humiliations of 1812
and 1813 would not end until a properly funded, professionally trained
army took the place of the starved constabulary that Jefferson and Madison
had espoused. Wilkinson should have been tried for colluding with his political masters.

The first attempt to organize a court-martial a month after his suspension
from duty collapsed when he protested that of the five officers available to
try him, only three were generals. "General Wilkinson declines being tried
by a court of the smallest legal number unless wholly composed of General
officers," Armstrong regretfully explained to the president, "and the court
not being so composed was dissolved." It left Wilkinson, as he assured his
friend Solomon van Rensselaer, "quite at ease, a man at large, and a Maj.
Gen. without a command." Leaving Albany, he and van Rensselaer made a
poignant visit to the hillsides of Saratoga, where Wilkinson had first tasted
real military glory. From there he traveled by steamboat down the Hudson
to New York City, where another friend, General Morgan Lewis, in charge
of the city's defenses, welcomed him. In June, he at last rejoined the divine
Celestine in Frederick, Maryland, but no one could suppose that Wilkinson
would be at ease until his trial took place.

During the summer, he and Celestine suffered the loss of their seven-
month-old girl, Marie, who had been born in November 1813 while the
general was in the north. For Wilkinson, it was in a sense a double tragedy,
because the girl had taken the place of James Biddle, killed two months
earlier on September 17 in Florida on active service. Yet the general's grief
was soon dissipated by the larger shock of a British fleet sailing into Chesapeake Bay.

As early as July 17, 1814, Wilkinson was convinced that British threats of
retaliation for the burning of the Parliament House in York were more
than mere words and had raged that Armstrong's "malignant spirit" prevented him from taking any action to defend the capital. The secretary of
war himself firmly denied that Washington was in danger, although he had
seen the ships sail into the Patuxent River. "They certainly do not come
here!" he insisted. "What the devil will they do here? No! No! Baltimore's
the place." On August 17, while General William H. Winder in command
of six thousand militia still debated whether to throw up defenses on the
Bladensburg road leading into the city, and Armstrong remained incapable
of recommending any action, Wilkinson pleaded with the secretary of

state, James Monroe, to be allowed to intervene: "Could my arrest be suspended and my sword restored for a short period, I would take command
of the militia and save the city or forfeit my life."

There was no reply. On August 24, in less than three hours, General
Robert Ross's column of forty-five hundred British regulars scattered
Winder's force from the vital Bladensburg bridge, which had been left un-
fortified and intact. By nightfall, flames were rising from the Capitol. In the
aftermath of the catastrophe, Armstrong at last resigned, leaving James
Monroe to run the War and State departments in tandem.

In such circumstances, the task of finding enough generals for Wilkinson's court-martial hardly ranked as a priority. It was not until November,
after the general had sent Madison a personal letter begging for his trial to
begin, that a date was set. The place selected was Utica, New York, uncomfortable and cold in winter, but convenient for the senior officers of the
Ninth Military District, who would have to attend. On January 3, 1815,
General Henry Dearborn opened the proceedings of a court-martial made
up of six other generals and six colonels and prepared to listen to one of
the most experienced and skillful military lawyers conduct his own defense. Everyone in the court knew the general, most had served with him,
and some, such as General Morgan Lewis, were his friends. The man on
trial was the incarnation of a military ethos discredited by the war, but
since each of his judges had subscribed to the same compromised values,
they were not likely to find him guilty.

At the outset, Wilkinson disposed of the danger presented by the special
judge advocate appointed by Monroe to prosecute him, Martin Van Buren.
Arguing that a civilian could have no standing in a military court, Wilkinson had the brilliant advocate thrown out, thus ensuring that he would not
fall victim to unexpected legal booby traps. On the military charges, his defense was a straightforward claim that the handicaps imposed on the commander of the Montreal expedition by the weather, the secretary of war,
and a treacherous colleague made success impossible. The official correspondence supported him, and Wilkinson had no difficulty in showing that
the deficiencies of the supply system, patchily supervised by General Swartwout among his other duties as an infantry brigadier, could not be blamed
on the commander. And although the action at La Colle Mill undoubtedly could be, Wilkinson diminished its significance by suggesting his
force was conducting an armed reconnaissance and simply turned back
having discovered the enemy's strength.

The more serious accusations Wilkinson had to face were the personal ones of intoxication, swearing, and cowardice. Yet here, too, the court was unlikely to find against him. The general's record of taking harsh measures against drunkenness was well-known, and no one questioned his assertion that it was "a vice my soul detests and which I have always exerted my authority to eradicate from the army." That he should instead have been taking laudanum, as Colonel Swift suggested, was a different matter. Not only did Swift testify that "the campaign was in no wise influenced" by its effects, every officer in court had at some time suffered from diarrhea and been forced to make use of the drug's binding properties. Colonel King's story about the general's damning the army must have raised a secret smile among generals often driven to still worse profanities by subordinates who had let them down. As to the imputation of cowardice, four grizzled generals and colonels with more than a century of service among them testified to his courage, and Colonel Jacob Kingsbury recalled that at Fallen Timbers two aides standing next to the general had fallen to enemy fire while Wilkinson "had exposed himself more than necessary" to the bullets.

The verdict of the court-martial delivered by General Henry Dearborn on March 21, 1815, was not a surprise: "He is hereby honourably acquitted of all and every one of the charges and specifications against him." On April 15, this was formally approved by the president. But while the court was still in session, a more damning judgment had been brought in, not just on General James Wilkinson but on the entire era that he represented.

IN DECEMBER 1814, the Treaty of Ghent brought an end to the disastrous war. Before the news arrived, General Andrew Jackson, defending a strong position in front of New Orleans with six thousand militia, routed an attack across open ground by eight thousand seasoned regulars led by General Edward Pakenham on January 8, 1815. His victory was taken by most civilians, and many historians, to be the war's crowning achievement. For professional soldiers, however, what mattered in military terms was the change that took place in the north.

During 1814, the experience of war coupled with an intense system of training instituted by General Winfield Scott had brought about a material change in the ability of the troops to withstand the shock of battle. It was first apparent at the battle of Chippewa on July 5, 1814, when the superiority of Scott's troops in infantry maneuvers and artillery fire won what an exultant General Jacob Brown declared to be "the first victory gained over the enemy on a plain"—that is, without advantage of ground or surprise.

Two weeks later, Scott's soldiers, now led by Brown in person, took part in the bloodiest conflict of the war, the confusing, terrifying battle of Lundy's Lane. There was no victory, but the uncompromising, disciplined gallantry the soldiers showed throughout most of a day when they were forced to fight on two sides, first in the front and then the rear, was, if any-thing, still more impressive. They matched the firepower and ferocity of British troops honed over fifteen years of war, volley for volley, and charge for charge, until nightfall and exhaustion brought the bloodshed to an in-decisive end. No one could doubt the difference compared with the per-formance in previous engagements from Detroit to Crysler's Field. As John Fortescue, the foremost authority on the nineteenth-century British army, admitted, "The British were beaten. It was evident that the experience of two campaigns had at last turned the Americans into soldiers who were not to be trifled with."

In earlier days, the gains might have been thrown away. Republican ideol-ogy demanded that a professional army be reduced to a skeleton, and defense entrusted to the mythical qualities of a citizen army. But at Bladensburg, a shocked Madison had seen with his own eyes the difference between profes-sional soldiers and amateurs. "I could never have believed," he exclaimed to a friend just before the White House was torched, "that so great a difference existed between regular troops and a militia force, if I had not witnessed the scenes of this day."

The proof that a new era had arrived lay in Congress's belated willing-ness to accept that reality and the consequences that flowed from it. Al-though the peacetime army was reduced, its size of ten thousand men commanded by two major generals, and four brigadier generals, made swift expansion possible. The criterion for selecting officers was whether they were "competent to engage an enemy on the field of battle," without ref-erence to how they might vote. Under a new secretary of war, William Crawford, funding was provided for a permanent general staff to take re-sponsibility for military organization, for an expanded military academy at West Point to train young officers in their profession, and for improved conditions and a uniform drill for new recruits. Much of their training was to be implemented by Scott, who by the time of his retirement in 1861 had set in motion the evolution of the modern U.S. army.

The passing of the old guard was signaled by the dismissal of four fifths of the army's existing officers. Their culling was brutal. A commission headed by General Jacob Brown removed an entire generation who had enlisted during the Revolution or in the first years of independence. Weeks after his appearance at Wilkinson's trial, Jacob Kingsbury, a veteran from the Revolutionary War, was cut off without a pension, leaving him, as he movingly revealed, "at the advanced age of sixty turned out upon the world, destitute of support, with a large and helpless family, and can expect no relief but from the Government whom I have served faithfully for more than forty years." To avoid starvation, Thomas Cushing, who had been at Wilkinson's side at every crucial phase of his career, begged for employment as a justice of the peace.

There was no place either for General James Wilkinson in this modern age. Like his old friends, he, too, was returned to civilian life without ceremony. But at least the executive felt obligated to find him some federal job—in which "no money is handled," specified one administration official—that would provide a salary. "I am willing to do the best we can for Wilkinson," Madison assured Monroe in May 1815, "and hope he will not frustrate our dispositions by insinuations or threats which must be defied." The War Department even showed itself ready to accept his notoriously unreliable accounts for $3,317 of secret service expenditure, and for a further $7,700 spent on compensation for military damage and other unexpected costs. But nothing the executive offered him could make up for the wound that forcible retirement inflicted on his vanity.

There was talk of a post with the navy in New York, a place on the boundary commission with Canada, and a job as commissioner of Indian affairs, but he rejected every suggestion, not politely but angrily. "General Wilkinson has broken through all decorum and indulges the most malignant rage in every conversation," A. J. Dallas, Monroe's deputy at the War Department, warned Madison. "He will leave Washington next week for active mischief elsewhere."

Dallas's prediction was correct. The general's finances made it folly to refuse these well-paid appointments, but Wilkinson was determined not to feel under an obligation to the administration that had dismissed him. What he wanted was revenge. He became a vocal member of the Association of Disbanded Officers, campaigning for pensions or lump-sum payoffs from the federal government. He wrote vituperative articles for William Duane's anti-administration newspaper, *Aurora*, denouncing Madison for throwing old soldiers to the wolves,, and Monroe for "the disorganization of the army." In New York, he was guest of honor at a Federalist Tammany Society dinner, where he was toasted as "The Hero of '76 who sustains the principles of '76, and who detected and exposed treason in its infancy," and his speeches in response lambasted Madison's administration for its vicious betrayal of the servants of the Revolution.

But he had only one way to demonstrate how badly he had been treated. On October 28, 1815, a discreet announcement appeared in the newspapers: "Mr. Small of Philadelphia, has issued proposals for publishing, in 3 vols. 8vo. a work entitled—*Memoirs of my own times*, by James Wilkinson, late major-general in the service of the United States." Three volumes, each of five hundred pages, would tell his and the nation's story from Bunker Hill onward.

His research, like his reconnaissance, was detailed and prodigious. He had been in the habit of retaining all important letters, and making duplicates of his own correspondence, but now he began to badger friends, colleagues, and the clerks at the War Department for copies of letters sent and received. This, the third version of his memoirs, was the first to begin with his birth and early years. The theme of selfless patriotism betrayed by mean-minded politicians was apparent in its opening paragraph. "My *youth* furnished objections to my unsolicited promotion, and *my age* has since afforded President Madison *a pretext* for turning me out of the service," he wrote with italicized emotion. "And thus it appears that from *youth to age* I have been a subject of persecution; yet it is my pride and my boast that my life has been devoted to my country."

There were no domestic distractions to his writing. In the summer of 1815, Celestine and her Trudeau entourage of sister and servants and slaves set sail for New Orleans. His young wife was pregnant again and anxious to be at home for the birth. Left alone, the general rented a house near Philadelphia, still the nation's largest city, at the "3 mile Stone near the Red Hart [tavern] on the Road to the City." Recovered in health, with something like his old ebullient vigor, he transported trunkfuls of documents to his new home and prepared to lash out at every enemy and repay every insult. The news created wide interest. Former governor of Pennsylvania Thomas McKean, a friend of John Adams's, thought that with his experience "he is better qualified to give a description of the [Revolution] than any other gentleman I know."

Visitors to the Red Hart found the general hard at work, one of them leaving a sharp portrait of Wilkinson as author: "A short, (stout) man, round faced, remarkably active, put his hand on his horse's saddle and sprang into it . . . He was in the midst of his paper, knee-deep, all around him on the floor. He was preparing his memoirs in vindication of himself."

For the first time in his life, he was forced to live economically, but as he boasted to Dearborn "most agreeably and independently at $5 a week." Between assembling his book, he fired off letters to van Rensselaer, either denouncing Armstrong as a "rascal" and his successor, James Monroe, as a "big liar," or fishing for a job as De Witt Clinton's military adviser—"You will perceive I am still a temporizing office hunter," he confessed. In January 1816, he achieved some financial security by persuading Maryland's legislature to commute the half-pay due to him as a colonel in the Revolutionary War to a lump sum of thirty-five hundred dollars. But his real hopes rested on the book. Not only would it expose Madison's treachery, but "protect my old age from penury."

The publication of the *Memoirs* in 1817 created an immediate impact. *Aurora* applauded the attack on the administration—"they *unmask imposture in a spirit worthy of Sallust, and with an energy worthy of Tacitus*"—and William Duane organized an author's tour, where the general was guest of honor at a series of political dinners and introduced as "the meritorious persecuted veteran." Wilkinson claimed that the first printing of fifteen hundred quickly sold out at $12.50 retail, and as a special deal $10 direct from the author. Recklessly he invested the profits in a second printing.

Its virtues are less immediately obvious to a modern reader. The first volume of what begins as a conventional autobiography abruptly breaks off when he resigned from the army in 1778; it then awkwardly resumes in 1797, shortly after his appointment as commanding general; and the last section is simply a reprint of his 1811 *Burr's Conspiracy exposed and General Wilkinson vindicated*. The second volume consists entirely of his defense to the charges assembled by Madison and Eustis in 1812, while the third is his defense to the charges drawn up by Armstrong for his 1815 court-martial. As a result the *Memoirs* lack continuity and any sense of historical development; the long list of charges and convoluted refutations emphasize the author's unreliability; and the obsessive, paranoid tone, occasionally reminiscent of Thomas De Quincey's *Confessions of an English Opium Eater*, suggests that some at least was written under the influence of laudanum.

Yet they contain a mine of information about military and political life. Most people telling the story of their life rely on their integrity to make the account credible. Because James Wilkinson's double life was based on invention, he felt bound to back up assertions with documentary proof. Consequently, much of the *Memoirs* consists simply of correspondence, depositions, contracts, and army regulations, which together offer an inimitable view of the stage on which he acted. Thus for all their faults, the *Memoirs* succeed in illustrating Wilkinson's historical importance in the two arenas for which he deserves to be remembered—opening up the Mississippi to western settlers, and ensuring that a restive army remained subject to civilian control.

In his preface, he admitted to a small regret, that having devoted so much space to "the illustration of my persecutions . . . I have not been able to touch the last twenty-five years of my service." Even the brief summary of what had been left out—eight voyages by sea, four descents of the Mississippi, and "I traversed a trackless wilderness four times from the borders of Louisiana to the frontiers of Georgia"—suggested the physical resilience that helped distinguish him among the generals of his time. The omission would, he promised, be made good in future volumes.

ON THE FRONTISPIECE, the general had printed a couplet from Richard Savage's play *Sir Thomas Overbury* that he felt applied to his experience:

> For patriots still must fall for statesmen's safety,
> And perish by the country they preserve.

The target, as he made obvious, was "cold, selfish, timid" James Madison, but the statesman for whose safety the patriotic Wilkinson ultimately fell escaped any hint of criticism. Unlike every other authority figure in Wilkinson's life, Thomas Jefferson was immune to even private attack. Their relationship dominated Wilkinson's career and clearly went further than was apparent on the surface.

Occasionally, the general would hint as much. In January 1811, he sent Jefferson a letter denying a rumor that he had boasted, "As to Long Tom—meaning you—he dare say nothing, for I have got him under my thumb," to which the president replied dismissively, "My consciousness that no man on earth has me under his thumb is evidence enough that you never used the expression." But Wilkinson returned to the topic. A year later Monroe heard it said that when the general intervened with Morales in 1803 after the withdrawal of American rights to use New Orleans as a depot, he did so at the president's suggestion. Jefferson's alleged purpose was not to discourage Morales, but to encourage him in his high-handed action in order to manipulate public opinion in favor of U.S. intervention. This time Jefferson reacted with fury. Which was more likely, he demanded of Monroe, "that I should descend to so unmeaning an act of treason, or that [Wilkinson] in the wreck now threatening him [his court-martial], should wildly lay hold of any plank."

Yet Wilkinson was not the only source of such rumors. One evening in January 1797, the adventurer John D. Chisholm, who was making detailed plans on behalf of William Blount to capture West Florida and Louisiana, went to Blount's Philadelphia house and was shown by his son into the dining room. "Instead of finding him alone as usual," Chisholm reported, "I found Mr Jefferson and Genl. Wilkinson at Table with him." What they were talking about, Chisholm could not tell, but he made a guess. "It immediately struck me, but I might be wrong, that [Blount] sent for me in order to open my Plan to these Gentlemen."

Chisholm kept his mouth shut and learned nothing more, but it is plausible that the three men were indeed discussing how the Spanish colonies might be taken, and in particular the best way to reach Santa Fe. Later that year Wilkinson sent his personal assistant to Jefferson with a message that ran, "In the Bearer of this Letter—Mr. P. Nolan, you will behold the Mexican traveler, a specimen of whose discoveries I had the honor to submit to you in the Winter 1797."

Jefferson was always eager to acquire Spanish territory, not by war but by economic and diplomatic pressure. Often the first point of contact had to be unofficial, and sometimes more probing than could be admitted. This must have been one motive for appointing Wilkinson governor of Louisiana Territory, and for the unofficial permission to send out exploration and spying parties. A similar impulse led him to select Wilkinson to discover whether Captain General Someruelos might be ready to take Cuba out of the Spanish empire. In short, the general's sinuous morality made him the ideal candidate for the dirty and deniable work that an upright president needed doing without knowing how it was done.

Naturally enough, Jefferson always remained aloof. "I have ever and carefully restrained myself from the expression of any opinion respecting General Wilkinson, except in the case of Burr's conspiracy," he told Monroe. "As to the rest of his life, I have left it to his friends and his enemies, to whom it furnishes matter enough for disputation. I classed myself with neither." It was a wise way to treat someone whose likes and hatreds were so unpredictable, and operationally necessary. And it was presidential in tone. But considering how much the general had done for him, it lacked warmth.

For his part, Wilkinson, who never remained faithful to any other superior, was always Jefferson's man. He gave him the army's loyalty, Burr's conspiracy, Louisiana's border. Long after he had damned every other statesman to perdition, he attempted to win Jefferson's constantly withheld friendship. And the crux of his life proved to be the moment when he sacrificed a career of treachery to be steadfast not just to his nation but to his president.

In June 1817 the general sailed for New Orleans. The *Memoirs* had not made him rich. The printing costs were high, and his hopes for the sales of a second printing overoptimistic. Scores of copies were sent to the long-suffering van Rensselaer to sell "at any reasonable sacrifice," and other friends were enlisted to take up remaindered volumes. But he had enough cash—four hundred dollars, to be exact—to pay the deposit on a fourteen-hundred-dollar cotton plantation fifteen miles south of New Orleans on the west bank of the Mississippi. With cotton prices climbing to thirty-five cents a pound and sugar at nine cents a pound, he intended, he announced, to grow both and "with the will of God to make a fortune in five years." Although the words were addressed to van Rensselaer, the audience most captivated by his dreams was always Wilkinson himself. "Suppose I get you a plantation adjoining me on the Mississippi on a spot as healthy as Albany," he wrote, "where you may so invest a Capital of $30,000 as to yield you $5,000 the first year, and $10,000 the Third, will you sell, pack up and em-bark and land at New Orleans where I will meet you and carry you home in a Steam Boat?"

The reality of the van Rensselaer estates in New York, vast, well settled, and productive, outweighed the attractions of swampland in the Mississippi delta. But Wilkinson continued to believe in his rural idyll. His reunion with Celestine had allowed him to meet for the first time his twin daugh-ters, Stephanie and the delightfully named Theofannie, who had been born in January 1816. Having only known sons before, he was enchanted.

"Blessed with my Celestine and two beloved little daughters, as good and beautiful as angels, with a bare subsistence which I am endeavouring to improve by my labours," he declared, "I hold myself above the attractions of the world, envy no man's condition, enjoy tranquillity and happiness without alloy." Having transported all his archives to New Orleans, he intended to of-fer the public more reminiscences because he had so far only been able "to glance at one fifth of my public life." In this new drama, he would devote himself to nothing but farming and writing. "I decline all company, refuse all public appointments, and in my Books, my Pen, my divine little Creole, and our charming little girls, Stephanie and Theofannie, I enjoy more tranquillity and happiness than I have experienced in my variegated life."

For a time the role suited him. Even when he fell sick and fever reduced him after three weeks in bed to "a mere skeleton," he soon bounced back to health, "new flushed, as elastic as [a] Billiard Ball, and with the grace of Heven will not have another maladay of any kind for ten or fifteen years to come." Evidence of the sixty-two-year-old general's happiness was the birth of another child, Theodore, in 1819.

The serpent in his Eden was lack of money. The plantation did not generate profits on the scale he imagined, and his wealthy Trudeau relations may well have contributed to the family's upkeep as the Biddles had thirty years before. In 1819 Celestine's sister, Josephine, "the same lively Dame" who had accompanied her to Maryland, married "a Creole of 3 or 400,000$ fortune," and the struggling Wilkinsons must have been something of an embarrassment. That same year General John Adair brought a civil suit against him in Natchez for false imprisonment during the Burr Conspiracy and was awarded twenty-five hundred dollars in damages, a sum far beyond Wilkinson's ability to pay. Within twelve months, Congress rescued him from ruin by voting three thousand dollars for his relief, but poverty took the gloss off his rural dream. Then, writing to van Rensselaer in 1821, he revealed a wider dissatisfaction with his surroundings.

His letter was devoted to the crisis created by Missouri's insistence in 1820 that it be admitted to the Union as a new slave state. From the old-established slave society of New Orleans, Wilkinson wrote, "You can not find any one of virtue & Intelligence who, viewing negro slavery in the abstract, & to probable results, will not condemn it as a curse. Yet yielding to Habit, indolence and ease, we approve the curse. The Missourians will discover too late that the opponents to the introduction of Slavery among them were their best friends." As a slave owner himself, this was neither a popular nor an easy line to argue, but he was clear about the risk of the Union's splitting over the spread of slavery. "[The Union] is the Rock of our political Salvation," he argued. "The Southerns and Westerns have most to dread from the Catastrophe, yet they are accelerating it by their insatiate desire for limitless domain."

Although the argument came strangely from a former Spanish conspirator, it illustrated the critical ingredient he had contributed to the idea of the Union during his lifetime. When Wilkinson swung the army against Burr's conspiracy, an alien element was introduced into the concept of the United States. At that moment, the strand of thought, advocated most vehemently by Samuel Adams and John Randolph, that pictured a standing army as a threat to a citizens' republic was turned upside down. Without a standing army, the republic must constantly be at the mercy of adventurers like Rogers Clark, Blount, and Burr. In the last resort, a republican government

did not depend only on the will of the people, but also on its ability to enforce their will.

THE GENERAL'S EXIT from his plantation stage took place in March 1822.
His strongest emotional bond to the place was severed by the death of the
angelic Theofannie early in the year, leaving Wilkinson distraught. The
child was "too good and too perfect for this world," he wrote in grief, "so
God took her." He still had Stephanie and Theodore, and the son of his
first marriage, Joseph Biddle, who had come south to join his father, but
Theofannie was his favorite. The old man's unpopular views on slavery,
and the imperative need to earn a fortune, removed most of the attractions
that the Magnolia Grove plantation once possessed. They also directed his
imagination toward Mexico, where land was as cheap as it had once been in
Kentucky, and the newly independent nation had outlawed slavery.

When he sailed to Veracruz in March 1822, he took with him his gold-
braided general's uniform, a full-length portrait of George Washington
by Gilbert Stuart, and a commission to recover debts owed to merchants
trading with the old Spanish empire, but his most valuable assets were
intangible—his military reputation among the Spanish-trained army, his
quick intelligence, and the remains of his abundant charm. With supreme
self-confidence, he used the brief delay while his vessel was kept waiting
outside the harbor, and before he had set foot in the country, to write a proposal for reform of Mexico's trading policies. Events in Mexico, moreover,
made it an opportune moment to offer advice.

One year earlier, Agustín de Iturbide, a Spanish-trained soldier who had
defected to the rebels, established Mexico's first independent government,
bringing an end to eleven years of warfare with both Spanish and rival revolutionary forces. His administration was still taking shape, and the new
congress had just voted to make him emperor with the title Agustín I.

Once arrived in the capital, Mexico City, Wilkinson flourished among
the crush of petitioners, lobbyists, and adventurers who had congregated
there to take advantage of the region's first stable government in a decade.
Dressed in his general's uniform, sympathetic to Hispanic manners and
customs, and exhibiting the elaborate courtesy that was his trademark, he
immediately created a favorable impression. Among the crowds was Stephen
F. Austin, seeking confirmation from the new government of the grant of
Texas land made to his father under the Spanish empire. With surprise and
admiration, he saw Wilkinson gain the confidence of Iturbide's regency
council "to a high degree." The newcomer was invited to stay with the

captain general of the province and had several meetings with Iturbide himself. When Austin sent in his petition, he took the precaution of asking Wilkinson for a letter of recommendation to go with it.

Emperor Agustín was to disappoint everyone. Dull and reactionary, he lacked the boldness of a real leader despite the powers granted him— "more the Lamb than the Lion, the Spinster than the Soldier," in Wilkinson's pungent judgment. Wilkinson's own preference was for the most enterprising of the emperor's lieutenants, Antonio Cordero y Bustamante, the future president of Mexico. As governor of Texas in 1806, Cordero had confronted Wilkinson at the height of the Burr Conspiracy, and the experience of having been on opposite sides during those convulsive days created an immediate friendship. Cordero was, according to the general, "literally a Washington in all his great qualities . . . bravest of the brave, judicious, modest to timidity yet daring to Death."

With Cordero's assistance, Wilkinson's effortless rise to influence seemed destined to continue. He delivered to the emperor a second paper on the settlement of Texas, suggesting that it be divided in half, with the eastern, and more desirable, province being renamed Iturbide. Instead of being settled by Anglo settlers, such as Austin proposed, who were "slothful, ready to vice, insensible to social affection and [to] really permanent social life," Wilkinson recommended that Iturbide should be "inhabited by cultured Catholic people, dedicated to manufacturing and all kinds of industry." This was shrewd salesmanship, aimed at an emperor who was revealing himself to be a Catholic hard-liner, anxious to bring back the Inquisition and restore Jesuit supervision of religion. What the general really had in mind became apparent only at the end of the document, when he suggested that the governor of this Catholic province should be "an official of honor, fidelity, intelligence, adaptability, and political sagacity." In short, himself.

Occasionally he reduced his dream to ownership of two hundred thousand acres near Galveston, "divinely situated on the Coast of the Gulph with a good harbour & salubrious climate, with Fish and oysters at the Door and droves of Buffalo & wild horses in thousands on our rear." But none of it was realistic. Resistance to the emperor's autocratic rule led to his abdication early in 1823, leaving Wilkinson to start all over again.

Running short of money, he moved from the center of Mexico City to a house on the outskirts. There he acted as a consultant to a stream of business and political visitors from the United States. "We stopped at the lodgings of our countryman, General W[ilkinson], who received us in the kindest manner," the first U.S. ambassador to Mexico, Joel Poinsett, reported. "He has been sometime here, and we sat up to a late hour, listening to his interesting account of the country." His expertise and his introductions to people in government earned him enough to live quietly while the prospect of his great prize hovered just beyond his reach. Mexico wanted Texas settled, but whether by immigrants from the United States or elsewhere, and whether under central or provincial government control, could not be decided. Nor were the successors to Iturbide's rule much more secure than the emperor. Meanwhile, as the tone of Poinsett's letter suggested, the general was in danger of turning into a curiosity on the sidelines rather than a power at the center.

That summer he played his trump card and presented to the congress of the newly reestablished republic of Mexico his full-length portrait of George Washington, the republican statesman, standing with peaceful hand outstretched, and dressed in civilian black, the garb almost obscuring his military sword. The gesture won Wilkinson great acclaim and a sympathetic hearing for his claims for unpaid debts, for unawarded land, and for a new payment of fifteen thousand dollars, which may have been recompense for himself. But gratitude did not immediately translate into action. Slowly the general was becoming an exile. He said as much in a letter to Thomas Jefferson written in March 1824.

They had corresponded only once since the unfortunate reference to "Long Tom." In 1818, Jefferson decided that he had been unfairly criticized in Alexander Wilson's classic *American Ornithology* for failing to send the ornithologist on Zebulon Pike's Red River expedition. Sensitive to the charge of impeding scientific study, Jefferson asked Wilkinson to remind him of the circumstances. From the Magnolia Grove plantation, Wilkinson assured his president that he was not to blame. Pike's mission was to explore the Red and Arkansas rivers. It was not an expedition suitable for scientists, and it was sent without the president's specific knowledge.

Jefferson had not acknowledged this helpful reply, and other letters Wilkinson had written had gone astray. Consequently the general had to invent a reason for getting in touch from Mexico. The way to catch Thomas Jefferson was through his curiosity. Writing in early 1824, Wilkinson sent packets of Mexican seeds—for parsley, lettuces, beans, cantaloupes, avocados, red corn, peas, tomatoes, and chilies. With the last of these came cooking suggestions—they were best "when young mixed with meat for ragout, when ripe, clean out seed, mixed with syrup makes a sweetmeat." Superficially his letter was in the same vein, the intrepid intelligence officer reporting back matters of interest to his commander, and as usual the truth required some dressing up. He had been intending to leave the country when he "unexpectedly became entangled" in the American claims for compensation, and as a result "I have been detained here in involuntary exile." Ruefully he admitted being unable to tell whether "I have been duped and deceived more by the Republican or Imperial governments." But his detention at least made it possible to pass on information about Mexican politics, and about his own efforts to help "the People of the Western hemisphere form a close knit League of National Republicks."

Only toward the end of six closely scrawled pages did the guise slip. What he really wanted was some reply to all the messages he had sent Jefferson, some acknowledgment from the father figure who had never entirely failed nor ever quite fulfilled the general's need for approval, "a letter sent under cover to [the] consul of the United States would certainly reach me here." In a shaky hand, the aged Thomas Jefferson wrote on the envelope, "Arrived May 21," but still there was no reply.

Desperate for a response, Wilkinson wrote again to Jefferson on July 1, now portraying himself on the verge of such success that people would "envy the good fortune I have acquired by patience, perseverance and long suffering." But his letter ended with the same yearning for the smallest sign of approval: "I shall be detained here still two months, I beg you to write me as a mere spirit of recognition." This time, however, the words were not even read. The last tenuous link with Thomas Jefferson had been broken.

DESPITE HIS SHOW OF OPTIMISM, the general's affairs were no closer to a solution. In September 1824 he told his son Joseph, "I have just made a contract apparently for a claims adjustment." He expected to be paid and to leave in two or three weeks. But six months later he was still in Mexico City, and now in such dire financial straits that he had to ask Joseph to send him some money. In return, his son could have one hundred thousand acres either in Galveston or farther north in Texas where the general expected to be given land. But without money or influence his dream was no longer really credible. In the summer of 1825, he even had to ask Poinsett, the ambassador, to give him an introduction to the new governor of Texas and Coahuila.

Age had crept up on the general. He still rode in the morning outside his little villa, but he grew tired easily. There was a constant pain in his stomach, and though he dosed himself regularly with laudanum, the relief was short-lived, and the discomfort longer. The animal energy that had given credibility to James Wilkinson's fantasies was running out. At a deeper level, he had lost the impetus to keep the show going. Jefferson's continuing silence removed the one audience he craved. The only person to influence his life more profoundly had been the original model of deceit, his real father, Joseph Wilkinson. The adoration the boy had given him had been transferred from one powerful successor to another, but none had come as close as Jefferson to occupying his father's place. Now, without a figure of authority to observe and applaud the performance, James Wilkinson may have felt that it was hardly worth going onstage anymore.

News of his deteriorating health brought Celestine to Mexico City shortly before Christmas. Nothing more could be done for him except to keep the pain at bay with laudanum. On December 28, 1825, at the age of sixty-eight, Major General James Wilkinson, once commander in chief of the U.S. army, and sometimes known as Agent 13, died.

He would have been gratified to learn that a distinguished congregation, including the future president Cordero y Bustamante and the American ambassador, assembled in the Church of St. Michael in Mexico City for his funeral. Outward appearances were always important. The inward reality was less easy to discern, and for the general it never counted for much. Thus the final disposal of his mortal remains was oddly appropriate.

In 1872 the cemetery of the Church of St. Michael where Wilkinson was buried was scheduled for development. When the news reached Washington, the Senate decided that the body of such a distinguished soldier deserved a proper resting place. Orders were given to exhume his body for transfer to the National Cemetery in Mexico City. The embassy sent an official party to supervise the ceremony with due honor. When they arrived, however, they discovered the graves had already been dug up and their contents consigned to a common vault. American bones were mixed with Mexican, and it was no longer possible to tell one from the other, friend from enemy, patriot from traitor, general from spy. Whoever was behind the outward appearance once known as James Wilkinson had simply disappeared.

ACKNOWLEDGMENTS

The centripetal process of conception, research, and writing that results in a book incurs many debts to the generosity and knowledge of others. I should like to acknowledge my gratitude to Frank Wilson, former books editor of the *Philadelphia Inquirer*, for initially focusing my attention on the bizarre nature of General James Wilkinson's double-faced career, and to my friend George Gibson, publishing director of Bloomsbury USA/Walker Books, for his encouraging response to my enthusiasm for the dark convolutions of the general's character.

My research has depended heavily on the professional expertise of librarians in the Manuscripts Division of the Library of Congress, the New York Public Library, the Chicago History Museum, the American Philosophical Society, the United States Military Academy Library at West Point, the Archivo General de Indias in Seville, the British Library in London, and the London Library. At one remove, I have also benefited from the resources, both human and online, of the Filson Historical Society, the Maryland Historical Society, the Maryland State Archives, the Massachusetts Historical Society, the State Historical Society of Missouri, and the Texas State Historical Society. The ability to access online original manuscripts and publications from the period is invaluable, and so at two removes, I should like to pay tribute to the many organizations that have digitized their records and made them available to researchers.

The outward expression of this inward absorption is my own responsibility, but for their deeply valued contributions to the churning of ideas, I would like to thank Paul Houlton, Alan Smith, Lyn Cole, Professor Tom Schmiedeler, and Philip Evans. Finally, but primarily, for the love and support of my wife, Marie-Louise, throughout the entire autogamic process I am eternally grateful.

APPENDIX 1

The real record of payments made to James Wilkinson was kept by his Spanish handlers. As printed by Jacobs in *Tarnished Warrior*, it reads as follows:

STATEMENT OF WILKINSON'S ACCOUNT

Pension from 1st January 89 to 1st January 96	14000
to so much advanced by advice of Carondelet & Gayoso to retard, disjoint and defeat the mediated irruption of General Clark in La.	8640
Credit	22640
Received from Miró	7000
Received from Carondelet by La Cassagne	4000
Received from Carondelet by Collins	6000
	17000
Of the taken credited	
L[a] C[assagne] has paid	2600
Collins has paid	2500

the balance is disipated [*sic*] or fraudently applyd [*sic*]
A true account upon honour W.

Ingeniously, Jacobs points out that the difference between what Wilkinson was due and what he had been paid was $5,640. Jacobs argues that when Carondelet sent Power north with $9,640, it was to pay Wilkinson the difference plus $4,000 representing two years' unpaid salary.

Appendix 2

In 1929, Lieutenant Mark Rhoads of the U.S. Army's Signal Corps, and soon to be the first instructor employed by the army's cryptanalysis training section, the Signal Intelligence School, undertook to analyze the ciphers used by James Wilkinson. He started with ciphered messages sent to New Orleans, most of which were already decoded, and worked back to find out what ciphering method had been used. Rhoads learned that, in addition to the basic cipher based on dictionaries, Wilkinson added complications of his own—substitution codes, doubled ciphering, and arbitrary transposition of symbols and letters. His notes are preserved in the Library of Congress files.

A code refers to the substitution of specific words in the original plain text with an arbitrary and predetermined set of words or symbols—e.g., the president was represented by O, the vice president by ⊙. A cipher refers to the substitution of the plain text with words, numerals, or other symbols selected according to a predetermined rule. A code is necessarily limited to the previously selected words. A cipher is as elastic as an alphabet.

Wilkinson's most commonly used code was based on the 1800 edition of John Entick's *The New Spelling Dictionary*. The coded text appeared as numbers separated by a decimal point. The digits up to the decimal point indicated the page of the dictionary; the digits after the point indicated the number of the word on the page; e.g., 261.37 stood for page 261, word on line 37; thus "able" = 2.18; "yourself" = 765.$\bar{\bar{2}}$. (Since there were two columns on each page of Entick's dictionary, the second column was indicated by two lines over the first digit after the decimal point; no marking meant the first column.)

This code was relatively easy to compose; Wilkinson's reports were long and chatty, spread over up to thirty pages, suggesting that he could easily remember the code for most words. It was also relatively simple to decode. As Rhoads himself pointed out, a quick study of the coded text revealed the maximum number of pages in the book, and the maximum number of lines. From this, it would have been possible to deduce the volume being used, a task made easier by the supposition that the likeliest choice was a dictionary or encyclopedia that had all the words needed. Accordingly Wilkinson also used substitution ciphers based on a keyword such as CUBA. This also produced a ciphered text in digits, following the rules below:

1	C	U	B	A
2	d	v	c	b
3	e	w	d	c
4	f	x	e	d
. . . .				
24	z	r	y	x
25	a	s	z	y
26	b	t	a	z

This required each letter to be ciphered in relation to the keyword. The first letter was taken from the first column, second from the second, and for a word of more than four letters, the substitution continued with the fifth letter from the first column, etc. Each letter was separated by a comma, each word by a period. Thus "bare" would be 26, 7, 18, 5. The keyword could be changed according to a predetermined order from paragraph to paragraph. Wilkinson's preference for ornate, polysyllabic words led him to select long keywords such as NORTHUMBERLANDSHIRE.

Finally, very sensitive information was coded replacing individual letters for arbitrarily selected substitutes, but repeated the process several times: e.g., $A = K = N = I; N = A = R = -$.

NOTES

INTRODUCTION: A TEST OF LOYALTY

The pivotal test of General James Wilkinson's (JW) uncertain loyalties received considerable publicity at Aaron Burr's trials in the summer of 1807. Lieutenant Colonel Thomas Cushing's sworn affidavit was presented in court; see T. Carpenter's *The Trial of Colonel Aaron Burr on an Indictment of Treason,* and reprinted in JW's *Burr's Conspiracy exposed and General Wilkinson vindicated against the slanders of his enemies on that important occasion.* JW's own reactions were recorded in *Burr's Conspiracy.* The widespread belief that he was in the pay of Spain, a "Spanish pensioner," provided the basis of Burr's defense. In their words, "General Wilkinson had an interest with the king of Spain."

CHAPTER 1: THE PENNILESS ARISTOCRAT

The main sources for colonial Maryland's aristocratic and tobacco culture are Aubrey C. Land's rather old-fashioned *Colonial Maryland—A History* (Kraus International); Trevor Burnard's *Creole Gentlemen: The Maryland Elite, 1691–1776* (New York and London: Routledge, 2002); and Arthur Pierce Middleton's *Tobacco Coast: A Maritime History of Chesapeake Bay in the Colonial Era* (Newport, VA: Mariners' Museum, 1953). The background of JW's ancestry and upbringing is taken from his *Memoirs* and from his two earlier biographies; James R. Jacobs's meticulously researched *Tarnished Warrior: Major-General James Wilkinson*; and Thomas R. Hay and M. R. Werner's *Admirable Trumpeter: A Biography of General James Wilkinson.* None of these sources refer to the near bankruptcy of Joseph Wilkinson. Evidence for this appears in the colonial probate records in the Maryland State Archives, Liber 52, 54, and 86 with relevant folios; in Calvert County tax assessments for 1783, MSA 1437; and in genealogical records of the Wilkinson and Heighe families.

8   "these bold and indigent strangers": Quoted in *The Conquest of the Old Southwest* by Archibald Henderson (New York: Century, 1920).

8   "The Manners of Maryland are somewhat peculiar": John Adams diary, November 21, 1777, Adams Family Papers (AFP), Massachusetts Historical Society, (digital) www.masshist.org/digitaladams/aea.

10   "The last words my father spoke to me": *Memoirs*, 1:7–9.

12   For colonial Philadelphia, see *The Private City: Philadelphia in Three Periods of Its Growth* by Sam Bass Warner, Jr. (Philadelphia: University of Pennsylvania Press, 1987).

12   "These inclinations were seconded" and JW's time in Philadelphia: *Memoirs*, 1:11–13.

13   "The *Rage Militaire*": quoted in Margaret Wheeler Willard, ed., *Letters on the American Revolution, 1774–1776* (Boston, 1925).

CHAPTER 2: CITIZENS AND SOLDIERS

The rivalry between supporters of militia and professional soldiers in the Revolutionary War has been the subject of extensive research. I have consulted the following: Lawrence D. Cress's *Citizens in Arms: The Army and the Militia in American Society to the War of 1812* (Chapel Hill: University of North Carolina Press, 1982), and his chapter "Reassessing American Military Requirements, 1783–1807" in *Against All Enemies: Interpretations of American Military History from Colonial Times to the Present*, edited by Kenneth J. Hagan and William R. Roberts (Westport, CT: Greenwood Press, 1986); Ricardo A. Herrera, "Self-Governance and the American Citizen as Soldier, 1775–1861," *Journal of Military History* 65, no. 1 (January 2001); Paul David Nelson, "Citizen Soldiers or Regulars: The Views of American General Officers on the Military Establishment, 1775–1781," *Military Affairs* 43, no. 3 (October 1979); William B. Skelton, "The Confederation's Regulars: A Social Profile of Enlisted Service in America's First Standing Army," *William and Mary Quarterly*, 3rd ser., 46, no. 4 (October 1989); and Skelton's "Social Roots of the American Military Profession: The Officer Corps of America's First Peacetime Army, 1784–1789," *Journal of Military History* 54, no. 4 (October 1990).

15   "the familiarity which prevailed": *Memoirs*, 1:33–34.

16   "no Dependence can be put on the Militia": General George Washington to John Hancock, July 10, 1775.

16   "When I look to the consequences of it": Quoted in *The Correspondence of King George the Third from 1760 to December 1783*, ed. John Fortescue (London: Frank Cass & Co., 1967).

16   "never desired to see better soldiers": Quoted in Nelson, "Citizen Soldiers or Regulars."

16   "A Standing Army, however necessary": Samuel Adams to James Warren, January 7, 1776, Warren-Adams Letters, I.

16   "Our troops are animated": Address of the Continental Congress to "The Inhabitants of the Colonies," February 13, 1776, JCC.

17   "Men may speculate as they will": Washington to John Banester, April 21, 1778, *Writings of George Washington*.

17   "The regiment was ordered for muster": *Memoirs*, 1:34–35.

18   Grover court-martial: Washington to John Hancock, president of Congress, May 5, 1776, JCC.
19   For Benedict Arnold's reputation, see Willard S. Randall's *Benedict Arnold, Patriot and Traitor.*
20   "We are now in a sweet situation": JW to General Nathanael Greene, May 24, 1776, *Memoirs,* 1:43–44.
20   "Captn Wilkinson . . . is truly alarming": Washington to John Hancock, June 7, 1776, JCC.
20   "Captn Wilkinson's Conjectures were not realized": General Schuyler to Washington, June 10, 1776, JCC.
20   JW's relationship with Arnold: *Memoirs,* 1:46–49.
21   JW and General Sullivan: Ibid., 1:51–59.
22   "a Gentleman who I have always esteemed as a friend": General Wayne to James Wilkinson, June 16, 1792, quoted in Nelson, *Anthony Wayne, Soldier of the Early Republic.*

CHAPTER 3: WOOING GENERAL GATES

The first volume of JW's memoirs provides the story of his relationship with General Horatio Gates. Despite JW's unreliability, the depth of his feeling for Gates is unmistakable. For Gates's character and career, see Nelson, *General Horatio Gates: A Biography,* and his "Legacy of Controversy: Gates, Schuyler, and Arnold at Saratoga, 1777."
24   "my dear General's affectionate friend": JW to Gates, June 10, 1776, *Memoirs,* vol. 1.
24   "an old granny looking fellow": Quoted in Nelson's "Legacy of Controversy."
25   "the intrepid, generous, friendly, upright, Honest man": JW to Varick, quoted in James R. Jacobs, *Tarnished Warrior.*
26   "the first officer in Military knowledge": Washington to Jack Washington, March 5, 1776, GWP.
26   "a certain great man is damnably deficient": Lee to Gates, December 13, 1776, *Memoirs,* 1:108.
27   General Lee's capture: *Memoirs,* 1:101–10.
27   JW's account of the battle of Trenton: *Memoirs,* 1:125–31; also Ferling, *Almost a Miracle.*
29   Evidence of the interest Washington took in Wilkinson's career appears in a letter from William Fitzhugh, Washington's neighbor and friend: "With respect to Wilkinson, who I verily believe is a young Fellow of Great Merrit, I will Endeavor, as you are Pleas'd to Advise, to get Him Provided for in The Battalions to be rais'd Here." Fitzhugh to Washington, October 17, 1776.
29   The diatribes against the militia: Quoted in Nelson, "Citizen Soldiers or Regulars."
30   For the reorganization of the Continental Army, see Cress, *Citizens in Arms,* and Wright, *Continental Army.*
30   "to remedy his polite manners": *Memoirs,* 1:156. Washington would have attached him to a regiment commanded by the notoriously rough-tempered Nathanael Guest had JW not protested, so Hartley represented the soft option.

31   Every recorded word written about Ann Biddle makes her sound adorable—
adventurous, tenderhearted, generous-spirited—just as Peale painted her. For John
Biddle and the Indian King, see Earle, "The Taverns of Colonial Philadelphia"; for
other members of the family, see Hay, "Letters of Mrs. Ann Biddle Wilkinson," and
Radbill, "Quaker Patriots: The Leadership of Owen Biddle and John Lacey."

CHAPTER 4: THE TRIUMPH OF SARATOGA

In addition to Nelson, *General Horatio Gates*, and his "Legacy of Controversy," sources
used include Wright, *Continental Army*; Upham, "Burgoyne's Great Mistake," and
Hudleston's *Gentleman Johnny Burgoyne*.

33   "My young heart leaped with joy": *Memoirs*, 1:154.

33   "I would to God, gentlemen could for once know their own minds": Ibid.

34   "John Burgoyne wagers": Quoted in Frothingham, *Washington: Commander-in-chief*.

34   "The perfidy of mankind": *Memoirs*, 1:172.

34   "It wrung my heart": Ibid., 1:174–75. Gates's order, issued on May 24, 1777,
read in full, "Colonel James Wilkinson is appointed deputy adjutant-general to the
army in the northen department; all orders written or verbal coming from him are
to be considered as the orders of the general in chief." Schuyler read a copy of JW's
letter to Gates and commented, "I admire warmth and affection in young gentlemen of your age . . . I hope you may find cause to give me a share of the regard
you now bear General Gates."

35   "these Mortals must be led and not drove": Horatio Gates to Joseph Trumbull of
Connecticut, quoted in Nelson, "Citizen Soldiers or Regulars."

35   "Gates' arrival raised us as if by magic": Udney Hay to Governor Clinton, August 13, 1777, quoted in Nelson, "Legacy of Controversy."

36   "He has great merit": General St. Clair to Gates, quoted in *Memoirs*, 1:352.

36   "His conduct . . . endeared him to me": Matthew Lyon, deposition to Ezekiel
Bacon's committee of the House of Representatives, 1811, ibid., 3:341.

37   "Such an explosion of fire I had never heard": James Phinney Baxter, *The
British Invasion from the North: The Campaigns of General Carleton and Burgoyne with
the Journal of Lieut. William Digby* (Albany, NY: Munsell's, 1887).

37   The battle of Freeman's Farm: *Memoirs*, 1:263–66. JW's account places him at
the center of events from the days before the battle when he purportedly took out
the reconnaissance party that found Burgoyne's army and selected Bemis Heights as
a strongpoint for Gates's force. During the fighting at Freeman's Farm, he also
claimed to have gone to the battleground in person and strengthened the morale of
the commanders Henry Dearborn and Daniel Morgan, the latter having been reduced to tears. Without corroboration it is impossible to know what degree of
credibility, if any, should be attached to these claims. However, the angry accusation
of Richard Varick, Arnold's staff officer, confirms that JW's intervention was responsible for effectively removing Arnold from his command.

39   "he is an old gamester": October 4, 1777, Gates to Governor George Clinton,
quoted in Nelson, "Legacy of Controversy."

39   "Our cannon were surrounded": Baxter, *British Invasion*.
40   "the likeliest young man I ever saw": Lyon to Thomas Jefferson, August 12, 1802, TJP.
40   JW's leading role in the negotiations for Burgoyne's surrender are described in *Memoirs*, 1:290–317, and largely substantiated by Nelson and Hudleston. Burgoyne's ascription of failure to "the fortune of war" rather than his own inadequacy was characteristic.
43   JW blamed his illness on "the strong excitements produced by the important scenes in which I had been engaged": Ibid., 1:321.

CHAPTER 5: BETRAYING GENERAL GATES

Necessarily JW's private quarrel with Gates is told without corroboration. But his role in the betrayal of the Conway cabal was very public, fully documented in the George Washington Papers, and both the *Journals of the Continental Congress* and the *Letters of Delegates to Congress*.
44   "The standing corps which I have seen are disciplined": John Burgoyne, *A State of the Expedition from Canada* (London, 1780).
44   "to Coax, to wheedle and even to Lye": Schuyler to Washington, November 22, 1776, quoted in Randall, *Benedict Arnold, Patriot and Traitor*.
44   "We can allow a certain Citizen to be wise": John Adams to Abigail Adams, October 26, 1777, AFP.
44   "From a well-regulated militia we have nothing to fear": John Hancock, 1774, quoted in Kohn, *Eagle and Sword*.
45   "We want you in different places": James Lovell to Gates, November 22, 1777, quoted in June Lloyd's "BeWare of Your Board of War," Pennsylvania Historical Society, *Pennsylvania Legacies*, November 2008.
45   "The northern army has shown us": Benjamin Rush (anonymously) to Patrick Henry, January 12, 1778, *Letters of Benjamin Rush*, vol. 1, ed. L. H. Butterfield (Princeton, NJ: Princeton University Press, 1951).
45   "the new Board of War is Composed": James Craik to Washington, January 6, 1778, GWP.
46   "New Jersey is *our* country": Quoted in Warren Burger, "Obstacles to the Constitution," Supreme Court Historical Society, 1977.
46   "If he *has* an Enemy": Henry Laurens to the Marquis de Lafayette, January 12, 1778, LCC.
46   "General Gates was to be exalted": Washington to Patrick Henry, March 28, 1778, GWP.
46   "I have been a Slave to the service": Washington to Richard Henry Lee, October 17, 1777, GWP.
46   "I have never seen any stroke of ill fortune": Tench Tilghman to Robert Morris, October 21, 1777, quoted in Preston Russell, "The Conway Cabal," *American Heritage Magazine*, March/April 1995.
46   The great storm that held up JW in Reading, see *Memoirs*, 1:338–40, and froze the defeated Brunswickers, see *Letters of Brunswick and Hessian Officers during the*

American Revolution, translated by William Stone, but drove others landing on Staten Island to think of deserting and swamped the huts of Washington's drenched troops.

47 "The Prospect is chilling": John Adams diary, September 16, 1777, AFP. Crammed into a small, German-speaking town, other delegates voiced equally depressed comments, for example, Cornelius Harnett of North Carolina: "It is the most Inhospitable Scandalous place I ever was in."

47 "and poaching in the heavyest Rain": John Adams to Abigail Adams, October 28, 1777, AFP.

48 JW's account of the dinner party with Stirling is studiously vague—"conversation too copious and diffuse for me to have charged my memory," *Memoirs*, 1:331–32—so it is not entirely clear whether he or McWilliams misquoted Conway's letter to Gates.

49 "Had I known that he had fallen in love": Adams to Thomas McKean, November 26, 1815, AFP.

49 The figures for British armaments captured at Saratoga are taken from the official returns to Congress, October 31, 1777, JCC.

49 "make the best and most immediate use of this intelligence": Letter by Richard Henry Lee and James Lovell to the U.S. representatives in France, October 31, 1777.

50 "Your Name Sir will be written": Henry Laurens to Horatio Gates, November 5, 1777, JCC.

50 "I have not met with a more promising military genius": Gates to John Hancock, October 20, 1777, JCC. On November 6, 1777, the Continental Congress meeting in the courthouse of York, Pennsylvania, passed the following resolution: "That Colonel James Wilkinson, adjutant general in the northern army, in consideration of his services in that department, and being strongly recommended by General Gates as a gallant officer, and a promising military genius . . ." JCC.

50 "My dear General and loved Friend" JW to Gates, November 1, 1777, *Memoirs*, 1:335. JW also referred to his discomfort at finding Congress had already heard unofficially from the general: "Through the industry of your friends, whom you indulged with copies the articles of the treaty (with their diabolical comments I suppose) reached the grand army before I did the Congress."

51 Gates "was too polite to make the Lieut. General and his troops prisoners of discretion": Quoted in David Duncan Wallace, *The Life of Henry Laurens* (New York, 1915), 247.

51 "Had an Attack been carried": JW to Congress, November 3, 1777, manuscript letter in Papers of the Continental Congress.

52 "a weak General or bad Counsellors": Washington to Conway, November 4, 1777, GWP.

52 "Your modesty is such": Conway to Washington, November 5, 1777, GWP.

52 "your generosity and frank disposition": General Thomas Mifflin to Gates, November 28, 1777, *Memoirs*, 1:371.

52 "No punishment is too severe": Gates to Mifflin, December 4, 1777, PCC.

53 "Those letters have been stealingly copied": Gates to Washington, December 8, 1777, GWP.

53   "I am under the disagreeable necessity": Washington to Gates, January 4, 1778, GWP.

53   "read [Conway's] letter publicly in my presence": *Memoirs*, 1:372–73. JW's full self-exculpation was wonderfully sinuous: "Conscious as I was that I had never spoken of that letter with evil intentions, or at all except when it was mentioned to me; and considering it, as it really was, nothing more than the vehicle of the opinions of an individual . . . which General Gates himself had not treated confidentially because he had read it publicly in my presence as matter of information from the grand army; I felt no personal solicitude about it, nor could I ascribe to it the importance which was subsequently given to it; and therefore I did not dream of the foul imputations it was destined to draw down upon me, and the strife and trouble it would occasion me."

53   "communicated by Colonl. Wilkinson to Major McWilliams": Washington to Gates, January 4, 1778, GWP.

54   "I never had any sort of intimacy": Gates to Washington, January 23, 1778, GWP.

54   In an attempt to clear up the inconsistency between Conway's letter and JW's misremembered version, Stirling asked him to produce the original letter. Stirling to Wilkinson, January 6, 1778, *Memoirs*, 1:382–83. JW replied angrily, "I may have been indiscreet, my Lord, but be assured I am not dishonourable."

54   "I always before heard": Abraham Clark to William Alexander, January 15, 1778, PCC. In this letter Clark voiced an oddly prescient suspicion: "If he betrayed the Confidence of his Pattron he may do the same by his Country."

55   "dissention among the principle Officers of the Army": Ibid.

55   "I earnestly hope no more of that time": Gates to Washington, February 19, 1778, GWP.

55   "I am as averse to controversy": Washington to Gates, February 22, 1778, GWP.

55   "the very improper steps": Anthony Wayne to Colonel Walter Stewart, quoted in Stewart's letter to Gates, *Memoirs*, 1:390. JW also quoted General Charles Lee's comment to Gates, March 29, 1779: "With respect to Wilkinson, I really think he had been a man more sinned against than any."

55   "I ever was sensible of Wilky's volatility": Ibid.

55   "Your generous Conduct at Albany": Colonel Robert Troup to JW, quoted in JW's letter to Washington, March 28, 1778, GWP.

55   "General Gates had denounced me": *Memoirs*, 1:385. The version of what happened between him and Gates is inescapably JW's. It can be partially confirmed by Gates's reply, quoted in full in the *Memoirs*, and by JW's letter of March 28, 1778, to Washington, in which he recounted substantially the same sequence of events.

57   "My Lord shall bleed for his conduct": JW to Gates, February 22, 1778, *Memoirs*, 1:385–86.

57   "flitted away like a vision of the morn": Ibid., 1:391.

57   "passed in a private company during a convivial Hour": JW to Stirling, March 18, 1778, ibid., 1:391–92.

57   "under no injunction of secrecy": Stirling to JW, ibid., 1:392.

58   "he seemed a good deal surprized": Washington to Stirling, March 21, 1778, GWP.

58   "after the act of *treachery*": JW to Laurens, March 29, 1778, *Memoirs*, 1:409–10.
58   "improper to remain on the files of Congress": Quoted in Jacobs, *Tarnished Warrior*, 47.
58   JW passes over the second duel, but Jacobs's description in *Tarnished Warrior* is taken from contemporary accounts: *New York Packet* (Fishkill, NY), September 17, 24, October 8, 1778; and *Continental Journal and Weekly Advertiser*, November 12, 1778.

CHAPTER 6: LOVE AND INDEPENDENCE

JW's recollections skip over the period between his leaving the army and his arriving in Kentucky almost six years later. However, his period as clothier general is well documented in the War Department Papers, as well as the *Papers of George Washington* and Papers of the Continental Congress. The Biddle family connections are based on Radbill, "The Leadership of Owen Biddle and John Lacey," and Hay, "The Letters of Mrs. Ann Biddle Wilkinson." The main sources for Pennsylvania politics are Wood, *Creation of the American Republic*; Reed, *Life and Correspondence of Joseph Reed*; William S. Hanna, *Benjamin Franklin and Pennsylvania Politics* (Stanford, CA: 1964); and Ireland, "The Ethnic-Religious Dimension of Pennsylvania Politics, 1778–1779."
62   JW's ownership of Trevose: Jacobs, *Tarnished Warrior*, 55–59.
62   land "sold for three pounds an acre": Benjamin Franklin, "Information to those who would remove to America," September 1782, *Writings*, 8:603–14.
62   For Arnold's time in Philadelphia, see Randall, *Benedict Arnold*.
62   "borrowed a sum of money of the Commissaries": JW to Joseph Reed, May 1779, quoted in Hay, *Admirable Trumpeter*, 45.
63   "If your Excellency thinks me criminal": Arnold to Washington, May 5, 1779, quoted in Randall, *Benedict Arnold*.
63   "If we review the rise and progress": Silas Deane to Robert Morris, quoted in Linklater, *Measuring America*, 166.
64   "Men without Cloathes to cover their nakedness": Washington to John Bannister, April 21, 1778, GWP.
64   The duties of the clothier general were a work in progress until the last years of the war. For their changing nature, see Wright, *Continental Army*.
64   "The clothing department has occasioned more trouble to me": Quoted in Hay, *Admirable Trumpeter*, 48.
64   "For when a Soldier is convinced": Washington to James Mease, April 17, 1777, quoted in Wright, *Continental Army*.
64   "I am again reduced": Washington to General William Heath, November 18, 1779, quoted in Erna Risch, "Supplying Washington's Army," *Special Studies Series*, ed. Maurice Matloff (Washington, DC: Center of Military History, 1981).
65   "I shall expect to see you": Washington's correspondence with JW is quoted in Hay, *Admirable Trumpeter*, 50–52.
65   For JW's Philadelphia distractions, see Hay, *Admirable Trumpeter.*
66   "Is it not a possible Thing to revive": General Huntington to Jeremiah Wadsworth, May 5, 1780, quoted in Royster, "Nature of Treason."
67   For the profound shock of Arnold's treason, see Royster, "Nature of Treason."

Next to Washington himself, no one could be thought more patriotic. In 1776, Mercy Otis Warren thought "the name of Washington and Arnold [would be linked] to the latest posterity, with the laurel on their brow."

67   "Address of Confidence": Jacobs, *Tarnished Warrior*, 62.

68   "Direct the Commander-in Chief": New York's 1780 petition cited by Baack, "Forging a Nation State."

68   "I should be wanting in Personal Candour": JW to Samuel Huntington, president of Congress, March 27, 1781, PCC.

69   "I think General Wilkinson too desponding": Reed to General Lacy, commander of the Pennsylvania militia, quoted in Hay, *Admirable Trumpeter*, 52.

69   "It is a pity so good an officer is lost to the service": Nathanael Greene to Clement Biddle, June 26, 1780, quoted in Reed, *Life and Correspondence*.

69   without "cash or credit": Wilkinson to Henry Lee, quoted in Davis, "By Invitation of Mrs. Wilkinson," 156.

CHAPTER 7: THE KENTUCKY PIONEER

For JW's early years in Kentucky, the Harry Innes Papers are indispensable. Yet the chaos of land titles as illustrated in Abernethy, *Western Lands and the American Revolution*; Aron, *How the West Was Lost*; Sakolski, *Great American Land Bubble*; and Dunaway, "Speculators and Settler Capitalists"—allied to JW's habitual exaggeration—lend mystery to his speculations.

71   "The vallies are of the richest soil": John William de Braham, "De Braham's Account," in *Early Travels in the Tennessee Country: 1540–1800*, ed. Samuel Cole Williams (Johnson City, TN, 1928).

71   "more frequent than I have seen cattle in the settlements": "The Adventures of Colonel Daniel Boon," in John Filson, *The Discovery, Settlement and Present State of Kentucké* (Wilmington: James Adams, 1784).

71   "The country might invite a prince" quoted in Archibald Henderson, *The Conquest of the Old Southwest etc, 1740–1790* (New York: Century, 1920).

72   "A person not quite tall enough": Humphrey Marshall, *History of Kentucky*, 1:165.

72   For JW's links to Hugh Shiell, see Hay, "Letters of Mrs. Ann Biddle Wilkinson."

73   JW's "wonderful address" in borrowing money: William Leavy, "A Memoir of Lexington and Its Vicinity," *Kentucky Historical Society Register* 40 (April 1942).

73   JW's traveling hardships were described in "Letters of General James Wilkinson," *Kentucky Historical Society Register* 24 (September 1926).

73   John Lewis dealings: July 3, 1784, agreement with JW for locating land, John Lewis papers, *First American West: The Ohio River Valley, 1750–1820*, LoC.

73   "Be sure you bring a double stock of great variety": JW to Scott, July 4, 1784, ibid.

74   "Our country is now a continued Flower Bed": JW to Scott, quoted in Hay, *Admirable Trumpeter*, 62.

74   "It is impossible for me to describe the torture," "I feel so Stupid": Ann Wilkinson to John Biddle, February 14, 1788, Hay, "Letters of Mrs. Ann Biddle Wilkinson."

74   A detailed study of Kentucky's chaotic system of land registration and confusion over multiple claims appears in Wilma A. Dunaway, "Speculators and Settler Capitalists," in *Appalachia in the Making: The Mountain South in the Nineteenth Century* (University of North Carolina Press, 1995). In 1821 Judge Joseph Story attributed the confusion to the decision to allow settlers to appropriate land "by entries and descriptions of their own, without any previous survey under public authority, and without any such boundaries as were precise, permanent, and unquestionable." "An address delivered before Members of the Suffolk Bar" (Boston, 1829).

76   "And when arrivd at this Heaven in idea": "Memorandum of M. Austin's Journey from the Lead Mines in the County of Wythe in the State of Virginia to the Lead Mines in the Province of Louisiana, 1796–1797," *American Historical Review* 5 (1899–1900): 525–26.

76   "The titles in Kentucky w[ill] be Disputed for a Century": Quoted in Dunaway, "Speculators and Settler Capitalists."

76   "under the necessity of employing about £40 of your cash": JW to Shiell, "Letters of James Wilkinson."

76   "far from affluent": *Memoirs*, 2:109.

77   The many Danville conventions were made necessary by the impossibility of achieving any agreement between the large speculator settlers and the smaller landholders whose titles were less secure. The arguments could be as fierce as they were inscrutable.

77   "There is nothing which binds one country": GW to Richard Henry Lee, August 22, 1785, GWP.

77   "The People of Kentucky alone," "I pleased myself": JW to James Hutchinson, "Letters of James Wilkinson."

78   "They shall be Informed": JW to unknown correspondent, April 1786, quoted in Hay, *Admirable Trumpeter*, 77.

79   "throw them into the hands eventually of a foreign power": James Monroe to James Madison, quoted in Harry Ammon, *James Monroe: The Quest for National Identity* (Richmond: University of Virginia Press, 1990).

79   "this country will in a few years Revolt": Harry Innes to Patrick Henry, quoted in Linklater, *Fabric of America*, 98.

79   "an outrage . . . generally disavowed": JW to Francisco Cruzat, quoted in Whitaker, "James Wilkinson's First Descent to New Orleans in 1787."

CHAPTER 8: SPANISH TEMPTATION

From the moment that JW descended to New Orleans, his actions become the subject of at least three differently motivated accounts: JW's version in volume 2 of his *Memoirs*, designed to demonstrate his patriotism; Daniel Clark's *Proofs of the Corruption of General James Wilkinson and His Connexion to Aaron Burr*, composed, as the title suggests, to prove the opposite; and the relevant legajos in the *Papeles Procedentes de Cuba*, together with some other documents in the Archivo General de Indias, written in triplicate to show that JW's influence and information were being used to Spain's best advantage. Apart from those already cited, the later historians involved are William

Shepherd, an early pioneer in the Spanish archives, Isaac Joslin Cox, and Arthur P. Whitaker.

81   "a considerable annual supply of tobacco": *Memoirs*, 2:113.

82   "thence round the western shores of Lakes Erie and Huron": John Jay's account of negotiations with the Spanish envoy Count d'Arande in Paris in July 1782, quoted in *The Life of John Jay: With selections from his correspondence and miscellaneous papers by his son, William Jay* (1833: repr. 2000), Bridgewater, VA: American Foundation Publications, 2:472.

82   JW's first journey to New Orleans: Arthur P. Whitaker, "James Wilkinson's First Descent to New Orleans in 1787," *Hispanic American Historical Review* 8, no. 1 (February 1928).

83   Humboldt's estimate might have been too low; silver production in Mexico mint in 1783 is estimated to have been 23.1 million pesos in Stanley J. Stein and Barbara H. Stein, *Apogee of Empire: Spain and New Spain in the Age of Charles III* (Baltimore: Johns Hopkins University Press, 2003).

83   Navarro's dispatch dated September 25, 1780, No. 23, cited in Whitaker, "The Commerce of Louisiana and the Floridas at the End of the Eighteenth Century." See also Navarro to Marquis de la Sonora, minister for the treasury and the Indies: "The only way to check them [the Americans] is with a proportionate population, and it is not by imposing commercial restrictions that this population is to be acquired, but by granting a prudent expansion and freedom of trade." February 12, 1787, quoted in Gayarré, *History of Louisiana*.

84   Miró and Navarro to Antonio de Valdes y Bazan, September 25, 1787, *Papeles de Cuba,* legajo 3893A, cited in Shepherd, "Wilkinson and the Beginnings of the Spanish Conspiracy." This document, given the number 13 *reservado* (secret) among papers sent to Madrid by Miró and Navarro, gave rise to JW's *nom d'espionnage*. In another document from Navarro to the king, dated April 30, 1789, JW is referred to as "a person endowed with high talents, and in whom the aforesaid [western] settlements have placed their hope of future happiness; and he informed the governor and myself that it was the intention of all to put themselves under the protection or vassalage of his Catholic Majesty." Museo-Biblioteca de Ultramar, Madrid, *Papeles relativos á la Luisiana*, vol. 3, quoted Shepherd, "Wilkinson and the Beginnings." The reference to Kentucky being prepared to seek protection as "vassals" of the Spanish king was the major difference between the "First Memorial" as sent to Madrid and as referred to later by JW.

84   "He is a young man": Miró and Navarro, document No. 13.

84   "Negroes, live Stock, tobacco": JW's "First Memorial," document No. 13.

85   "First Memorial": Document No. 13.

86   Instruction to McIlvain: May 10, 1790, Harry Innes Papers, LoC.

86   "[Self]-interest regulates the passions of Nations": document No. 13.

87   "the prediction of our transatlantic foe!": Washington to James Madison, November 5, 1786, GWP.

88   "one of the most complex ciphers": Document No. 13.

88   "be rewarded generously": Ibid.

89   "I have look'd for my Wilkinson": quoted in Hay, "Letters of Mrs. Ann Biddle Wilkinson." See the same source for her circumstances in Kentucky.

90   "your business was so pressing": Washington to JW, February 20, 1788. As was his
     habit, JW had sent Washington a present of seeds and "Indian fabricks." The rise in
     prices following JW's visit is vouched for by Daniel Clark in testimony to the
     House of Representatives, January 11, 1808, *Annals of Congress* (AC).
90   "My much esteemed and honored friend": JW to Miró, quoted Gayarré, *History
     of Louisiana*, 242.
91   For the New Orleans fire, see Gayarré, *History of Louisiana*, 204.
91   "you cannot be at a loss to know": Dunn to Wilkinson, June 15, 1788, Wilkinson
     Papers, vol. 1, Chicago Historical Society.
91   JW's profits were presented by Daniel Clark in *Proofs of the Corruption of General
     James Wilkinson*, 55.
91   "It is exceedingly important": Miró to Valdes, August 28, 1788, quoted in
     Gayarré, *History of Louisiana*, 219.

CHAPTER 9: CASH AND CONSPIRACY

The spread of the Spanish Conspiracy was guessed at in 1824 by Humphrey Marshall
in his *History of Kentucky* and given considerable substance in 1867 by Charles
Gayarré's *History of Louisiana*, written with the assistance of some Spanish documents
discovered in Baton Rouge. But William Shepherd first found the documents in
Madrid and Seville originally sent by Miró that provided proof of the conspiracy's
existence.
93   "the mischief that might arise from vexing him": Miró to Valdes, June 15, 1788,
     legajo 3893A.
94   "The consequences of depending on a body": JW to Miró, February 12, 1789,
     legajo 3893A, quoted in Gayarré, *History of Louisiana*, 224–26.
94   "This affair progresses more rapidly": Miró to Valdes, November 3, 1788, ibid.
94   The seventh Danville convention was covered in detail by Marshall, whose uncle,
     Thomas, apparently took verbatim notes of the proceedings.
94   John Brown wrote to George Muter, July 10, 1788, about his talks with Gardo-
     qui, "I have been assured by him in the most explicit terms, that if Kentucky will
     declare her independence, and impower some proper person to negociate with him,
     that he has authority, and will engage to open the navigation of the Mississippi, for
     the exportation of their produce, on terms of mutual advantage." This was the let-
     ter published in the *Kentucké Gazette*, September 4, 1790. It became a central doc-
     ument in the abortive charges against JW and Brown for their parts in the Spanish
     Conspiracy in September 1806.
95   "He is a young man of respectable talents": JW to Miró, February 14, 1789,
     legajo 3893.
95   JW's account of the convention and his speech was contained in his February 14
     message.
96   "I am aware that it may be possible": Miró to Valdes, June 15, 1789, legajo
     3893A. This remarkable assessment is quoted at length in Gayarré, *History of
     Louisiana*, 212–13. Jon Kukla, *A Wilderness So Immense: The Louisiana Purchase and
     the Destiny of America* (New York: Knopf, 2003).

96 "to attract to our side the inhabitants of the Ohio and Mississippi": José, Count of Floridablanca, to Diego de Gardoqui, May 24, 1788, in Kukla, *A Wilderness So Immense.*

97 "unanimous in their vehement desire": John Sevier to Gardoqui, September 12, 1788, quoted by Gardoqui to Miró, legajo 104, cited in Whitaker, "Spanish Intrigue in the Old Southwest."

97 JW's story about Connolly, and St. Clair's letter deploring JW's involvement with the conspirators, were part of his February 14, 1789, message; also referred to in Jacobs, *Tarnished Warrior,* 77.

98 The *Speedwell* saga was referred to repeatedly in Clark's *Proofs,* notes 30, and by Miró to Madrid, legajo 2373.

99 "I still continue to hold you as the principal actor in our favor": Miró to JW, April 23, 1789, Gayarré, *History of Louisiana.*

99 Dunn's suicide: Jacobs, *Tarnished Warrior,* 87.

99 Ballinger's carriage of silver to pay the tobacco farmer was presented in Clark's *Proofs* as evidence of Spanish payment to JW for his services as a spy. His clumsy lie was easily exposed by an affidavit from Ballinger: "I arrived at Frankfort and delivered the money to General Wilkinson in the presence of many person who were expecting it. They were Lincoln county farmers and were much disappointed because the entire shipment of money had not been sent." Clark's lie thus strengthened JW's claims that all Spanish payments were for commercial transactions.

100 Second memorial quoted extensively in Clark's *Proofs,* appendix 105, and referred to in JW's *Memoirs* 2:113. Jacobs and Hay were both at pains to play down JW's assistance to Spain, but there was real value in his specific recommendation for a garrison of two hundred men and galleys with fifty rowers at New Madrid, and for organizing the militia on American lines by companies, battalions, and regiments "officered by the most respectable of their countrymen" so that military duty would be seen as patriotic and socially desirable.

101 "My anxiety about him is so great": Hay, "Letters of Mrs. Ann Biddle Wilkinson."

102 "a valuable tract of land of 10,000 acres": Ibid.

CHAPTER 10: ENSHACKLED BY DEBT

Details of JW's increasing indebtedness are to be found in the Harry Innes Papers and Daniel Clark's *Proofs* and demonstrate his failings in respectively real estate and commerce.

103 "On my arrival here": JW to Miró, January 26, 1790, legajo 2374, quoted in Gayarré, *History of Louisiana,* 278.

104 "The great falling off which I observe": Miró to Valdes, May 22, 1790, ibid.

104 "that Congress strongly suspects my connection with you": ibid.

104 "I much regret": Miró to JW, April 30, 1790, ibid.

105 "I am of opinion that said brigadier-general": Miró to Valdes, May 22, 1790, ibid.

105 "Let me conjure you to be rigid": JW to Miró, undated, legajo 2374.

106 For JW's partnership with Peyton Short, see Clark, *Proofs.* Clark wrote, "I am authorised without the fear of contradiction to state, that this gentleman felt for years the embarrassments caused by the connection," 38.

106 "appalled my Spirit": JW to Michael La Cassagne (also written "Lacassagne"), January 20, 1790, *First American West: The Ohio River Valley, 1750–1820*, LoC.

107 For the impact of General Harmar's defeat, see especially Kohn, *Eagle and Sword*, and Cress, "Reassessing American Military Requirements."

107 "The voice of all ranks called me": JW to Miró, February 14, 1791, legajo 2374, cited in Jacobs, *Tarnished Warrior*, 98.

107 "The consternation arising": Henry Knox to George Washington, September 22, 1791, GWP.

107 "During a residence of more than seven years in these woods": JW to Knox, August 26, 1791, GWP.

108 "in the name of the President of the United States": Knox to St. Clair, September 29, 1791, GWP, requiring him to pass on the message.

108 "to effect a violent seperation from the United States": Thomas Marshall to Washington, February 12, 1789, GWP.

108 "I was greatly alarmed": Washington to Marshall, March 27, 1789, GWP.

108 James O'Fallon's letter to Washington, September 30, 1790, GWP.

109 "To hold a post of such responsibility": Washington to Alexander Hamilton, June 25, 1799, GWP.

109 For the evolution and composition of the army after 1783, see especially Kohn, *Eagle and Sword*; Cress, *Citizens in Arms*; and Skelton, *An American Profession of Arms.*

111 "My views in entering the Military Line are 'Bread & Fame' ": JW to Peyton Short, December 28, 1791, quoted in Jacobs, *Tarnished Warrior*, 102.

CHAPTER 11: A GENERAL AGAIN

Information after JW rejoins the army divides into three types: they relate to his public duties as an officer, to his private ambitions to gain command, and to his activities in relation to New Orleans. Regarding the first, the sources already cited are invaluable; for the second, JW's letters to Congressman, later Senator, John Brown, and Harry Innes (the Innes Papers) are useful; for the third, the Spanish archives remain essential. JW's *Memoirs*, volume 2, throw an unreliable light on all three strands.

113 Of the many excellent and harrowing accounts of St. Clair's defeat, William Darke's firsthand version in his letter to Washington has an unequaled immediacy. William Darke to Washington, November 9, 1791, GWP.

114 "The [regular] Troops were instantly formed": Ibid.

114 "[The Indians] could skip out of reach": *The Military Journal of Major Ebenezer Denny* (Philadelphia: Historical Society of Pennsylvania, 1849).

114 "To suffer that army to be cut to pieces": Recounted by Tobias Lear to Dr. Benjamin Rush and retold by Richard Rush in *Washington in Domestic Life* (Philadelphia: Lippincott, 1857).

115 "my private interest": JW to Miró, December 4, 1791, legajo 2374.

115 "The depth of the snow": JW to Samuel Hodgdon, March 12, 1792.

116 Comments on candidates for commanding officer: "Memorandum on General Officers," Philadelphia, March 9, 1792, PGW.

117   Thomas Jefferson's notes: *Annals of Thomas Jefferson,* ed. Franklin Sawvel (New York: Round Table Press, 1904), 62.

117   "I regret much": Hay, "Letters of Mrs. Ann Biddle Wilkinson."

118   "Brigadier Wilkinson's attention": Washington to Knox, August 13, 1791, PGW.

119   "Political Conditions of the Province of Louisiana": Original in *Papeles de Cuba, Estados de Misisipi,* 313, quoted by James Alexander Robertson, *Louisiana under the Rule of Spain, France, and the United States, 1785–1807* (Cleveland: Clark, 1911), 1:280–83.

119   Carondelet's message confirming JW's pension of two thousand dollars a year: Carondelet to JW, February 1, 1792, legajo 2374.

120   "To save me in this": Peyton Short to JW, December 21, 1791, Innes Papers, vol. 23.

120   "I pray you, my friend": JW to Innes, February 29, 1792, ibid.

120   "uncontrolled power over my whole property": JW to Innes, April 10, 1792, ibid.

121   "The Vice of drunkenness": Knox to Washington, September 17, 1792, GWP, 248.

121   "Be pleased therefore, Madam": Major Armstrong to JW, June 1, 1792, quoted in Jacobs, *Tarnished Warrior,* 110.

122   The St. Tammany's Day celebration: Jacobs, *Tarnished Warrior,* 110.

122   "2000 select troops composed of Musketeers": JW to Carondelet, December 15, 1792, legajo 2374.

CHAPTER 12: DISCIPLINE AND DECEIT

For the creation of the Legion of the United States, the military sources are those cited earlier, but of particular relevance is Birtle, "The Origins of the Legion of the United States." For Wayne's side of the toxic battle with JW, Paul David Nelson's biography *Anthony Wayne, Soldier of the Early Republic* remains indispensable. The sources for JW's double life are those cited earlier.

124   "It is painful to consider": Knox to Washington, July 17, 1789, GWP.

126   Mad Anthony: The origin of Wayne's nickname reflected his character. See Nelson, *Anthony Wayne.*

126   For the composition of the army, see Skelton, "Social Roots of the American Military Profession."

128   "send as soon as possible a canoe to New Madrid": Carondelet to Gayoso, October 29, 1793, quoted in Hay, *Admirable Trumpeter,* 136.

128   "the projected attack against Louisiana": JW to Carondelet, November 23, 1793, ibid.

129   "Hell on earth": Quoted in Jacobs, *Tarnished Warrior,* 113.

130   *Journal of a Journey through the United States, 1795–6* (Morrisiana, N.Y., 1869).

130   "filled with ardent poison & Caitiff wretches": quoted in Nelson, *Anthony Wayne,* 241.

130   "I am persuaded your good sense": Knox to JW, May 17, 1793, WDP.

131   "I have often expressed to her and to Colonel Biddle": Knox to JW, ibid.

131   "the novelty of the thing": JW to Washington, November 1, 1792, PGW.

131   "There is no calculating on anything but insult": Quoted in Nelson, *Anthony Wayne,* 249.

132 "the old man really is mad": Ibid., 250.
132 "My General treats me with great civility": JW to Innes, October 3, 1793, Innes Papers, vol. 23.
132 "into the nature and degree of the Confusion of Stores": Knox to Wayne, December 28, 1793, WDP.
132 "Your remarks of the disproportionate punishments of death": Knox to JW, July 17, 1792, WDP.
132 "Mrs. W. ventures to hope your Excellency": JW to Wayne, December 20, 1793, quoted in Jacobs, *Tarnished Warrior*, 118.
133 "to retard, disjoint and defeat the mediated irruption": JW's accounts presented to Carondelet, September 22, 1796, legajo 2375.

CHAPTER 13: POISONED VICTORY

The sources here are also those of the previous chapter.
134 "two distinct Parties": Nelson, *Anthony Wayne*, 251.
134 "I am unsettled in my purpose": JW to Innes, March 12, 1794, Innes Papers, vol. 23.
134 "I owe so much to my own feelings": JW to John Brown, August 28, 1794, Innes Papers, vol. 23.
135 Article signed "Army Wretched": Nelson, *Anthony Wayne*, 255.
135 "During my stay I found him attending": Ibid.
138 The Battle of Fallen Timbers: JW's jaundiced account of the march and battle was conveyed in a long letter to John Brown written after the fighting, JW to Brown, August 28, 1794. See Quaife, "General James Wilkinson's Narrative of the Fallen Timbers Campaign," *Mississippi Valley Historical Review*, June 1929, 81–90.

CHAPTER 14: THE BATTLE FOR COMMAND

JW's relentless battle for command and his desperate need for money from New Orleans swamped all other considerations, leaving the correspondence with Henry Knox and Carondelet as the major sources of information for this period in his life.
140 Official report on the battle: Wayne to Knox, August 29, 1794, American State Papers, 3rd Cong., 2nd sess., Indian Affairs, vol. 1.
140 "Yet the specious name of Victory": JW to Brown, August 28, 1794, Innes Papers, vol. 23.
140 "The whole operation presents": November 10, 1794, JW to Innes, ibid.
141 "a liar, a drunkard": December 1794, JW to Innes, ibid.
141 "You must rest assured that your military reputation": December 4, marked "private"; followed by December 5, 1794, Henry Knox to JW, WDP.
141 For the military costs involved, see Kohn, *Eagle and Sword*.
142 "I always indulged the Brigadier": Wayne to Knox, January 25, 1795, quoted, with comments on Wayne's surprise at JW's animosity, in Nelson, *Anthony Wayne*, 276.

142 The Robert Newman affair was almost certainly contrived by Wayne to destroy JW's connections to the British in Canada, which he believed had led to the sabotage of the Legion's supplies. JW's outrage, after Nolan tracked down Newman and got an inkling of what had happened, crystallized his hatred of Wayne.

143 Wilkinson's claim for financial reward for defeating Clark: JW to Carondelet, April 30, 1794, Archivo Histórico Nacional, Madrid, estado legajo 3898.

143 "Do not believe me avaricious": JW to Carondelet, undated, *Papeles de Cuba*, legajo 2374.

144 The story of Owens, the silver dollars, and the arrest of his murderers was extensively covered in Clark's *Proofs*, 17–19, and in the attached affidavit of Thomas Power, *Proofs*, 115.

147 The political campaign and Sedam's remark "by many Genl. Wayne has been Sensured": Nelson, *Anthony Wayne*, 277.

CHAPTER 15: DEATH OF A RIVAL

In addition to the military sources already cited, the diplomatic background is detailed in Kukla's *A Wilderness So Immense*, and JW's double triumph in securing command of the army and silver from Carondelet is also sourced in War Department documents and Spanish archives.

148 "vile assassin": Wayne to Knox, January 29, 1795, quoted in Jacobs, *Tarnished Warrior.*

149 JW's replies to Knox's private and public letters: JW to Knox, January 1 and January 2, 1795, WDP.

149 Of Timothy Pickering, David McCullough wrote in *John Adams* (Simon & Schuster, 2001), "In many ways, Pickering might have served as the model New Englander for those who disliked the type. Tall, lean, and severe looking with a lantern jaw and hard blue eyes, he was Salem-born and bred, a Harvard graduate, proud, opinionated, self-righteous, and utterly humorless," 472.

150 "If my very damned and unparalleled crosses": JW to John Adair, August 7, 1795, Clark, *Proofs*, notes 32. Polishing his frank, open guise, JW described himself as "a man of Mercury, whose heart and tongue are in unison."

150 For the background to the San Lorenzo treaty, see Kukla, *A Wilderness So Immense.*

151 In April 1790, JW specifically advised Miró to add a garrison of two hundred to the fort at New Madrid, and fifty oarsmen for the galleys. To the total of his treacherous assistance should be added his betrayal of a reconnaissance party under Major Doughty exploring a route from Kentucky to New Orleans in 1790. After JW warned Miró of their movements and suggested an armed response, Miró sent Creek warriors to attack them, and several in the party were killed. Cox, in "Louisiana-Texas Frontier III," suggests JW also briefed the Spanish on the proper border to defend during the 1805 negotiations with Monroe and Pinckney.

151 Harry Innes's correspondence with Gayoso, and his involvement in the Spanish Conspiracy, are covered in detail in Whitaker, "Harry Innes and the Spanish Intrigue: 1794–1795."

152   Joseph de Pontalba's memorandum and career in New Orleans, where he lived for eighteen years, are described in Gayarré, *History of Louisiana*. But his subsequent imprisonment and emotional torture of his wealthy daughter-in-law, ending in her murder and his suicide, is an operatic tragedy that falls outside Gayarré's canvas.

152   "And G.W. can aspire to the same dignity": Carondelet to JW, July 16, 1795, legajo 2374.

152   Clark's *Proofs* and Power's affidavit are the primary sources for Carondelet and Gayoso's contacts with JW, but JW provides his own defensive gloss in *Memoirs*, volume 2, repeatedly between pages 37 and 219.

154   "This accomplished, you will most probably have me for a neighbour": JW to Innes, September 4, 1796, Harry Innes Papers, vol. 23.

154   "determination to inculcate": JW's general order, December 13, 1795.

155   Power's second visit to JW was again the subject of Clark's *Proofs* and his own testimony and was again rebutted by JW's *Memoirs*, vol. 2.

156   The military consequences of the three treaties, Jay, Greeneville, and San Lorenzo, are detailed in Kohn, *Eagle and Sword*, 183, and Cress, *Citizens in Arms*, 133.

157   "to get rid of Genl Wayne": Quoted in Nelson, *Anthony Wayne*, 291.

157   The drama of smuggling $9,640 past Fort Massac to JW's bank account was described by Thomas Power in note 36 in Clark, *Proofs*.

159   "My views at Philadelphia": JW to Carondelet, September 22, 1796, legajo 2375.

159   JW's encounter with Andrew Ellicott was described in *The Journal of Andrew Ellicott*.

160   "I am proud of my little Sons": Hay, "Letters of Mrs. Ann Biddle Wilkinson."

160   "The fact is my presence with the army": Wayne to James McHenry, July 28, 1796, quoted in Nelson, *Anthony Wayne*, 296.

161   "It is generally agreed that some cavalry": Washington to the House of Representatives, February 28, 1797, PGW.

CHAPTER 16: THE NEW COMMANDER IN CHIEF

Despite its mendacity, JW's *Memoirs* becomes the crucial text during the brief period when his public life as commanding general came close to coinciding with his private interests.

164   "You will endeavour to discover, with your natural penetration": Carondelet to Power, May 26, 1797, Clark, *Proofs*, note 38.

164   "General Wilkinson received me very coolly": Power to Carondelet and Gayoso, undated, Clark, *Proofs*, note 43.

166   James McHenry's directive to General James Wilkinson: McHenry to JW, March 12, 1797, WDP.

166   "There is strict discipline observed": Power to Carondelet and Gayoso, Clark, *Proofs*, note 43.

166   "In fact the American peasant": Murray, *Travels in North America, 1834, 1835 & 1836* (New York: Harper, 1839), 2: 67–68, quoted in Prucha, "The United States Army as Viewed by British Travelers, 1825–1860."

167   The challenge of peacetime soldiering in the period is detailed in Ricardo A. Herrera, "Self-Governance and the American Citizen as Soldier, 1775–1861."

168   The fort "presents a frightful picture to the scientific soldier": JW to Captain James Bruff, June 1797, quoted in Hay, *Admirable Trumpeter,* 163.

168   For JW's disciplinary methods, see general orders issued from Fort Washington, May 22, 1797, and from Detroit, July 4, 20, and November 3, 10, 1797, cited in Hay, *Admirable Trumpeter,* 148.

169   Carondelet "ought not to be apprehensive": Power to Carondelet and Gayoso, Clark, *Proofs,* note 43.

169   For Gayoso's delaying tactics, see Ellicott, *Journal of Andrew Ellicott,* and Linklater, *Fabric of America.*

170   "that there is too much ground to think": Pickering to Winthrop Sargent, August 1797, quoted in Hay, *Admirable Trumpeter,* 171.

170   "was strongly attached to the interest and welfare of our country": Ellicott, *Journal of Andrew Ellicott.*

170   "a child of my own raising": JW to Gayoso, February 6, 1797, Clark, *Proofs,* 42.

171   "You have a warm place in my affections": JW to Ellicott, September 13, 1797, quoted in Ellicott, *Journal of Andrew Ellicott.*

171   "the chain of dependence": JW to McHenry, August 1797. The argument continued through the end of the year, when McHenry proposed new regulations for the army. JW replied January 8, 1798, that they would result in "the destruction of subordination and Discipline." McHenry then backed off, letting it be known that they were proposals only. WDP.

172   Ellicott's dispatch to Pickering: Ellicott to Pickering, November 14, 1797, quoted in Catherine van C. Mathews, *Andrew Ellicott: His Life and Letters* (New York: Grafton Press, 1908), 161–63.

172   The Little Turtle saga, "Could I be made instrumental": JW to John Adams, December 26, 1797, quoted in James Wilkinson (grandson), "Paper Prepared and Read," and John Adams's reply, Adams to JW, February 4, 1798, *The Works of John Adams,* ed. Charles Francis Adams (Boston: Little, Brown, 1856).

173   "I most sincerely wish an inquiry": Wilkinson, "Paper Prepared and Read."

173   "I esteem your talents": Adams, *Works.*

174   "How is the subordination of the military to the civil power to be supported?": "Review of the Propositions of Mr. Hillhouse," 1808, ibid., vol 5.

174   "that provisions will always be made at Headquarters": JW to Samuel Hodgdon, July 7, 1797, WDP.

175   "My Ann unusually hearty": JW to Owen Biddle, December 24, 1797, quoted in Hay, *Admirable Trumpeter,* 169.

175   Ellicott report on Captain Guion's behavior: Ellicott to Pickering, February 10, 1798, Ellicott Papers, LoC.

175   "Observed everywhere, I dare not communicate": JW to Gayoso, March 5, 1798, legajo 2374.

CHAPTER 17: ELLICOTT'S DISCOVERY

My admiration and affection for Andrew Ellicott led me to include a study of him in *The Fabric of America*, and together with his *Journal* and the Andrew Ellicott Papers in the Library of Congress, this provides much of the background to this chapter.

177   "My Love,—I have at length worried the Spaniards out": Ellicott to Sarah Ellicott, quoted in Mathews, *Andrew Ellicott*, 128.

177   JW's visit to Ellicott's camp followed by Clark's to Loftus Heights were explored in Clark, *Proofs*, 62, 64, 79–80, and in *Memoirs*, 2:37, 133, 183.

178   "My friend, you are warranted": Quoted in Linklater, *Fabric of America*.

180   Ellicott's report: Ellicott to Pickering, November 8, 1798, quoted in *Memoirs*, 2:171. The original letter from Gayoso to Power was dated October 23, 1798.

180   "I have seen a letter of Mr. Power's": Ellicott to JW, December 16, 1798, quoted in *Memoirs*, 2:172.

180   "a beastly, criminal, and disgraceful intercourse": Testimony of Thomas Freeman, April 10, 1811, at the court-martial of JW.

CHAPTER 18: THE FEDERALIST FAVORITE

The short-lived expansion of the army in the wake of the XYZ affair receives detailed attention from military historians cited earlier; it forms part of Theodore Crackel's *Mr. Jefferson's Army* and is the particular focus of Murphy, "John Adams: The Politics of the Additional Army, 1798–1800."

182   "Four times from 1786 to 1792": Pontalba's memorandum, Gayarré, *History of Louisiana*, 410.

183   JW's mutually admiring relationship with Hamilton was reported in *Memoirs*, 1:442–51, and as JW admitted, the latter's friendly attitude "excited my admiration and gladdened my self love."

183   "I am aware that some doubts have been entertained of him": Hamilton to Washington, June 15, 1799; Washington to Hamilton, June 25, 1799, PGW.

184   "The anxiety of my wife at the idea of our separation": JW to Gayoso, May 14, 1799, legajo 2375.

184   "a few cranberries": JW to Gayoso, May 15, 1799, ibid.

184   "Would you take the trouble": JW to Gayoso, Arpil 20, 1799, ibid.

184   "I left Mrs. Wilkinson": JW to Ellicott, June 12, 1799, Ellicott Papers, LoC.

185   The ban on wearers of the "French cockade": Reported in *Centinel*, quoted in Crackel, *Mr. Jefferson's Army*.

185   "when a clever force has been collected": Hamilton to Sedgwick, February 2, 1799, *The Works of Alexander Hamilton*, federal ed., ed. Henry Cabot Lodge (New York: G. P. Putnam's Sons, 1904), vol. 10.

185   "whenever the Government appears in arms": Hamilton to McHenry, March 18, 1799, ibid.

186   "brave, enterprising, active and diligent": Hamilton to Adams, September 7, 1799, quoted in *Memoirs*, 2:157.

186   Washington's last strategic advice: Washington to Hamilton, September 15, 1799, PGW.

186   "I cannot more safely consign my own Interest": quoted in Hay, *Admirable Trumpeter*, 184.

CHAPTER 19: JEFFERSON'S GENERAL

The constitutional importance of JW's relationship with Jefferson makes the military studies of this period exceptionally useful, especially Crackel's distinguished *Mr. Jefferson's Army*, Skelton's counterbalancing *An American Profession of Arms*, and Jackson's "Jefferson, Meriwether Lewis, and the Reduction of the United States Army."

188   "Blooming still as Hebe": JW to Hamilton, March 24, 1800, Lodge, *Works of Alexander Hamilton*.

188   "I defy the most prized of mortal": JW to Hamilton, June 27, 1800, ibid.

189   "Through all parts of the Country": Adams to McHenry, May 8, 1800, Adams, *Works of John Adams*.

189   Absolutely no evidence suggests that JW was responsible for the War Department fire—except for the answer to the age-old question asked of any unsolved crime: Cui bono? Who benefited from the fire?

191   "It is understood on all sides": Thomas Cushing to JW, February 26, 1800, quoted in Crackel, *Mr. Jefferson's Army*.

191   "The Army is undergoing a chaste reformation": Jefferson to Nathanael Macon, May 14, 1801, ibid.

191   "possessing a knoledge": Jefferson to JW, February 23, 1800, PTJ.

192   Opinions differ about the effectiveness of Jefferson's policy of political cleansing (JW was ultimately the chief beneficiary), but no one could doubt the result he intended.

193   "What do you think of the surveyor-general's office": JW to Ellicott, March 1801, Ellicott Papers.

193   "I now find that I am inevitably ruined": Quoted in Linklater, *Fabric of America*.

193   Ellicott wrote Jefferson: Ellicott testified on January 30, 1808, that he had sent this letter to Jefferson in "the month of June 1801," Clark, *Proofs*, 148.

194   "I was determined not to [cut my hair]": Bissell to D. Bissell, July 9, 1802, quoted in Jacobs, *Beginning of the U.S. Army, 1783–1812*.

194   In the battle of Butler's queue, what must have most hurt Wilkinson's vanity was the ridicule directed at him in Washington Irving's satire Diedrich Knickerbocker's *History of New York*, published in 1809. Irving caricatured JW as the bombastic General Jacobus Van Poffenburgh, with "large, glassy blinking eyes which protruded like those of a lobster." The best line in the book went to Butler, who told his friends on his deathbed, "Bore a hole in the bottom of my coffin right under my head, and let my queue hang through it, that the d—d old rascal may see that, even when dead, I refuse to obey his order."

195   "placed under the protection of faithful officers": Elbridge Gerry to Jefferson, May 4, 1801, PTJ.

196   " 'To which of the political creeds do you adhere?' ": Quoted in Crackel, *Mr. Jefferson's Army.*

196   On October 7, 1802, the result of JW's boundary-making was a treaty with the Choctaws signed at Fort Confederation, containing the following clause: "The said Choctaw Nation, for, and in consideration of one dollar, to them in hand paid, by the said United States, the receipt whereof is hereby acknowledged, do hereby release to the said United States, and quit claim forever, to all that tract of land [in southern Alabama measuring about a million and a half acres]."

197   JW's application for the surveyor general's post was made on May 30, 1802.

197   "In the first case . . . my intimacy with the inhabitants": Quoted in Hay, *Admirable Trumpeter*, 195.

198   "If Mr Monroe succeeds all will be well": JW to Jacob Kingsbury, February 27, 1803, quoted in Crackel, *Mr. Jefferson's Army.*

198   "If anything professional is to be done": JW to Dearborn, ibid.

198   "I have extended my capacities for utility": JW to Hamilton, undated, quoted in Hay, *Admirable Trumpeter*, 199.

199   "to act towards him so as to convince": Hamilton to Adams, September 4, 1799, quoted in *Memoirs*, 2:157.

200   For the reception of JW and Claiborne in New Orleans, see Hay, *Admirable Trumpeter*, 204–6.

CHAPTER 20: AGENT 13 REBORN

The meticulous researches of Isaac J. Cox and Arthur P. Whitaker in the first half of the twentieth century underpin the narrative of JW's later connections with the Spanish.

202   "It was hardly possible": Pierre-Clement de Laussat, *Memoirs of My Life*, quoted in Hay, *Admirable Trumpeter*, 210.

203   The battle of the ballroom is taken from Hay, *Admirable Trumpeter*, 205–6.

204   "I apprehend no Danger": JW to Dearborn, January 6, 1804, American State Papers, Military Affairs, L.C.

204   Nolan's cinematic life is described in Cox, "Louisiana-Texas Frontier I."

206   JW's intricate maneuverings with Folch and Casa Calvo are the subject of Cox, "General Wilkinson and His Later Intrigues with the Spaniards."

207   The importance attached to "Reflections" is best gauged by the readiness of Casa Calvo to pay the massive sum of twelve thousand dollars in one installment. It clearly played a significant role in forming and reinforcing Spanish border policy.

209   "You have taken no notice of any of my letters": Dearborn to JW, February 1804, quoted in Crackel, *Mr. Jefferson's Army.*

209   "It is so important that Wilkenson's [sic] maneuvers": Jefferson to Dearborn, February 17, 1804, PTJ.

209   Twenty-two-page strategy document: Sent to Dearborn, July 13, 1804.

211   Cox's three articles on the Louisiana-Texas frontier explore Spain's border strategy in detail.

212   On the day that he was to meet Humboldt, Monday, June 11, 1804, JW bombarded Jefferson with detailed queries to be put to Humboldt about routes leading

into Texas and Mexico. He signed himself "Jabeil Kingan," a pseudonym that was in some ways the equivalent of Agent 13, in that he seemed to use it mostly for communicating secret information about Mexico to Americans.

Wilkinson copied Humboldt's chart and passed it on to young Zebulon Pike when he set out on his expedition to the west in 1806. And Pike, knowing no better, later published it as an American map, provoking Humboldt to protest angrily to Jefferson at the use of information "which he undoubtedly obtained in Washington with the copy of my map . . . a quick glance at Mr. Pike's map may prove to you from where he got it." By then years had passed, and Jefferson brushed the matter aside, although he certainly knew how Pike came by his information.

CHAPTER 21: BURR'S AMBITION

The wealth of excellent studies of the Burr Conspiracy poses its own challenge. While juggling JW's, Burr's, and Clark's competing versions, all remarkable for their tendentious way with information, Roger Kennedy's *Burr, Hamilton, and Jefferson: A Study in Character*, and Gordon Wood's "The Real Treason of Aaron Burr," have been useful correctives. But I still incline to Henry Adams's view in *History of the United States of America* that Creole unrest was, next to the loyalty of the army's commander, the critical ingredient.

215   "To save time of which I need much and have little": JW to Burr, May 23, 1804, quoted in Jacobs, *Tarnished Warrior*, 191.

216   "never known, in any country, the prejudice in favor of birth, parentage, and descent": Quoted in Wood, "Real Treason."

216   "Mr. Burr's career is generally looked upon as finished": Quoted in Adams, *History of the United States.*

217   "his conduct very soon inspired me with distrust": Jefferson, "Conversations with Aaron Burr," 1804, PTJ.

217   "He is sanguine enough to hope every thing": Hamilton to Gouverneur Morris, December 24, 1800, WAH.

218   "to effect a separation of the Western Part of the United States": Anthony Merry, quoted in Adams, *History of the United States.*

218   "You have appointed General Wilkinson": Joseph Daveiss to Jefferson, January 10, 1806, PTJ.

219   "one of the most agreeable, best informed, most genteel, moderate": Gideon Granger to William Easton, March 16, 1805.

219   "Of the General I have no very exalted opinion":Albert Gallatin to Jefferson, February 12, 1806, *Writings of Albert Gallatin*, ed. Henry Adams Philadelphia: Lippincott, 1879. Gallatin's comments were evidently in response to Jefferson's query about his loyalty. In his next sentence Gallatin refers specifically to Ellicott's warning, demonstrating that Jefferson had not only received his message, but remembered its contents.

219   "in the meantime I can only say the country is a healthy one": JW to Charles Biddle, March 18, 1805, quoted in Jacobs, *Tarnished Warrior.*

220   "The Kentuckians are full of enterprise": John Adair to JW, December 10, 1804, ibid.

220   "We must have a *peep* at the unknown world": JW to Adair, May 28, 1805, Clark, *Proofs*, 120.

220   "he talked as if the business was indispensable": Lyon's deposition to Ezekiel Bacon, congressional committee of inquiry.

220   "two or three frigates": Adams, *History of the United States*.

222   Morally, the battle of the queues had been won in 1804 when Jefferson himself cropped his pigtail. It went with a general tidying up of the president's style. "He has improved much in the article of dress," wrote Senator Plumer in December 1804; "he has laid aside the old slippers, red waistcoat, and soiled corduroy small-clothes, and was dressed all in black, with clean linen and powdered hair."

CHAPTER 22: BETRAYER BETRAYED

The sources for this chapter are those cited earlier.

225   "the gentle Aurora with lighted taper": The quote and the reception scene come from Hay, *Admirable Trumpeter*, 222.

226   "There has been Leaves cut out of the Books": Quoted in Linklater, *Measuring America*, 274.

227   "From a rank Federalist to a suspected Republican": Edward Hempstead, quoted in Jacobs, *Tarnished Warrior*, 207.

228   "Not a single fact has appeared": Jefferson to Samuel Smith, May 5, 1806, PTJ.

228   "an elegant barge, [with] sails, colors, ten oars": Aaron Burr to Theodosia Alston, *Memoirs of Aaron Burr*.

228   "whose worth you know well how to estimate": JW to Clark, June 9, 1805, Clark, *Proofs*, 119.

229   "many absurd and evil reports circulated here": Clark to JW, September 7, 1805, Wilkinson, *Burr's Conspiracy exposed*, 82.

229   "particularly of the garrison-towns between Vera Cruz and Mexico [City]": John Graham's deposition to the court of inquiry, January 1806.

229   "I have encouraged, and will continue to encourage": October 10, 1804, *Burr's Conspiracy exposed*, 81.

229   "He has often said that the Union could not last": Claiborne quoted in Gayarré, *History of Louisiana*, ch. 4.

230   "because I do not acknowledge his superiority," JW to Samuel Smith, November 14, 1806, quoted in Jacobs, *Tarnished Warrior*, 207.

230   "My friend, no person was ever more mistaken!" and subsequent quotes: *Memoirs*, 2:304.

231   "a Corps of 100 Artillerists, 400 Cavalry": JW to Dearborn, September 8, 1805, American State Papers, Military Affairs, L.C.

232   "Burr is about something": *Burr's Conspiracy exposed*, 13.

232   "You observe to me": Adair to JW, January 27, 1806, *Burr's conspiracy exposed*, 19.

233   "Nothing has been heard from the Brigadier since October": Burr to JW, April 16, 1806, *Memoirs*, vol. 2, appendix 86.

235   "Aliens and Suspicious Characters mingling with the Natives": JW to Jefferson, December 23, 1805, PTJ.

236 "You will therefore with as little delay as possible repair to the Territory of New Orleans": Dearborn to JW, May 6, 1806, American State Papers, Military Affairs, L.C.

237 "Bruff, Lucas &c say it is done to get me out": JW to Samuel Smith, June 17, 1806, ibid.

CHAPTER 23: THE GENERAL AT BAY

The sources for the Burr Conspiracy are those cited earlier.

238 "General Wilkinson being expressly declared": Quoted in Crackel, *Mr. Jefferson's Army*.

239 "Genrl Wilkinson had not left St Louis on 28th July": Dearborn to Jefferson, September 2, 1806, PTJ.

240 The abortive approach to the naval captains: See Crackel, *Mr. Jefferson's Army*.

241 "It is now well ascertained that you are to be displaced in the next session": Dayton to JW, July 24, 1806, *Burr's Conspiracy exposed*, 16.

242 "[Even] if I had no regard for my own health and constitution": Journal entry, October 16, 1805, Zebulon M. Pike, *An Account of Expeditions to the Sources of the Mississippi and Through the Western Parts of Louisiana* . . . (Philadelphia: C. & A. Conrad, 1810).

242 "Any number of men who may reasonably be calculated on": October 2, 1806, Pike to JW, quoted in Hollon, "Zebulon Montgomery Pike and the Wilkinson-Burr Conspiracy." For evidence that papers taken from Pike suggested that he expected to be taken by the Spanish, Bolton, "Papers of Zebulon M. Pike."

243 "It must appear strange to you, friend Briggs": Deposition of Isaac Briggs, *Memoirs*, vol. 2, Appendix 53.

244 "The time looked for by many": JW to Adair, September 27, 1806.

245 Swartwout's arrival and transfer of the letter was described by both JW and in Cushing's deposition at Burr's trial. T. Carpenter, *Trial of Colonel Aaron Burr*, 236, 355.

245 Burr's letter was, according to the modern editor of his papers, Mary-Jo Kline, probably written by Dayton. However, for all practical purposes it was Burr's, and he did not demur when Chief Justice Marshall explicitly referred to it as Burr's letter.

CHAPTER 24: HIS COUNTRY'S SAVIOR

The sources are those cited earlier for the Burr Conspiracy.

247 The events were described by Cushing and JW at Burr's trial. T. Carpenter, *Trial of Colonel Aaron Burr*.

248 "If I had faultered [sic]": *Memoirs*, 2:326.

249 "The agency of the Army": John Randolph, February 1808, quoted in Crackel, *Mr. Jefferson's Army*.

249 Deposition of Eaton: *Louisiana Gazette*, March 8, 1807, quoted by Wilkinson, "Paper Prepared and Read."

250 "I have never, in my whole life": JW to Jefferson, October 21, 1806, *Memoirs*, vol. 2, appendix 95.

251   "I had not formed a decided opinion": *Memoirs*, 2:327.
251   Donaldson's letter: Ibid., appendix 98.
253   "a deep, dark and wide-spread conspiracy": JW to Jefferson, November 12, 1806, ibid., appendix 100.
253   "I have made up my mind to perish": JW to Freeman, November 12, 1806, ibid., appendix 101.
253   "you are surrounded by disaffection": JW to Claiborne, November 12, 1806, ibid., 2:328.
253   "Integrity of the Union is menaced": JW to Samuel Smith, November 12, 1806, quoted in Hay, *Admirable Trumpeter*, 259. This letter ends with a wild swipe at one of his St. Louis enemies, Judge Return J. Meigs, "a poor, pimping, hypocritical Yankee."
253   "spring like Leonidas": JW to José de Iturrigaray, November 12, 1806, ibid.
254   "I confess I approached him with caution": Deposition of Isaac Briggs, *Memoirs*, vol. 2, appendix 53.

CHAPTER 25: THE GENERAL REDEEMED

The sources are those cited earlier for the Burr Conspiracy. Much of the detail of JW's "reign of terror" in New Orleans comes from Charles Gayarré's *History of Louisiana*.
256   "Two days after the receipt of General Wilkinson's information": Jefferson's message to Congress, January 27, 1807, PTJ.
257   "Under circumstances so imperious": Quoted in Gayarré, *History of Louisiana*, 163.
257   "Burr may come": Mead to Claiborne, December 24, 1806, ibid., 169.
258   JW and Claiborne's exchanges: Ibid., ch. 3.
259   "This was acknowledging the fact": Ibid., 173.
261   "dispose of the troops in such manner": Dearborn to JW, November 27, 1806, American State Papers.
261   "After a most arduous journey": Briggs testimony, *Memoirs*, vol. 2, appendix 53.
262   "in a nation tender as to anything infringing liberty": Jefferson to JW, February 3, 1807, ibid., appendix 30.
262   "A strict observance of the written laws": Jefferson to John Colvin, September 20, 1810, PTJ.
263   "I have never attempted to justify": JW to Clark, May 24, 1807, Clark, *Proofs*, 153.

CHAPTER 26: TWO TRAITORS ON TRIAL

Among the Burr Conspiracy sources cited earlier, Daniel Clark's *Proofs* and Carpenter's shorthand version of Burr's trial in September were particularly useful for this chapter.
264   JW's approach to Folch, and the latter's testimony in his support, are detailed in Folch, "An Interview of Governor Folch with General Wilkinson."
265   "to forget any personal animosity towards the Governor": Clark, *Proofs*, note 65.

265 The exchange of veiled menaces between JW and Clark are the subject of notes 70 to 76 in Clark, *Proofs*.

266 "As to any projects or plans": Testimony of George Poindexter, Carpenter, *Trial of Colonel Aaron Burr*, 273.

266 "Our ground of defence is": Ibid., 390.

266 "Why, something would have been done": Adair quoted in *Burr's Conspiracy exposed*, 25.

267 "he would lash General Wilkinson into tortures": Quoted in Carpenter, *Trial of Colonel Aaron Burr*, 356.

268 "The president has undertaken to prejudge": Martin to Marshall at the grand jury hearing, quoted in Adams, *History of the United States*.

268 "treason against the United States": Chief Justice John Marshall, Ex Parte Bollman and Ex Parte Swartwout, 8 U.S. 4 Cranch 75 (1807).

268 "Wilkinson strutted into court": Washington Irving, quoted in Hay, *Admirable Trumpeter*, 274.

269 "I was introduced to a position within the bar": JW to Jefferson, ibid., 276.

269 "He is a very slight man but of the common stature": William Plumer, letter to his son, February 22, 1803, quoted in Albert Beveridge, *The Life of John Marshall* (Boston: Houghton Mifflin, 1965), 83.

270 "Your enemies have filled the public ear": Jefferson to JW, *Memoirs*, vol. 2, appendix 30.

270 Proceedings of the September trial are taken from Carpenter, *Trial of Colonel Aaron Burr.*

272 "he must hang Mr. Burr": Ibid., 390.

272 "He exhibited the manner of a sergeant": Blennerhassett, quoted in Hay, *Admirable Trumpeter*, 275.

CHAPTER 27: THE WAR WITH RANDOLPH

Randolph's hostility enmeshed JW in a series of inquiries. Because JW's biographical works, *A Plain Tale, Memoirs,* and *Burr's Conspiracy exposed*, are composed of the arguments that he deployed in rebuttal, they are central to this and the following chapters.

276 "I can distinctly trace the source of my persecutions": *Memoirs*, vols. 2, 3.

276 "I recognize no right to hold me accountable": Jacobs, *Tarnished Warrior*, 218.

276 "I denounce John Randolph": Quoted in Crackel, *Mr. Jefferson's Army.*

277 The story of the Annapolis party: *Memoirs* 2:7.

277 "I [was] a secret agent of the Spanish government": January 7, 1808, *Annals of Congress*, 10th Cong., 1st sess.

279 Jefferson's assertion that Clark's evidence "is the first direct testimony ever made known to me" was contradicted not just by Ellicott, but by the contents of Gallatin's note in 1806.

279 "the present administration has been minutely informed": Ellicott to Clark, January 10, 1808, Clark, *Proofs.*

280 "If I could believe that there was the least danger to the liberties": Taylor, February 1808, quoted in Crackel, *Mr. Jefferson's Army.*

281 "The armed resistance to the embargo laws on the Canada line": Jefferson to JW, August 13, 1808, PTJ.

282 "it multiplies our wants, depresses our tastes": JW to Jefferson, October 6, 1808, PTJ. For Jefferson's decision to send JW to Cuba, see Cox, "The Pan-American Policy of Jefferson and Wilkinson."

282 "Many of the appointments were positively bad": Winfield Scott, *Memoirs of Lieutenant-General Scott*, quoted in Crackel, *Mr. Jefferson's Army*.

283 "as large a proportion of our regular troops at New Orleans": Dearborn to JW, December 2, 1808.

283 "His Majesty had some relations [with] No. 13": quoted in Szaszdi, "Governor Folch and the Burr Conspiracy."

284 "Sweet was the song sung on Monday evening": *Pensioner's Mirror* (New Orleans), April 20, 1809, quoted in Jacobs, *Tarnished Warrior*.

285 The melancholy narrative of Terre aux Boeufs is based largely on the "Report of the Committee appointed to inquire into the great Mortality in the Troops at New Orleans," *Annals of Congress*, April 1810, and JW's defense in *Memoirs*, vol. 2.

CHAPTER 28: MADISON'S ACCUSATIONS

The remorseless accumulation of documents by JW in his defense to an avalanche of accusations makes *Memoirs*, vol. 2, a prime source. Theodore Crackel's *Mr. Jefferson's Army* and William Skelton's *An American Profession of Arms* provide essential ballast. For the diplomatic and political lead-up to the war of 1812, see Stagg, *Mr. Madison's War.*

289 "I confess, the strength of my mind was shaken": *Memoirs* 2:22.

290 "Mr. Eustis received me with great cordiality": Ibid., 2:25.

292 "the untarnished companion of my thigh for forty years": Hay, *Admirable Trumpeter*, 306.

292 The story of the court-martial proceeding is primarily drawn from *Memoirs*, 2:3–577. The faked Nolan account that explained his Spanish payments appeared on page 119, as follows:

General Wilkinson in Account with Don E. M[iró].
Dr[awn].

1790 June 2,	
To Cash paid Philip Nolan—	$1800
1792 Aug. 4, To do. remitted by Lacassang—	4000
1794 July 29, To do. remitted by Owen—	6000
To do. paid insurance 12½ percent	750
To do. remitted by J. E. Collins	6350
1796 Jan. 4, To do. paid Philip Nolan per receipt	9000
To balance due J. W.	2095
	29,995

Cr[edit].

By net proceeds of 235 hogshead of Tobacco condemned in the year 1790 by Arietta, and passed in the year 1791 by Brion—	17874

By so much recovered for loss sustained on the cargo
of the boat Speedwell— 6121
By so much sent by H. Owen, insured— 6000
29,995
Balance due James Wilkinson $2095
New Orleans, January 4, 1796.
(Errors excepted) for Don E. M.
Gilbert Leonard.

This should be compared to the real account kept by his Spanish handlers: see Appendix 1.
295 "to vary or expunge any rank Epithet": Jacobs, *Tarnished Warrior*, 251.
296 "to take care of the interests of the North:" Samuel Perkins, *History of the Political and Military Events of the Late War between the United States and Great Britain.*
297 "I therefore feel anxious not only to add the Floridas to the South": Grundy, December 9, 1811, *Annals of Congress.*
298 "It has been hinted to me that I may be recalled": Hay, *Admirable Trumpeter*, 313.
299 The capture of Mobile: *Memoirs*, 3:339–41.
300 "Why should you remain in your land of *cypress*": John Armstrong to JW, March 12, 1813, ibid., 3:342.

CHAPTER 29: THE LAST BATTLE

JW's role in the Canadian campaign is reflected darkly through *Memoirs*, vol. 3, written around the defense he presented in his last trial. The military background comes primarily from Quimby, *The U.S. Army in the War of 1812: An Operational and Command Study*; Skelton, *An American Profession of Arms*; Stagg, *Mr. Madison's War*; and as always Henry Adams provided the broader view.
302 "a general officer does not expose his person": JW's comment represents the shift from the front-led collisions of eighteenth-century warfare, to the distantly generaled battles of maneuver that Napoléon bequeathed to the nineteenth century. It was unfortunate for JW, and the entire army, that Armstrong remained mired in the earlier era.
302 "struck at the very foundation of military character": *Memoirs*, 3:345.
305 "Two heads on the same shoulder": JW to Armstrong, August 24, 1813, American State Papers, Military Affairs.
306 "I have escaped my pallet and with a giddy head": September 16, 1813, ibid.
306 "General Wilkinson arrived this day in Sackett's Harbor": Armstrong's entry quoted in *Memoirs*, 3:69.
307 "in my feeble condition": Ibid., 3:71.
307 The story of the St. Lawrence campaign comes from Adams, *History of the United States*, 7:193–98; the testimony of General Lewis in *Memoirs*, 3:128–29; and JW's reports in American State Papers, Military Affairs, 1: 462–79.
308 JW's poor health was apparent in a flood of references: October 28 he was "very ill"; on November 2 "very feeble"; on November 30 "sick"; and on

December 7 "seriously indisposed." Colonel Joseph Swift thought that between the two commanders, "Wilkinson and Lewis had not a day of sound health." November 21, 1813, Swift, *Memoirs*, 122.

310   "The mortality spread so deep a gloom over our camps": *Memoirs*, vol. 3, appendix 9.

310   "on which a box is placed to receive my bed": Hay, *Admirable Trumpeter*, 323.

310   "He threatens to make a dash soon": Daniel Tompkins to Armstrong, ibid., 324.

310   "blasted all my hopes": *Memoirs*, vol. 3, appendix 53.

310   La Colle Mill skirmish: Ibid., 3:102.

CHAPTER 30: THE CHANGING OF THE GUARD

The proceedings of JW's court-martial form the core of *Memoirs*, vol. 3. The final stages of his life are covered by his letters, the autobiographical torrent finally running dry with the publication of *Memoirs*, vol. 2, in 1816. Academic sources are Thomas R. Hay, "Some Reflections on the Career of General James Wilkinson," and for his last days in Mexico, Bolton, "General James Wilkinson as Advisor to Emperor Iturbide."

313   JW's successful protest against his court-martial: *Memoirs*, 3:492–93.

313   JW's family loss left Celestine distraught: Jacobs, *Tarnished Warrior*, 282. JW was seemingly a caring father; shortly before James Biddle left with Pike's expedition in 1806, JW wrote anxiously to the hard-driving Pike, "My Son has the foundation of a good Constitution but it must be tempered by degrees, do not push Him beyond his capacities in hardships too suddenly. He will I hope attempt any thing but let the stuff be hardened by degrees."

314   Henry Adams's scathing account of the burning of Washington ends with a bitter jab: "Before midnight the flames of three great conflagrations made the whole country light, and from the distant hills of Maryland and Virginia the flying President and Cabinet caught glimpses of the ruin their incompetence had caused."

314   JW's account of the opening of the court-martial, and his success in disposing of Van Buren, *Memoirs*, 3:4–22.

315   "a vice my soul detests": Supported by the testimony of several witnesses, ibid., 3:104, 144–45, 163, 211.

315   "He is hereby honourably acquitted": Ibid., 3:496.

315   "the first victory gained over the enemy on a plain": Quoted in Kimball, "The Battle of Chippawa: Infantry Tactics in the War of 1812."

316   "The British were beaten. It was evident": Fortescue, *History of the British Army*, 10:109–10.

316   "that so great a difference existed between regular troops and a militia force": Madison quoted in Carl Benn, *The War of 1812* (New York: Osprey Publishing, 2002), 20.

317   "The Die is Cast," Cushing wrote when he heard of his forcible retirement, "unless it should please the President of the United States to reward me for long and faithful services by a civil office, I shall be left on the verge of sixty years of age, after devoting almost forty years to the military service of my country, with no

other prospect before me but that of spending the remnant of my days in poverty and wretchedness." Quoted in Skelton, "Social Roots of the American Military Profession."

317   "General Wilkinson has broken through all decorum": Dallas to Madison, August 3, 1815, Dallas, *Life of Dallas*, 436.

320   "As to Long Tom—meaning you": JW to Jefferson, January 21, 1811, PTJ.

320   "that I should descend to so unmeaning an act of treason": Jefferson to Monroe, January 11 or 12, 1812, PTJ.

321   The story of Chisholm's unexpected encounter with Jefferson and JW appears in Isaac Joslin Cox, "The Louisiana-Texas Frontier I." Cox's authority lends weight to his conclusion: "We are led to believe that Jefferson's interest in Nolan extended farther than to the latter's description of the wild horses of Texas."

321   "I have ever and carefully restrained myself": Jefferson to Monroe, January 11 or 12, 1812, PTJ.

322   "Suppose I get you a plantation adjoining me": JW to van Rensselaer, December 29, 1815, Wilkinson Papers, N.Y. State Library.

322   "Blessed with my Celestine and two beloved little daughters": JW to M. R. Thompson, January 14, 1818, Darlington MSS, University of Pittsburgh. Thompson, a wealthy Baltimore merchant, was a new friend who brought out the best of JW's domestic side.

323   "new flushed, as elastic as [a] Billiard Ball": Ibid.

323   "You can not find any one of virtue & Intelligence": JW to van Rensselaer, January 16, 1821, Wilkinson Papers, N.Y. State Library.

325   "more the Lamb than the Lion, the Spinster than the Soldier" and "literally a Washington in all his great qualities": JW to Jefferson, March 21, 1824, PTJ.

325   "slothful, ready to vice, insensible to social affection": JW's memorial to Iturbide appears in Bolton, "General James Wilkinson as Advisor to Emperor Iturbide."

325   "divinely situated on the Coast of the Gulph": JW to Jonathan Williams, December 1822, quoted in Jacobs, *Tarnished Warior*, 308.

327   That JW was caught on the horns of a dilemma, unable to make his fortune and too proud to return penniless, was made clear in a letter to Thomas Aspinwall, U.S. consul in London. JW said he needed to make a fortune in order not to have to depend on "gifts and graces" from the "little Jesuit Madison or his Bi-faced friend Monroe." JW to Aspinwall, April 17, 1823, printed in *Bulletin N.Y. State Library* 3:362.

327   "I have just made a contract apparently": JW to Joseph Wilkinson, February 25, 1825, *Tarnished Warrior*, 311.

BIBLIOGRAPHY

NOTES ON SOURCES

There has never been a shortage of material on James Wilkinson. He hoarded letters and papers obsessively, and his notoriety in his own lifetime ensured that many people either corresponded directly with him or made reference to his activities. The only problem is to make sense of information, which was rarely biased toward the truth.

James Wilkinson's papers are widely distributed. The largest single collection, the James Wilkinson Papers, containing about 650 documents, is held by the Chicago Historical Society. Other notable sources are the Filson Historical Society of Louisville, Kentucky, covering the period 1784 to 1805, especially Wilkinson's land deals and separatist activity; the Pennsylvania Historical Society, for papers relating to the Biddle family and Wilkinson's political activities to 1807; the Mississippi Department of Archives and History, the Winthrop Sargent and William Claiborne Letters for the period 1795 to 1807; the Missouri Historical Society, covering Wilkinson's governorship and exploration; and the Library of Congress (LoC). In this last location are also to be found important collections relevant to Wilkinson's life: the Andrew Ellicott Papers relating to their connection, 1795 to 1807; Harry Innes Papers, particularly volumes 19, 22, and 23, containing Wilkinson's business correspondence, 1784 to 1805; Thomas Jefferson Papers (TJP), correspondence from 1800 to 1824; George Washington Papers (GWP), letters and references, 1776 to 1799; and the *Papeles Procedentes de Cuba* of the Archivo General de Indias, in particular photostats of legajos (bundles) numbers 2373, 2374, and 2375, containing most of Wilkinson's coded communications.

The Jefferson and Washington Papers are also available online at, respectively, http:// memory.loc.gov/ammem/collections/jefferson_papers/index.html., and http://rotunda .upress.virginia.edu:8080/founders/GEWN.html, as are other LoC sources: American State Papers; Journals of the Continental Congress (JCC); Letters of the Continental Congress; and the Annals of Congress—at http://memory.loc.gov/ammem/browse/ index.html. The Adams Family Papers (AFP) have been assembled online by the Massachusetts Historical Society, and the War Department Papers (WDP), once widely scattered, have been brought together at the Center for History and New Media, George Mason University, also available online.

Many of Wilkinson's official letters were also published in his different volumes of memoirs.

UNPUBLISHED PAPERS

Archivo General de Indias. *Papeles Procedentes de Cuba* (PPC), legajos 2373, 2374, and 2375. LoC. The library also has photostats of manuscripts from the Archivo Histórico Nacional, Madrid, containing references to Wilkinson.
Andrew Ellicott Papers. LoC.
Harry Innes Papers. LoC.
War Department Papers. Center for History and New Media. George Mason University. http://wardepartmentpapers.org/index.php.
James Wilkinson Papers. Chicago Historical Society.

CONTEMPORARY SOURCES

Adams, Charles F. *Memoirs of John Quincy Adams*. 12 vols. Vol 9. Philadelphia: 1874–77.
Adams Family Papers (AFP). Massachusetts Historical Society. (digital) www.masshist .org/digitaladams/aea.
American State Papers. LoC. (ASP)
    —Foreign Relations. Vol. 1, 1789–1819.
    —Indian Affairs. Vol. 1, 1789–1819.
    —Military Affairs. Vol. 1, 1789–1819.
Annals of Congress (AC)
Burke, Edmund. *Reflections on the Revolution in France*. 1790. Reprint, New York and London: Penguin Classics, 1986.
Burr, Aaron. *Memoirs of Aaron Burr with Miscellaneous Selections from His Correspondence*. Ed. Matthew West. New York: Harper & Bros., 1834.
———. *The Private Journal of Aaron Burr During His Residence of Four Years in Europe*. 2 vols. New York: Harper, 1838.
Carpenter, T. *The Trial of Colonel Aaron Burr on an Indictment of Treason*. Washington, DC: Westcott, 1808.
Clark, Daniel. *Proofs of the Corruption of General James Wilkinson and of His Connexion with Aaron Burr*. Philadelphia: Hall & Pierie, 1809.
Ellicott, Andrew. *The Journal of Andrew Ellicott, late Commissioner on behalf of the United States . . . for determining the boundary between the United States and the possessions of his Catholic Majesty in America . . . With six maps . . . To which is added an appendix containing all the astronomical observations made, etc.* Philadelphia, 1803.
Filson, John. *The Discovery, Settlement and Present State of Kentucké*. Wilmington, Adams, 1784.
Foster, Thomas, ed. *The Collected Works of Benjamin Hawkins, 1796–1810*. Tuscaloosa: University of Alabama Press, 2003.

Imlay, Gilbert. *A Topographical Description of the Western Territory of North America*. 3rd ed. London: J. Debrett, 1797. Reprint, New York: Augustus M. Kelley, 1969.

Kilty, John. *Land Holder's Assistant and Land Office Guide*. Baltimore: G. Dobbin & Murphy, 1808. MSA L 25529.

Jefferson, Thomas. *Notes on the State of Virginia*. 1785. Reprint, New York, Evanston, London: Harper Torchbook, 1964.

———. *The Papers of Thomas Jefferson*. Ed. Julian P. Boyd. Princeton, NJ: Princeton University Press, 1950–74. Online: American Memory, LoC (PTJ).

Journals of the Continental Congress, 1774–1789. Ed. Worthington C. Ford et al. Washington, DC, 1904–37 (JCC).

Letters of Brunswick and Hessian Officers during the American Revolution. Trans. William Stone. Albany, NY: Munsell's Son, 1891.

Letters of Delegates to Congress, 1774–1789. 25 vols. Ed. Paul H. Smith et al. Washington, DC: Library of Congress, 1976–2000 (LDC).

Lodge, Henry Cabot. *The Works of Alexander Hamilton*, vol. 10. Federal edition. New York: G.P. Putnam's Sons, 1904. (WAH)

Marshall, Humphrey. *The History of Kentucky, Exhibiting an Account of the Modern Discovery; Settlement; Progressive Improvement; Civil and Military Transactions; and the Present State of the Country*. 2 vols. Frankfort, KY: George S. Robinson, 1824.

Papers of the Continental Congress. American Memory, LoC (PCC).

Reed, Joseph. *The Life and Correspondence of Joseph Reed*. Philadelphia: Lindsay and Blakiston, 1847.

Washington, George. *The Papers of George Washington*. Digital ed. Ed. Theodore J. Crackel. Charlottesville: University of Virginia Press, Rotunda, 2007 (PGW).

———. *The Writings of George Washington*. Ed. Jared Sparks. Boston, 1834 (WGP).

Wilkinson, James. *Burr's Conspiracy exposed and General Wilkinson vindicated against the slanders of his enemies on that important occasion*. Washington, 1811.

———. *Memoirs of My Own Times*. 3 vols. and an atlas. Philadelphia: A. Small, 1816.

———. ("A Kentuckian," i.e., Wilkinson). *A Plain Tale, Supported by Authentic Documents, Justifying the Character of General Wilkinson*. Richmond, KY: The Inquirer, 1807.

JOURNAL ARTICLES

Baack, Ben. "Forging a Nation State: The Continental Congress and the Financing of the War of American Independence." *Economic History Review*, n.s., 54, no. 4 (November 2001).

Birtle, Andrew J. "The Origins of the Legion of the United States." *Journal of Military History* 67, no. 4 (October 2003).

Bolton, Herbert E. "General James Wilkinson as Advisor to Emperor Iturbide." *Hispanic American Historical Review* 1, no. 2 (May 1918).

———. "Papers of Zebulon M. Pike, 1806–1807." *American Historical Review* 13, no. 4 (July 1908).

Brooks, Philip C. "Spain's Farewell to Louisiana, 1803–1821." *Mississippi Valley Historical Review* 27, no. 1 (June 1940).

Cox, Isaac Joslin. "The American Intervention in West Florida." *American Historical Review* 17, no. 2 (January 1912).

———. "The Freeman Red River Expedition." *Proceedings of the American Philosophical Society* 92, no. 2 (May 5, 1948).

———. "General Wilkinson and His Later Intrigues with the Spaniards." *American Historical Review* 19 (1914).

———. "Hispanic-American Phases of the 'Burr Conspiracy.'" *Hispanic American Historical Review* 12, no. 2 (May 1932).

———. "The Louisiana-Texas Frontier I." *Southwestern Historical Quarterly* 10, no. 1 (July 1906).

———. "The Louisiana-Texas Frontier II." *Southwestern Historical Quarterly* 17, no. 1 (July 1913).

———. "The Louisiana-Texas Frontier III." *Southwestern Historical Quarterly* 017, no. 2. Online, p. 140.

———. "The Louisiana-Texas Frontier During the Burr Conspiracy." *Mississippi Valley Historical Review* 10, no. 3 (December 1923).

———. "The Pan-American Policy of Jefferson and Wilkinson." *Mississippi Valley Historical Review* 1, no. 2 (September 1914).

———. "Spanish Papers Relating to the Treachery of General James Wilkinson." *American Historical Review* 21 (1916).

Davis, Elvert. "By Invitation of Mrs. Wilkinson: An incident of life at Fort Fayette." *Western Pennsylvania Historical Magazine* 13 (July 1930): 145–81.

Earle, Robert G. "The Taverns of Colonial Philadelphia." *Transactions of the American Philosophical Society*, n.s., 43, no. 1 (1953).

Ekirch, Arthur A. "The Idea of a Citizen Army." *Military Affairs* 17, no. 1 (Spring 1953).

Folch, Vincent. "An Interview of Governor Folch with General Wilkinson." *American Historical Review* 10 (July 1905).

Hay, Thomas R. "Letters of Mrs. Ann Biddle Wilkinson from Kentucky, 1788–1789." *Pennsylvania Magazine of History and Biography* 56 (January 1932): 33–55.

———. "Some Reflections on the Career of General James Wilkinson." *Mississippi Valley Historical Review* 21 (March 1935): 471–94.

Herrera, Ricardo A. "Self-Governance and the American Citizen as Soldier, 1775–1861." *Journal of Military History* 65, no. 1 (January 2001).

Hollon, Eugene W. "Zebulon Montgomery Pike and the Wilkinson-Burr Conspiracy." *Proceedings of the American Philosophical Society* 91, no. 5 (December 3, 1947).

Horsmann, Reginald. "American Indian Policy in the Old Northwest, 1783–1812." *William and Mary Quarterly*, 3rd ser., 18 (January 1961): 35–53.

Ireland, Owen S. "The Ethnic-Religious Dimension of Pennsylvania Politics, 1778–1779." *William and Mary Quarterly*, 3rd ser., 30, no. 3 (July 1973).

Jackson, Donald. "Jefferson, Meriwether Lewis, and the Reduction of the United States Army." *Proceedings of the American Philosophical Society* 124, no. 2 (April 29, 1980).

Johnson, Leland R. "The Doyle Mission to Massac, 1794." *Journal of the Illinois State Historical Society* 73, no. 1 (Spring 1980).

Kimball, Jeffrey. "The Battle of Chippawa: Infantry Tactics in the War of 1812." *Military Affairs* 31, no. 4 (Winter 1967–68).

McDowell, George T. "General James Wilkinson in the Knickerbocker History of New York." *Modern Language Notes* 41, no. 6 (June 1926).

Murphy, William J., Jr. "John Adams: The Politics of the Additional Army, 1798–1800." *New England Quarterly* 52, no. 2 (June 1979).

Nelson, Paul David. "Citizen Soldiers or Regulars: The Views of American General Officers on the Military Establishment, 1775–1781." *Military Affairs* 43, no. 3 (October 1979).

———. "Legacy of Controversy: Gates, Schuyler, and Arnold at Saratoga, 1777." *Military Affairs* 37, no. 2 (April 1973).

Prucha, Francis Paul. "The United States Army as Viewed by British Travelers, 1825–1860." *Military Affairs* 17 (Autumn 1953).

Quaife, M. M. "General James Wilkinson's Narrative of the Fallen Timbers Campaign." *Mississippi Valley Historical Review* 16, no. 1 (June 1929).

Radbill, Kenneth A. "Quaker Patriots: The Leadership of Owen Biddle and John Lacey." *Pennsylvania History* 45, no. 1 (January 1978).

Reps, John. "New Madrid on the Mississippi." *Journal of the Society of Architectural Historians* 18, no. 1 (March 1959).

Royster, Charles. " 'The Nature of Treason': Revolutionary Virtue and American Reactions to Benedict Arnold." *William and Mary Quarterly*, 3rd ser., 36, no. 2 (April 1979).

Schaffel, Kenneth. "The American Board of War, 1776–1781." *Military Affairs* 50, no. 4 (October 1986).

Shepherd, William R. "Papers Bearing on James Wilkinson's Relations with Spain, 1787–1816." *American Historical Review* 9, no. 4 (July 1904).

———. "Wilkinson and the Beginnings of the Spanish Conspiracy." *American Historical Review* 9 (April 1904).

Skelton, William B. "The Confederation's Regulars: A Social Profile of Enlisted Service in America's First Standing Army." *William and Mary Quarterly*, 3rd ser., 46, no. 4 (October 1989).

———. "Social Roots of the American Military Profession: The Officer Corps of America's First Peacetime Army, 1784–1789." *Journal of Military History* 54, no. 4 (October 1990).

Smithers, Harriet. "English Abolitionism and the Annexation of Texas." *Southwestern Historical Quarterly* 32 (1929).

Stewart, Donald H. "The Press and Political Corruption During the Federalist Administrations." *Political Science Quarterly* 67, no. 3 (September 1952).

Szaszdi, Adam. "Governor Folch and the Burr Conspiracy." *Florida Historical Quarterly* 38, no. 3 (January 1960).

Tapson, Alfred J. "The Sutler and the Soldier." *Military Affairs* 21, no. 4 (Winter 1957).

Turner, Frederick J. "Documents on the Blount Conspiracy, 1795–1797." *American Historical Review* 10, no. 3 (April 1905).

Upham, George Baxter. "Burgoyne's Great Mistake." *New England Quarterly* 3, no. 4 (October 1930).

Wade, Arthur. "A Military Offspring of the American Philosophical Society." *Military Affairs* 38, no. 3 (October 1974).

Wheeler, Joseph Towne. "The Maryland Press, 1777–1790." Baltimore: Maryland Historical Society, 1938.

Whitaker, Arthur P. "Another Dispatch from the United States Consulate in New Orleans." *American Historical Review* 38, no. 2 (January 1933).

———. "The Commerce of Louisiana and the Floridas at the End of the Eighteenth Century." *Hispanic American Historical Review* 8, no. 2 (May 1928).

———. "Harry Innes and the Spanish Intrigue: 1794–1795." *Mississippi Valley Historical Review* 15, no. 2 (September 1928).

———. "James Wilkinson's First Descent to New Orleans in 1787." *Hispanic American Historical Review* 8, no. 1 (February 1928).

———. "Spanish Intrigue in the Old Southwest: An Episode, 1788–89." *Mississippi Valley Historical Review* 12, no. 2 (September 1925).

Wilkinson, James. "Letters of Gen. James Wilkinson Addressed to Dr. James Hutchinson, of Philadelphia." *Pennsylvania Magazine of History and Biography* 12 (1888): 55–64.

———. "A Paper Prepared and Read by His Great-Grandson James Wilkinson." *Louisiana Historical Quarterly* 1, no. 2 (1918).

Wood, Gordon S. "The Real Treason of Aaron Burr." *Proceedings of the American Philosophical Society* 143, no. 2 (June 1999).

Wright, Louis B., and Julia Macleod. "William Eaton's Relations with Aaron Burr." *Mississippi Valley Historical Review* 31, no. 4 (March 1945).

BOOKS

Abernethy, Thomas P. *Western Lands and the American Revolution.* New York: Appleton-Century, 1937.

Adams, Henry. *History of the United States of America under the Administrations of Thomas Jefferson and James Madison.* 9 vols. New York: Scribner, 1921.

Aron, Stephen. *How the West Was Lost: The Transformation of Kentucky from Daniel Boone to Henry Clay.* Baltimore and London: Johns Hopkins University Press, 1996.

Boyd, Thomas A. *Mad Anthony Wayne.* New York: Scribner, 1929.

Burnard, Trevor. *Creole Gentlemen: The Maryland Elite, 1691–1776.* New York and London: Routledge, 2002.

Clark, Thomas D., and John W. Guice. *Frontiers in Conflict: The Old Southwest, 1795–1830.* Albuquerque: University of New Mexico Press, 1989.

Crackel, Theodore J. *Mr. Jefferson's Army: Political and Societal Reform of the Military Establishment, 1801–9.* New York and London: New York University Press, 1987.

Cress, Lawrence Delbert. *Citizens in Arms: The Army and the Militia in American Society to the War of 1812.* Chapel Hill: University of North Carolina Press, 1982.

———. "Reassessing American Military Requirements, 1783–1807." In *Against All Enemies: Interpretations of American Military History from Colonial Times to the Present,* ed. Kenneth J. Hagan and William R. Roberts. Westport, CT: Greenwood Press, 1986.

Cronon, William, George Miles, and Jay Gitlin, eds. *Under an Open Sky: Rethinking America's Western Past.* New York: W. W. Norton, 1992.

Davis, W. H. *The History of Bucks County, Pennsylvania.* Philadelphia, 1905.

Dunaway, Wilma A. "Speculators and Settler Capitalists: Unthinking the Mythology about Appalachian Landholdings, 1790–1860." In *Appalachia in the Making: The Mountain South in the Nineteenth Century*, ed. Mary Beth Pudup, Dwight Billings, and Altina Waller. Chapel Hill: University of North Carolina Press, 1995.

Faragher, John M. *Sugar Creek: Life on the Illinois Prairie*. New Haven: Yale University Press, 1986.

Ferling, John. *Almost a Miracle*. New York: Oxford University Press, 2007.

————. *A Wilderness of Miseries: War and Warriors in Early America*. Westport, CT: Greenwood Press, 1980.

Ford, Paul L., ed. *The Works of Thomas Jefferson*. New York and London: G. P. Putnam's Sons, 1904–5.

Foster, Thomas, ed. *The Collected Works of Benjamin Hawkins, 1796–1810*. Tuscaloosa: University of Alabama Press, 2003.

Frothingham, Thomas G. *Washington: Commander-in-chief*. Boston: Houghton Mifflin, 1930.

Gayarré, Charles. *History of Louisiana*. New York: William J. Widdleton, 1867.

Guy and Sheridan, eds. *Contested Ground: Comparative Frontiers on the Northern and Southern Edges of the Spanish Empire*. Tucson: University of Arizona Press, 1998.

Halliday, E. M. *Understanding Thomas Jefferson*. New York: HarperCollins, 2001.

Hay, Thomas R., and M. R. Werner. *The Admirable Trumpeter: A Biography of General James Wilkinson*. Garden City, NY: Doubleday, Doran, 1941.

Holmes, Jack D. L. *Gayoso: The Life of a Spanish Governor in the Mississippi Valley, 1789–1799*. Baton Rouge: Louisiana State University Press, 1965.

Hudleston, F. J., *Gentleman Johnny Burgoyne: Misadventures of an English General in the Revolution*. Garden City, NY: Garden City Publishing, 1927.

Jacobs, James Ripley. *The Beginning of the U.S. Army, 1783–1812*. Princeton: Princeton University Press, 1947.

————. *Tarnished Warrior: Major-General James Wilkinson*. New York: Macmillan, 1938.

Kennedy, Roger G. *Burr, Hamilton, and Jefferson: A Study in Character*. Oxford: Oxford University Press, 2000.

Kohn, Richard H. *Eagle and Sword: The Federalists and the Creation of the Military Establishment in America, 1783–1802*. New York and London: Free Press, 1975.

Kukla, Jon. *A Wilderness So Immense: The Louisiana Purchase and the Destiny of America*. New York: Knopf, 2003.

Land, Aubrey C. *Colonial Maryland—A History*. Mishawaka, IN: Kraus International, 1981.

Linklater, Andro. *The Fabric of America: How Our Borders and Boundaries Shaped the Country and Forged Our National Identity*. New York: Walker Books, 2007.

————. *Measuring America: How an Untamed Wilderness Shaped the United States and Fulfilled the Promise of Democracy*. New York: Walker Books, 2002.

Mackesy, Piers. *The War for America: 1775–1783*. Lincoln: University of Nebraska Press, 1993.

Masteron, William Henry. *William Blount*. Baton Rouge: Louisiana State University Press, 1954.

Mathews, Catherine van C. *Andrew Ellicott: His Life and Letters*. New York: Grafton Press, 1908.

McCullough, David. *John Adams*. New York: Simon & Schuster, 2001.

Melish, John. *Travels in the United States 1806, 1807 & 1809*. 2 vols. Philadelphia, 1811.

Merrell, James. *Into the American Woods: Negotiators on the Pennsylvania Frontier*. New York: W. W. Norton, 1999.

Middleton, Arthur Pierce. *Tobacco Coast: A Maritime History of Chesapeake Bay in the Colonial Era*. Newport, VA: Mariners' Museum, 1953.

Nelson, Paul David. *Anthony Wayne, Soldier of the Early Republic*. Bloomington: Indiana University Press, 1985.

———. *General Horatio Gates: A Biography*. Baton Rouge: Louisiana State University Press, 1976.

Nobles, Gregory H. *American Frontiers: Cultural Encounters and Continental Conquest*. New York: Hill & Wang, 1997.

Prucha, Paul. *The Sword of the Republic: The US Army on the Frontier, 1783–1846*. New York: Macmillan, 1969.

Quimby, Robert S. *The U.S. Army in the War of 1812: An Operational and Command Study*. Lansing: Michigan State University Press, 1997.

Randall, Willard S. *Benedict Arnold, Patriot and Traitor*. New York: William Morrow, 1990.

Richards, Leonard L. *Shays's Rebellion: The American Revolution's Final Battle*. Philadelphia: University of Pennsylvania Press, 2002.

Robertson, David B. *The Constitution and America's Destiny*. St. Louis: University of Missouri, 2005.

Roosevelt, Theodore. *The Winning of the West*. 3 vols. New York: Putnam, 1894–96.

Rutman, Darrett B., ed. *The Old Dominion: Essays for Thomas Perkins Abernethy*. Charlottesville: University Press of Virginia, 1964.

Sakolski, A. M. *The Great American Land Bubble: The Amazing Story of Land-Grabbing, Speculations, and Booms from Colonial Days to the Present Time*. New York: Harper & Brothers, 1932.

Scott, Winfield. *Memoirs of Lieutenant-General Scott*. 2 vols. New York: Sheldon, 1864.

Shepherd, William R. *Guide to the Materials for the History of the United States in Spanish Archives*. Washington, DC: Carnegie Institution, 1907.

Skelton, William B. *An American Profession of Arms: The Army Officer Corps, 1784–1861*. Lawrence, KS: University Press of Kansas, 1992.

Slaughter, Thomas P. *The Whiskey Rebellion: Frontier Epilogue to the American Revolution*. New York: Oxford University Press, 1986.

Smith, Henry Nash. *Virgin Land: The American West as Symbol and Myth*. Cambridge: Harvard University Press, 1950, 1978.

Stagg, J. C. A. *Mr. Madison's War: Politics, Diplomacy, and Warfare in the Early American Republic, 1783–1830*. Princeton: Princeton University Press, 1992.

Szatmary, David. *Shays' Rebellion: The Making of an Agrarian Insurrection*. Amherst: University of Massachusetts Press, 1980.

Taylor, Alan. The *Divided Ground: Indians, Settlers and the Northern Borderland of the American Revolution*. New York: Knopf, 2006.

Turner, Frederick J. *The Frontier in American History*. New York: Holt, 1921.

Wood, Gordon S. *The Creation of the American Republic, 1776–1787*. Chapel Hill: University of North Carolina Press, 1969.

Wright, Robert K. *The Continental Army*. Washington, DC: Center of Military History, 1983.

Young, Alfred F., ed. *The American Revolution: Explorations in the History of American Radicalism*. DeKalb: Northern Illinois University Press, 1976.

INDEX